ETERNITY NOW

WOJCIECH TWOREK

ETERNITY NOW
RABBI SHNEUR ZALMAN OF LIADY AND TEMPORALITY

Published by State University of New York Press, Albany

© 2019 State University of New York

All rights reserved

No part of this book may be used or reproduced in any manner whatsoever without written permission. No part of this book may be stored in a retrieval system or transmitted in any form or by any means including electronic, electrostatic, magnetic tape, mechanical, photocopying, recording, or otherwise without the prior permission in writing of the publisher.

For information, contact State University of New York Press, Albany, NY
www.sunypress.edu

Library of Congress Cataloging-in-Publication Data

Names: Tworek, Wojciech, 1981– author.
Title: Eternity now : Rabbi Shneur Zalman of Liady and temporality / Wojciech Tworek.
Description: Albany : State University of New York Press, [2019] | Includes bibliographical references and index.
Identifiers: LCCN 2018040464 | ISBN 9781438475554 (hardcover) | ISBN 9781438475561 (ebook) | ISBN 9781438475547 (pbk.) Subjects: LCSH: Shneur Zalman, of Lyady, 1745-1812. | Habad. | Hasidism. Classification: LCC BM755.S525 T86 2019 | DDC 296.8/332--dc23 LC record available at https://lccn.loc.gov/2018040464

10 9 8 7 6 5 4 3 2 1

CONTENTS

	Acknowledgments	vii
	A Note on the Presentation of Source Materials	xi
	Introduction	xiii
1.	Toward a Definition of Time	1
2.	History: From Creation to the End of Time	31
3.	The End of Days	69
4.	Time and Religious Praxis	101
5.	Time's Gender Twist	123
	Conclusion	151
	Notes	155
	Bibliography	225
	Index	241

ACKNOWLEDGMENTS

This book has developed out of my doctoral dissertation written at the Department of Hebrew and Jewish Studies of University College London. I wish to thank the following institutions for their support: the Rothschild Foundation Hanadiv Europe, the Posen Foundation, the Memorial Foundation for Jewish Culture, the Berendel Foundation, the Ian Karten Foundation, the YIVO Institute for Jewish Research, and the Department of Hebrew and Jewish Studies, UCL. I would also like to acknowledge the Paideia Institute in Stockholm and the Center for Urban History in Lviv. I owe my deepest gratitude to my supervisors, Ada Rapoport-Albert and Naftali Loewenthal. Their support and faith in both my project and me cannot be emphasised enough. Their wisdom, understanding, and knowledge will always be a source of inspiration.

I have completed the writing of this book as a postdoctoral fellow at the Department of Jewish Studies at the University of Wrocław, and later as the Ray D. Wolfe Postdoctoral Fellow at the Anne Tanenbaum Centre for Jewish Studies at the University of Toronto. I wish to thank my colleagues and students at both of these institutions for providing a fruitful and stimulating environment for research and writing.

My adventure with Habad began during my undergraduate studies at the Hebrew Studies Department of the University of Warsaw. I would like to use this opportunity to thank my then tutor, Maciej Tomal, whose knowledge and erudition have made him a role model for the entire generation of Jewish Studies students in Poland. I would also like to thank Helen Beer, my Yiddish mentor at UCL. Her commitment to Yiddish culture, dedication to students, and good-hearted humor is an example I have been trying to emulate in my own life. I thank Agata Paluch for the most valuable friendship and unwaning confidence in me and in this project. Our conversations have inspired me to constantly revise my thinking and to strive for excellence. Michał Jastrzębski, Selim Korycki, Małgorzata Lipska, Aleksandra Rawska, Maciek Wilk, Kuba Wesołowski, Imran Sheikh, and Udi Tsabari have been there to help me up in the most difficult moments. I thank Sonia Gollance for helping me with the revisions of this book. The doors of Gosha Zaremba and Hershl Glasser's warm home have always been open to me. Irit Klein with her family, and Ronen Kroitoro with his, spontaneously volunteered to be my *mishpahot me'ametsot* in Israel. David and Danielle Chaimovitz-Basok did the same in Wrocław. Thanks to Luiza and Alex Moshkin, I have called Toronto home. Long coffee breaks with my friends from the British Library—Azadeh Shokouhi, Daniel Lowe, Maria Kekki, Nur Sobers-Khan, Sara Taghdimi, and Suhanna Shafiq—led to the most fascinating conversations. Working with Ilana Tahan and Ulrike Koch in the British Library, and with Jonathan Fishburn at Fishburn Books, was a pleasure and taught me a lot. I should probably add that performing other, mostly dead-end menial jobs in Poland, Sweden, Israel, and the United Kingdom, while not contributing to my expertise in Jewish studies, did help me pay my bills and was certainly an experience that shaped me into who I am today. I thank the members of the unforgettable UCL Max Nordau Society, the Ur Circle in Wrocław, and all my dear friends from Nankiera 212. Without you, my life would have been dull and incomplete.

I remain grateful to my parents, who have always supported my passion for Jewish studies, even though they would have preferred their son to become an engineer or a physician, and to my brother and sister with their families, for their love and patience. I would also like to honor my late grandparents. Thanks to their financial support I was able to pursue my undergraduate degree relatively carefree, even if sometimes hungry and in torn shoes. May their memory be a blessing.

I thank Ezra Margulies and Sarah Hussell who edited the early versions of the manuscript, and Rafael Chaiken and SUNY Press for recognizing its potential, and for their efforts to bring my project to completion. Last but not least, I am grateful to all the anonymous readers for their valuable comments. For any errors or inadequacies that may remain in this work, the responsibility is entirely my own.

Acknowledgments

* * *

Part of this study has been published elsewhere:

Chapter 4 is a revised version of "Setting Times for Torah Study in R. Shneur Zalman of Liady's Thought," *AJS Review* 38, no. 1 (2014): 29–57. © Cambridge University Press. Reprinted with permission.

Chapter 5 is an expanded version of a Hebrew article "Time in the Teachings of Rabbi Shneur Zalman of Liady," in *Habad Hasidism: History, Theology and Image*, edited by Jonatan Meir and Gadi Sagiv (Jerusalem: Zalman Shazar Center, 2016), 57–76.

I thank the original publishers for their permission to use these works.

A NOTE ON THE PRESENTATION OF SOURCE MATERIALS

Published English translations (with some modifications, as necessary) have been used wherever possible. All other translations from the Hebrew sources are my own. Biblical quotations follow the *Tanakh: The Holy Scriptures* (Philadelphia, PA: Jewish Publication Society of America, 1985). Quotations from the liturgy follow S. Singer and J. Sacks, ed., *The Authorised Daily Prayer Book of the United Hebrew Congregations of the Commonwealth* (London: Collins, 2007). *Tanya* translations follow the bilingual Kehot-Soncino edition (London: Soncino, 1973). All of the above translations have been modified by me, where necessary.

The transliteration of Hebrew aims to reflect contemporary Modern Hebrew pronunciation while generally following the Library of Congress's romanization system, with the following exceptions: there is no distinction between *alef* and *'ayin* (both are represented by the same inverted comma and disregarded when *alef* is appearing as an initial letter), *tet* and *tav*, *samekh* and *sin*, *het* and *he*. The consonants *vav* and *kuf* are represented by *v* and *k*, respectively. Consonants marked with a *dagesh* are not doubled in transliteration. Hebrew words in transliteration are generally italicized, with the exception of those in common English use (i.e., kabbalah), where the common English spelling has been preserved.

Tanya is abbreviated throughout as T followed by a section number (1—Sefer shel beinonim, 2—Sha'ar ha-yihud veha-emunah, 3—Igeret ha-teshuvah, 4—Igeret ha-kodesh, 5—Kuntres ha-aharon), chapter number, and folio. *Torah or* is abbreviated as TO, *Likute Torah* as LT, *Ma'mere Admor ha-Zaken* as MAHZ, *Hilkhot talmud Torah* as HTT, and *Zohar* as Z. Mishnah, Tosefta, and the Palestinian and Babylonian

Talmuds are referred to throughout as *m, t, y,* and *b* followed by a tractate title.

Shneur Zalman's teachings were directed first and foremost to male audiences. In the contexts in which Shneur Zalman's teachings would be relevant only to his male followers, exclusively masculine pronouns have been used. More inclusive pronouns have been used to avoid gender bias only if the context of the teachings suggested that Shneur Zalman would consider them to be relevant to all Jews (or, in some cases, to all people).

INTRODUCTION

Time plays an essential role in Jewish practices and beliefs. Many of the 613 commandments prescribed by *Halakhah* (Jewish law) are bound by time and operate, therefore, according to a precise framework. The rhythm of the observant Jew's life is set by time-bound rituals: from prayers that punctuate the day, to the weekly Sabbath, monthly celebrations of the new moon, and annual festivals. The cycle of Jewish calendar points also toward different temporal realms: the mythical past of the Jewish people and humankind on the one hand, and the anticipated future of redemption, on the other. The centrality of the belief in the telos of history was sealed when Moses Maimonides's thirteen principles of faith, which include the belief in the coming of the Messiah, were widely embraced by Jewish communities around the world (despite initial resistance and controversies).[1]

Given the centrality of time in Judaism, it is not surprising that the emergence of Hasidism in Eastern Europe in the eighteenth century, and the rejuvenation of Jewish religious life that it led to, left its mark on the Jewish experience and conceptualization of time. Yet initially, only two of the movement's characteristic features caught the interest of scholars. The first was the practice of delaying prayers beyond the halakhically prescribed times, which earned Hasidim accusations of heresy on the part of their opponents, *mitnagedim*. These charges waned away with time, as Hasidism grew into a massive movement, and merged with the *mitnagedim* into the emergent Jewish orthodoxy, in which their ideological differences became of secondary importance.[2] The second was the role of messianism in the Hasidic movement's early years. Eventually, the pioneering scholar of Jewish mysticism, Gershom Scholem, set the course of the discussion when he declared that Hasidism had neutralized the messianic message of Lurianic kabbalah in response to Sabbateanism's heretical messianism.[3] Scholem's view steered scholars away from the historiosophical dimension of early Hasidic sources on the assumption that if the Hasidic masters were not oriented toward the messianic future, but strove instead to enable their followers to cleave to God in the here-and-now, then the appropriate approach was to investigate Hasidism as an atemporal doctrine.

Still, the idea of the Hasidic neutralization of messianism has not gone unquestioned. Scholars, most notably, Moshe Idel showed various ways of considering messianism in early Hasidism beyond the idea of neutralization.[4] What really brought the concepts of messianism and messianic times back to the center of the discussion of Hasidic ideas and practice, however, was the eruption of Habad messianism in the late-twentieth century.

From the Preacher of Liozna to the "Messiah of Brooklyn"[5]

Habad emerged at the end of the eighteenth century in the present-day Belarussian-Russian borderland as a local and ideological variety of Hasidism. Hasidism began not much earlier, in the first half of the eighteenth century, in Podolia, a region located farther south, in what is now Western Ukraine and by then was the southeastern corner of the Polish-Lithuanian Commonwealth. Hasidim trace the roots back to the figure of Israel Ba'al Shem Tov (also known as the Besht, who died around 1760) and the circle of his disciples and fellow mystics in Mezhbizh. Although Ba'al Shem Tov did not intend to initiate a new religious movement, and his circle may not have been something extraordinary in the Podolian landscape, his late followers, who carried on his teachings and acquired disciples of their own, retroactively projected on him the image of a religious innovator and visionary founder of Hasidism.[6]

The founder of Habad, Shneur Zalman, was born in 1745 in the town of Liozna, which at that time was still part of the Polish-Lithuanian Commonwealth, but soon, following the partitions of Poland, was incorporated into tsarist Russia.[7] His life overlapped with Ba'al Shem Tov's, yet, apparently, they never met.[8] As a young man, Shneur Zalman became a follower of Dov Ber of Mezrich, also known as the Great Maggid (1704–1772), an important student of Ba'al Shem Tov.[9] Shneur Zalman's time at the Maggid's court, while doubtlessly formative, is very poorly documented and shrouded in Hasidic legend.[10] Certainly, he was among the youngest in the circle of the Maggid's followers, some of whom acted as Hasidic leaders either after, or even during the Maggid's life. It was these individuals, as well as other Hasidic leaders independent of this circle, who would later transform Hasidism from loosely connected elitist fraternities into a religious movement with its self-conscious identity, key concepts, literary corpus, core institutions, and organizational structure.[11] All these aspects of Hasidism would take shape only after the Maggid's death, and Shneur Zalman would play an important role in this process as a teacher, writer, and communal leader at the forefront of the conflict with the opponents of the nascent Hasidism: the *mitnagedim*.

The Maggid's circle was by no means uniform and even its scope is difficult to ascertain.[12] It consisted of around fifteen individuals, including people who left a very deep imprint on Hasidism and whose teachings are widely studied in the present day, such as Levi Yitshak of Berdichev (1740–1809), Elimelekh of Lizhensk (1717–1787), Menahem Nahum of Chernobyl (1730–1797), or Aharon of Karlin (1736–1772), to name just a few. Members of the Maggid's circle differed with regard to their understanding of Hasidic worship, and their relationships were not always ideal. We know, for example, about a conflict between the Maggid and Avraham of Kalisk (1741–1810), which broke out shortly before the former's death and concerned the style of worship of the latter that exposed Hasidim to attacks from the *mitnagedim*.[13] In many cases, however, they would cultivate their friendships long after the Maggid's death in 1772, and even strengthen them by marital ties. According to Habad traditions, Shneur Zalman was particularly close to the Maggid's son, Avraham "the Angel" (1739–1776), and Levi Yitshak of Berdichev. His two granddaughters, Sarah (d. 1809?) and Devorah Leah (d. 1876), were married into families of prominent *tsadikim*. Sarah married Eliezer Derbaremdiker, a grandson of Levi Yitshak of Berdichev, and Devorah married Ya'akov Yisra'el of Cherkasy, a son of Mordekhai of Chernobyl (1770–1830) and a grandson of Menahem Nahum.[14]

According to later Habad traditions, Shneur Zalman's colleagues considered him *primus inter pares* and, following the death of the Maggid, entrusted him with coordinating all the new centers of Hasidism. This image, however, has been debunked as an anachronistic description that projects the structure of a nineteenth-century Hasidic court on the early, decentralized and disorganized circle of the Maggid's disciples and comrades.[15] Shneur Zalman himself did not immediately pursue leadership of any sorts. Instead of engaging in forming his community, he joined the group that gathered around two prominent

Hasidic leaders, Menahem Mendel of Vitebsk (ca. 1730–1788) and Avraham of Kalisk. Following their emigration in 1777 to Ottoman Palestine, Shneur Zalman was appointed their representative in White Russia. The idea of leading Hasidim from the Land of Israel through Shneur Zalman failed, however, as the Hasidim, looking for a more direct and intimate mode of leadership, soon began to travel to *tsadikim* in Volhynia and Lithuania. This trend eventually encouraged Menahem Mendel and Avraham of Kalisk to convince Shneur Zalman to become a Hasidic *tsadik* in his own right, which he reluctantly did, according to Etkes, around the year 1786. Although several members of the local Hasidic elite initially voiced some opposition to Shneur Zalman's leadership, within a few years it became uncontested.[16]

Shneur Zalman's ideas concerning a *tsadik*'s obligations contrasted with those of other *tsadikim*. His fellow Maggid's disciples—for example, Levi Yitshak of Berdichev or Elimelekh of Lizhensk—considered the *tsadik* responsible for both the material and spiritual well-being of his community. Their primary interest was, therefore, on the *tsadik* and his worship, as the vehicle for the rank-and-file Hasidim's attachment to God. Shneur Zalman, conversely, emphasized the role of the worship of an individual Hasid, and saw himself merely as his followers' guide in spirituality and the leader of a growing network of communities. Unlike his peers, he denied having the capability to perform miracles and substantially limited the possibility for his Hasidim to ask his advice concerning their earthly needs.[17]

Despite taking a different path than the leaders of more popular, *tsadik*-centered versions of Hasidism, Shneur Zalman succeeded in expanding the community he inherited from Menahem Mendel of Vitebsk. He proved to be such an inspirational preacher, first as *magid* (preacher) in Liozna, and then as a Hasidic *tsadik*, that he was eventually forced to impose regulations limiting access to his court by issuing the so-called Liozna Ordinances.[18] He was also a brilliant writer; his *Tanya* (1796) is an unprecedented example of a systematic elucidation of Hasidic thought.

In his book on early Habad, Naftali Loewenthal described the Habad's way as "the third dimension of Hasidism,"[19] bridging the gap between the scholarly and/or mystically inclined elites and the simple followers. Shneur Zalman's sermons and, most of all, his *Tanya*, created a language capable of transmitting the Hasidic experience, and thus empowering the rank-and-file Hasidim. Still, to process Shneur Zalman's teachings required a certain level of articulacy in Jewish sources, which suggest that the core members of his following, to whom his teachings were primarily addressed, were people with a considerable cultural and financial capital.[20] Shneur Zalman's sophisticated teachings, his reluctance toward miracle making, and the relatively high level of Torah education among his Hasidim contributed to the common perception of his enterprise as an intellectual one. This, in turn, was reflected in the name *Habad*, an acronym of *Hokhmah, Binah, Da'at* (Wisdom, Understanding, Knowledge), which had already come into use during Shneur Zalman's lifetime.[21]

The strategies, employed by Shneur Zalman to make the Habad experience more inclusive will be discussed in detail in chapter 4. While Shneur Zalman's eloquence, erudition, and charisma were surely decisive for the growth of Habad, one other factor should also be mentioned. Before becoming a leader in his own right, Shneur Zalman operated a fund-raising network (*kollel*) in White Russia for the Hasidic settlement in Ottoman Palestine. He used correspondence and emissaries to maintain communication with local communities engaged in the fund-raising, and to keep the monies flowing. After becoming a Hasidic leader, he adapted the already existing network and used the same channels that served to collect funds to disseminate knowledge and to exercise his control. In sum, the structure of the fund-raising network prepared the ground for a relatively decentralized Habad community, where local leaders, who earlier collected donations for the Hasidim in the Land of Israel, would now enforce his ordinances, control the traffic from the peripheries to the *tsadik*'s court, offer advice and transmit the *tsadik*'s teachings to the local population.[22]

While exact numbers are not available, anecdotal evidence testifies to the impressive growth of the Habad community. A document from 1800 of the Russian Senate's Secret Department estimates the number of Shneur Zalman's followers as being as many as 40,000.[23] Other sources proposed still higher-inflated numbers: both a Hasidic *tsadik*, Nahman of Bratslav (1772–1810), and a maskilic writer famous for his virulent anti-Hasidic satires, Yosef Perl (1773–1839), estimated the size of the Habad community at 80,000 people![24] While these estimates are considered to be widely exaggerated, scholars agree that already in the 1790s, festivals when all Hasidim were allowed to visit the *tsadik* could attract anywhere between a thousand and one-and-a-half thousand men.[25]

Not everyone was equally thrilled by the growing influence of Shneur Zalman. The opponents arose both within and without of the Hasidic community. In 1797, a controversy erupted when Avraham of Kalisk sent Shneur Zalman a letter from Tiberias, in which he criticized his leadership. In the letter, he denounced Shneur Zalman's attempts to popularize the esoterics through the *Tanya*; a concept he considered dangerous. Instead, the proper way would be to teach Hasidim ethics and instill in them simple faith. The conflict between these two former disciples of the Maggid, which was as much a theological dispute as it was a power struggle, continued with ebbs and flows until 1806. It provoked several other *tsadikim* to become involved on both sides, but, at the end of the day, confirmed Shneur Zalman's status as the leader of a distinctive Habad community.[26]

A stronger blow came from outside of the Hasidic world. Shneur Zalman eventually became a burning threat to the *mitnagedim*, and following their denunciations, he was twice arrested on trumped-up charges by the tsarist authorities, in 1798 and 1800. In these instances, too, he had the upper hand and was cleared of both charges. This, in turn, was commonly seen as Habad's victory over the *mitnagedim* and a stamp of approval from the authorities, which only helped consolidate the Habad camp and further strengthened Shneur Zalman's position within the Jewish community.[27] He spent his final years in the town of Liady (hence his cognomen), delivering regular sermons to his followers, and died in 1813 (1812 according to the Old Style calendar), while fleeing Napoleon's army. His grave in Hadiach (Ukraine) attracts Hasidic pilgrims from all around the world.[28]

Following Shneur Zalman's death, Habad's center moved to the town of Lyubavichi, from which the movement got the second part of its name: Habad-Lubavitch. Fragmented into several courts led by scions of the Schneersohn family, Habad remained for over a century merely one of many available Jewish Orthodox affiliations. Its influence did not extend far beyond its original territory, with additional enclaves in Ottoman Palestine and the United States. It did, however, engage in the shaping of the social and political reality of Jews in Russia.[29] In addition, further Habad books were published, contributing to the strengthening of the Habad presence within the Jewish community. The input of the third Habad leader, Menahem Mendel Schneersohn the Tsemah Tsedek (1789–1866), was of particular importance, both as a publisher and a prolific author in his own right. The Tsemah Tsedek was not only instrumental in the publication of some of the sermons of his grandfather, Shneur Zalman, but also produced a multivolume collection of both mystical sermons (published in forty-two volumes posthumously as *Or ha-Torah* between 1913 and 1987) and halakhic writings (published, also posthumously, as *Tsemah Tsedek*; the first volume came out in 1871, the last in 1999).

Importantly for the topic of this book, the Tsemah Tsedek also authored a philosophical book titled *Sefer ha-hakirah* (as his other writings, this book was also published posthumously, in 1912), in which he raised, among other issues, the question of the nature of time. Using a genre unprecedented in the Habad tradition, the Tsemah Tsedek engaged in *Sefer ha-hakirah* works of medieval Jewish philosophers. *Sefer ha-hakirah* remains somewhat of an oddity in the Habad corpus, as even the author distanced himself from it and stressed that the ad hoc use of philosophical investigation, strange to Habad mystical thinking, was merely a tool in the struggle against the Haskalah. Nonetheless, it is a rare example of the Habad encounter with philosophy, even if in a very limited scope.[30]

The historical, political, and cultural developments in Eastern Europe did not leave the Hasidic community unaffected, and Habad leaders put the movement at the forefront of the struggle against what they perceived as the threat of secularization. While it may seem a paradox, the Habad leaders showed a great deal of attunement to modern trends in their antimodernization methods. Particularly noteworthy was the use of Habad in iconography and press,[31] and the establishment of the modern Habad yeshiva *Tomkhe temimim* by the fifth leader, Shalom Dovber Schneersohn (1860–1920).[32] Finally, contemporary trends in literature, sciences, and arts began to trickle into Habad.[33] The love/hate relationship of Habad with modernity reached its symbolic climax in the 1920s and 1930s, when the scion of the Schneersohn clan, who would later become the rebbe himself, Menahem Mendel Schneerson (1902–1994), embarked on academic studies in Berlin and Paris. The impact of his academic training on his later worldview as the leader of Habad, including on his grasp of temporality, remains a desideratum.[34]

But the radical change for Habad came together with the World War I, the October Revolution, and the establishment of the Soviet Union. Antireligious persecutions in the new Soviet state stifled Habad institutions in Russia and forced the then *tsadik*, Yosef Yitshak Schneersohn (1880–1950), to emigrate. The transplantation of the Habad school from its traditional strongholds in Lithuania-Belarus to an alien Polish environment in the 1920s deeply influenced the self-perception, ideology, and politics of Habad. In the new environment, away from its traditional constituency, Habad had to develop new fund-raising networks and educational institutions, as well as adjust the content and methods of its teachings to engage the new, Polish-Jewish audience.[35]

The institutional and doctrinal transformation of Habad in the interwar years prepared the ground for the rapid revival of Habad in the USA after the Holocaust. Under the leadership of the seventh and last rebbe, Menahem Mendel Schneerson, Habad emerged as one of the leading forces within the orthodox Jewish community. Young Habad Hasidic men and women followed their leader's call and went out to the streets looking to convince nonobservant Jews to put on phylacteries or light Sabbath candles. In so doing, these individuals placed themselves at the forefront of Orthodox outreach. Young families of *sheluhim* (emissaries) relocated to often far-flung locations to assist and lead the local religious community. Over the course of the second half of the twentieth century, the movement succeeded in building an extensive network of Habad houses all over the world, attracting thousands of new followers and forcing other, even non-Hasidic orthodox groups, to adopt some of its outreach strategies. This activity was fuelled by a strong messianic fervor and the belief that every commandment could tip the scales of history and bring the arrival of the Messiah.[36] Heated debates concerning the life and works of the rebbe Schneerson, as well as the controversial belief that he is the Messiah, continue to this day, more than two decades after his death.[37]

Habad and Temporality

The literature of twentieth-century Habad is infused with temporality, with references to the mythologized past of the movement, on the one hand, and to the anticipated messianic future, on the other. Its last two rebbes, Yosef Yitshak and Menahem Mendel Schneerson, are widely credited with inculcating in their followers the belief in the imminent arrival of the Messiah, and thus the imminent end of teleological history. Historical events, such as the Holocaust, the establishment of the State of Israel, the Six-Day War, and the collapse of the Soviet Union have been used by Habad followers in an attempt to prove the validity of their concept of history, and by academics to pinpoint landmarks in Habad's acute messianism.[38] The passing of Schneerson in 1994 did not extinguish Habad's messianic flame. Rituals centered around the figure of the now-absent rebbe-Messiah, or the Brooklyn building that served as his headquarters, are used to shape a consciousness that defies the apparent lack of any tangible evidence that the final redemption he promised has already materialized. These rituals have enabled believers to rise above history, transcend time, and experience the world as redeemed. Moreover, the active dissemination among Jews and non-Jews throughout the world of Habad's messianic credo has spread this redemptive consciousness beyond the fluid boundaries of the Habad community itself.[39]

Following Naftali Loewenthal, this book regards Shneur Zalman's teachings not as abstract concepts, but as the means by which he communicated a particular religious experience to his followers.[40] It was the richness of the ideas he adapted to his community's needs that made Shneur Zalman such a successful Hasidic leader. His teachings convey a multidimensional worldview that cannot be reduced either to a complex of theological ideas or to a set of practical instructions on how to lead an ideal religious or spiritual life. In fact, his vast corpus of teachings imparts the sense of a complete religious experience. This experience is governed by the daily, weekly and yearly cycles of the individual's mundane life, but at the same time, it connects him to the multigenerational congregation of Israel which, although subject to history, aims at transcending it by integration in the supratemporal divine. In focusing on the concept of time, this book explores the mystical and the mundane, the intellectual and the experiential, and finally, the individual and the communal dimensions of Shneur Zalman's teachings.

A Brief History of Jewish Time

Despite the fact that the concept of time has been a crucial factor for the understanding of Jewish religious experience, it has rarely been examined in research on kabbalah and Hasidism. Moshe Idel has discussed possible reasons for this state of affairs, including the long shadow of Mircea Eliade's categorization of Jewish time as linear and historical, notwithstanding the fact that it hardly fits the diversity of temporary experience in the various forms of Judaism that have developed over the course of history.[41]

The literature of the Sages, for example, is much less interested in linear history than it is with the cycles of days, weeks, years, *shemitah*, and jubilee, which, according to Jeffrey L. Rubenstein, serve as a springboard toward primordial, mythical time. The experience of Sabbath or festivals is for the Talmudic rabbis not only a reminder, but also a reenactment of God's act of creation. The Sages effectively translate the biblical drama into cyclical rituals, which, in turn, "dramatize paradigmatic or archetypal events, which, although they may have originated within history, are no longer conceived in historical terms."[42] The question has been raised of whether or not the Sages actually conceptualized time as an abstract entity. As Sacha Stern has argued, the Sages did not think of time as an existing being that can be measured, experienced, and described in ontological terms. Rather, they experienced reality through "process, change and motion, without having to resort to the abstract concept of a time dimension."[43] The cyclical recurrence of events and rituals does not equal the concept of cyclical time, but only, as Stern has argued, "a concept of cyclical events."[44] Stern has also pointed at what Rubenstein calls the dehistoricization of Israel's experience: the Sages perceived historical events as occuring within a cyclical, calendric pattern. This did not spring from the Sages' idea of time as a cyclical entity, but from associating particular types of events with certain days of the year. Historical events were reduced to events that occur in a cycle determined, in the end, by astronomical factors.[45] Time as an independent entity, Stern has argued, emerges in the rabbinic world only with the development of medieval Jewish philosophy, predominantly with the works of Moses Maimonides (1135–1204).[46]

Maimonides cannot be credited with being the first Jewish philosopher to refer to time as an abstract entity;[47] nonetheless, he provided an influential definition of time as "an accident consequent upon motion [which] is necessarily attached to it."[48] The definition, influenced by the Aristotelian definition of time as a measure of movement,[49] proved problematic for Maimonides's successors: Aristotle's definition is connected to his belief in an eternal universe, which stands in contrast to the image conveyed by the Torah according to which God created the world in six days. Whether Maimonides shared this tenet of Aristotelian philosophy remains a matter of dispute.[50] Be that as it may, in order to disconnect time from movement, Maimonides's prominent critic, Hasdai Crescas (1340–1410/11), proposed to view time as the measure of duration. As such, time's status was no longer dependent on creation, and in fact, time, or its essence, could exist prior to the creation of the world.[51] Medieval philosophy had a significant impact on the development of kabbalah and, directly and indirectly, also on Hasidism. As Jonathan Dauber has demonstrated in his recent book, the ethos of the early kabbalah developed following the transplantation of philosophy, developed in the sphere of the Islamic culture, to Christian lands. The kabbalah adopted the philosophical ethos, with the investigation of God as its highest religious value, and creatively incorporated some philosophical concepts and terms.[52] Several authors have pointed at the presence of temporal reflection in various kabbalistic and Hasidic discourses and attempted to present it in a broader framework of temporal models of religious times. Moshe Idel, while criticizing Eliade's unidimensional representation of time in Judaism as linear, constructed three temporal models in Judaism, all the while emphasizing that in the course of history these models intertwined, with some gaining dominance in certain periods and types of literature. These three models are: *micro-, meso-* and *macrochronos*. *Michrochronos* relates to the time of cyclical repetitions of shared rituals, which both connects Jews with God but also relates them to events from their mythical past. *Mesochronos* is the time understood as a linear development from the past through the present to the future. The events that take place in *mesochronos* are singular. While the *michrochronic* model has at its center the congregation of Israel united in enduring worship, the *mesochronic* model focuses on the Jewish people's history and covenant with God. Finally, the third, *macrochronic* model, deals with the macrocycles of cosmic time, in which the whole universe comes into being and perishes in the cycles of cosmic *shemitot*.[53]

Yet, there is still more to the kabbalistic-Hasidic temporal discourse. Some kabbalistic and Hasidic thinkers, inspired by philosophical concepts of time, also embarked on both theoretical and practical investigations into that which transcends time and into eternity. As Moshe Idel and Adam Afterman have pointed out, some mystical traditions informed by Jewish early neoplatonic and neoaristotelic philosophy saw time as an obstacle on the way to the true reality that transcends time; a way from multiplicity to unity, from dynamic to static, and from profane to holy. According to Abraham Abulafia's ecstatic kabbalah (1240–ca. 1291), for instance, the clinging of the soul to the supratemporal divinity constituted the religious ideal and the way of achieving eternal life, whereas clinging to worldly matters, which by nature fall under the category of temporality, condemned the soul to temporal existence and eventual doom.[54]

Other traditions, influenced by later Neoplatonism, transcended the dichotomy of time and eternity. Theosophical kabbalists strove to experience a higher, divine or sacred form of time. According to the kabbalistic traditions of, most prominently, Azriel of Gerona (ca. 1160–1238) or Moshe Cordovero (1522–1570), time has relevance for some aspects of the divine pleroma and is related to the movement and order of *sefirot*. The order of *sefirot*, in turn, corresponds to the days of creation and the days of the week. Just as in the past, medieval philosophers associated the root of time experienced in sublunar reality with the movements of heavenly spheres,[55] so these kabbalists associated the origins of worldly time with the dynamic of the divine emanations—the *sefirot*. Needless to say, these traditions still wished to preserve the ontological difference between our world and the Godhead, as well as between our time and the temporality of the *sefirot*. To that end, they created a distinction between worldly time, and the "order of time" (*seder ha-zemanim*) of the *sefirot*.[56] The changes that occur within the world of the divine emanations, albeit beyond the dimensions of past, present, and future, can be described in terms of relations of priority and posteriority. These relations are the divine, eternal matrix above for the temporal modes of past and future, experienced in the passing of time in the world below.

Hasidic masters had at their disposal, and made use of in their work, a plethora of earlier kabbalistic and philosophical works and ideas.[57] It is hardly surprising that the Hasidic concepts of time, eternity, temporality, and atemporality also draw on and combine a variety of earlier concepts. Hasidic masters therefore retained the idea of the soul's imperative to transcend the temporal world and experience the divine unity that is higher than time, yet still subjected some aspects of the divine—the seven lower *sefirot*—to the order of time. As Idel has concluded, the Hasidic concept of time exemplifies the movement's synthetic commitment to theosophical and ecstatic kabbalah.[58]

Hasidic doctrines deal with the ways a person may transcend the constraints of time and delve into the various aspects of eternity and supratemporality, be it in the sphere of the "order of time" of the seven lower *sefirot*, or in the divine unity that is above this subtle domain. Idel demonstrates that Dov Ber of Mezrich introduced this idea to Hasidism and disseminated it through his teachings and students: Ze'ev Volf of Zhitomir, Levi Yitshak of Berdichev, Elimelekh of Lizhensk, Menahem Nahum of Chernobyl, and last but not least, Shneur Zalman of Liady.[59] These Hasidic masters taught that the supratemporal reality is to be reached from within the Jewish body and through Jewish religious praxis. The special connection that Jews share with the supratemporal God and which they keep by dint of performing the commandments in the physical world enables them to transform the multiplicity of time into the unity of that which is above time.

Shneur Zalman of Liady adopted a singular position among this group of students. While, for example, Levi Yitshak of Berdichev emphasized the role of the *tsadik* in serving the material and spiritual needs of the community, Shneur Zalman placed in the center a common Hasid's worship and personal struggle against the evil inclination. While Elimelekh of Lizhensk in his *No'am Elimelekh* strove to maintain the elitist character of the fraternity of *tsadikim*, Shneur Zalman made his teachings available to all educated readers. While Avraham of Kalisk was protective of Hasidic mystical traditions, set very demanding standards for mystical worship capable for transcending time and space, and postulated promoting simple faith among the Hasidim, Shneur Zalman believed the mystical experience could and should be communicated broadly, and taught intellectual contemplation as a means leading toward the transcendence.[60] Against Menahem Mendel of Vitebsk, who valued most worship leading to complete divestment from corporeality, Shneur Zalman stressed the role of body and corporeal commandments in reaching the divine.[61] Moreover, the vivid interest in messianism connects Shneur Zalman with Nahman of Bratslav, a maverick *tsadik* unrelated to the Maggid's circle. Although Shneur Zalman offered different understanding with regard to the role of the rank-and-file and the *tsadik* in the messianic process, he shared with his controversial contemporary the intense expectation of the messianic times and the belief in their harmonistic and all-encompassing character.[62]

Regardless of later attempts by Habad writers to posthumously portray Shneur Zalman as the Great Maggid's (and therefore, the Ba'al Shem Tov's) main student and successor, his teachings deserve particular attention. His mystical lore contains subtle and nuanced discussions of the concept of time, its relation to individual existence, and to collective anticipation of the messianic advent and the end of history. The abundance of sources, superior in number to those in the writings of contemporaneous Hasidic masters, allow the careful reader to get a well-rounded idea of the Hasidic discourse of time developed in the school of the Great Maggid, which combines earlier kabbalistic and philosophical ideas and integrates the various modes of *micro-*, *macro-* and, to some extent, *mesochronos*. It is not a purely theoretical issue but a concept that is directly related to the existential struggle of every Jew, whose very condition as a dualist—torn between his or her animal and divine soul and between his or her evil and good inclination—is a constant struggle between the unredeemed present and the redeemed future, and between temporality and eternity, not only from the perspective of the entire world expecting the advent of the Messiah, but also, importantly, from the perspective of the microcosm (*'olam katan*)—a human being.[63]

Sources

Shneur Zalman's corpus consists of over thirty volumes, the majority of which were published posthumously. His homilies (*derushim*) or discourses (*ma'amarim*) make up the largest category within this corpus.[64] Delivered orally in Yiddish, they were translated into Hebrew even as they were being transcribed by his followers.[65] The homilies circulated in manuscript form for many years, until the third Lubavitcher Rebbe, Menahem Mendel Schneersohn the Tsemah Tsedek, initiated the process of making them available in print. He published two volumes of Shneur Zalman's homilies on the weekly Torah portions, *Torah or* and *Likute Torah*, in 1837 in Kapust and 1848 in Zhitomir. Teachings pertaining to prayer were included in Shneur Zalman's prayerbook, *Seder tefilot mi-kol ha-shanah*, first published in Kapust in 1816. An additional collection of unpublished *ma'amarim* appeared in Jerusalem in 1926 as *Boneh Yerushalayim*. However, the more comprehensive publication of Shneur Zalman's sermons began only in the second half of the twentieth century, when Habad's Kehot Publishing House brought out a series of volumes titled *Ma'mere Admor ha-Zaken*. This process continues to some extent to the present day, as brochures of rediscovered copies of homilies are published occasionally in print and online.

Another important segment of Shneur Zalman's corpus, generally overlooked by scholars interested in the philosophical or theological dimensions of the Habad tradition, are his halakhic works. Two of them were published in Shneur Zalman's lifetime in Shklov: *Hilkhot talmud Torah* in 1794 (Compendium of the Laws of Torah Study), and *Seder birkhot ha-nehenin* in 1800 (Laws of Blessings for Enjoyment, republished in 1801 alongside *Dine netilat yadayim* [*Laws of Ritual Washing of the Hands*]). His other legal writings were compiled posthumously into *Shulhan 'arukh Rabenu ha-Zaken*, published by his sons in Kopys and Shklov in 1814 and 1816.[66]

Shneur Zalman's writings also include a large number of letters, addressed to his Hasidic followers collectively or to certain individuals. Some contain mystical teachings, others issue instructions to remote Habad communities, others still relate to his involvement in fund-raising for Hasidic settlements in the Land of Israel, and more again testify to his controversies with other Hasidic leaders or with *mitnagedim*. In general, the letters provide invaluable insights not only into Shneur Zalman's style of leadership but also into the model of spirituality he propagated. They were first collected and published by David Zvi Hillman in Jerusalem, in 1953, as *Igerot Ba'al ha-Tanya u-vene doro*. Later, Kehot published a new edition of Shneur Zalman's letters in two volumes, entitled *Igerot kodesh* (together with the letters of Dov Ber Shneuri [1773–1827] and Menahem Mendel the Tsemah Tsedek).

Finally, there is the book *Tanya*, the publication of which in Slavuta in 1796 established one of the unique features of the Habad school of Hasidism: the *Tanya* is the first more or less systematic exposition of a Hasidic model of spirituality.⁶⁷ It is one of four of Shneur Zalman's books to be published during his lifetime, and the only one that concentrates on his mystical teachings. He explains in a letter that precedes the printed versions that he wrote the work to provide his followers with a manual of direct spiritual guidance so as to render regular personal contact with him unnecessary. Effectively, the book was to serve as a substitute for a personal meeting with the *tsadik* (the so-called *yehidut*).⁶⁸ Still, the discrepancies between the content of *ma'amarim* and the *Tanya* prompted some scholars to draw a firm line between them, and while the distinction between exoteric *Tanya* and esoteric *ma'amarim* proposed by Isaiah Tishby and Joseph Dan was generally rejected, many still attempt a content-oriented analysis in their scholarship.⁶⁹ Form-oriented research of Habad writings, focusing on their transition from oral to written form and from Yiddish to Hebrew, remains a desideratum.

A brief review of Shneur Zalman's works reveals that the vast majority were, in fact, written by his followers. In other words, what is known as Shneur Zalman's body of writings was largely compiled from manuscripts prepared, copied, and preserved by others. Shneur Zalman's writings indicate that he was aware of the unrestrained dissemination of his teachings through these manuscripts and attempted to control this process by appointing editors responsible for checking and correcting them.⁷⁰ But despite these efforts, in many cases it remains difficult to determine where Shneur Zalman's words end and scribal or editorial interpolations begin.⁷¹ There is also some disagreement among Habad scholars about the attribution of some of the discourses. For example, *Shene ha-me'orot* and *Be'ure ha-Zohar*, which are usually attributed to Dov Ber, appear in Foxbrunner's work as Shneur Zalman's own.⁷² All in all, many factors contributed to the fact that Shneur Zalman's writings vary greatly, be it the time of their production, their genre, the way they were preserved and edited, and so on. His output, therefore, should not be seen as a whole, self-contained doctrine, but as a dynamic and often inharmonious body that changes and adjusts according to temporal circumstances.

This Book's Structure

The book is divided into five chapters. The chapter 1 sets out the conceptual framework for analyzing Shneur Zalman's idea of time. In it, I explore the various contexts in which time features in his works, focusing first on the relation between God and time, and its place in the process of creation. I discuss its location within the *sefirotic* structure and the discourse on divine names, locating the sources of Shneur Zalman's treatment of time within the earlier strands of the Jewish mystical tradition he inherited. I demonstrate how Shneur Zalman's attempts to conceptualize time intertwine with his kabbalistic mind-set, giving birth to the notion of continuous cycles of creation and annihilation by way of *ratso va-shov*—the perpetual rhythm of descent and ascent by which the life-giving energy of the divine illuminates creation and sustains its existence.

Chapter 2 discusses the historiosophical underpinnings of Shneur Zalman's teachings. I discuss his idea that cosmic history is the product of the dynamic tension between creation, identified with exile, and redemption, perceived as the telos of creation. This leads to a detailed analysis of Shneur Zalman's interpretation of Israel's historical exiles, which he transforms into spiritual states of enslavement as punishment for sin, impurity and the absorption of gentile wisdom, all amounting to detachment from God. The main focus is placed on the Egyptian exile, which—based on a recurring wordplay in Shneur Zalman's teachings that reads the Hebrew name for Egypt, *Mitsrayim*, as *metsarim*, "constraints"—is taken to represent the limitations of materiality and corporeality. I discuss the exile in Egypt as the paradigm of both the enslavements experienced by the Jewish people throughout history and the personal enslavement of each and every individual within the material world. The hard labor performed by the Israelites during their enslavement in Egypt becomes an allegory for worship in the state of ontological exile, namely during life in the material world. This is followed by a discussion of Shneur Zalman's presentation of the biblical Exodus as the paradigm of redemption. I analyze his concept of worship within the material world by means of prayer, Torah study, and the performance of the commandments as the only means of attaining redemption by way of building God's "dwelling place in the lower worlds" (*dirah ba-tahtonim*).

While chapter 2 discusses cosmic history as the process that ultimately leads to redemption, chapter 3 focuses on Shneur Zalman's eschatology. In this chapter, I highlight the distinction he makes between the messianic days and the time of the resurrection of the dead, exploring the place and role of the gentile nations in the world-to-come in view of his conviction that the end of days will bring about the ultimate eradication of evil and impurity, which are clearly associated with the gentile nations throughout his writings. I also explore the role of the Messiah in Shneur Zalman's teachings, especially against the background of the scope he allows for individual redemption within the unredeemed world, which takes place irrespectively of time and place and is achievable by means of the daily performance of religious rituals. I conclude the chapter with an examination of the future-to-come as the end of history, namely, as the era in which the dynamics of *ratso va-shov*—the continuous creation and annihilation of worlds by the descent and ascent of the life-giving divine energy—will be replaced by a state of permanent *shov*, the overflowing abundance of godliness. I distinguish between the two paradigms of this everlasting future that are discernible in Shneur Zalman's teachings: the future-to-come as the everlasting Sabbath, and as the eighth day that is "entirely long and good," which is connected to the ritual of circumcision and the abundance of God's blessings that come as a result.

In chapter 4 I discuss the temporal experience in the everyday life of Shneur Zalman's followers. I concentrate on the rituals of prayer and Torah study (in particular on the study of Torah at set times) as a means of transcending temporal limitations. Two aspects of these rituals are of particular interest. First, both rituals are time-bound: the times of prayer are determined by Jewish law, and the times for Torah study are set by the student. Second, the significance of the ritual of setting times for Torah study in Shneur Zalman's doctrine tells us much about his target audience and his idea of Hasidism in general. I unpack the various ways in which he reinterpreted this seemingly minor halakhic precept in order to empower and enrich the religious experience of middle-class businessmen who were hardly as spiritually and intellectually accomplished as the elite core of the Habad movement. This chapter bridges the gap between Shneur Zalman's concepts of time and history, on the one hand, and the everyday experience of his followers, on the other. It shows how the emphasis he placed on the power of time-bound rituals to enhance the spiritual experience of each and every one of his Hasidim helped turn Habad into a broad movement without ever compromising on its intellectual and spiritual ideals.

Chapter 5, the last chapter, deals with the nexus of time and gender. It investigates some hagiographical traditions about Shneur Zalman's unique attitude toward women in an attempt to show that there is hardly any convincing evidence that he shared the more inclusive attitude toward women of the last two Lubavitcher rebbes. I take as my starting point the fact that Shneur Zalman locates the source of time within the *sefirotic* tree in the feminine constellation of Nukba. I then discuss the function of gender categories in Shneur Zalman's thought inasmuch as they relate to the polarity of giver and recipient in the *sefirotic* structure. I analyze the *ma'amarim*, in which gender imagery is employed to depict the exilic present and the envisioned redemption, including those that feature the elevation of the feminine aspect of the divine in the future-to-come. In relation to these, I attempt to determine whether there is any correlation between the elevation of the cosmic female and the status of flesh-and-blood women on earth. I look closely at his attitude toward women's exemption from time-bound commandments, and to the commandments generally considered feminine (such as the lighting of the Sabbath candles) in order to comment on his attitude toward feminine spirituality.

❖ 1 ❖

TOWARD A DEFINITION OF TIME

Setting the Stage

Our discussion of time in Shneur Zalman's teachings begins with two basic and seemingly straightforward questions: what is time and what kind of conceptual tools may be used to investigate it?

It may seem paradoxical to discuss Shneur Zalman's teachings on time from a philosophical perspective, since he had a complicated attitude toward philosophy. Yet his teachings did not emerge in a vacuum, nor did his concept of time. He was familiar with medieval Jewish philosophy and its attempts to grasp reality in all its manifestations, including the temporal one. As a thinker influenced by kabbalistic writings and by the founding figures of Hasidism, Shneur Zalman had at his disposal other, nonphilosophical conceptual frameworks and, like many of his predecessors, he considered philosophical tools inadequate for understanding reality.[1] First, he had a generally negative view of philosophy as a non-Jewish wisdom of demonic provenance that pollutes the three intellectual attributes of the divine soul in every Jew: Wisdom, Understanding, and Knowledge.[2] He discouraged Jews from studying philosophy, and only permitted outstanding scholars to do so for a living.[3] Second, he believed that non-Jewish philosophy simply did not deliver on its promises: no matter how hard they try, philosophers fail to express the most important issue, which Shneur Zalman considers to be at the core of Jewish faith: the unity of God. Paradoxically, although this concept lies beyond the grasp of even the brightest philosophers, it can be comprehended by those whom Shneur Zalman describes as the simplest Jews, for "even women, the youth and the children have faith in the one God."[4] It is a truth every Jewish child receives once old enough to develop "a bit of knowledge."[5]

While it is true that Shneur Zalman softens his criticism with regard to Jewish philosophy, he nevertheless maintains his reservations concerning its attempts to comprehend God intellectually.[6] Thus, in *Hilkhot talmud Torah*, his compendium of laws concerning Torah study, the prohibition on inquiring into the books of non-Jewish philosophers is followed by a warning against reading Jewish books containing non-Jewish philosophical ideas. Shneur Zalman even states explicitly that those who study books of this kind commit such a grave offence that they lose their share in the world-to-come! While medieval rabbis may have had good reasons to deal with philosophy, the same certainly does not apply to the average Jew.[7]

Shneur Zalman even suggests that the greatest of Jewish philosophers, Maimonides, had a somewhat limited understanding of the divine. Drawing on kabbalah, he explains that there are four worlds arranged in a fixed hierarchy ranging from the closest to God to the furthest from God: Emanation (*atsilut*), Creation (*beri'ah*), Formation (*yetsirah*), and Making (*'asiyah*). Each comprises ten *sefirot*, which in Habad teachings are *Hokhmah* (Wisdom), *Binah* (Understanding), *Da'at* (Knowledge), *Hesed* (Mercy), *Gevurah* (Power), *Tif'eret* (Beauty), *Netsah* (Lasting Endurance), *Hod* (Majesty), *Yesod* (Foundation), and *Malkhut* (Kingdom).[8] In Shneur Zalman's theosophy, *Keter* (Crown) is not included in the ten *sefirot* but plays the role of intermediary between the *sefirotic* world and its transcendent source above.[9] When evaluating the relevance of Maimonides's philosophy, he balances his preference for kabbalah over philosophy, on the one hand, and his respect for the great medieval thinker and halakhist, on the other. He concedes that Maimonides's philosophy is indeed valid, but only with regard to the reality below the three upper *sefirot* of the World of Emanation. Anything above that, he maintains, is attainable only to the masters of kabbalah.[10] Moreover, as Yosef Stamler has noted, Shneur Zalman's ambivalence regarding Jewish philosophy finds expression in the sources he selects to quote. While Maimonides does indeed feature in his teachings, Shneur Zalman rarely refers to his philosophical ideas and work, and when he mentions Maimonides in *Tanya*, he often finds it necessary to adduce additional support from the kabbalists for the ideas put forward.[11]

Given Shneur Zalman's doubts concerning philosophy, it may be surprising that his teachings on time are so strongly influenced by medieval philosophical discourse. He might not point his readers directly to his sources, but his language betrays the fact that he did precisely what he advised against: allowing philosophical ideas to influence his worldview. The conceptual framework of his temporal discourse is informed first and foremost by the Aristotelian concept of time as a "number" or a "measure of movement" that was embraced by the medieval Jewish philosophers.[12] This Aristotelian underpinning is particularly conspicuous when he describes time as "an aspect of number and division [*behinat mispar ve-hithalkut*],"[13] a definition that in turn establishes the opposition between temporality and God who, "blessed be he, is above time [. . .], for he is the simple one [*ehad pashut*] with no division at all, heaven forfend, but rather everything is united [in Him]."[14]

The polarity of God and time follows the dichotomy between the simple and the compound, as well as the philosophical assumption that the infinite and immeasurable is superior to the finite and measurable. The latter assumption not only concerns the gap between God and time, but also the general difference between the infinite God and the finite creation. It is true, argues Shneur Zalman in *Tanya*, that when we compare the numbers of one and one million, we may be impressed by the disparity between them and the magnitude of the latter. This, however, cannot be compared to the relation between any set of numbers and the infinity, as the latter cannot be expressed in numerical figures. There is an ontological gap between the divine Light of Infinity (*Or Ein Sof*) and the contracted illumination that brings about the lower worlds. This gap results from a qualitative rather than a quantitative difference: the finite cannot be compared to the infinite, and regardless of its size, it is always considered "as nothing" when seen from the perspective of the infinite.[15]

Even though in this particular case Shneur Zalman does not refer explicitly to time, the fact that it is an aspect of number makes the connection evident. This understanding of time as number/finitude allows him to reaffirm the view expressed by some Jewish philosophers and kabbalists[16] that time belongs to the realm of creation, and is separate from God, who is defined as Infinity (*Ein Sof*),[17] which precedes creation. According to Shneur Zalman, God's infinity and supratemporality are hinted at in God's ineffable name.

> He [God], may he be blessed, is verily in the nature of *Ein Sof*. He was, he is and he will be [*hayah, hoveh, ve-yihyeh*][18] verily with no change, as in the statement [in the daily morning service]: "It was you who existed before the world was created, it is you now that the world has been created," etc.[19]

Shneur Zalman goes to great lengths to emphasize that the act of creation does not limit or influence God in any way. Since he is indifferent to temporal change, even as dramatic an event as the creation of the world does not represent a turning point in the history of the divine. In other words, God precedes creation in an ontological sense and not just in a temporal sense. This principle would later be formulated explicitly by Menachem Mendel Schneersohn, the Tsemah Tsedek.

> He [God], blessed be he, is not dependent on time at all. That being the case we say [about Him] the Ancient One [kadmon], but not [in the sense of] temporal precedence [kedimah zemanit], heaven forfend, which would mean that he preceded the world in time. [. . .] Rather the precedence, which we ascribe to Him, means that he preceded everything, including the aspect of time. [. . .] He, blessed be he, was alone prior to the existence of world, and when he created the world, he created time, too.[20]

What his successor spells out, Shneur Zalman signals by employing an expression from the daily morning service, which describes God as the "king exalted alone since the beginning of time [. . .] extolled from days of old [ha-mitnase mi-yemot 'olam]." According to his explanation, God is exalted and extolled not "from" (or "since") but rather above and beyond yemot 'olam, which Shneur Zalman understands literally as the "days of the world," namely, worldly days, symbolizing temporality. The liturgical verse therefore reaffirms God's supratemporal character and the status of time as a product of creation.

The view of time as a product of creation helps Shneur Zalman find illuminating solutions to some earlier debates with regard to the timing of creation. The Sages entertained the idea that the creation could have occurred, at least theoretically, at any other point in time, whether earlier or later than it actually did. This presumption occurs in the midrash, where Rabbi Tanhuma declares: "The world was created at the proper time. The world was not ready to be created prior to then."[21] While Rabbi Tanhuma's statement merely alludes to the possibility of an earlier or a later creation, the Talmudic argument between Rabbi Eliezer and Rabbi Yehoshua concerning whether the world was created in the month of Tishri or Nissan clearly assumes the prior existence not only of time, but also of the Jewish calendar.[22] Shneur Zalman, however, dismisses the whole problem of the proper time of the creation by referring to the kabbalistic conception of creation as a heuristic model, amended according to the teachings of his Hasidic teacher, Dov Ber the Maggid of Mezrich. According to Hayim Vital's

'Ets ḥayim, the sequential emanation of the *sefirot* must have taken place before the actual event of the creation.[23] The duration of the process must, therefore, have determined the timing of the subsequent creation. Shneur Zalman, however, points out that this answer is not satisfactory, for one could further ask why the process of emanation began at that particular point in time rather than earlier or later. In order to resolve this difficulty, he refers to the teachings of Dov Ber,[24] who explains that time itself was created ex nihilo (*yesh me-'ayin*) and could not therefore have predated the creation or in any way conditioned it. For that reason, the very problem that *'Ets ḥayim* tackled appears to be merely the result of a misconception of the nature of time and the limits of the temporal discourse.

Not only does Shneur Zalman argue that time did not exist before the creation of the world, and therefore that the temporal categories of "earlier" and "later" simply do not apply to that context, he also states unequivocally that time was created from the divine nothingness.[25] Like generations of Jewish philosophers before him, he adopts a conception of time as a unit of measurement and thus as something that out of necessity entails finitude and multiplicity, and uses it as an underpinning for his exposition of the kabbalistic understanding of time as a product of the creation of the infinite God, who acts through his infinite light.

Between an Eternal God and a Temporal World

The dichotomy of the infinite God versus temporal creation does not clarify the nature of relations between them. At first glance, the chasm seems unbridgeable. In Shneur Zalman's teachings, however, one rarely finds descriptions of the absolute, time-bound immanency or isolated, supratemporal transcendence.[26] In most cases, Shneur Zalman is interested in God's involvement in the world. His main obstacle is how to reconcile God's transcendence with his presence within the creation.

Shneur Zalman's argument is based on the assumption that one can understand God's transcendence in both the strong and the weak senses of the term. On the one hand, when understood in the strong sense, God's transcendence represents the state of his absolute separation and self-confinement. Such transcendence can be talked about, but never fully comprehended, since whenever we consider the idea discursively we adjust it to our conceptual apparatus. We thus deprive the transcendence of its absolute character. Shneur Zalman describes this aspect as God's essence (*'atsmut*) and it may become comprehensible only in the messianic future, when human cognitive abilities change.[27] On the other hand, God's transcendence can be understood in the weak sense as relational. God transcends the world but is not detached from it entirely, as he brings it to existence. This aspect, his outworldly existence in which, and through which, everything else can exist, is intelligible for Jews even in the current condition of life in exile.

Somewhat paradoxically, in order to grasp God's existence, one must contemplate the notion of time. Shneur Zalman deduces this from the Maimonidean statement according to which the awareness of God's deeds in the world indirectly leads to the knowledge of God Himself, even though such knowledge offers no insight into the essence of the divine being.[28] If God is, as Maimonides states, the existent (*matsui*) who brings all beings into existence (*mamtsi*), then in order to be able to create all beings as they are, the creator must already in some way possess their qualities.[29] Shneur Zalman proceeds to apply this logic to the existence of time: he infers from the fact that time affects all created beings the claim that temporality somehow also relates to God. Through the contemplation of the past, present, and future of beings, therefore, one can comprehend that God, the one who brings temporal creatures to life, must necessarily comprise time. Indeed, God is not subject to time, but he comprises time in a state preceding its division into past, present, and future. This divine aspect in which the three tenses are one, prior to their actualization in the created reality, is reflected in the Tetragrammaton, interpreted as comprising the past, present, and future forms of the Hebrew verb "to be."[30]

What makes time so special is its universal character. The entirety of creation is subject to the category of time. Thus, contemplation of the temporality of one being reveals the character of creation in its totality and, at the same time, points toward its creator. In fact, as Shneur Zalman explains in another sermon, time is one of the three properties, which are present in all created beings.[31] This sermon borrows from an ancient mystical tradition according to which three properties—world, year, and soul (*'olam, shanah, nefesh*)—are present in "all created beings." It differs, however, from the original, when it interprets this triad as space, time, and the divine life force.[32] The fact that they are initially contained within God creates a link between the transcendent God—the source of all beings—and the created beings, a link which Hasidic sources refer to as "the secret of smoke," in which the smoke refers to the revelation on Mount Sinai, depicted in rabbinical literature as the moment when the heavens and the earth met.[33] Shneur Zalman writes,

Surely, the Light of Infinity [*Or Ein Sof*], blessed be he, is drawn down into everything, as Scripture says: "Now Mount Sinai was all in smoke" [Exod. 19:18]. [The word *'ashan* is to be interpreted as an acronym of the Hebrew for] world, year, soul. World is a reference to space [*makom*, literally "place"], into which the Infinity is drawn, as Scripture says: "See, there is a place near me" [Exod. 33:21]. Likewise, with regard to year, which is a reference to time: "He reigned, he reigns, and he will reign"—past, future, and present, all are in the nature of Infinity, etc. In the soul, too, there is an illumination of the Infinite.[34]

'Olam, *shanah*, and *nefesh*, or, in other words, space, time, and the divine life force, represent three different aspects of the divine illumination in the world. Even though all these terms belong to the created reality, Shneur Zalman cites Scripture to show that their source lies within the Godhead. He also links these notions with the Sinaitic revelation by reading the Hebrew word for smoke, *'ashan*, which in the Exodus narrative surrounded Mount Sinai, as an acronym for *'olam, shanah, nefesh*. The Sinaitic revelation serves therefore as a paradigm for the incorporation and ultimate annihilation (*bitul*) of these three worldly categories within God,[35] seemingly because, at Mount Sinai, the borders between transcendence and immanence, or the supratemporal and infratemporal realities, were dissolved. Shneur Zalman thus considers time, space, and the divine life force as transcendental notions that permeate all finite created beings and which originate in the divine infinity.

The passage quoted above underscores the complexity of the relation between God and time in Shneur Zalman's writing. Although he borrows from the Maggid of Mezrich the dichotomy of the supratemporal versus the infratemporal, it serves only as a point of departure for his discussion of temporality. The picture he presents in his teachings is ultimately much more nuanced.[36] In fact, the God of Shneur Zalman is above time, is the source of time, and most of all, manifests himself through time. The divine revelation which occurred at Mount Sinai bridges the gap between the two seemingly irreconcilable poles of the dichotomy: God, who is higher than time, and the temporal world. Moreover, as we shall see further, Shneur Zalman does not consider the Sinaitic experience as only an event from the past of the Jewish people, but as something that is reenacted each and every day. As the philosophical discourse fails to describe God's revelation, Shneur Zalman turns to kabbalistic terminology. He employs three models to demonstrate the divine revelation in temporality: through God's will (*ratson*) enclosed in the Torah, through the divine names and, finally, through God's kingship (*malkhut*).

The Sinaitic revelation, mentioned as the moment of the disintegration of boundaries between the transcendent and the immanent, points to the role of the Torah as a bond that ties the eternal God to the temporal world. This idea occurs in the classical rabbinical literature. The Sages held that the eternal Torah preceded and served as a blueprint for the creation of the world.[37] Shneur Zalman, following in the footsteps of the Maggid, revises this idea.[38] In his teachings, the Torah becomes an epitome of God's will and wisdom, located within the sefirotic structure in *Keter* and *Hokhmah* (and therefore higher than time),[39] which penetrates and manifests itself in the physical world. In a sermon elaborating on the words of the *Shema'* prayer ("Hear, O Israel," Deut. 6:4–9), he says:

> [God] said: "and these words which I command you this day" [Deut. 6:6]. That is to say, the Torah, which is his wisdom, [. . .] descends from a high to a low place. [. . .] The low place is time and space, which are a contrary thing [to God]. [. . .] And this is his true will, for even though he himself is above time and space, [. . .] nevertheless his wisdom, blessed be he, is within time and space, that is to say, the entire Torah is [subject to time and space] like the [commandments of wearing the] fringed garment [*tsitsit*], [laying] the phylacteries [*tefilin*], reciting the *Shema'* and [observing] the Sabbath and festivals at set times. Therefore, the Torah is the source of the life force of all the worlds, for his wisdom, blessed be he, required that his will should be within time and space. This is how all the worlds were revealed at the point at which [the divine will] entered time and space.[40]

The biblical verse with which Shneur Zalman opens his exegesis carries several meanings. First, "words" are taken to refer to the Torah, whose descent from its transcendent divine source (the divine Wisdom, *Hokhmah*) to the people of Israel in the lower world is a result of the arbitrary divine will (*Keter*), expressed by the word "command." Second, "this day" (*ha-yom*) introduces a temporal perspective: the fact that God, unbounded by time, is associated in the verse with a period of time (a day) underscores the role of the Torah as the intermediary between supratemporal and infratemporal realities.[41]

The expression "this day" in the Deuteronomy verse can also be approached from another perspective. It could point to the eternal relevance of the Torah. As Shneur Zalman says: "It has already been three thousand years since the Torah was given, but to you it should be as if it was given today [ha-yom]."[42] In other words, despite the fact that the Torah was given at a certain moment in history, it remains unaffected by the passing of time, and provides access to the Sinaitic experience to every Jewish person through the rituals of Torah reading and study.

The presence of the eternal Torah in the temporal world results from the divine's will to bring God's wisdom into the lowest domain of reality. This reality is the physical world, described as a "contrary thing" to God, on account of its separateness and ultimate distance from the divine unity. The presence of divine wisdom in the physical world is established through rituals and objects prescribed by the Torah. Indeed, items such as the phylacteries, the ritual fringes or the parchment of the mezuzah are subject to spatiality, while the Sabbath and festivals are subject to temporality, yet since they are commanded by the Torah, they also belong in the eternal divine wisdom and will.

The significance of Torah, commandments, and ritual objects will become apparent in the discussion of the divine service of the individual in the next chapters. Here, it is important to stress the role that the Torah plays as the vehicle of the manifestation of the supratemporal divinity in temporality, a relationship that Shneur Zalman expresses in even stronger terms when he proclaims that the Torah is the very reason for the existence of the world. As he explains, it was God's will that his wisdom (the Torah) should extend down to the spatiotemporal reality, and to fulfill his will, he created and sustained time and space. Consequently, the Torah is what causes the life force to be drawn into the worlds.

Furthermore, if the Torah is the cause of the existence of the world, it must have preceded creation. Shneur Zalman explains the eternity and preexistence of the Torah not in the simplistic terms of the midrash, which speaks of the two thousand years that separated the Torah from the world,[43] but rather by transposing the idea of the midrash to the *sefirotic* scheme: the Torah, being God's will and wisdom, originates in *Keter*, an entity that transcends the *sefirotic* tree, and in *Hokhmah*, the highest of all the *sefirot*, which Hasidic masters located above the realm of temporality.[44] Thus, the Torah precedes the lower worlds in the ontological rather than the temporal order. At the same time, it reveals itself in the most tangible everyday objects, allowing every observant person to grasp the supratemporal through daily practices.

The figure of the Torah as God's will and wisdom serves as one possible interpretative model for the manifestation of the supratemporal realm in temporality. Another strategy that Shneur Zalman adopts relates to the dynamics of the divine names representing different aspects of God's relationship, whether separateness from or involvement in temporal reality, and in more general terms, aspects of God's transcendence and immanence. The juxtaposition of the Tetragrammaton, on the one hand, and the names Elohim (a name often associated with nature, since the Hebrew word for nature, *ha-teva'*, and Elohim have the same numerical value of 286[45]) and Adonai ("the Lord"), on the other, plays a prominent role in Shneur Zalman's model of the creation, of which the discourse on time constitutes only a part. Used as a hermeneutical model for the contraction of the divine light in the process of creation, it appears in the second part of the *Tanya* ("The Gate of Unity and the Faith"),[46] as well as in some of his *ma'amarim*.

> Now, Scripture says that "the Lord [YHVH] God [Elohim] is sun and shield" [Ps. 84:11]. Just as the sun has its covering that can bear its radiance, [. . .] so, by way of allegory, [the name] Elohim is the covering for the name HVYH, which conceals [the name] HVYH. [. . .] Elohim stands for the general contraction and the aspect of time: "YHVH reigned, YHVH reigns, [and YHVH will reign]," whereas Adonai stands for the particular contraction, for [. . .] the aspect of Lord [*adon*] refers to the Blessed One only with respect to separate beings, and therefore this contraction is particular.[47]

In this excerpt, Shneur Zalman refers to the Lurianic myth of creation, a crucial stage of which is the contraction (*tsimtsum*) in which God's infinite light limits itself in order to make space for nondivine beings.[48] He compares the Tetragrammaton and Elohim to the sun and to the shield that covers it, protecting the world below and preventing it from being burned. The names Elohim and Adonai restrain the unbound divine light originating in the Tetragrammaton so as to enable creation to take place.[49] The divine light mediated through these lower divine names provides the created beings with life while simultaneously allowing them to preserve their individual existence. Thanks to these filters, they are not at risk of dissolving in the divine light because it reaches them in diminished form rather than in full force.

Shneur Zalman connects the Tetragrammaton with God's supratemporal dimension, pointing to the past, present, and future forms of the verb "to be" comprised in it. This step allows him to employ the concept of *tsimtsum*—the divine contraction—in the discourse on God and temporality. On the whole, there are two dimensions of the contraction: the general and the particular. The particular contraction gives rise to the existence of individual beings, presumably because it adjusts the radiance of the divine light to each and every one of them. It is also associated with the name Adonai (traditionally used in the liturgy as a substitute for the Tetragrammaton), as the idea of lordship reflects both God's supremacy and the gap separating Him from created beings.[50] The general contraction, linked to the name Elohim for nature, diminishes the divine light in order to create the temporal framework in which these beings can exist.[51]

The discourse on divine names shows that time is a created entity, which conditions all worldly things. Temporality is created from the concealment of God's four-lettered name by the name Elohim, since both often appear together in the Bible. The creation of individual beings comes as a result of the contraction of the Tetragrammaton's life force into Adonai, an idea based on the ritual replacement of the ineffable four-lettered name of God with its liturgical euphemism.

It is worth noting that the distinction between the roles of the two contractions of the Tetragrammaton, by Elohim on the one hand and Adonai on the other, is not maintained rigidly in Shneur Zalman's texts. In another *ma'amar*, he infers the occurrence of time and space from the integration of the Tetragrammaton within Adonai rather than Elohim.[52] The two possible ways of integrating the Tetragrammaton with Adonai reflect the twofold relation between God and the physical world. The integration of Adonai within YHVH reflects the nullity of the creation against divine wholeness, whereas the integration of YHVH within Adonai shows that the divinity permeates the spatiotemporal reality:

> Time and space, too, are from Him, blessed be he, and they are not a thing that is separate from Him. [. . .] Only from the point of view of the recipients it is an individual thing and a real opposite [to God], whereas in truth, [even his mode of] surrounding all worlds [*sovev kol 'almin*] fills the dimensions of time and space.[53]

In other words, the polarity of God and the physical reality is not absolute, as it might seem from the human perspective. In fact, they are united in twofold unity, and "The Gate of Unity and the Faith" elaborates on this issue. The twofold unity of God in Shneur Zalman's thought has been the subject of scholarly examination;[54] here, it is sufficient to say that he employs zoharic terminology to describe these two aspects of the relation between God and creation, naming them the "upper unity" and the "lower unity" (*yihuda 'ila'ah* and *yihuda tata'a*).[55] The "upper unity" represents the unity and uniqueness of the divine as the only true being, as opposed to all other worldly beings, whereas the "lower unity" means that the world, perceived by humans as a separate entity, is also permeated with the divine. Although from the perspective of the created beings, time and space are nondivine entities, they are in fact both permeated by *sovev kol 'almin*, the transcendent aspect of God.

The dynamics of the divine names thus enable Shneur Zalman to depict the transition from a supratemporal God to an infratemporal reality. It presents time as a side effect of the contraction of the ineffable four-letter divine name into its euphemistic substitutes. From this perspective, time becomes an expression of God's lordship in the world, and a framework wherein individual beings can exist by God's will.

The twofold unity of God and the world finds its expression in the first two verses of the *Shema'* prayer. The first verse, "Listen, Israel, YHVH is our God [Elohenu], YHVH is one," corresponds to the upper unity, while the second, "Blessed be the name of his glorious kingdom for ever and ever," corresponds to the lower unity.[56] The words of the prayer not only explain the two unifications and the relation between the two divine names mentioned in it; they also make it possible to locate the source of time and space within *Malkhut*, the lowest level within the *sefirotic* structure.

Shneur Zalman discerns in the *Shema'* prayer several parallels between the upper unity and the lower unity. First, the divine transcendence expressed by the word *one* (*ehad*) in the first verse is paralleled by the expression, in the second, of God's presence in the world, which will last forever "and ever" (*va-'ed*). The interchangeability of *ehad* and *va-'ed* serves to demonstrate that the divine transcendence and immanence are but two modes of expression of the divine unity.[57] Second, whereas the Tetragrammaton in the first verse expresses the upper unity, the "kingdom" (*malkhuto*) in the second verse points to the lower unity of God within the world.

The word *Malkhut*, which could be translated as kingdom or kingship, defines God's relation with his creation. In Shneur Zalman's teachings, God is compared to a king who must therefore have subjects. It is not enough for the king to rule over his family or his court; in order to display his power to the full, he needs to be able to subdue people who are remote from him. In this allegory, the class of the king's subjects refers to individual beings in the world whose existence ultimately stands in contrast to the unity of God. As the allegory intends to show, God creates these beings in order to demonstrate that he exercises dominion over them, while at the same time proving the impossibility of any existence which does not result from his will.[58] As in the *ma'amar*, quoted above, in which Shneur Zalman referred to the physical world as the lowest place into which the Torah descends, here too he describes the spatiotemporal reality as the entity that is opposed to the divine being. He underscores the absolute transcendence of God, but then brings *Malkhut* into the picture as the divine agent in which time and space originate and that acts through his immanence.

The interpretation of God's relation to the world in terms of kingship or dominion has further consequences: it transposes the contraction of the name YHVH into Adonai or Elohim, which takes place in the process of the creation, to the *sefirotic* realm. The displacement, which plays on the similar meanings of *adnut* (lordship) and *malkhut* (kingship),[59] makes the *sefirah Malkhut* into the intermediary between transcendence and immanence,[60] where time and space are created out of nothing.[61]

Elsewhere, Shneur Zalman provides a biblical source for this idea that both the dimensions of time and space originate within *Malkhut*.

> Your kingship [*malkhutekha*] is an eternal kingship, and your dominion is for all generations [Ps. 145:13]: "eternal" [*kol 'olamim*, literally "all worlds"] [refers to] space; "all generations" [*khol dor va-dor*] to time.[62]

As Elliot Wolfson has noted, a parallel is drawn here between the upper and lower unities within the conceptual framework of the Habad temporal discourse.[63] In the liturgical phrase "YHVH reigns, YHVH reigned YHVH will reign" (*melekh, malakh, yimlokh*), the four-lettered name of God, which "indicates that he transcends time, that he was, he is, and he will be—all at the same instant,"[64] is placed alongside *Malkhut*, conjugated in three tenses: the past, present, and future. The parallel comes to show that even though time comes into being only in *Malkhut*, its roots reach much higher.

On the symbolic level, God's involvement in the world remains unaffected by the multiple conjugations of the verb "to reign." In order to preserve the concept of divine immutability despite the constant changes that affect the world, Shneur Zalman employs the idea of the disclosure of God in the world.

> *Malkhut* of the world of Emanation [...] is the root and the source of the coming into being of time. [...] As is known, the coming into

being of the past, present, and future in the worlds of Creation, Formation, and Making comes from the aspect of "[YHVH] reigned, [YHVH] reigns, [YHVH] will reign," etc., which is the aspect of world, year, etc. [and soul], as is written elsewhere. And the source of time is only in *Malkhut*, which is the disclosure of the [world of] Emanation, the World of Disclosure. [. . .] This, however, is not the case above, where the aspect of World of Concealment does not fall into the category of the source of time, for it belongs in the mode of surrounding all worlds, which is the aspect of concealment of the essence.[65]

The *sefirah Malkhut* of the World of Emanation brings the divine essence out of the state of concealment, so that it is disclosed in the world, namely within the categories of time and space. This statement conveys a paradox: elsewhere, Shneur Zalman maintains the absolute incomprehensibility of God's essence, which means that the disclosure in the world of God's essence comes at the same time as its concealment.[66] Shneur Zalman plays on the ambiguity of the Hebrew root *'ayin-lamed-mem*, which is shared by the words for "world" (*'olam*) and "concealment" (*he'lem*).[67] The world reveals God's essence, which otherwise is concealed in the absolute divine transcendence; at the same time, however, it conceals it, since the transcendence can no longer be transcendent when it is revealed in immanence: "The world [*ha-'olam*] [. . .] is essentially a form of concealment [*he'lem*]—it conceals the light so that it may be revealed, as there can be no extension without withholding, no showing without hiding, no presence without absence."[68] The process of disclosure itself is in turn related to the concept of "world, year, soul," where "world" stands for the lower worlds in which the divinity is revealed, "year" stands for *Malkhut*, which is the source of time, and "soul" represents the divine life force flowing down from *Ze'ir anpin* (the Small Countenance, the constellation of six *sefirot* from *Hesed* to *Yesod*) to *Malkhut*.[69]

Malkhut, therefore, is a liminal entity that stands on the border between the temporal and timeless realities. On the one hand, it separates the three lower worlds from the World of Emanation, which is often described by Shneur Zalman as one with the divine.[70] It also distinguishes God's transcendence (surrounding all worlds) from his immanence (filling all worlds); the World of Concealment from the World of Disclosure; and what is higher than time from what is within the temporal realm. On the other hand, *Malkhut* is an intermediary, through which the infinite God is revealed in the finite world within time and space. When it ascends to the World of Emanation, it is united with the timelessness symbolized by the Tetragrammaton, where "He was, he is and he will be—all at the same instant."[71] Yet, when *Malkhut* of the World of Emanation descends to bring the divine influx into the World of Creation, it becomes the source of time in the lower worlds.[72] As Shneur Zalman calls it, resorting to the kabbalistic jargon, *Malkhut* of the higher world becomes *'Atik*[73] of the lower. By describing *Malkhut* of the World of Emanation as *'Atik* (the ancient one) of the World of Creation, Shneur Zalman presents *Malkhut* of the upper world as the source of the worlds that lie beneath it, and at the same time, as the pretemporal source of time in this world. In this way, he highlights the continuity between the upper and the lower worlds while at the same time keeping them apart.

It is clear, then, that the relation between God and creation cannot be exhausted by the dichotomy of supratemporality versus infratemporality, or eternal versus temporal. Rather, Shneur Zalman proposes a more sophisticated model of the transition from the ultimate unity of God to the multiplicity of the temporal world. The realm that lies beneath *Malkhut* of Emanation is clearly temporal. What is directly above it, however, is not necessarily deemed to be supratemporal.

> The notion of eternity [. . .] refers only to that which falls within the category and limitation of time, [even though] it endures for a very long time. But the duration of time does not have any relevance to that which is not within the category and limitation of time; rather, [it refers to] "He was, he is, and he will be"—all at once. This category and this notion refers only to [. . .] his Kingship [*malkhuto*], blessed be he, which is within the category and limitation of time: "He reigned, he reigns, he will reign."[74]

Echoing Aristotle, Shneur Zalman considers eternity to be a mode of temporality, regardless of the duration of time it denotes.[75] The notion of eternity thus cannot apply to the transcendent aspect of the divine, which is above any temporal characterization. The idea of the divine that is above eternity is alluded to by the Tetragrammaton when it is used as the symbol of the one instant which comprises the aspects of "was," "is," and "will be," namely, the past, present, and future. As I will explain below, this aspect of the Godhead relates to the sequence of events taking place within the theosophical structure rather than to the passage of time within the world; it is identified as the "order of time" (*seder ha-zemanim*),[76] and as such precedes ontically the existence of time in the world.[77]

The various models of divine revelation demonstrate that the relation between God and the world is much more complex than the opposition between the "higher than time" infinity and the temporal finitude. Not only does it reveal the modes in which infinity manifests itself within the world without becoming in any way limited in its infiniteness, it also points to a domain in the *sefirotic* world which is caught in between, above the *Malkhut* of Emanation, and therefore not subject to time, but still below the absolutely infinite and undivided *Ein Sof*. Since *Ein Sof* is utterly beyond temporal characterization, there must be an entity that mediates it to the temporal reality of the lower worlds as they come into being.

In order to understand the relation between the time in the lower worlds and the quasi-temporal mode in the World of Emanation, one needs to refer to Shneur Zalman's model of creation of the four worlds. The four worlds—Emanation, Creation, Formation, and Making—come into being in two stages. The first stage is the emergence of the World of Emanation, in which all ten *sefirot* remain in a state of unity with God. The second comprises the three worlds that lie beneath Emanation, which are in a state of separation and multiplicity. These two stages require two different intermediaries to connect them to their supernal source. As was shown above, *Malkhut* of the World of Emanation mediates between the domain that lies above time and the three lower worlds that are subject to temporality, a role that renders *Malkhut* the effective source of time. An analogous role is ascribed to the more elevated entity of "Primordial Man" (*Adam kadmon*), which mediates between the transcendent God and the World of Emanation and itself precedes the creation of time but is subject to the "order of time." In the spirit of Lurianic kabbalah,[78] Shneur Zalman presents *Adam kadmon* as an entity that emanates from *Ein Sof* prior to the emergence of the four worlds. But he strips *Adam kadmon* of the mythical characteristics often attributed to it and presents it instead as a simple and instantaneous divine thought that comprises the totality of creation with all its future developments. Since time is a part of creation, some mode of temporality features in *Adam kadmon*, too. At first, temporality develops into the "order of time," but with the creation of separate beings, this turns into time proper as it is experienced in the lower worlds.[79]

These gradations of temporality show that Habad thinkers in general, and Shneur Zalman in particular, struggled to fill the ontological gap between creation and a God who is beyond any positive characterization. Habad discourse on time draws from a wide range of midrashic, kabbalistic, and philosophical traditions. The complexity of the different worldviews stemming from all of these earlier sources led to the proliferation in Habad thought of a variety of intertwining entities whose role is to mediate between the supratemporal and the infratemporal realities. Moreover, the vast ontological gap between unity and multiplicity provoked Habad thinkers to further negotiate the distance between God and temporal reality by borrowing from kabbalah the "the order of time."[80] Admittedly, this notion remained marginal for Shneur Zalman, possibly on account of its highly theoretical character. However, it was discussed extensively by his grandson, the Tsemah Tsedek in his philosophical book, *Sefer ha-hakirah*.

Before we get to the core of the discussion of "the order of time," a few words about the origins of this term. The very notion of the order of the time, or a quasi-temporal order of events that precedes the coming into being of time, is inspired by the language of an ancient midrash.

> Said Rabbi Yehudah bar Simon: "Scripture does not say: 'there shall be evening,' but rather 'and there was evening' [Gen. 1:5], for there was a prior order of time [*seder ha-zemanim*]." Rabbi Abbahu said: "this comes to teach that he was creating worlds and destroying them, until he created these [worlds]."[81]

The two Amoras in the midrash question the significance of the *vav* consecutive in the Hebrew account of creation, which changes the meaning of the verse from "there shall be evening" (*yehi 'erev*) into "and there was evening" (*va-yehi 'erev*). The former would have meant that evening and morning were to follow the creation of light, whereas the latter suggests that they had already passed before light was created. Rabbi Yehudah intimates that even though time had not yet come into being, there must already have existed a certain "order of time." To Abbahu, in contrast, the creation of the world as we know it was preceded by a number of aborted creations. In any case, following Stern's interpretation of rabbinic culture as devoid of the abstract concept of time, the midrashic "order of time" appears to be a preestablished order, in which the events unfolded prior to the emergence of the natural phenomena used by the rabbis to measure processes and intervals between them.[82]

Both these resolutions reverberate in Habad teachings. The created and destroyed worlds that preceded the creation of ours is substituted, under the influence of kabbalah, by a sequence of emanated upper worlds.

And behold: in truth, "I am the Lord, I have not changed" [Mal. 3:6], for there is no change in Him, blessed be he [...] for "He, with his name alone existed" [*Pirke de-Rabi Eli'ezer*, ch. 3, 2b] for several thousands and myriads of years before the creation of the world (and similarly, before the coming into being of time, for time, too, is created. But there was an order of time before the creation of this world, that is, from the time of the emanation and coming into being of spiritual worlds, as is written in *'Ets hayim*, [Gate of] Circles and Linearity [Gate 1, Section 1, 25]. But prior to this, even the order of time was not applicable, for he, blessed be he, is completely above time).[83]

The main point in this passage is the immutability of God in the face of creation, which is a recurrent idea in Shneur Zalman's teaching. But much more interesting is the difficulty he faces when explaining this idea using temporal notions, such as in the description of God, who remained unchanged during the thousands of years preceding the creation of the world. This stands in obvious contradiction to Shneur Zalman's belief that time itself is a created entity, forcing him to provide an additional explanation: the gap between God and the creation is measured by the order of time rather than by time proper.

In order to explain the midrashic expression of the order of time, Shneur Zalman uses the very same passage from Vital's *'Ets hayim* that he refuted elsewhere as an insufficient explanation of the timing of the creation.[84] In this passage, Vital argues that creation was preceded by a sequence of emanations, the duration of which determined the exact timing of the creation of the worlds. Shneur Zalman does not accept Vital's argument with regard to time and the creation but is willing to use the idea that lies behind it—the notion that the order of time explains the sequence of the coming into being of the *sefirot* of the World of Emanation.

This idea, hinted at in Shneur Zalman's teaching, is further elaborated by the Tsemah Tsedek, whose attitude toward philosophical discussion was much warmer than his grandfather's. He comments on the medieval discussion of the preexistence of time in order to explain what Hasdai Crescas may have had in mind when he claimed that time had somehow existed before the creation of the world.

It would seem from the words of the author of the *'Akedah*[85] that Rabbi Hasdai came to the conclusion that [the categories of] prior and posterior apply [to God]. But he may have argued that they apply to the essence of the Creator only from the moment of the emanation of the ten *sefirot*, for only then do [the categories of] prior and posterior apply. This is what is called the order of time, that is to say, a priori and posteriori, for the attribute of *Hesed* was emanated first, and only then the attribute of *Gevurah* and *Din*, and after that the attribute of *Rahamim*, etc.[86]

The Tsemah Tsedek revises Crescas' critique of Aristotle and Maimonides (as mediated by Yitshak Arama's fifteenth-century *'Akedat Yitshak*). Contrary to Aristotle, Crescas maintained that time is not related to motion. Instead, he proposed the idea of time as duration.[87] This implies that time predated creation, and that it conditions even eternal and immobile entities, such as God. Crescas therefore takes the midrashic statement according to which the order of time preceded the creation literally.[88] The author of the *'Akedat Yitshak* disagrees with him, claiming that time could not have existed before creation, and that the midrashic statement must therefore refer to something else. According to Arama, the midrash attempts to resolve a much more specific issue than the one Crescas deals with, namely, the existence of time before the creation of the celestial spheres. The question that occupied the Sages was not whether time is bound to motion in general, but rather whether it is bound specifically to the motion of the celestial spheres. According to the biblical account of the creation (Gen. 1:14–19), stars and planets were created on the fourth day; nonetheless, temporal characteristics such as the division between day and night feature in the creation from its very beginning. The order of time, according to Arama, refers to the first three days of creation, when the duration of time had already been established, despite the fact that there were no celestial spheres by which it could be measured. Crescas was therefore wrong when he maintained the existence of the duration of time prior to creation.[89]

The Tsemah Tsedek refutes both views. He reinterprets Crescas in line with his Habad predecessors, arguing that to refer to God in temporal terms, as in Crescas's interpretation of the order of time, would imply that there was an a priori and a posteriori in the divine before creation. This cannot possibly apply to the essence of God, which according to Shneur Zalman lies above and beyond any temporal characterization, but only to the World of Emanation, which is in a state of absolute unity with God and is thus above time, since time exists only from the *sefirah* of *Malkhut* of the World of Emanation downward.

Although the World of Emanation is one with the divine, its ten constituent *sefirot* emanated from God in a precise order. The Tsemah Tsedek, following his grandfather, identifies this order as the "order of times" mentioned in the midrash. In this way, he transposes the account of the creation into his theosophical discourse. The order of time, which Crescas ascribes to the divine prior to creation, is ascribed by the Tsemah Tsedek to the *sefirot* above the worlds of Creation, Formation, and Making; time, which Yitshak Arama attributes to the subcelestial realm, he ascribes to the *sefirot* and to the worlds below *Malkhut* of the World of Emanation. The order of time is indeed something that exists prior to the created worlds, but it is still contained within the boundaries of the World of Emanation. It exists, as Shneur Zalman puts it, "from the time of the emanation and coming into being of spiritual worlds,"[90] with "spiritual worlds" meaning either the World of Emanation or the previous worlds created and destroyed by God.[91] Finally, the order of time is seen not only as something that precedes time but also as the paradigm of time and the source of its existence.[92] It is not surprising, therefore, that Shneur Zalman identifies the order of time with the Tetragrammaton: "He was, he is, and he will be," from which the temporal modes of past, present, and future develop in the lower worlds.[93]

The Nature of Time

The transposition of the order of time to the theosophic structure utterly changes the sense in which the Sages understood the concept. Shneur Zalman does not see the emergence from the infinite divine of the order of time and then time proper as a chain of events in cosmic history, but rather as an order of ontological relations between time and its source. This does not at all mean that he is not interested in cosmic history (he discusses the subject in his teachings, as will be shown in detail in the next chapter). But it is important to emphasize that, for Shneur Zalman, the order of time did not cease with the creation of the world or with the establishment of the luminaries in the firmament. Rather, it continues to exist in the upper realms and to influence the passing of time in the lower worlds. This aspect of his discourse on time is related to his view of creation as a continuous rather than a one-off event, which he shares with other Hasidic masters.[94] Not only does the model of continuous creation present time as being constantly renewed rather than enduring unchanged from the moment of creation, but it also yields a tentative definition of time.

How does one grasp the true character of creation? As indicated earlier, Shneur Zalman maintains that one can learn about God by studying his deeds. This principle applies here, too. The cyclical rhythm of nature hints at the true character of all beings: they are not created once, but rather are continuously created and re-created. The Hasidic masters read this idea into a particular liturgical phrase. Levi Yitshak of Berdichev (1740–1809), Shneur Zalman's friend and a Hasidic *tsadik* in his own right, noted the peculiar phrasing of the blessing *yotser or*:[95] "'Who *forms* light and *creates* darkness' rather than 'Who *formed* light and *created* darkness.' We use the present tense, because God is constantly forming, revitalizing all of life, moment to moment."[96] Shneur Zalman's mentor, Menachem Mendel of Vitebsk, also attached special significance to the words of this blessing, but focused on the subsequent words (in the *nusah Sefarad*, the kabbalistic version of the prayer book used by the Hasidim): "[God] daily, continually, renews the work of creation." However, he modifies the meaning of the verse to suggest that since the world's existence is entirely dependent on God's will, it is only "as if" (*ke-ilu*) he creates and destroys it at each moment.[97] Shneur Zalman, in contrast, understands the statement quite literally: the divine life force constantly descends and ascends again, annihilating the created beings and bringing them back to life anew, ex nihilo (*me-ayin le-yesh*). He likens this to the alternation of sleep and wakefulness: when people are asleep, their life force departs from them, but when they wake up and the life force returns, it is as if they had been created anew. By contemplating the alternation of such contrasting phenomena as sleep and wakefulness, day and night, and so on, one can grasp the idea of the continuous creation.[98]

To describe the rhythm of the world's perpetual alternation between materialization and annihilation, Shneur Zalman employs the term *ratso va-shov*, borrowed from the vision of Ezekiel in which "the living creatures ran and returned" (Ezek. 1:14).[99] This biblical expression, meaning literally "run and return," recurs throughout his teachings in reference either to the nature of divine service or, in theosophical terms, to the dynamics of the relations among various entities within the divine sphere. The rhythm of *ratso va-shov* is comparable to that of a heartbeat, which continuously gathers and pumps the life force within a body.[100]

According to Shneur Zalman, the acknowledgment that creation takes places continuously is also an expression of faith in God's providence. He stated that while gentiles and heretics[101] may believe that God created the world, they maintain that his involvement ceased past that point. Jews, in contrast, believe that God, as Shneur Zalman puts it elsewhere, "brings life to everything, creates it out of nothing, and renews it, by his goodness, on every day and at every moment."[102] In other words, he contrasts the deistic view of divine providence attributed to gentiles and heretics with the Habad version of occasionalism, whereby God is involved in every occurrence in the world by virtue of his constant re-creation of it.[103]

It is worth noting that Shneur Zalman attributes the split between these two beliefs not to a divergence of theological approaches, but rather to the difference between the gentile and the Jewish soul in terms of their respective relations to temporality. The gentile soul originates in the domain that lies within the temporal realm, and therefore it is incapable of perceiving God's acts, which transcend time; all that it is able to see is the self-regulating natural order within the world. By contrast, the Jewish soul stems from the transcendent domain of "supernal thought," which lies above time. Accordingly, the Jewish soul's perception transcends nature and allows it to recognize God's acts that come into the world from above nature.[104] This distinction originates in the broader discussion on the nature of the gentile soul and Jewish soul, the main principles of which Shneur Zalman lays out in the famous first chapter of *Tanya*.[105] According to Shneur Zalman, the gentile soul's subjugation to time is clearly related to the fact that gentiles possess only the animal soul, whereas the Jewish soul's ability to transcend time is related to the additional, divine soul, which is "the part of the God above,"[106] and which only the Jews possess. As a result, he believed gentiles remain completely subjugated to nature, which, as the gentiles supposedly claim, was once created and now runs its course, whereas Jews can transcend nature and its temporal limitations and, in a way, have power over time.

Among the Hasidic masters who focused on the difference between the Jewish and gentile experience of time was, notably, Shneur Zalman's teacher, the Maggid of Mezrich. While, unlike his student, he did not delve into the core of the difference between Jews and gentiles, he recognized the uniqueness of Israel in that respect.

> "And who is like your people of Israel, a unique nation on earth?" [1 Chr. 17:21] [. . .] as they reach the state of unity which transcends number [. . .] for time is under their control to do whatever they want, as they are higher than time.[107]

In the eyes of the Maggid, Israel's exceptionality among the nations, besides indicating its ethnic uniqueness, points also to its unique ontological status. Israel exists in the state of unity, which corresponds with the unity of God. The Maggid learns about this correspondence from the Talmudic dictum, according to which God dons phylacteries, just as the Jews do. While Jews' phylacteries proclaim God's unity in *Shema'*, as is inscribed on the phylacteries' parchment, God's phylacteries, which bear the formula from the book of Chronicles, proclaim the oneness of Israel.[108] The oneness of Israel means that it is beyond the dominion of multiplicity, and, consequently, time. On the most basic level, the control that Jews exert over time means that they set times of study, determine the times of festivals, the arrival and departure of the Sabbath, and so on. The Hasidic masters, including Shneur Zalman, take this observation one step further: Jews may use time-related rituals to arrive at and unite with the infinite, supratemporal source of time. Particular applications of this principle in Shneur Zalman's teachings will be discussed in details in chapter 4.

In addition to continuous creation, Shneur Zalman viewed continuous annihilation and revival as inherently related to time.[109] The philosophers who influenced him defined time as a derivative of motion or duration. Shneur Zalman transposes the physical concept of motion to the metaphysical concept of divine influx. Even though he does not produce a rigorous definition of time, he clearly conceptualizes it as deriving from the *ratso va-shov*, and as a measure of the intervals that punctuate the cycles of the worlds' annihilation and revival.[110]

Shneur Zalman provides a number of explanations for the genesis of *ratso va-shov*, which gives rise to time. In some of his teachings, the phenomenon appears to be an effect of certain permutations of divine names, following the concept that the twelve hours of the day correspond to the twelve permutations of the Tetragrammaton, whereas the twelve hours of night correspond to the twelve permutations of the name Adonai.[111] Each and every permutation draws down a particular aspect of the divine life force. When one permutation replaces another, the life force related to the former permutation departs, and that of the latter descends into the world, creating the passing of time. To illustrate this process, Shneur Zalman presents the invented etymology of the Hebrew word for hour (*sha'ah*) as semantically connected to the homonymous verb that means "to turn toward something," for in the passing of time "the divine life force turns downwards from up above, by way of *ratso va-shov*."[112]

Elsewhere, Shneur Zalman refers, on the one hand, to the pretemporal order of the emanation of the *sefirot* as the source of *ratso va-shov*, and on the other, to the dynamics of their emergence. The former corresponds to the idea of the order of time as described above (the sequence of the emanation of the *sefirot* precedes time and serves as its paradigm), while the latter points to the opposing forces of *Hesed* and *Gevurah* that emerge in the process of the emanation. The dialectical relation of unity and opposition between the emerging *sefirot* constitutes a form of *ratso va-shov* from which time emerges.

> For they [the *sefirot*] are in the nature of *ratso va-shov*, which is the order of time, from which branches out the cause of time as the duration that effects from [the motion of] *ratso va-shov*, which is comparable to a heartbeat. Since the motion of *ratso va-shov* comprises both an affirmation and its own negation, it causes there to be a passage of brief duration[113] of the *shov* and the *ratso* which follows it. This is [the cycle of] disclosure and absence of the influx, etc. which may be compared to a clock, [where] the movement from side to side (of what we call a pendulum), which is comparable to a heartbeat, causes a momentary passage of time.[114]

Time's *ratso va-shov* is compared both to a heartbeat, which underscores the aspect of creation and annihilation inscribed in the rhythm of time, and to the motion of a pendulum, so as to emphasize the connection between the bipolar dynamics of *ratso va-shov* and the progress of time. The opposite phases of *ratso va-shov* are affirmation and negation, or the influx and withdrawal of the divine energy. In the phase of *shov*, the divine reveals itself and permeates the worlds, while in the phase of *ratso* it returns to its supernal source. The duration of the cycle constitutes a unit of time, a moment (*rega'*). In short, time is measured by the intervals in the flow of the divine life force into the world. By means of this intermittent influx of life force the world is annihilated and created anew, thus giving the impression of time's passing.

The analogy of the pendulum illustrates the relativity of time. Shneur Zalman duly notes that the lowest end of the pendulum has to cover a greater distance with each of its movements than any other point along its arm. For this reason, units of time can have different values, depending on the position in which they are being measured: the higher the position on the arm, the smaller the value. So it is with the *ratso va-shov* in relation to time: the further the divine influx descends down the hierarchy of worlds, the longer the distance it has to cover, and consequently the higher the value of the time unit.[115] Thus, according to Shneur Zalman, when the Psalmist addresses God with the words, "For in your sight a thousand years are like yesterday that has past" (Ps. 90:4), he tells us literally that the duration of a day in the upper worlds equates to the duration of a thousand years in our world below. The days, according to Shneur Zalman, refer to the six *sefirot* of the World of Emanation (the constellation of *Ze'ir anpin*: *Hesed, Gevurah, Tif'eret, Netsah, Hod,* and *Yesod*; the *sefirah* of *Malkhut* corresponds to Sabbath), traditionally called "supernal days,"[116] each one of which comprises six thousand years of the world's history (whereas *Malkhut* corresponds to the seventh messianic millennium).[117]

Shneur Zalman therefore defines time by using the concept of *ratso va-shov*. Time results from the divine life force's continuous cycle of descent and ascent. With every ascent the life force nullifies the existence of the world, and with every descent it creates it anew, thus giving the impression that time flows. The moment of the life force's presence constitutes the time unit. In this way, Shneur Zalman transposes the philosophers' definition of time as the measurement of the movement of heavenly spheres to the theosophic structure, seeing in it the measurement of the movement of the divine life force, which in turn results from the movements of the *sefirot* (an idea which may have originated in the kabbalah of Moses Cordovero, who also explained the flow of time in his commentary on the prayer book as dependent on the revolutions of the *sefirot*).[118]

The image of the pendulum is just an application of a common paradigm in Shneur Zalman's teachings, according to which a higher entity in the hierarchy of worlds always comprises a lower one, by way of the general comprising the particular. The time-transcending God encapsulates all temporal aspects and historical developments in his one simple thought, which comprises everything "at a glance, with no duration of time, either prior or posterior,"[119] as in the prayer describing God as one who "looks and sees to the end of all generations."[120] In the course of creation and the development of the hierarchy of worlds, time is formed, compartmentalized, concretized, and extended, as it grows from an instant to six supernal days to the six thousand years in our world. At the same time, one should keep in mind the fact that the creation and division of time is a continuous process, which should be seen as a part of the continuous creation of the world. Therefore, God constantly re-creates time in the lower worlds, or as Shneur Zalman puts it, the renewal of time (*hithadshut ha-zeman*) comes from above time, when the divine life force returns to its source in *shov*.[121] He employs several hermeneutical models to explain this process.

The first explains the division of time in terms of the potentiality that existed prior to the instantaneous divine thought. This is said to be comparable to the rabbinic exegetical method of following a general statement with a particular claim (*kelal u-ferat*),[122] which in turn becomes the general statement on which the next particular claim is based. The whole process culminates in a final stage of interpretation, which in the case of the evolution of time, corresponds to the World of Making. Just as the Gemara does not generate any new laws but merely develops the mishnaic laws in greater detail, so time in the lower worlds is only an actualization of the potential concealed within God's supra-temporal instantaneous thought.[123]

The interpretative model of the division of time is not limited to the metaphor of the source-commentary relation. The "interweaving of temporality and textuality," as Wolfson calls it,[124] is an offshoot of Shneur Zalman's doctrine of creation, in which the divine speech plays a prominent role.[125] It is also a result of associating *Malkhut* both with divine speech and with time.

> [This is] the root of the matter of "time for loving" [Eccl. 3:8], etc. As is explained in the *Zohar*, the Yanuka interpreted it to mean that it refers to love within *Malkhut*, which is called time ['*et*, which is spelled with the letter '*ayin*],[126] but it is also called *et*, [spelled] with an *alef*, for [all] "*alefs* [interchange with] '*ayins*,"[127] etc. So the issue of time begins in *Malkhut*, and these are the letters *alef* [and] *tav* which are set in the mouth, as is written in *Sefer yetsirah* [2:3], and this is sufficient for him who understands.[128]

This passage illustrates the relationship of *Malkhut* with time and speech. Basing himself on the zoharic source, Shneur Zalman ascribes Ecclesiastes's "time for loving" to *Malkhut*, since, following the *Zohar*, he identifies *Malkhut-Shekhinah* with time.[129] He then draws on a Talmudic tradition ascribed to the school of Rabbi Eliezer, which tended to pronounce the Hebrew gutturals '*ayin* and *alef* in the same way. The reference to this tradition provides Shneur Zalman with the ambiguity he seeks: the time of *Malkhut* ('*et*) can be read as the particle *et*, which contains the first and last letters of the Hebrew alphabet and therefore points to all the letters of the alphabet by means of which God created the world, but also perhaps to the duration of time from its beginning to its end.[130]

Shneur Zalman compares the forming of time to the process of articulation. Every act of speech originates in a thought, which in turns is rooted in the individual's will. The thought is associated with limitlessness, as any single thought can comprise an unlimited number of topics. In the process of articulation, however, the thought is channeled into an act of speech, which takes place at a particular time and place and can relate only to a single topic.[131] Analogously, all aspects of time, and the future developments of history, are included in the instantaneous divine thought, which is like an "illumination and a lightning in the world."[132] Yet when it comes to realization in the world, this thought splits into past, present, and future, and into the six supernal days, which in turn divide into six thousand years,[133] each dividing into 365 days, the days into hours, and so on. Effectively, God renews the act of creation by releasing each day into the world only "a number of combinations of letters" out of his unique divine thought.[134]

The sequential stages of this hermeneutical model correspond to the levels of the sefirotic structure: the divine thought parallels the three upper attributes, the supernal days are the six attributes constituting *Ze'ir anpin*, and speech is located within the *sefirah* of *Malkhut*. As Shneur Zalman mentions briefly elsewhere,[135] the source of time is in the conjunction of *Hokhmah* and *Binah* and is expressed in *Malkhut*. In other words, in the process of verbalizing a thought, intuitive wisdom (*Hokhmah*) is instantaneously conceptualized in *Binah*,[136] but it takes time for it to be verbalized at the stage of *Malkhut*. Analogously, the renewal of the divine life force, which results from the union of *Hokhmah* and *Binah*, or from nonbeing and being, is immediate, but when mediated by *Malkhut*, it is noticeable only as the change between day and night. In sum, the flow and division of time in the lower worlds is a reverberation of the dynamics of the *sefirot* in the upper worlds, which Shneur Zalman explains in terms of the verbalization of the divine thought.

In his attempts to describe the flow and division of time, Shneur Zalman also resorts to the images of light and the divine life force as an alternative hermeneutic model. By doing so, he roots his teachings deeply in the kabbalistic tradition: time in the kabbalah is so closely related to the metaphysics of light that, in Wolfson's terms, "The kabbalistic conception of time is based on the intermingling of temporality and luminosity; the motion of the infinite light refracted through the prism of the emanations produces the sensibility of duration."[137] In Shneur Zalman's teachings, however, the image of light is rarely associated with time, even though the term *light* often seems to be used interchangeably with the "divine life force" (*hiyut*).[138] Otherwise, it is usually the flow and division of the divine life force into a number of particular levels that determines the passing and order of time in Shneur Zalman's teachings.

The introduction of the divine life force into the model of the development of worldly temporal dimensions calls to mind the triad of *'olam*, *shanah, nefesh*, in which world (or space), time, and the divine life force are interconnected. According to this paradigm, the divine life force (or the divine light) descends and unveils itself in the lower worlds on multiple levels, determined by their degree of materiality. The higher a world is in the hierarchy, the more spiritual it is, and the life force and light are unveiled in it with greater intensity. The distance that the divine life force has to cross in order to reach the lower worlds, which it does by way of the continuous pulse of *ratso va-shov*, affects the evolution of time.[139] Thus, by connecting the flow of time to the flow of divine influx into the world, Shneur Zalman conceptualizes time in spatial terms. The connection between time and space is evident in the sources quoted in this chapter, for example, in the discussion of the triad *world, year, soul*, where two of the three characteristics present in every creation are time and space; in the description of *Malkhut* as a source of both time and space; and finally, in the description of God who is "above" time, as opposed to the world, which falls "under" time, as if time was a category applicable to a particular stage in the vertical hierarchy of worlds. The blurred boundary between the notions of time and space is also visible in the fact that Shneur Zalman often resorts to the language of temporal units when he illustrates the spatial limits of the lower worlds, which, he claims, measure "from the earth to the firmament the distance of five hundred years."[140]

Conclusion

Shneur Zalman's teachings reveal a complex concept of time informed by philosophical, midrashic, and kabbalistic sources. Despite his animosity toward both gentile and Jewish philosophy, Shneur Zalman relies on an Aristotelian philosophical conceptual framework, filtered by Jewish medieval philosophers. Time in his theosophic system is described as created and finite, and its finitude places it in opposition to its infinite creator. Consequently, no temporal features can be ascribed to God or to anything that preceded creation. Shneur Zalman adjusts a philosophical concept of time to the kabbalistic model of reality, which consists of a gradation of *sefirot* and worlds; a vertical hierarchy, flowing from God's unity down to the multiplicity of the lower world. In this model of partly emanated and partly created worlds, relation to the created time also varies. In order to render this variety of temporalities and bridge the gap between God's supratemporality and the worlds' temporality, Shneur Zalman and his Habad successors resort to the notion of the "order of time," which according to the Sages measured the course of cosmic events before our world was created, but which Shneur Zalman understands as the proto-temporal order of concatenation of the ten *sefirot* in the World of Emanation, which itself remains above time.

Shneur Zalman pays much attention to the transition from an infinite and supratemporal God to a finite and temporal reality. Time is expressed in the preexistent divine, and, in much the same way as the multiplicity of the cosmos itself is included in the infinite God. So, creation is a moment in which alterity emerges, including physical phenomena but also the entirety of temporal structure. He offers several explanations for this process based on kabbalistic concepts such as the triad of "world, year, soul," the dynamics of the divine names, or the mystical concepts of Torah and commandments that bind the temporal to the supratemporal. He locates the source of time in *Malkhut* of the World of Emanation, namely, the final *sefirah* of the world that is united with God.

For Shneur Zalman, time is the *ratso va-shov* pulse of the divine life force engaged in the process of continuous creation. This concept derives from two main ideas: Shneur Zalman's occasionalist view of reality as being continuously nullified and re-created by the flow of the divine life force, and the philosophical idea of time as the measure of movement. He merges these two concepts by presenting time as a measure of the divine influx's movement between expansion and contraction. In short, it is the measurement of the cycles of the flow of God's creative energy.

The idea that time is nullified with every ascent of the divine force and substantiated again with each of its descents yields the concept of the division of time in the hierarchy of the worlds. This aspect of Shneur Zalman's teachings, perhaps more than anything else, shows yet another aspect of his temporal discourse; namely, its dependence on spatial terminology. Not only is the dimension of time, like space, a product of the *sefirah* of *Malkhut*, but any explanation of time, its flow and division, also refers to spatial concepts.

The definition of time, and the description of the flow of time as the rhythmic pulse of the divine light that continuously re-creates it from nothing into being does not exhaust the concept of time. This chapter discussed the development of circular time from the infinite source to the finite world. The next chapter will consider linear time, as it develops in the course of the divine history.

✧ 2 ✧

HISTORY

FROM CREATION TO THE END OF TIME

Using Moshe Idel's typology, Shneur Zalman's definition of time as the measurement of the perpetual pulse of the divine energy represents the *michrochronic* model, which relates to the yearly cycle, such as Sabbath and festivals.[1] Indeed, Shneur Zalman refers to the New Moon and Rosh Hashanah as the moments in the yearly cycle when the new portion of divine energy, allotted for the month or year, respectively, comes down to the world to renew it and sustain it. Shneur Zalman, however, further develops this model of *microchronos*. In kabbalah, *microchronos* relates to the time of cyclical repetitions of Jewish rituals, which connects the people to God, but also to the events of the mythical past. While in Shneur Zalman's teachings time's *ratso va-shov* relates to the cyclical repetition of creation, which indeed connects the Jewish people to God's life-giving energy, it also refers to God's first creative act, which began this perpetual cycle of creation. This reference to God's first creation in every time unit points to another aspect of time, which Idel calls the *mesochronos*—the linear, historical time. Shneur Zalman's concept of time therefore relies on a paradox: while God's energy constantly annihilates and re-creates the world, the re-creation is never an identical copy of what existed beforehand. Rather, the repetition of creation is always a new creation, even though it always refers to God's original creative act, as described in Genesis. Thanks to this paradoxical relation between continuity and change, cyclical time develops into linear time, which begins with the creation of time and the worlds and ends, as we shall learn, on the everlasting day at the end of history.

Discussing linear time in Shneur Zalman's thought begs a preliminary question: what kind of history is he interested in? Shneur Zalman was not a historian, and one will not find in his teachings many direct references to current affairs or to past events. This, however, does not mean that he was detached from the reality of his time and place. On the contrary, he was a fully engaged leader in his local Hasidic community, which had been entrusted to him by Menahem Mendel of Vitebsk. He responds to contemporary events, such as the controversy between the Hasidim and *mitnagedim*[2] or conflicts within his own community (e.g., over access to *arenda* leases) in his letters.[3] He and his followers sided with the Russians in the war against Napoleon, and even became involved in espionage on their behalf.[4] His *ma'amarim*, however, generally lack direct reference to these events, and on the few occasions when they do mention, for example, the gentile nations among which the Hasidim live, they clothe them with the biblical names of Esau or Ishmael. The nations are therefore removed from Shneur Zalman's immediate sociopolitical reality into the sphere of mythical history, where Israel carries their perpetual struggle against their perennial enemies, goes into the Egyptian, Babylonian, and Roman exiles, and gradually advances toward the Promised Land. In his teachings, as in rabbinic literature in general, profane history becomes part of the larger divine history that begins with creation and unravels toward the ultimate redemption.[5]

From Exile to Redemption

Shneur Zalman sees history as teleological, and its telos as being determined by the very moment of creation. History as we know it, or linear time as we experience it, is in fact a process of finalization of the creation, the ultimate purpose of which is the revelation of God's kingship in the universe. As the creation of the universe was mediated by the divine aspect of *Malkhut* (Kingship), which facilitated the emergence of alterity and multiplicity, so its final fulfillment will also be related to the revelation of God's unity in the world through the revelation of his kingship in the material realms.[6] Shneur Zalman illustrates in *Tanya* the dialectical relation between creation and revelation by sharing the allegory of a king and his subjects.

> It is known to all that the purpose of the creation of the world is for the sake of the revelation of his kingdom, may he be blessed, for "There is no king without a nation." The word '*am* [nation] is related etymologically to the world '*omemot* [dimmed], for they are separate entities, distinct and distant from the level of the king. For even if the king had very many sons, the name kingdom would not apply to

them, nor even to the nobles alone. Only "A numerous people is the glory of a king" [Prov. 14:28].[7]

God is a king who needs to assert his power. He cannot accomplish this by subduing to his will only family members or courtiers, as they are already part of his domain. He must therefore exercise his power over the common folk, that is, over people who, by their number and status, stand inferior to his unique and exalted rank. Shneur Zalman uses Rashi's invented etymology to link the word *'am* ("nation" or "folk") to the word *'omemot* ("those which are dimmed") to convey this message.[8] Thus, in his allegory, the common folk are "dimmed,'" remote and separate from God, just as the dimmed coals are remote and separate from the source of fire. God creates a multiplicity of ostensibly separate beings in order to demonstrate that they, too, are his and belong under his dominion. This also underscores the notion that no existence is possible that is not a product of the divine will, as even those entities whose very existence would seem to contradict God's unity are, nevertheless, a part of his creation.[9]

The allegory of the king and his subjects also allows for a reevaluation of the Lurianic model of creation, where the process of creation is dramatically interrupted by the cosmic catastrophe known as the breaking of the vessels (*shevirat ha-kelim*). The basic framework of the Lurianic model is as follows. The light that emanated from the divine pleroma was too strong for the vessels assigned to contain it. The vessels shattered into pieces containing concealed sparks of the divine light, creating a world different from the one originally intended, and which consequently required repair (*tikun*). The shattering of the vessels is a concept broad enough to allow for various interpretations, from a chaotic eruption to an orderly process governed by certain rules. Shneur Zalman, however, goes one step further. In his teachings, the breaking of the vessels is an integral part of the creative process; it is a condition for the emergence of nondivine entities and enables God to become "king over [his] people."[10] The notions of the contraction and the breaking of the vessels are thus stripped from the negative connotations of their original Lurianic context (where the shattering of the containers designed to hold the infinite divine light causes a violent rupture in the creative process, as a result of which the demonic forces assume an ontological status of their own).[11] For Shneur Zalman, the breaking of the vessels stands primarily as the transition point between the divine unity and worldly multiplicity—a relation, which he explains in a sermon, that conflates the Lurianic and philosophical discourses.

> The Emanator, blessed be he, in his essence is alone and unique, in a state of ultimate unity, as is known. It is for this reason that the coming into being of the created entities must have taken place by means of the breaking of the vessels. For [the created entities] are marked by great multiplicity and separation, and they fall into the category of being that exists in its own right, which entirely contradicts the truth of his unity, blessed be he, whereby there is nothing but him. Thus, the multiplicity of the created entities must have come about because the vessels had split into a multiplicity of small parts, and by dint of this splitting, every created entity became a thing in its own right.[12]

For Shneur Zalman, the numerous vessel shards in the divine world above correspond to the numerous individual entities in the created worlds below. The use of purely theoretical, philosophical notions in this passage is striking, as they stand in contrast to the original dynamic, mythical concept of the imperfect vessels shattered by the overflowing, unlimited divine light. Rather than being the dramatic and unforeseen result of a flaw in the divine plan of creation, the breaking of the vessels constitutes an integral and deliberate stage in this plan that is necessary for the coming into being of separate entities, which in turn are God's way of expressing his own fullness. Thus, even though the physical reality contradicts the divine unity, it is neither evil, nor erroneous, nor destined ultimately to be cast away; rather, it is to be rediscovered as a part of God's domain.

The concept presented above, whereby God creates a world that is ostensibly separate from his unity in order to claim his power over it, acquires powerful messianic overtones, as Shneur Zalman defines God's kingship over separate entities as God's ultimate "dwelling place in the lower worlds" (*dirah ba-tahtonim*), from which he derives delight (*ta'anug*).[13] Two striking ideas are present here. The first is the radical revision of an old midrashic idea according to which God wants to dwell in our material world. The second is that God, in some way, experiences and is driven by the delight he draws from his creative acts.

Understanding Shneur Zalman's creative take on the idea of God's dwelling place in the lower worlds requires recourse to *Midrash Tanhuma*, where this concept appears for the first time. In the midrash, following the creation of the universe, God desires to establish for himself a dwelling place in the lower worlds.[14] For this reason, he creates man and commands him to cultivate the Garden of Eden. However, in Shneur Zalman's teachings (following in the footsteps of the Maggid of Mezrich and his circle), the understanding of what is meant by God's dwelling place radically changes. First, in Shneur Zalman's teachings, God's desire to enjoy his dwelling place in the lower worlds clearly precedes and serves as the reason for creation, in general, not specifically for the creation of humans. In fact, it was this desire, arising from God's wish to fully express his own unity by ruling over the separate entities whose existence would seem to contradict it, which necessitated the contraction of his fullness and the creation of separate entities. Second, while the midrash locates God's desired dwelling place in the past—first in the Garden of Eden and later at Mount Sinai at the Giving of the Torah—Shneur Zalman defines it in eschatological terms as the ultimate goal of the creative process.[15] As the midrash, Shneur Zalman also understands God's dwelling place in the lower worlds as man's duty. However, he replaces man's labor, which prepares God's dwelling place in the Garden of Eden, with acts of religious observance: prayer, Torah study, and fulfillment of the commandments.

An explicit expression of Shneur Zalman's concept of history as the teleological process spanning from creation to redemption appears in the *Tanya*, in the chapter explaining the meaning of God's dwelling place in the lower worlds. Shneur Zalman states that the physical world will be transformed into God's dwelling place in the messianic future, which is the "fulfillment and culmination of the creation of the world, for which purpose it was originally created."[16] Even though he acknowledges in the same chapter that God had already revealed himself to the Israelites on Mount Sinai, their experience at that time was only fragmentary, or, as he puts it, it was merely "something" of the future revelation, when God will establish his dwelling place in the lower worlds.[17] This will take place in the future, described somewhat imprecisely as the days of the Messiah and the resurrection of the dead. The messianic days and the resurrection are not just an outcome of the internal dynamics of Jewish history; rather, they are the ultimate goal of cosmic history for which the universe was created in the first place.[18]

The view that the redemption is no longer determined historically but inheres in the first act of creation has implications for the idea of exile. Just as redemption concludes the act of creation by revealing the presence of godliness therein, so does exile mark the withdrawal of godliness. The exile is, therefore, first and foremost the exile of God, an idea that occurs already in the classical rabbinic sources. God's presence is said to have been exiled to Edom and Babylonia together with Israel.[19] In Shneur Zalman's teachings, however, the divine presence was exiled into the world as part of the process of creation, and it accompanies Israel only inasmuch as Israel is the major force driving the process of redemption.[20] This emphasizes a paradox that underlines the very existence of created beings: despite being removed from God, an existential bond connects them with the divine, even in their preredemptive state.[21] They are created and sustained by the divine vitality which has been diminished through numerous contractions in the course of its emanation from the pleroma right down to the lower worlds. According to this model, the contraction subtly oscillates between the disclosure and concealment of the divine vitality. The world owes its existence to this balance. On the one hand, increased disclosure would cause the absorption of the separate beings back into the divine pleroma; on the other, a further concealment would result with the separate being reverting to nothingness, as it would lack its only source of life, namely, the divine vitality. Shneur Zalman explains that following the multiple contractions, "a separate thing in its own right does not receive its vitality from the holiness of God, [that is,] from the inner essence and substance of holiness itself, but rather from its hind-side."[22] This, in turn, allows him to declare that the world of beings, seemingly removed and independent from God, is "the world of husks and the 'other side' [demonic force]." The "hind-side" (*ahorayim*) of the divine life energy sustains it, so it belongs to the "other [demonic] side" (*sitra ahra*).[23]

The mystery of creation is its paradoxical nature: the full revelation of God's creative powers necessarily occurs through their own concealment. The descent and limitation of the divine vitality to the point where it gives life to apparently separate beings is, in fact, the exile of the divine presence, the *Shekhinah*. The exile of the *Shekhinah* is therefore identical with the creation of separate beings ex nihilo (*yesh me-ayin*), which brings into existence ostensibly nondivine entities constituting part of the domain of the husks (*kelipot*)—the shattered pieces of the vessels that Lurianic kabbalah associates with impurity, sin, and evil. Moreover, creation qua exile is a manifestation of the inherent materiality and corporeality of the separate entities, and this too associates them with the realm of evil.[24]

As a blend of divine and nondivine elements—spirituality and corporeality—the human being embodies the exile in a microscale. Consequently, the concept of exile as a confinement of the life force in nondivine, material beings has its parallel in the concept of the person, as the macrocosm has its counterpart in the microcosm.

For the faculty of Wisdom that is in the divine soul, together with the spark of Godliness [that comes] from the light of the blessed *Ein Sof* in which it is clothed, are in [a state of] exile within their body, [namely], within the animal soul that comes from the husk within the left-hand-side of the heart, which reigns and holds sway over their body by way of the esoteric doctrine of the exile of the *Shekhinah*.[25]

In human nature, as in the rest of creation—"good" and "'evil," the "holy spark" and the "profane husk," "spirituality" and "materiality"— are all juxtaposed. This duality expresses itself in the relation between the two souls that every Jewish person possesses. The divine soul, which is "the portion of God from above" (Job 31:2), is exiled into the realm of the husks, to the animal soul and the body.[26] In the exile, that is, during the time when the divine life force resides within both divine and nondivine entities, all people have the opportunity to draw it down by their "three garments of the soul" (thought, speech, and deed),[27] either from the "palaces of holiness" or, conversely, from the "palaces of the evil 'other side.'"[28] It is similarly up to the individual whether the divine vitality continues to flow down into the pure side or the impure side of the universe. The act of channeling the divine life-energy to the realm of the husks (through deeds that are not directed solely to God) parallels the concealment of the divine energy within separate beings in the process of creation. Similarly, all the thoughts, words, and deeds that are not oriented to the good side of creation but instead empower the evil side drive the *Shekhinah* into exile.[29] Consequently, the thoughts, words, and deeds that draw down the divine energy to the good side advance the end of the exile.

This definition may seem counterintuitive since it overtly ignores the primary meaning of exile, namely a dispersion of the Jewish people. Nonetheless, Shneur Zalman maintains the connection between theosophy and politics, and between confinement of the divine life-force in the lower worlds and the existence of the gentile nations and their power over Israel. The key to understanding the exile of people is to understand the channels through which the divine energy flows down to Israel and the nations. As Shneur Zalman explains, the vitality of the people in the Land of Israel is drawn directly from *Malkhut* of the Word of Making, while the vitality of the other seventy nations descends through the mediation of the seventy patron-angels appointed over them. Even though the patron-angels receive a life force that is already diminished, the idol-worshiping nations still mistakenly consider them as divine since from their perspective these angels are the source rather than merely the channels of vitality. On the one hand, the creation of the patron-angels and the seventy nations over which these angels rule created conditions for idolatry, and so the exile of *Shekhinah* among the idolatrous nations is embedded in the process of creation (or, alternatively, in the sin of the Tree of Knowledge) rather than being directly related to the historical tribulations of the Jewish people. On the other hand, however, the state of exile intensifies when the Jews live under gentile rule in the diaspora, since the innermost aspect of the divinity that resides among Israel is exiled with them.[30]

The diaspora, therefore, is primarily a displacement of the divine life force; the physical displacement of the people is secondary. By sinning, the Jews channel the life force to the gentile nations, and thereby intensify the state of divine exile. The confusion caused by the displacement of the divine life force leads to the intermingling of good and evil in the world, which is also the reason why the wicked prosper and the righteous suffer.[31] As well as providing a tentative answer to the perennial question of theodicy, Shneur Zalman effectively achieves two important things: he explains why the Jews remain in exile and indicates how it can be brought to an end.

That being said, Shneur Zalman refrains from applying this model of exile (as the presence of the divine vitality within ostensibly nondivine beings) directly to his own political context (the condition of Jews in the Russian Empire) or to other contexts in the long and complex history of Jewish displacement. While this strategy may seem to be an indication of detachment of Shneur Zalman's mystical teachings from the here-and-now of his community in Russia, we shall see that it actually helps him to apply the metaphysical exilic condition to the existential and spiritual state of his followers and provides them with an accessible model of devotional redemption. Instead, he refers to the exile in Egypt, described in the book of Exodus, or to the four exiles listed in the midrash (the Babylonian, the Median-Persian, the Greek, and the Roman).[32] Yet, he does so in a way that dehistoricizes each of these major events, as well as the idea of exile in general.

In fact, Shneur Zalman is not even particularly eager to distinguish between the various historical (or mythical) exiles. Rarely, and with no particular consistence, he inscribes the subsequent exiles onto the *sefirotic* scheme of the world of husks—the theosophical counterpart of the divine *sefirot*.[33] He often refers to several of them simultaneously or speaks about them in general terms without specifying which particular one he has in mind. The only exception is the Egyptian exile, which provides a paradigm for all subsequent exiles, just as the Exodus from Egypt prefigures the future redemption. It is only seldom that the other exiles display any distinguishing traits, and references to particular historical exiles appear only in order to shed light on the current state of Israel's spiritual enslavement.

Babylonia is therefore turned into an allegory: it is presented as the state in which the individual is unable to serve God "from the depth of their heart," where the radiance of the divine Wisdom transcends the categories of reason and understanding. In this state, the innermost point of the individual's heart is completely covered by the "foreskin" of exile—mundane affairs and worldly desires in which he is engrossed—and he cannot access it even when he engages in divine service.[34] It is not entirely clear why Babylonia corresponds to the state of engrossment in worldly affairs. It is possible that Shneur Zalman draws inspiration from the Hebrew wordplay on the words *Babylonia* (*bavel*) and *heart* (*levav*), which mirrors the relation between these two entities: *levav* read backward is *bavel*.[35] In the epistle, which reiterates the idea of symmetry of good versus evil in the created world,[36] Babylonia, representing mundane affairs and desires, is the unholy counterpart of the holy innermost point of the heart. Another plausible source for the idea is the rabbinic depiction of Babylonia as the lowest of all lands.[37] Service from the depths of the heart fulfills the words of the Psalmist: "Out of the depths I call you, O Lord" (Ps. 130:1).[38] Since service from the innermost point of the heart originates in the highest point of the *sefirotic* hierarchy, namely, *Hokhmah*, its opposite must be located in the lowest of all worldly realms: Babylonia.[39]

In the grand scheme of things, however, the Babylonian exile had its telos, too, and it is the renewal of the divine worship. Shneur Zalman demonstrates this idea using a midrash on the weekly Torah portion *Terumah* (Exod. 25:1–27:19),[40] which anachronistically connects two biblical motifs: the statue in the book of Daniel (Dan. 2:31–33), whose "head was of fine gold, his breast and his arms of silver, his belly and his thighs of brass, his legs of iron, his feet part of iron and part of clay," and the offerings of gold, silver, and brass collected for the construction of the Tabernacle (Exod. 25:2). The three precious metals mentioned in both texts refer, respectively, to Babylonia, Media, and Greece, indicating that, at the end of days, the Messiah will incorporate these three gentile nations in his redemptive project. However, when the prophet Zechariah encourages his compatriots to return to Judah from Babylonia, he sees in one of his visions the menorah made only of gold (Zech. 4:2). The ancient Babylonian exile, described in the Bible and filtered through rabbinic imaginations, exemplifies here the timeless idea that only from the lowest level can one reach the greatest heights. The return to God in the Temple cult was therefore made possible by the experience of exile in Babylonia.[41]

Other exiles are similarly seen as aspects of displacement and concealment of divinity in the world, and Shneur Zalman uses some rather creative readings to find hints in classical sources that would shed light on their particularities. For instance, rabbinic sources often mention Persia and Media together, and Shneur Zalman explores this feature in his teachings to describe both nations as more than merely the impure forces that mirror the divine agents of creation. Sometimes, they stand for the powers of the *Shekhinah* itself—Media as the external lights of the divinity and Persia as the internal lights (*orot makifim* and *orot penimiyim*). These two types of light, which descended into the lower worlds together with the *Shekhinah* when she accompanied Israel into exile, became embodied, respectively, in the Torah and the commandments. Shneur Zalman once again relies on an invented etymology for the names of Persia and Media to support this claim. Persia (*paras*) he derives from the Hebrew word *perusah*, meaning a slice of bread; just as bread nourishes the body, so the Torah nourishes the soul, and just as the bread must be sliced and divided into small pieces to be fit for consumption, so the Torah, as it descends to the lower worlds together with the internal lights, divides into books, *parashiyot*, words, commandments, and so on, in order to provide Israel with spiritual nourishment in all respects. The name Media (*madai*) he derives from the word *madim* (1 Sam. 17:38), meaning "garment," which is supposedly an allusion to the external lights surrounding the soul; just as garments envelop the body, so the commandments envelop the soul.[42]

The Greek exile features in Shneur Zalman's teachings even less frequently than the exiles of Persia and Media. He mentions it occasionally as the *Hokhmah* of the world of husks, as explained above. The Greek wisdom of the husks stands against the wisdom of God, for in Shneur Zalman's interpretation, the Greek philosophers at the time of the Hasmoneans negated prophecy. The fact that there was very little oil in the Temple after the Maccabean campaign symbolizes the Greeks' attempts to uproot the Torah,[43] as oil stands for the Torah.[44]

Finally, the exile of Edom, traditionally associated either with the conquest of the Land of Israel by the Romans or with the current diaspora, which began with the destruction of the Second Temple, is similarly reinterpreted in spiritual terms. It no longer signifies political subjugation by a foreign nation or an idolatrous religious cult, but rather an aberrant mode of divine service. The *Tanya* describes the exile of the *Shekhinah* to Edom as the fall of the divine presence into the grasp of external (evil) forces (*hitsonim*):

> As our rabbis, of blessed memory, state: "When they [the Israelites] were exiled into Edom, the *Shekhinah* went with them."[45] That is to say, when a person practices the acts of "Edom," he degrades and brings down thither the divine spark, which vitalizes his [three levels of the soul:] *nefesh*, *ruah* and *neshamah*.[46]

Shneur Zalman identifies the exile in Edom with the "act of Edom," namely sin, and points out that every sinful act draws down the divine presence toward the external forces, supplying them with the vitality that increases their strength. The term *external forces* is only one of several other names for the demonic side, but it is used in this context to emphasize a particular method by which sin reinforces the powers of evil: it raises an "iron barrier" between the sinner and God.[47] Underlying this claim is yet another wordplay, this time on the words *mehitsah*, the iron "barrier" that separates the individual from God, and *hitsoniyut*, "externality," with which one is connected when separated from God. Both words Shneur Zalman derives from the same root, while taking the metal "iron" again to be an allusion to Edom.[48] Thus, the iron barrier is created specifically by the "deed of Edom" and leads to the exile of Edom. Sins are the essence of this exile. They are not a theological rationalization of the historical subjugation of Israel to Edom (or Christian rulers), but rather should be understood simply as creating a condition in which a Jewish person separates him- or herself from God—a state of spiritual exile.

One may ponder, however, why the Babylonian exile, described in such strongly negative terms, stands out from other Jewish exiles with its relative brevity. After all, it lasted only seventy years, which seems surprisingly short in comparison to the lengthy exile that followed the destruction of the Second Temple and which, by Shneur Zalman's lifetime, had already lasted seventeen centuries. The comparison seems all the more stunning when considering the Sages' view that the First Temple was destroyed because of the sins of idolatry, incest, and bloodshed, while the second one was destroyed for the lesser sin of baseless hatred.[49]

Shneur Zalman addresses this paradox by weaving the rabbinical discourse of the exiles into the kabbalistic framework. The three cardinal sins committed by Israel are associated with the presence of the remains of the seven gentile nations in the land of Canaan. As it turns out, these nations were not completely eliminated during the conquest of the land, and eventually they drove Israel to sin, fulfilling God's warning that those who remain of the original inhabitants "shall be stings in your eyes, and thorns in your sides, and they shall harass you in the land in which you live" (Num. 33:55). These seven nations, in turn, correspond on the theosophical plane to the seven evil attributes of the world of husks.[50] In other words, the destruction of the First Temple was, paradoxically, the final stage of the conquest of Canaan, as it completed the eradication of the seven nations and their evil influence. The gravity of Israel's sins makes repentance relatively straightforward: there is no dispute of the wickedness of murder, incest, and idolatry. The exact number of seventy years points to the theosophic roots of these sins in the seven attributes of the world of husks. The multiplication of the seven attributes by ten (as each comprises ten attributes) yields a total of seventy years of exile.[51]

The case of the current exile is more complex. Although the sin that has caused it—baseless hatred—was not as grave as murder, idolatry, and incest, the appropriate emendation is much more complex and time-consuming. Interestingly, although the Second Temple was destroyed by the Roman Empire, which in rabbinic parlance is associated with Edom, Shneur Zalman looks for the roots of the destruction in the exile of Media (probably because of a wordplay on the Hebrew name for Media [*midyan*] and the word for contention [*madon*]).[52] Contention represents division and multiplicity, which contradict the divine unity. Analogously, baseless hatred, while not an obvious sin like murder, represents the root of all evil, as Shneur Zalman deduces from Hillel the Elder's answer to a prospective convert: "What is hateful to you, do not to your neighbor."[53] In other words, any unbecoming conduct can be, in the end, reduced to its source in hatred. There is no simple remedy for baseless hatred, and the process of emendation is long and excruciating, hence the seventeen centuries of exile in Shneur Zalman's times.[54]

In short, despite occasional references to specific historical circumstances or personalities, Shneur Zalman subordinates the historical perspective to the metaphysical one, thereby making it almost impossible to distinguish any historical exile from the continuous state of the Jews' spiritual exile within the created world. This dual understanding of exile, as a succession of historical events that took place at particular times in the past and as a condition of existence that has lasted since the beginning of time itself, has important implications for his understanding of redemption. It allows him to develop a range of interconnected redemptive motifs: collective redemption from a particular exile in history, cosmic redemption at the end of days, and personal redemption in the here and now.

The Exodus

The elucidating descriptions of the four exiles notwithstanding, it is the exile in Egypt that occupies a special place in Shneur Zalman's teachings. It encapsulates the historical, the communal, and the personal perspectives as the first exile in the history of the Jewish people, which is remembered during everyday prayer and celebrated and reenacted every year at Passover throughout the Jewish world.[55] The story of this exile is therefore important primarily as a rich narrative of redemption, with the hasty flight from Egypt on the night of the Exodus, the splitting of the Red Sea, the Giving of the Torah at Sinai, and the conquest of the Land of Israel as its main landmarks. Shneur Zalman consciously exploits these themes, which are intertwined in his conception of exile as a metaphysical condition rather than a political one. The Egyptian exile not only reflects the exile of the *Shekhinah* in the process of creation, it also forms the paradigm of the future redemption. As Shneur Zalman states explicitly: "Every exile is in the nature of the Egyptian exile."[56]

Once again, Shneur Zalman focuses on the Hebrew name for Egypt as a key to understanding the exile's essential features.

> Now, the Sages said: "When they were exiled to Egypt, the *Shekhinah* was with them," [bMegilah 29a] for Scripture says: "I myself will go down with you to Egypt" [Gen. 46:4], that is, *Malkhut* [of the world] of Emanation actually clothes itself in [the worlds of] Creation, Formation, and Making. Thus, the *Shekhinah*'s exile to Egypt means that the *Shekhinah*, which is *Malkhut* [of the world] of Emanation, is in exile within limits and borders.[57]

This passage inscribes the Egyptian exile in the theosophical structure of the *sefirot*. Despite the presence of a biblical reference to the historical Egyptian exile, the actual enslavement of the Israelites in Egypt seems to be less significant here, with the main focus on the dynamics of the *sefirot* within the four kabbalistic worlds. The transition from history to theosophy is facilitated by a pun on the Hebrew name for Egypt (*mitsrayim*) which, vocalized differently, can be read as "limits" or "straits" (*metsarim*). This reading transforms Egypt from a political entity into the metaphysical embodiment of limitation and boundaries, which define the lower worlds of Creation, Formation, and Making and distinguish them from the supernal World of Emanation. The exile of the *Shekhinah* into Egypt therefore symbolizes the descent of the *sefirah Malkhut* from the World of Emanation, characterized by its complete unity with the divine,[58] into the worlds of plurality, division, and limitation. In other words, the Egyptian exile represents the transference of the divinity from infinitude to finitude. In the instance of the World of Making, the lowest of the four worlds, the divine immanence is captured within the "real limitation" of time and space, as this world is limited in time by the six thousand years of history, and in space by the distance of five hundred-years' walk from earth to the firmament.[59] The description of the exile in Egypt and, in particular, the reinterpretation of its Hebrew name therefore make it eponymous with exile in general, understood as God's creation and continued maintenance of the nondivine reality. Moreover, the submission of the Israelites to Pharaoh's authority features throughout Shneur Zalman's teachings as the drawing down of the divine influx into the "hind-parts" (*ahorayim*) of the *sefirotic* structure, thus enhancing the power of the evil forces. Here too, the Egyptian exile is interpreted on the basis of wordplay: the name *far'oh* ("Pharaoh") read backward gives *'oref* ("the back of the neck"), namely, the rear part of the body.[60]

This idea is further reinforced by other readings of the name *mitsrayim* as *makom tsar* (a narrow space)[61] or *metsar yam* (a sea strait), a pun on the strait to the "sea of Wisdom,"[62] where the exile in Egypt stands specifically for the contraction of the *sefirah Hokhmah* into *Binah*, the intuitive and unbounded wisdom into discursive knowledge. When projected onto the anthropomorphic scheme of the *sefirotic* hierarchy, *mitsrayim* is identified with the throat, a narrow channel that connects the brain (namely the intellectual *sefirot* of *Hokhmah*, *Binah*, and *Da'at*) with the heart (the emotional attributes associated with *Hesed*, *Gevurah*, *Tif'eret*, *Netsah*, *Hod*, and *Yesod*).[63] The Egyptian exile, therefore, stands for the disclosure of God's intellectual attributes in the lower, sensual realm—disclosure by contraction of the loftier divine aspects in order to make them fitting for the revelation in the lower, coarser spheres of reality.

The contraction from the intellectual to the sensual in the condition of exile is further explored in Shneur Zalman's interpretation of the story of Joseph's service and subsequent imprisonment in Egypt. In this case, the function of Egypt as the throat is embodied in the chief cupbearer and baker (Gen. 39:1–41:12), and related to the worldly pleasures they represent, which stand in the way of the disclosure in the heart of the divine light residing in the brain.[64] Following "the way of the kabbalists [*yod'e hen*]," Shneur Zalman also reads the Hebrew word *garon* ("throat") interchangeably with *haron* ("anger"), linking it to the story of Jacob, who set out for Haran from Be'er Sheva.[65] The verse "Jacob left Beer-sheba and set out for Haran" (Gen. 28:10) is in turn interpreted figuratively as an illustration of the flow of the divine energy downward, toward the separated beings that inhabit the lower worlds. This connection between Haran and the throat enables Shneur Zalman to expound his own idea of creation by means of divine speech:[66] out of the throat comes the voice, which is identified with the life-giving energy of the divine, and it continues to do so until it dries out (*nihar geroni*), that is, until the voice ceases to be audible and it seems as if the words it uttered exist in their own right.[67] From a national perspective, this interruption reflects the state of exile, while from a personal perspective, it reflects the divine service that is not entirely selfless.[68]

The exile can thus be perceived on two levels, sometimes referred to as Upper and Lower Egypt:[69] the theosophic level (Upper Egypt), where it stands for the concealment of the divine vitality behind the veil of materiality, parallels the personal level (Lower Egypt), which is the inability to serve God wholeheartedly on account of one's corporeality or immersion in mundane affairs. The limits and boundaries encoded in the Hebrew word for Egypt refer also to the "prison of the body" and the animal soul, in which the divine soul is confined.[70] Many of the features of the Egyptian exile overlap with those of other exiles, as Egypt is not only the paradigm of exile on which all subsequent exiles are modeled, but it is also a continuous state in which the world in general, and especially every individual, exists as long as it remains subject to the limits of time and space.

The Exodus mirrors some of the characteristic traits of the exile. Just as the exile traps the divine vitality within the spatiotemporal framework, so the Exodus frees it from the boundaries of time and space. To come out of Egypt means to cross the boundaries and limits (exemplified by temporality and spatiality) that conceal the true character of creation by giving the impression that it is a separate entity rather than an inherent part of the divine. In the Exodus, one transcends these boundaries and limits, clinging instead to the supratemporal and infinite God.[71]

The overcoming of the spatiotemporal dimensions of the created world on the redemption does not, however, mean that these limits are to be annihilated and creation overturned. If the exile was earlier likened to the narrow strait of the throat, in which the divine words of creation are obstructed and cease to be audible, then the Exodus is the time when the divine voice is heard, loud and clear, as it is revealed throughout the lower levels of creation.

> The coming out of Egypt refers to the brain as it emerges out of the strait [*metsar*] of the throat, to expand in the body. From there it [the brain] is drawn down as *Malkhut*, which is "a good and spacious land" [Exod. 3:8], [namely,] a wide space, unlike the throat, which is in the nature of Egypt [*mitsrayim*]—a narrow space [*makom tsar*].[72]

The use of figurative language further reinforces the connection between this theosophic process and the Egyptian exile. The intellectual attributes emerge out of the narrow strait of Egypt and expand onto the six emotional attributes. All of them gather together in the last *sefirah*: *Malkhut*. As the *sefirah* that contains and brings all the others downward to the lower worlds, *Malkhut* enables the disclosure of the divinity in its fullness.[73] Elsewhere, following the association of the throat with the divine voice of creation, Shneur Zalman describes the Exodus as the process of connecting the divine brain with the emotional attributes by means of the voice, specifically during the recitation of the Torah. Torah reading reveals God's wisdom encapsulated in the words of the Torah, but the act of recitation is also an intense experience, which triggers various emotions, such as the love and fear of God. Occasionally, Shneur Zalman uses more precise language and describes the Exodus as the revelation in the heart of the hidden love concealed within the brain.[74] The differences in phrasing are significant for the types of practice prescribed to achieve personal Exodus: the attribute of love and its full disclosure "in all your heart" (Deut. 6:5, 26:16, 30:6) points to the role of prayer ("service of the heart" in *b*Ta'anit 2a) in the experience of personal redemption, while the focus on the voice points to the role of Torah study. Both these issues will be discussed in chapter 4.

It is important to emphasize that during the Exodus, the lower realms were not obliterated or replaced by the upper realms. The Tetragrammaton did not replace the name Elohim but rather, as a result of the Exodus, revealed itself fully. The dynamic represented here by the two divine names is translated elsewhere into the conceptual framework of Shneur Zalman's metaphysics of light: the radiance of the light that fills all the worlds (*memale kol 'almin*) constitutes the metaphysical state of the Egyptian exile, as this aspect of the divine light radiates with different degrees of intensity on many different levels of reality, and as such, it is subject to limits and boundaries. In the Exodus, the infinite light that surrounds all the words (*sovev kol 'almin*) revealed itself within the domain of *memale kol 'almin*.[75] Whereas the messianic redemption is envisioned as God's "dwelling place in the lower worlds," so the deliverance from the Egyptian slavery saw God's transcendence reveal itself in the lower worlds and become one with them, yet in a way that does not obliterate their low-worldly nature.

All the exilic tribulations that result from the concealment of God's face[76] are but a preparation for the divine revelation on Mount Sinai.[77] As a necessary step preceding redemption, Shneur Zalman compares the Egyptian exile to the act of sowing, and the liberation of the Exodus to the act of reaping.[78] In this metaphor, Israel is the seed placed in the soil, which grows by drawing on the divine life-giving energy that has been concealed within the "husks" since the primordial breaking of the vessels.[79] Just as the seed must first decay in the soil and disintegrate in order to sprout, so Israel must go into exile, be enslaved, have its heart broken, and be "reduced to naught" before it can develop into a "great nation" (Deut. 4:7).[80] This dynamic yet again evokes the duality of *ratso va-shov*, with the enslavement in Egypt corresponding to the *ratso* and the Giving of the Torah to the *shov*. The former represents the state in which the divine vitality has seemingly departed from Israel and God remains hidden from the worlds below, while the latter is when the actions of those who inhabit the lower worlds draw down the light of *Ein Sof*, revealing it throughout their earthly domain. Moreover, in the *ratso*, the life-giving energy of the divine withdraws to a level from that it radiates down indiscriminately to both Israel and the gentile nations, thus enabling the latter to prevail over the former. In the *shov*, however, God bestows his *Shekhinah* on Israel alone.[81]

As pointed out above, Shneur Zalman describes the exile in Egypt as the descent of *Malkhut* of the supernal World of Emanation into the lower worlds of Creation, Formation, and Making. Correspondingly, he describes the Exodus as the emergence of this *Malkhut* out of its exile in the three lower worlds, to be reintegrated in the unity of the World of Emanation. However, the purpose of this is the descent from the realm of unity and infinitude into the realm of limitation and plurality, and this depends on the "arousal from below" (*ita'aruta dile-tata*), namely, the theurgic action of Israel, which is followed by the "arousal from above" (*ita'aruta dile-'ila*), the influx of divinity into the world.[82] The actions of Israel from below thus prepare them and the world for the divine revelation. Shneur Zalman takes their response to the Giving of the Torah—"we will do and we will hear" (see Exod. 24:7)—to be an indication of their perfect humility and the obliteration of their will before God's in the Torah.[83]

The "we will do" directly follows the sorrows of slavery endured in Egypt, which paved the way to the Sinaitic revelation. This "doing" refers, therefore, to the experience of hard labor in exile: the humility that preceded revelation begins with the humiliation of servitude in Egypt. The Israelites were enslaved by the Egyptians and were redeemed by becoming God's servants. The Hebrew noun signifying divine worship (*'avodah*) is the same as appears in Exod. 1:14 in relation to the "labor" carried out under the Egyptians.[84]

Shneur Zalman thus reevaluates the exile in Egypt, turning it into much more than a precondition for the revelation of God at Sinai. On account of the humiliation and the immersion in materiality of the Egyptian exile, Israel deserved a revelation of the divinity that originated above the order of emanation and pierced through the external, material aspect of reality. Shneur Zalman resorts to a yet another wordplay which connects the slavery in Egypt with materiality: "The Jews merited [the Giving of the Torah] thanks to their enslavement in Egypt 'at mortar and bricks' [Exod. 1:14], for by dint of this the *sitra ahra* was subjugated."[85] In other words, by employing the ambiguous Hebrew word *homer* (meaning either "mortar" or "matter"), Shneur Zalman suggests that the Israelites merited the redemption by virtue of their work (which could mean either "labor" or "worship," as both are designated by the word *'avodah*) within materiality.

By conditioning the Giving of the Torah with the Israelites' material labor, Shneur Zalman posits the Exodus as overcoming of the dichotomy of material and spiritual. The Exodus transforms the hard labor in materiality into divine worship and enables God's revelation in the physical world. Prior to the Exodus, God's will was revealed to people: according to the Sages, Abraham, who lived centuries before the Torah was given to Moses at Sinai, nevertheless fulfilled its commandments, albeit spiritually, in all of their details.[86] This means that the manner of Abraham's observance was different from that of the generations that came after the Exodus, as he fulfilled only the commandments' inner aspects of observance (*penimiyut*). The terms used here to distinguish between the inner and the outer aspects of observance carry certain axiological connotations: the inner aspect is associated with the essential and the spiritual, whereas the outer aspect is linked to the accidental and material. Abraham, who performed the commandments spiritually but not materially, did not resort to any ritual objects such as the mezuzah, phylacteries, or the Torah scroll. Moreover, *outer* or *external* may refer to the *other* in the sense of the non-Jewish or plainly evil, as, for example, in the expression "external wisdom," which stands for pagan philosophy, or "external forces," denoting the forces of evil. That Abraham observed the internal aspect of the Torah underscores his extraordinary spiritual stature, while simultaneously suggesting that his observance was incomplete as it lacked the all-important external aspect of worship. This external aspect has two connotations: on the one hand, it appears to be less refined than the internal aspect since it closely relates to the evil side of reality, but on the other hand, it is a vital part of one's divine service, even though—owing to its proximity to the evil side—it requires special effort. The effort involved in the enslavement in Egypt was a precondition for external worship (or service).

Having crossed the Red Sea and left Egypt, the Israelites, now liberated from slavery, embarked on a forty-year journey in the wilderness, divided into forty-two stages (see Numbers 33). This journey, too, constitutes a part of the redemptive process and a paradigm of the future redemption.[87] The wilderness symbolizes the domain of evil husks[88] and is associated with the gentile nations,[89] namely, the lowly and "external" aspect of creation sustained by the excess of life-giving energy that flows to them indirectly via Israel.[90] Accordingly, the purpose of Israel's forty-two-stage journey in the wilderness is to cut off the external forces from this flow. As long as the husks can draw on the life-giving energy, the Israelites are not entirely free; they are trapped within the limits and boundaries of the material world. The forty-two stops in the wilderness are the stages through which they set themselves free.

Just as the source of entrapment within boundaries lies in the creation of the world, so the ability to free oneself is rooted in the creation of man. The Jew was created as God's subject, a concept supported by the principle that "There is no king without a nation." His task is to transform the material world into God's dominion. For this reason, he was created as a dual entity: in God's image and after his likeness (see Gen. 1:26). These two aspects correspond to the upper and lower unities he embodies (*yihuda 'ila'ah* and *yihuda tata'ah*), and further to the two kinds of divine light that he draws down: surrounding all worlds and filling all worlds. By drawing down these lights and performing these unifications in the wilderness, the Israelites reveal that the forces within the world are indeed fully united with God and thereby "transform the darkness into light." This, in turn, explains the forty-two stages of their journeys: the number represents the multiplication of the seven attributes of *Ze'ir Anpin* by six, for each one of these attributes consists of six others. The transformation of the attributes in the wilderness concludes symbolically with the transformation of *Malkhut* from mute entity to God's creative speech.[91] In short, the wanderings of Israel in the wilderness can be perceived as a transition period in Israel's redemptive history. Over the course of their wanderings, the Israelites transform the realm of husks into one of divinity by reuniting the seven lower attributes with the Godhead. The forty-two stages of their journey represent the seven lower attributes (each comprising six other attributes) and the final stop before entering the Promised Land (Jericho by the Jordan [Num. 33:48–49]) marks the final stage of the process of transforming these attributes. The crossing of the Jordan and the ascent to the Land is thus theosophically paralleled by the rectification and ascension of the last of the *sefirot*, *Malkhut*, to its source in the Godhead.

Toward the Advent of the Messiah

Far from being a narrative of things past, in Shneur Zalman's teachings, the biblical account of the Exodus serves as a point of departure for speculation on the nature of the present exile and the future redemption. The Egyptian exile, the miraculous deliverance from it, and the experience of communion with God at the Giving of the Torah are all seen as analogous to the current exile and the anticipated final redemption. Moreover, as the Exodus is reenacted and reexperienced both communally (each Passover) and individually (every day in prayer), it shapes the ritual patterns of everyday life for Jews and binds them with the anticipated redemption. The messianic idea involves, therefore, a present-day reenactment of Exodus, one which involves the Jews' participation as individuals and as a community.

The claim that the Exodus prefigures the final redemption is something that Shneur Zalman presents not as his own contribution, but as a part of the biblical narrative, available to a reader careful enough to pick up on subtle hints left in the Torah.

> Now, Scripture says: "We came indeed down" [*yarod yaradnu*, Gen. 43:20], etc., [namely,] one descent followed the other. And about the Exodus and the redemption it says: "I myself will also bring you back" [*a'alekha gam 'aloh*, Gen. 46:4], etc., [and] "Let us by all means go up"

['*aloh na'aleh*, Num. 13:30], etc. In other words, [these verses refer to] two ascents, one following the other. In truth, during the Exodus, [the Israelites] ascended only once, as Scripture says: "I will take you out [*a'aleh etkhem*] of the misery of Egypt," etc., "to a land flowing with milk and honey" [Exod. 3:17]. But the second ascent alludes to the future redemption, may it come speedily in our days, amen.[92]

In the biblical text, even ostensibly stylistic features carry deep meaning. The duplication of a verb for rhetorical effect, which occurs commonly throughout the biblical corpus, is generally interpreted as an emphatic device. Shneur Zalman, however, employs the traditional exegetical method that ascribes to every such rhetorical repetition an additional meaning. He therefore reads *yarod yaradnu* literally as referring to two descents into exile, and *a'alekha gam 'aloh* or *'aloh na'aleh* as two ascents to the state of redemption. But since the biblical account of the Exodus mentions only one ascent from Egypt to the Land of Israel, the allusion to the second ascent must point to a redemption that is yet to take place, while the fact that it did not happen at the time of the historical Exodus suggests that exile is to some extent an enduring state.

When it comes to envisioning the future redemption, both the character and the purpose of the Egyptian exile are illuminating. First, the exile in Egypt was a preparation for the future revelation of the Torah on Mount Sinai; second, the hard labor and the bitterness of this exile were meant to bring about the revelation of the Torah in the external aspect of reality. The analogy, therefore, goes as follows: the future redemption will surpass the Sinaitic revelation inasmuch as it will bring about the revelation of the innermost aspect of the Torah (including its most abstruse element, the reasons for the commandments, *ta'ame ha-mitsvot*). Moreover, not only will this future revelation be heard, it will also be perceived visually.[93] In addition, while enslavement during the Egyptian exile paved the way for the Exodus, current "enslavement for the sake of one's livelihood" (namely, engaging in mundane occupations in order to earn a living rather than being totally dedicated to divine service) is a means to the much loftier end of the final redemption.[94] This is the reason why the Egyptian exile lasted only 210 years, whereas the current exile, by the time of Shneur Zalman, had already lasted for over seventeen centuries.[95]

Detaching the concepts of exile, redemption, and messianism from particular political or historical circumstances, Shneur Zalman often inscribes the preparative aspect of the current exile onto the Lurianic idea of the purification of sparks, which fell down and mixed with materiality.[96] The intermingling of the divine sparks with the husks resulted from the breaking of the vessels or from the sin of the Tree of Knowledge,[97] two events that are associated with the process of creation in general, not with any particular episode in Jewish or universal history. The task of purification is multifaceted. It can be seen from the theosophical perspective as a process that takes place within the sefirotic structure, in which *Ze'ir anpin*, the transcendent, supra-temporal aspect of the Godhead, purifies the fallen *Malkhut*. The "six extremities" of *Ze'ir anpin* (the six *sefirot* constituting it) correspond to the six thousand years for which the world is traditionally said to last until the messianic age, and to the six days of the week in which the purification of sparks takes place.[98] The reason why the state of exile has endured for so many years is the great number of fallen sparks awaiting purification. The initial 288[99] were split from their source in the process of the evolution of the worlds of Creation, Formation, and Action. In reality, however, the number of sparks trapped in the lower worlds significantly exceeds this initial number, and accordingly, more time is required to purify them. When the process of purification is complete, claims Shneur Zalman, the Messiah will come.[100]

The purification of sparks can also be seen from an axiological perspective, as a means of separating good from evil. To recognize the exile as part of the tension between the good and the evil elements of reality is to underscore the ahistorical character of the exile, since good and evil have existed since the creation of the world and had already become intermingled when humans ate from the Tree of Knowledge of Good and Evil. The task of separating one from the other prepares the ground for the messianic times, which Shneur Zalman often describes as the era when God "will destroy death forever" (Isa. 25:8) and "all wickedness shall be wholly consumed like smoke."[101]

Several important features of the exile appear from this description. First, as emphasized above, the exile is neither the product of a historical chain of events, nor is it limited to any particular point in time. Even the primordial sin of Adam did not cause the intermingling of good and evil that is an inherent quality of exile; its only consequence was that the process of separating good from evil would require hard labor (an allusion to Gen. 3:17–19) and that a constant struggle would exist between these two aspects of reality. Before the sin, separation took place as a harmonious and peaceful process.[102] The sin changed the character of the exile, but not its essence. In short, the world, from its creation until the final redemption, exists in the state of exile.

Second, the evil that must be separated from good is associated with materiality; this separation is a process of purification, the purpose of which is to reveal the godliness that resides within the ostensibly ungodly, material, lower worlds. Shneur Zalman's mentor, Menahem Mendel of Vitebsk, in one of his pastoral epistles, pointed to the duality of spirituality and materiality in the world, present in each individual through the duality of soul and body. Any activity in which a person cleaves to the spiritual aspect in order to "strip it of all aspects of corporeality, that is dust, and return it to the place of the [divine] will" is considered a redemptive act of "raising the *Shekhinah* from the dust."[103] Shneur Zalman follows his master's dualistic view of reality and occasionally compares the individual's character to a state in which the divine soul is imprisoned by the body and the animal soul. However, he does not claim that redemption involves stripping of the material. The separation of good from evil in the lower worlds is just the first stage in the process of purification. It is akin to the process of digestion, in which the energy is drawn from food and separated from refuse, with the body absorbing the former and rejecting the latter. At the second, higher stage, the impure, instead of being rejected, is transformed into the pure. The separation of good from evil is effected by the highest *sefirah*, *Hokhmah*. *Hokhmah* organizes reality from within the world without changing its elements: good remains good, evil remains evil, yet they are separated from one another. However, the transformation of evil into good or the purification of the impure changes the elements of the world and therefore must be carried out by an entity that is not part of it: it can be achieved only by means of *Keter*—an entity located above the internal hierarchy of the *sefirot*, which precedes the breaking of the vessels.[104]

Notwithstanding the processes of separation and transformation effected by the supernal forces, Shneur Zalman also emphasizes every individual's ability to purify the sparks precisely because of their immersion in materiality.

> Now, the celestial beings do not have the power to purify and elevate that which is in the husk of *nogah* as a result of the breaking [of the vessels]. Only the terrestrial beings [can achieve this], for they are vested in a material body [known] as the "hide of the serpent,"[105] which derives from the husk of *nogah*. These [embodied souls] weaken its strength by crushing the passions, thereby subjugating the *sitra ahra*, so that "all evildoers shall be scattered" [Ps. 92:10].[106]

Clearly, for Shneur Zalman, materiality and corporeality are as much a curse as they are a blessing. Indeed, as the product of the husks, the body is connected to sin and to the evil side of creation, but it is precisely this connection that enables the purification to take place. One can rectify materiality only by acting through and within it, which is why the task of purification has been given to "terrestrial beings," namely, to humans who are made up of an immaterial soul and a material body. By contrast, "celestial beings" such as angels, who are of a subtler composition than humans, as well as souls prior to incarnation, do not possess a material body and are therefore incapable of subjugating the Evil Side to the Good through its materiality. Furthermore, purification is the purpose of the soul's descent from its supernal source to the lower worlds where it is incarnated.[107] Thus, the body becomes a necessary redemptive tool, to the point where Shneur Zalman states that "The redemption depends on us who have bodies. We must quell and break all [worldly] passions. Through this merit we will be redeemed."[108] The redemption in this case is referred to as God's "dwelling place in the lower worlds," achieved by virtue of "our worship and our Torah."[109] By emphasizing the role of corporeality in the messianic enterprise, Shneur Zalman provides a theoretical underpinning for the Hasidic concept of worship through corporeality (*avodah be-gashmiyut*) and lays the ground for involving the working members of the Jewish community in the messianic project.[110]

The messianic task of establishing God's dwelling in the lower worlds is placed on the shoulders of Jews, both individually and collectively. It starts with the body of each and every individual and extends to the actions of the entire community throughout the generations. The idea of communal responsibility for realizing the messianic future features extensively in the thirty-seventh chapter of *Tanya*. This excerpt, which unequivocally lays the messianic responsibility on the shoulders of each and every Jew, has been an inspiration for the messianic fervor of twentieth-century Habad, and is worth quoting in full.

> This culminating fulfillment of the messianic era and of the resurrection of the dead, which is the revelation of the light of the blessed *Ein Sof* in this material world, depends on our actions and service throughout the duration of the exile. For what causes the reward of a commandment is the commandment itself,[111] because by virtue of performing it the person draws a flow of the blessed *Ein Sof*'s light from above downwards, to be clothed in the corporeality of this world, in something that was previously under the dominion of *kelipat nogah*.[112]

The advent of messianic times and the fulfillment of the messianic task are dependent on the Jews' everyday activity. This idea is discernible in the teachings of other Hasidic masters as well, such as the Maggid of Mezrich, Menahem Nahum of Chernobyl, or Nahman of Bratslav, who believed that the whole righteous and observant community of Jews constructs the stature of the Messiah and makes his coming possible. While these authors recognised the importance of the role of the leader of the community—the *tsadik*—in this collective effort, they all acknowledged that his actions would be futile without the communal involvement.[113] Even Nahman of Bratslav, who went so far as to claim the messianic role for him and for his infant son, Shlomo Efraim, believed that the community participates, to some extent, in the messianic effort, even though the major burden of bringing the redemption lies on the shoulders of the *tsadik*-Messiah.[114] In stark contrast to Shneur Zalman, Nahman of Bratslav hid his messianic message away from his followers. It was transmitted in an encoded manuscript, which was then accessed, supposedly, by only one person in a generation, until it was published for the first time by Zvi Mark in 2006.[115] Nahman's messianism, beyond its prerequisite simple faith in the *tsadik*, belonged to esoterics.[116] Conversely, by addressing this message in print to his readers, Shneur Zalman underscores the communal and egalitarian character of the messianic effort: all members of the Jewish community take part in it, both the representatives of the elite, such as himself, and the broader circle of his followers, to whom the book was addressed. The messianic enterprise is not a task for a *tsadik*, but for a person to which Shneur Zalman devotes the entire first part of the *Tanya*, the "intermediary man" (*beinoni*), who is engrossed in materiality and leads a constant internal struggle against the evil inclination.[117] As the core of the messianic effort lies in the performance of the commandments, there is nothing that takes Shneur Zalman's messianic concept beyond the nomian framework. He reinterprets the mishnaic saying that "the reward of the commandment is a commandment"[118] to claim that the ultimate reward (namely, the redemption) will be granted in return for the fulfillment of the commandments. In other words, the redemption, which is the full revelation of the light of *Ein Sof* in the lower worlds, is brought closer by the performance of commandments, each of which draws down a certain amount, however small, of the light of *Ein Sof*.

The messianic dimension of the commandments is further reinforced in the commentary on the laws of the ritual of the red heifer. About this ancient ritual it is said that, following the destruction of the Temple, only the king Messiah will perform it again.[119] In Shneur Zalman's opinion, the commandment of the red heifer represents the totality of the Torah and constitutes the purpose of the descent of the soul to the lower worlds and its embodiment.[120] It epitomizes the dynamics of *ratso va-shov* inherent in every one of the commandments: the ashes from the cremation of the heifer stand for *ratso*, while the purifying running water (Num. 19:17) stands for *shov*. The significance ascribed to the red heifer is rooted not only in the structure but also in the purpose of the ritual, which Shneur Zalman understands in much broader terms than the biblical source. While the purpose of the biblical ritual is to cleanse the Israelite who has come into contact with a corpse, Shneur Zalman transposes it to the theosophic structure of the kabbalistic world: the "impurity of the corpse" becomes the impurity of the seven Edomite kings (Gen. 36:31–39) whose death symbolizes the breaking of the vessels.[121] The red heifer cleanses the cosmic impurity caused by the breaking of the vessels and is thus invested with a redemptive value. In addition, the cremation of the heifer stands for the love of God as expressed by his mode of *ratso*:[122] the living water of Torah. The vessels in which the ashes and the water are mixed stand for the commandments and the letters that make up the text of the Torah.[123] Consequently, Shneur Zalman successfully reinterprets a ritual that has little relevance to daily life in exile as a metaphor for the purifying and redeeming powers of both Torah study and the performance of the commandments.

The redemptive role of the commandments starts with the individual. The commandments have a transformative value. This idea is further reinforced by the purported parallel between the commandments and the body parts:[124] the 365 negative commandments corresponding to the 365 blood vessels, and the 248 positive commandments to the 248 body parts. Every transgression of a negative commandment enables one blood vessel to draw vitality from the three impure husks, thus rendering the whole body impure and unable to ascend to God. Similarly, the prohibitive force of each negative commandment serves to protect a corresponding blood vessel from being penetrated by the impurity of the husks. By performing all 613 precepts of the Torah, one imbues one's body with holiness.[125] Moreover, the division of the commandments into positive and negative is reflected in their different functions within the body, and it is for this reason that one is obliged to perform all 613 of them. Since these commandments insulate the body from impure influences by blocking the channels from which the Evil Side draws its vitality, they actively diminish the power of the Evil Side and bring closer the messianic era, which is when—according to the prophecy of Zechariah—the spirit of impurity would "vanish from the land" (Zech. 13:2).[126]

By the same token, the positive commandments suffuse the body parts with divine vitality, thereby transforming every observant Jew into a perfect "chariot" or "vehicle" for the divine will. Among the 613 commandments that the individual must perform in order to become a chariot for the divine are the cardinal positive commandments of prayer and Torah study. Both are considered not only as spiritual or intellectual pursuits but also as physical actions, since "moving one's lips constitutes action."[127] They are, therefore, no less significant in the transformation of the body into a vehicle for divinity than the more material, practical commandments, such as donning phylacteries or placing a mezuzah on one's doorstep. Indeed, Torah study, prayer, and various other positive commandments, especially those relating to charity, often take on unique redemptive significance.[128]

The emphasis on prayer, Torah study, and charity recurs in Shneur Zalman's teachings and derives from the belief that these three commandments comprise the essence of divine service, following Shimon ha-Tsadik's dictum in *Pirke avot*: "The world is based upon three things: the Torah, divine service and the practice of kindness" (*m*Avot 1:2). Prayer, Torah study, and charity are not only the three pillars of worship, but they also correspond to the three garments of the soul: thought, speech, and deed. This correlation can be explained as follows: prayer as the "service of the heart" (*b*Ta'anit 2a) depends on the intention (*kavanah*) that is in one's thought. It is said of Torah study that "You shall meditate therein" (Josh. 1:8), but Shneur Zalman reads the word *meditate* (*hagita*) as "articulate," "utter," or "speak out," as an evocation of the halakhic rule that in Torah study, "thought is not the same as speech" (*b*Shabat 150a), which is why Torah must be recited aloud in fulfillment of the commandment of Torah study. Finally, charity is associated with deed (*ma'aseh*), following the biblical verse that refers to "the work of righteousness" (*ma'aseh tsedakah*, Isa. 32:17), which may be alternatively translated as "a deed of charity."[129]

In the collective messianic effort, a distinctive role is granted to individual worship. As Jonathan Garb has observed, "the existential struggle of the *beinoni* derives from the foundational structure of the Jewish psyche, which is ruled by profound duality of identity."[130] Namely, the distinction and conflict between the animal and the divine soul will be the key to the individual redemption. Some elements of the liturgy, such as the reading of the *Shema'*, preceded by *Pesuke de-Zimra* and the blessings *Yotser* and *Ahavah*, which arouse the "hidden love" residing in a person's divine soul, prompt it to reveal itself within the animal soul. Every Jewish person, regardless of his or her merits, possesses this "hidden love" for God. It comes from the divine soul, effectively a part of divinity in each Jew. While the hidden love cannot extinguish itself, it needs to be brought out from concealment to actualization in one's mind and body. Prayer, with intention and fervor, subjugates the individual's thoughts and senses to Godliness, and thereby fulfills this purpose of subduing the *kelipah* to an aspect of the divinity that exists within every single Jew. This constitutes a particular form of the purification of fallen divine sparks.[131] Similarly, Shneur Zalman credits the recitation of blessings with the power to draw down the divine influx into the world, or to bring the transcendent light (*sovev*) into the immanent (*memale*),[132] thus bringing the divine influx from above time into the physical world.[133] Moreover, at the time of prayer, a person's thought cleaves to God as an act of self-sacrifice,[134] since they submit their own will and heart to God and thereby become a vehicle or chariot for the divine.[135] In this way they bring down the divine life force into the world, becoming instrumental, on the one hand, in keeping the world in existence, and on the other hand, in establishing the divine kingdom on earth.[136] This amounts to creating God's dwelling place within the lower worlds, and ultimately, to bringing about the redemption. The kingdom of God established through the vitality drawn down by everyday prayer is related here explicitly to the idea that "there is no God without a people," which in turn appears throughout Shneur Zalman's teachings as the quintessence of God's dwelling place in the lower worlds, the promised redemptive state in which God confirms his dominion over ostensibly separate and independent beings in the lower worlds.

Prayer is but one redemptive practice available for every Jewish person. The redemptive role of Torah study is closely related to its legal function. As the criterion by which one distinguishes right from wrong, pure from impure, and the permitted from the forbidden, the Torah is an instrument of separation between good and evil in the world, and thus an agent of the redemption. Shneur Zalman explains this in a sermon that establishes an analogy between the slavery in Egypt, which led to the Giving of the Torah at Mount Sinai, on the one hand, and Torah studies in current times, which will lead to God's ultimate revelation and the final redemption on the other. The excerpt, which combines conclusions drawn from close reading of Scripture and a zoharic wordplay on the original biblical passage, demonstrates Shneur Zalman's exegetical mastery.

> Now, Scripture says: "I will show him wondrous deeds as in the days when you sallied forth from the land of Egypt" [Mic. 7:15]. This verse draws an analogy between the last redemption and the Exodus. [. . .]

And thus, what was said about the enslavement and exile in reference to the Egyptian exile: "They made life bitter for them with harsh labor at mortar and bricks and with all sorts of tasks in the field" [Exod. 1:14], applies also to recent times, [as the phrase] "And they made their lives bitter" refers to the Torah, which is our life; [the phrase] "with harsh labor" ['avodah kashah] refers to a challenging [Talmudic] question [kushiya]; "at mortar" [be-homer] refers to [the hermeneutical principle of] *a fortiori* [kal va-homer];[137] "in all sorts of tasks in the field" refers to the baraita;[138] and "and bricks" [bi-levenim] refers to the clarification [libun] of halakhah. [. . .] Therefore, just as [the Israelites] merited the Giving of the Torah through the Egyptian bondage "at mortar and bricks," so also, by means of clarifying the halakhah in our own time will they merit the disclosure of the inner aspect of Torah in the future-to-come, when "will I show unto him marvelous things."[139]

According to this interpretation, the verse in Micah refers to two exiles—one in the past and the other in the present—in order to highlight their common features and purpose. Just as the purpose of the Egyptian exile was the revelation of Torah at Sinai, so the purpose of the current exile is a revelation of Torah. While the Israelites witnessed at Sinai only the external aspect of the Torah, they will discover in the future its innermost aspect, including even the enigmatic rationales of the commandments. In the context of the present exile, the most important task, common to all Jews, is the labor they are expected to perform, the character of which is deduced from the types of work undertaken by the Israelites in Egypt. Following the *Zohar*,[140] Shneur Zalman interprets the Hebrew terms for these types of work by relating them etymologically to various elements of traditional Torah study: hard labor ('avodah kashah) signals tackling a Talmudic kushiya; mortar (homer) stands for kal va-homer; work in the field refers to the study of baraitot; and finally, bricks (levenim) are interpreted as clarification of the law (libun hilkheta). Torah study will ultimately lead to redemption because it will produce a final and unanimous exposition of the law that will establish a decisive separation between the pure and the impure, in contrast to the current presence of competing legal rulings in halakhah. It is therefore not surprising that Shneur Zalman defines Torah study for the sake of clarifying halakhah as the messianic process of purifying fallen divine sparks.[141]

The third rabbinic pillar that supports the world besides prayer and Torah study is charity.[142] As mentioned above, Shneur Zalman occasionally presents charity as the epitome of a commandment; it is the one commandment that comprises all the others (*kelalut ha-mitsvot*),[143] the quintessential commandment (*mitsvah setam*),[144] "truly God's commandment" (*mitsvat Hashem mamash*),[145] or an act that is "equivalent to all the commandments."[146] The prominent status of charity results from its association with giving the necessities of life, which in turn corresponds to the general purpose of all the commandments: to draw the divine life force down into the world. Giving charity in our own world is indeed a life-giving act, whereby the donor provides the poor with the necessities of life. As such, it is perhaps the most tangible example of the life-giving force of a commandment, for not only does it infuse the recipient of charity with the hidden divine vitality (*hiyut*), but it also provides him or her with material sustenance.[147] The act of charity, however, is a win-win situation, as it strengthens both recipient and giver. Charity is a protective act, which shields the donor from the influence of the husks (a claim Shneur Zalman derives from a literal reading of Isa. 59:17: "He donned righteousness [*tsedakah*, which can also mean 'charity'] as a coat of mail"). From the point of view of the donor, every coin given to charity adds up to build a coat of mail that protects him or her from the demonic *sitra ahra*.[148]

Shneur Zalman's descriptions hint also at theurgic, pietistic, and mystical dimensions of charity. Defining its purpose as "bring[ing] life, grace and kindness to him who has nothing of his own"[149] alludes to the *Zohar*, where these words refer to the *Shekhinah*, which, like the moon, "has no light of her own."[150] The act of giving charity in the lower worlds is "the arousal from below," which instigates the "arousal from above," namely, the flow of the divine light from above downward.[151] By displaying unwarranted kindness, it reenacts the creation by God's will, and hence serves as a vehicle of the primordial divine light[152] drawn down from the divine attribute of *Keter*.[153] Charity is an act of *imitatio dei*, for just as God gives life through creation, so humans give life through charity.[154] Finally, it results in the arousal of the hidden love for God, as well as in the elevation of the soul of the donor and its cleaving to the light of *Ein Sof*.[155]

The revelation of the divine light caused by practical commandments in general, and by the commandment of charity in particular, has an overtly eschatological meaning. It is described as the realization of the vision of God's "dwelling place in the lower worlds," at the point at which the materiality of the world has become so refined that it can receive God's infinite light without immediately dissolving in it. Charity, as a material commandment, is a very tangible way of transforming the material "darkness" into the divine "light," and an exemplary case of "worship through corporeality."[156] The concept of the purification of materiality through the purification of one's own body and one's surrounding "four cubits" (of space) was discussed above in the context of the commandments in general. Here, charity plays the leading role in this process.[157]

The emphasis that Shneur Zalman places on the commandment of charity is not surprising, given his involvement in collecting donations for the Hasidic settlement in the Land of Israel.[158] His teachings are replete with direct references to charity as a redemptive activity, and in *Tanya* one encounters such expressions as "Israel shall be redeemed only by virtue of charity,"[159] or "charity brings the redemption closer."[160] Like the practical commandment, the fulfillment of which draws down the divine life force into the world, the redemptive aspects of charity are usually presented in correspondences in similar terms as those found in Tanya or throughout the corpus of Shneur Zalman's *ma'amarim*. By referring also to the overtly redemptive characterization of charity in the classical rabbinic sources, he emphasizes the importance of donating money to the Hasidic settlement in Palestine. This seems to stem from the intrinsic value of the Land of Israel itself rather than from any sense of the immediacy of redemption or the power of charity as the last step required in order to bring it on at once.[161] Even though Shneur Zalman states in one place that charity constitutes the essence of divine service in the generation of the "footsteps of Messiah,"[162] it seems that his purpose in choosing this wording was to encourage his followers to donate regularly for the sake of their brethren in the Land of Israel. It seems that he considered the practical commandments in general, and especially charity, prayer, and Torah study, as no more than important components of divine service.[163]

The transformation that occurs in each individual by virtue of fulfilling all 613 commandments is part and parcel of the larger process that enables God to occupy "a dwelling place in the lower worlds," for the accumulation of many such individual transformations gives rise to a cosmic transformation.

> The whole community of Israel, comprising 600,000 particular souls, is the [source of] life for the world as a whole, which was created for their sake.[164] And each one of them contains and is related to the vitality of one part in 600,000 of the totality of the world, which [part] depends on his vital soul for its elevation to God through its own [the soul's] elevation, namely, by virtue of the individual's

partaking of this world for the needs of his body and vital soul in the service of God, that is to say [by] eating, drinking, and the like, [by his] dwelling and all his utensils.[165]

Shneur Zalman takes Rashi's view, whereby the opening verse of Genesis is a statement to the effect that the world was created for the sake of Israel, to suggest that it was created in order to enable the Jews to worship God. Every material object in a Jewish person's worldly environment is capable of being utilized for the purpose of divine service, and thus of being elevated to the divine, whether by serving as a ritual object or simply as a means of maintaining the individual in a state of physical well-being that renders him or her fit for worship. The commandments, which draw down the divine light into the material world, transport it from the domain of the husks into God's domain. By subjecting mundane objects to the rules of *halakhah*, the Jewish person enables divinity to pervade the "four cubits" of his or her everyday environment. This is particularly conspicuous with regard to ritual objects such as the mezuzah or the Torah scroll, which are but pieces of leather until they are incorporated in the ritual framework and acquire religious significance. Similarly, money donated to charity or items of food on which the appropriate blessing is recited conform to the divine will as expressed in the commandments and are therefore absorbed into the light of *Ein Sof*.[166] Food has an additional significance because it becomes new blood and can thus provide the body with energy. Blood, belonging to the animal soul, is a quintessential derivative of the impure, evil *kelipah*; yet when the energy it generates is used for Torah study and prayer, it is transformed into good and integrates the domain of holiness.[167] Moreover, following the Talmudic dictum whereby "As long as the Temple stood, the altar atoned for Israel, but now man's table atones for him" (*b*Berakhot 55a), Shneur Zalman compares eating food to offering sacrifices. Just as the purpose of the latter, as Shneur Zalman explains anachronically, was to purify the soul of the sacrificial animal and reunite it with its source, which lies above the breaking of the vessels, so eating—as long as it is accompanied by the appropriate blessing and intention—purifies the inanimate, vegetative, and animate elements concealed within food.[168]

Each and every soul in Israel therefore becomes responsible for elevating the world by utilizing it in serving the divine. The transformation of the whole world into God's dwelling place is an outcome of the accumulation of multiple such individual transformations. Altogether, the 600,000 souls of Israel correspond to the same number of particles of divine vitality (sparks) present in the world: when Israel have performed all the commandments, their animal souls and bodies, together with the lower worlds they inhabit, will be divinized by the light of *Ein Sof*.[169] A life governed by the *mitsvot* has the power to transform the body and the personal space of the individual, but at the same time it also sanctifies the dimension of time, since the purpose of both the individual's life span (set at seventy years, following the Scripture)[170] and the whole chain of his soul's incarnations from one generation to the next, is to perform every single commandment, as is required for the redemption to come.[171] In addition, the length of the current exile is understood as being determined by the large number of sparks,[172] or by certain aspects of the *sefirotic* tree, that still require purification.[173]

It is important to point out that the messianic concept described above does not aim to restore the order that preceded Adam's sin or the creation. This is because good and evil were intermingled in the Tree of Knowledge even before Adam tasted its fruit; his sin only complicated the process of purification, turning it into a war between good and evil.[174] It was not Adam's sin, but rather creation itself, that brought about the state of exile. Moreover, Shneur Zalman views the creation positively, as the means of God's self-expression within his so-called dwelling place in the lower world, namely, as a totality comprising even ostensibly separate and autonomous entities. The redemption concludes the process that began with the creation of the world rather than amending and restoring it to any primordial state untainted by sin.

Conclusion

A close reading of Shneur Zalman's *ma'amarim* uncovers their historio-sophical underpinnings. Contrary to their common depiction as an atemporal mystical doctrine focused on integration in the divine transcendence within the here-and-now, the teachings examined in this chapter show that the first Habad leader's model of spirituality depends on his understanding of history: the Jewish exilic past preconditions the present mode of divine service, the purpose of which is to bring about the messianic future. Admittedly, actual historical events or current affairs do not feature in his writings as much as one might have expected given his involvement in the life of the Hasidic communities of Belarus and the Land of Israel. They feature mostly in his letters rather than in his mystical teachings.

And yet history, understood primarily as the tension between the creation and the final redemption, plays a central role in his doctrine.

The redemption, defined as God's dwelling place in the lower worlds, is the ultimate goal and purpose of creation. Creation is thus, by definition, a state that requires redemption. It is the state in which the divine itself is in exile, when the one God invests his infinite light in a multitude of finite, separate beings. Shneur Zalman recalls all the historical exiles of the Jewish people first and foremost as an allegory for the ontological state of exile that began with creation itself and which will end only with the final redemption. The exile in Egypt occupies a prominent place, as it conveys the idea of confinement within the limitations of the material world (based on the wordplay *mitsrayim/metsarim*) and shows the way that leads from slavery to redemption by means of hard labor through and within materiality. The Israelites' hard labor in Egypt stands for worship in the state of ontological exile: through the labor of divine service, the body and the material reality of the lower worlds will be filled with the divine presence and redeemed. For Shneur Zalman, nomian worship has a distinctly redemptive value: prayer, Torah study, and the commandments (with special emphasis on charity) transform the individual and his or her surroundings into the dwelling place of the divine. Every member of the community participates in this process, and collective redemption is the result of their individual endeavors.

The redemptive model offered here eludes particular political, social, or economical ramifications of the Hasidic community at the turn of the nineteenth century, but is by no means irrelevant to it. On the contrary, it is an accessible and relevant model of devotional redemption, which not only could have been attractive for Shneur Zalman's growing circle of followers, but because of its universal character, could also be carried on long after his death. Indeed, Shneur Zalman's interpretation of the messianic component in Judaism had far-reaching consequences for the further developments of Hasidic doctrines, both within and outside of the world of Habad-Lubavitch. While a thorough comparative study lies beyond the scope of this book, many ideas formulated by Shneur Zalman have fueled the messianic concepts and activities of Habad in the twentieth century, when in the aftermath of the World War II and the destruction of European Jewry, messianism became the hallmark of the movement. In their studies, Elliot Wolfson and Dov Schwartz examined influences of Shneur Zalman on the messianism of Menahem Mendel Schneerson; Schwartz even attempted to sketch a gradual development of the concept of redemption from the inception of Habad until current times.[175] Here, I want to merely point out certain aspects of Shneur Zalman's teaching, which the twentieth-century Habad translated into tangible messianic activities.

The omnipresent Habad *sheluhim* (emissaries), who provide religious services both within established Jewish communities and in far-flung locations, are one of the inventions of the twentieth-century Habad but with ideological roots in Shneur Zalman's teachings. The *sheluhim* as an institution sprang from Shneur Zalman's call for creating God's dwelling place in the lower worlds, which Habad Hasidim took up with increased vigor in the twentieth century. The expectation of the imminent messianic advent resulted in the creation of an outreach framework as the Hasidim felt the need to actively include virtually all Jews in the final stages of the transformation of the material world into God's dwelling. They believed that the communal responsibility for the redemption, which features prominently in Shneur Zalman's teachings, is no longer limited to tending to one's "four cubits of *halakhah*," but that their task at the end of days is to ensure that other Jews would follow suit, too. In short, creating the outreach framework translated Shneur Zalman's concept of the collective responsibility for bringing the redemption through living an observant life into a social-religious activism.[176]

Since every commandment brings the divine light to shine through the material world, performance of every commandment matters. As in the case of the *sheluhim*, so in this case a theoretical precept proposed by Shneur Zalman, combined with the messianic fervor of postwar Habad and unprecedented creativity of Menahem Mendel Schneerson, resulted in a novel institutional framework for Habad messianic activity. The military-style *mitsvah* campaigns, announced in 1967 and continued until the present day, have focused on one commandment, or one aspect of Jewish observance, such as laying phylacteries, lighting Sabbath candles, keeping dietary or ritual purity requirements. The ultimate goal is to prepare the world for the ultimate redemption by infusing it with the light of commandments.[177] The campaigns have targeted Jews of all backgrounds,[178] also those completely estranged or hostile to religion, and often have not involved any systematic follow-up that would ensure that a performance of one random *mitsvah* would lead to increased observance. Despite the criticism they attracted, large numbers of Habad Hasidim continue to engage in the *mitsvah* campaigns, making the campaigns an even more prominent sign of emphasis on the communal participation in the redemption perhaps than the institution of the *sheluhim*.[179] In their outreach campaigns, contemporary Habad Hasidim follow in practice the concept of Shneur Zalman, whereby the messianic task lies on the shoulders of the entire Jewish people, the vast majority of whom may strive to reach the level of the *beinoni* at best. The messianic task is, therefore, not solely dependent on the *tsadik*—even the *tsadik* who is the Moses of his generation.[180]

Speaking generally, the rapid growth of the Habad outreach machine is also part of the much older Habad communication ethos, which strives to make the previously restricted esoteric knowledge accessible to everyday Jews.[181] At first glance, the contemporary Habad outreach might look very different from the communication strategies deployed by Shneur Zalman at the turn of the nineteenth century. On the one hand, contemporary Habad presents the outreach as a pan-Hasidic imperative derived from the famous letter of the Besht to his brother-in-law Gershon of Kuty, and therefore as being older than the Habad itself.[182] On the other hand, it uses modern media and cutting-edge technologies, and knows how to navigate meandering of law and politics in countries as different as Sweden, Russia, Israel, or China. Still, it is that same principle of making the esoteric available for the masses, which prompted Shneur Zalman to publish the *Tanya*, which motivates Habad Hasidim today to carry the teachings of Habad outside of its community and into less observant communities, the mass-media, college campuses, and academia.[183] Menahem Mendel Schneerson certainly strengthened the messianic undertones of the act of revealing the secrets.[184]

But even before the eruption of the messianic ferment in the twentieth-century Habad, Shneur Zalman's ideas resurfaced in the teachings of a different powerful Hasidic school: the Gur Hasidim. As Yoram Jacobson has pointed out, Shneur Zalman in general, and his concepts of exile and redemption, had a significant influence on the teachings of the second rebbe of Gur, Yehudah Aryeh Leib Alter, known after his posthumously published book as the Sefat Emet (1847–1905).[185] The Sefat Emet borrowed from Shneur Zalman the overarching concept of the cosmic history, whereby the redemption is an inherent part of the act of creation as its intrinsic and ultimate goal. Consistently, it is the act of creation itself that generates the condition of exile, which the Sefat Emet—just as Shneur Zalman—considers to be a necessary preparatory stage before the redemption. The Sefat Emet identifies the exile with nature (*teva'*), as it conceals the divine unity in spatio-temporal dimensions—a concept that recalls the dynamics of the Tetragrammaton and the name Elohim (equal to *ha-teva'*) in Shneur

Zalman's description of the creation, as discussed in chapter 1. Accordingly, bringing the redemption closer means transforming nature and elevating it back to the divine unity.[186]

In the context of the comparison between Shneur Zalman and the Sefat Emet, it is noteworthy that the latter extensively uses the triad of "world, year, soul" in his description of the redemptive process. In a similar vein to Shneur Zalman, the Sefat Emet describes the "world, year, and soul" as three transcendental categories through which the divine oneness brings about the created multiplicity. He adds, however, his novel interpretation by spelling out what in Shneur Zalman's sermons is only implicit: each of these categories contain certain aspects that allow connection with godliness from within the spatiotemporal world. These three clearings allowing the divine light to shine through in the world refer to a specifically Jewish experience. For "world," which stands for space, it will be the Land of Israel and Jerusalem; for "year," namely time, it will be the Sabbath and the Jewish festivals; finally, for the "soul," namely the divine life force, it will be the inner point (*nekudah penimit*) in the Jewish soul, untainted by materiality and coarse existence among the non-Jews.[187] The Land of Israel and Jerusalem, despite the growing influence of the Zionism in the times of the Sefat Emet, remained understood in spiritual terms as places of God's revelation and not as an actual geographic place entangled in conflicting religious, ethnic, and political conflicts. Shifting focus from an actual land to its spiritual hypostasis is coherent with two other poles of the triad: the year and the soul. The Sabbath, which is given specifically to the Jews only,[188] belongs to the sacred realm, elevated above the everyday hustle and bustle. The Jewish aspect of the soul separates and elevates the Jews above the nations, engrossed in the material world. Finally, the spiritualization of the Land of Israel allows the Sefat Emet to claim that the Jewish people operate outside of the constraints of space, in contrast to non-Jewish nations, each and every one of which has an allocated plot of land.[189] It seems that in this regard the Sefat Emet was also influenced by Shneur Zalman, who believed that through their worship, Jews redeem and sanctify the space around them causing the boundaries of the Land of Israel to spread around the entire globe, encompassing the lands of other nations, too.[190]

✧ 3 ✧

THE END OF DAYS

The Double-Ending Eschatology

Shneur Zalman's teachings, which encourage his followers to excel in the life of Torah and commandments and to bring the creation to his redemptive completion, also contain descriptions of the promised end of days. These descriptions, too, are fragmentary, uneven, eclectic, and not always mutually coherent, and generally they reflect the character of his teachings. The double-ending eschatology, whereby the arrival of the Messiah is followed by the ultimate redemption and the resurrection of the dead, is one dominating idea that recurs throughout Shneur Zalman's teachings. The division between these two stages in eschatology, however, is not always clear-cut; they often appear side-by-side, with no differentiation, in discussions about the era that will follow the end of exilic history.[1] Only on some other occasions does Shneur Zalman's wording clearly indicate that the days of the Messiah would precede the resurrection of the dead, as in a passage from *Tanya* (discussed in the previous chapter), in which "the messianic era, and *especially* the time of the resurrection of the dead" are said to be the fulfillment of creation.[2]

An important source for this distinction is one of Shneur Zalman's epistles, where he attempts to reconcile conflicting Talmudic and zoharic[3] statements about the observance of the commandments at the end of days.[4] In this fragment, he harmonizes these traditions by suggesting that the suspension of the commandments will occur in the days of the Messiah, while a messianic *halakhah* will come into force after the resurrection of the dead.

> How is it possible that in the days of the Messiah they will no longer need to know the laws of *isur* and *heter* [what is forbidden and permitted], and of impurity and purity? How will they slaughter the sacrifices, and also [the animals] for common use, when they will not know the laws of *derasah*, *haladah*, and *shehiyah*, which render the slaughtering unfit, and [the laws] of the defective knife?[5] Will there then be a man born who by his very nature will slaughter without *shehiyah* and *derasah*? Will the knife also be the way it should, and remain forever without defect? [There are] also many more laws [relating to] fat, and blood, and other prohibitions. They will also need to know about the impurity of a corpse, as Scripture says: "The child shall die a hundred years old" [Isa. 65:20]. It will be further necessary to know about the impurity of a woman in confinement, as Scripture says: "those with child and those in labor" [Jer. 31:8]. Even if a woman gives birth every day as a result of one marital union, nonetheless, with respect to the restrictions resulting from her impurity, the law will not change.[6]

The picture Shneur Zalman draws resembles the Maimonidean messianic future,[7] where "the world moves along its lines" (*'olam ke-minhago noheg*):[8] birth and death remain, and people still need to know the laws that regulate everyday life, such as ritual slaughter, purity, dietary restrictions, and so on.[9] Moreover, the laws of sacrifices are still in force, which indicates that the Temple has been rebuilt (another similarity to Maimonides). Even the idea that women in the messianic era will give birth every day does not suggest a break from the natural order but only its enhancement by the removal of obstacles that have hitherto limited women's procreative capabilities.

The messianic days appear, therefore, as a transitional stage between exile and ultimate redemption. Shneur Zalman himself is inconsistent as to whether the Messianic days still belong to the time of striving toward redemption through Torah and commandments, or whether they are to be considered the time for the reward, the latter option echoing the Talmudic dictum (commenting on Deut. 7:11): "Today [the present time] is for doing them [the commandments], tomorrow [the future-to-come] is for collecting the reward."[10] In the following passage, Shneur Zalman leans toward the former view.

> Now, our Sages of blessed memory said: "There is no difference between this world and the messianic era except for the oppression [of Israel by foreign kingdoms],"[11] because the days of the Messiah

are not the world-to-come that follows the resurrection [of the dead], which is the time of rewarding the righteous. Rather, the days of the Messiah are in the nature of what is referred to as "today is for doing," not of "collecting the reward." The essential part of "today is for doing," and the ultimate fulfillment of "doing" belong in the days of the Messiah, [. . .] for the essential part of doing is the sacrificial service, which we cannot perform in the exile, even though the prayers have been established as a substitute for the sacrifices during the exile. Yet this [kind of doing] is not truly "in accord with your will's commandment" [*Musaf* prayer for Sabbath and *rosh hodesh*].[12]

The messianic days appear in this passage as the time when worship reaches its culminating point, when the Jews can fulfill the commandments that they are not able to perform in exile, in the absence of the Temple. The establishment of prayer as a ritual substitute for sacrifices does not satisfy the need, felt even in exile, to perform all the commandments exactly as God commanded. The quote from the liturgy, which appears in a plea for God to gather all the Jews in the Land of Israel precisely in order to enable them to offer sacrifices, emphasizes this insufficiency. To the extent that this period allows for the fulfillment of all 613 commandments exactly as God willed them, entailing therefore the reinstatement of Temple service, the messianic days still count only as a stage in the redemptive process rather than its climax.[13] Redemption is what follows, when all the commandments have been performed in full; it features the resurrection of the dead, the time when the righteous receive the reward of their deeds.

From this viewpoint, the resurrection of the dead appears as the ultimate purpose of creation in general[14] and of the fulfillment of the commandments in particular.[15] The era of the resurrection is also associated with the reward granted to the righteous for their deeds, an association that plays down the difference between the exile and the messianic days.[16] This is why Shneur Zalman occasionally adds that the reward the righteous receive is material in the messianic days and spiritual at the time of the resurrection.[17] This spiritual reward exceeds the imaginable, in line with the prophetic claim that "such things had never been heard or noted, no eye has seen [them], o God, but you, who act for those who trust in you" (Isa. 64:3):[18] the righteous will be elevated and incorporated in the divine holiness, the divine will, and the supernal delight. Their material reward, as in the Talmudic statement, will amount to the overthrowing of the foreign nations that oppress the Jewish people in exile.[19]

The emphasis placed on the divine will and supernal delight, both of which are associated in the Godhead with *Keter*, links the idea of reward with the resurrection of the dead by means of the divine dew. Now, resurrection by dew is a common motif in rabbinic literature, which derives from the biblical verse: "Awake and sing, ye that dwell in dust: for thy dew is as the dew of herbs, and the earth shall cast out the dead" (Isa. 26:19).[20] *Pirke de-Rabi Eli'ezer* (ch. 34, 34a) also specifically mentions that the dew originates from the head of God, which can be the source of the connection that Shneur Zalman makes between *Keter* (Heb. "Crown") and the dew. Be that as it may, according to Shneur Zalman, this dew originates in *Keter* and represents the overflow of the life-giving light of *Ein Sof*, which is so intense that it revives the dead.[21] Since the light confined in the dew bypasses the order of emanation and enters the world directly from the most transcendent aspect of God, the world it redeems is no longer subject to the laws of nature, and the bodies it resurrects are subtler than those of ordinary mortals.[22]

The transformation of the body marks a transition point between the days of the Messiah and the resurrection of the dead. The soul and the body undergo parallel transformative processes, respectively, after death and the resurrection. The former ascends from the body to the Lower, and subsequently to the Upper Garden of Eden, passing on its way through the River of Fire (*nehar di-nur*), so as to annihilate all its previous cognitions and delights. Unlike the crossing of the soul into the afterworld, the transition from the messianic days to the resurrection involves both the soul and the body, as they are prepared for the ultimate delight,[23] which is the key to understanding the role of the body after the resurrection. In the previous chapter, the body was presented as a necessary tool for redemption: since its materiality and corporeality stem from the husks, only in and through it would the evil side of reality be transformed into good. An analogical reasoning underlies the persistence of corporeality in the redeemed world. By its nature, delight is associated with materiality and corporeality as all delights are experienced sensually. Now, material delights are only the "debris of the supernal delight." When righteous people die and cast off the external husk of their bodies, their souls can experience an inner, spiritual pleasure in the Garden of Eden, which is derived from all of the commandments they performed during their lifetimes.[24] However, this spiritual delight is merely the immediate source of the material delights confined within the framework of the emanated worlds, which are further contracted in order to be integrated in materiality. The real source of all spiritual, inner delight is the supernal delight, which transcends the hierarchy of the emanated worlds and the contractions that accompanied the process of their unfolding. As such, it lies beyond any value-charged differentiation between spirituality and materiality, externality and internality: it concerns both spheres equally. Although the soul achieves a higher level of delight after the death of the body within the unredeemed world, it is the body that grants the soul a higher level of delight after redemption.[25]

The redeemed bodies will be different from those conceived and born before the resurrection. Following the resurrection, the body will become a suitable vessel for the infinite light, and the illumination it receives will be similar to the one that a person receives at death. Accordingly, in the redeemed world, the sublime resurrected bodies will be capable of sensually perceiving God.[26] The sublimation of the body constitutes only one element of the bigger change, in which materiality is purified and the laws of nature, including mortality, are abolished. Purified materiality will be capable of receiving the divine world without obscuring it,[27] and as a result, the lights of *sovev* and *memale* will shine equally to everyone, there being no difference between light and darkness[28] since the *sitra ahra* and the husks will be annihilated.[29] For in the messianic days preceding the resurrection, evil will exist in *potentia*, not *in actu*, in a state of being subjugated by good (*itkafia*), whereas the resurrection entails its actual transformation into good (*ithapkha*).

Shneur Zalman's concept of the sublimation of the body juxtaposes midrashic and kabbalistic imagery. On the one hand, it draws on aggadic material, vividly describing the resurrection as a reconstruction of the body[30] sustained by the divine light that is clothed in the dew of resurrection (in contrast to the mortal body, which is sustained by the divine life force while being clothed in flesh).[31] As a result, there will be no need for drinking and eating after the resurrection.[32] On the other hand, the cessation of eating and drinking results from the transformation of the world by the transcendent light of *sovev*. Only the divine soul, which is "the portion of God from above,"[33] is sustained by the vitality that comes directly from the light of *Ein Sof*, whereas the animal soul receives the vitality that is mediated by the order of concatenation. Because the revelation of the vitality nowadays comes about mostly through the immanent light of *memale*, the animal soul must sustain itself by the vitality concealed in material food. In the future, however, when the light of *sovev* will shine through *memale*, materiality will not conceal the vitality and the animal soul will sustain itself directly by the light of *Ein Sof*, just like the divine soul.[34]

The totality of the resurrection finds yet another expression: because of the revelation of the radiance of *Ein Sof*, all Jews will have a share in the world-to-come after the resurrection.[35] This is not the case in the afterlife in the Garden of Eden, where only the souls of the righteous enjoy the radiance of *Shekhinah*, which comes from the revelation of the divine light through the order of the emanations of worlds.[36] Also, different classes of Jews will share in the elevation of the entire world to a higher status at the redemption: the Levites of today will be reborn as priests.[37]

Limitations of Redemption: Gentile Nations in the World-to-Come

According to Shneur Zalman, the status of the gentile nations at the end of days begs a question, given the description of the messianic times as the liberation from the nations' oppression, and the resurrection as the transformation of evil into good. The previous chapter mentioned the gentile nations as objects of history rather than as subjects: they provide the backdrop of world history in which Israel, who "originated in the beginning of thought" and for whose sake the world was created, play the key role. The nations are "matter" to be purified by the Jews who have been exiled among them.[38] Therefore, they play only an ancillary role, defined by their relation to Jews, even if they seemingly have an upper hand. In a rather drastic and extreme example, the Jews' historical role is to sanctify God's name by dying as martyrs in order to purify the traces of holiness trapped among the gentile citizens of Poland—their murderers.[39] Only within this limited scope can gentiles be considered Israel's partners in the redemption.

The difference between Jews and non-Jews is not primarily ethnic, political, confessional, or historical. The gentiles are ontologically different from the Jews: they do not possess the divine soul but only the baser animal soul, which stems from the three wholly impure husks. The Jews, on the other hand, possess not only the refined divine soul but also a superior animal soul originating in the husk of *nogah*, in which good and evil are mixed.[40] Moreover, in contrast to the gentiles, who do good only for their own benefit,[41] Jews are characterized by their capacity for selflessness. The very Hebrew word for a Jew, *Yehudi*, hints at *hoda'ah* (the thanksgiving benediction that acknowledges God by means of complete self-nullification, a capacity that guarantees every Jew a share in the world-to-come).[42]

Shneur Zalman's beliefs about the inherently base characteristics of gentiles would seem to be at odds with his notions of a universal redemption: as entities associated with absolute impurity, they should, presumably, be annihilated at the end of days, when all impurity as such would cease to exist. Yet, he often weaves into his sermons references to biblical prophecies that suggest the opposite. At least as far as the days of the Messiah are concerned, the presence of the impure gentiles is compatible with Shneur Zalman's vision, which reiterates Maimonides's description whereby the world will continue to move along its customary lines, the only exception being the ability of the Jews to live and worship freely under the rule of the king Messiah. In one passage from *Torah or*, Shneur Zalman compares the rule of the king Messiah to that of Solomon: as in the time of the latter, the nations will flock to the royal court to enjoy the king's wisdom—a vision that echoes the Maimonidean concept of a Messiah who improves the world by motivating all the nations to serve the one and only God.[43]

The idea of the king Messiah who teaches wisdom to the gentiles raises the question of the boundaries between the nations and the Jews. After all, the Messiah's wisdom stems from the Torah, which suggests that, through him, the nations will also access the Torah. Furthermore, some passages suggest that gentiles will be even more deeply involved in the life of Torah and commandments.

> [In the days of the Messiah] the principal occupation with Torah will [. . .] be with the inner aspect of the commandments and their hidden reasons. The revealed aspects, however, will be manifest and known to every Jew as an innate knowledge, which can never be forgotten. Only the mixed multitude will have to occupy themselves with these [revealed aspects of Torah], because they will not merit the taste of the Tree of Life[44] which is the inner aspect of the Torah and the Commandments. They will need to occupy themselves [as Torah study] with the *Mishnah* in order to weaken [by their occupation with Torah] the power of the *sitra ahra*, which cleaves unto them, so that it will not dominate them—causing them to sin. Thus, Scripture says: "But the sinner being a hundred years old shall be accursed" [Isa. 65:20]; this refers to the sinners of the mixed multitude.[45]

In the above excerpt, Shneur Zalman further elaborates on the status of the Torah and the commandments at the end of days. The commandments will indeed remain valid even in the days of the Messiah, and yet the Jews' access to them will become quite different: they will need to concern themselves only with the inner, mystical layers of the Torah (e.g., the reasons for the commandments), but they will not be occupied with the nonmystical layers, as these will have become their "innate knowledge," knowledge that does not need to be acquired and memorized by means of study. Only the "mixed multitude" will be compelled to study the revealed, nonmystical, halakhic facet of the Torah in order to know how to avoid transgressing it. In its original context, the biblical term *mixed multitude* (*'erev rav*, Exod. 12:38) refers to the people who accompanied the Israelites on their way out of Egypt at the Exodus. Rashi explains that these were "strangers" or "converts" (*gerim*),[46] and he later charges them with the idolatrous sin of the golden calf.[47] Shneur Zalman accordingly seems to understand *'erev rav* as the gentiles who will accompany Israel on their way toward the final redemption.[48] They will comprise those who accepted the yoke of Torah and commandments, remaining the only group that was still susceptible to sin. One of Israel's tasks during the exile has been to clarify the *halakhah* in order to purge the divine sparks of the husk of *nogah*.[49] But in the days of the Messiah, the sparks will be elevated and halakhic studies for the sake of purifying the sparks will become obsolete. This, in turn, will leave Israel free to delve only into the internal, mystical layers of the law.[50] By contrast, the mixed multitude, composed of the gentile nations who are ontologically linked to the husks, will remain bound by the revealed aspects of the Torah even in the days of the Messiah, and they will need to study and clarify the *halakhah* for themselves in order to stay on the right path and avoid repeating the sin of idolatry—the hallmark of the *'erev rav* ever since the Exodus.

The different function of the Jews and the non-Jews is based on a distinction between worship for the sake of the purification of sparks and worship for the sake of delving into the innermost aspects of the Torah. Once Israel has completed the task of purifying the sparks by means of its divine service, when it has freed itself from the need to expound *halakhah*, it becomes the gentile nations' task to carry on with this activity. The same idea undergoes an interesting twist in another of Shneur Zalman's *ma'amarim*, where the gentiles are said to be destined to be elevated in the messianic future while still remaining unequal to Israel, inasmuch as they will perform only the commandments that are incumbent upon women—an idea that stems from the theosophic notion whereby worship during the exile purifies the feminine aspect of the divinity (*Nukba*).[51] Here, too, the gentiles are allowed to merit the life of Torah and commandments, but their inferior status in relation to the Jews is not that of the convert versus the Israelite, but rather the status of the female versus the male in the traditional community.[52]

The texts discussed above provide a somewhat inclusive perspective on the messianic future as they welcome gentiles in the community of Torah students, albeit in an inferior position.[53] There are, however, many references throughout Shneur Zalman's corpus of teachings to some mode of gentile participation in the resurrection. These references follow the path of the rectification and sublimation of material reality in the future-to-come. For example, while acknowledging that the Israelites had already merited the dew of the resurrection at Sinai, Shneur Zalman goes on to say the following:

> The sin [of the golden calf] caused both [the Israelites] and the world to become gross again—until "the end of days," when the dross of the body and of the world will be purified, and they will be able to apprehend the revelation of the divine light which will shine forth to Israel by means of the Torah, called "might." And, as a result of the overflow of the illumination on Israel, the darkness of the gentiles will also be lit up, as Scripture says, "And nations shall walk by your light" [Isa. 60:3], etc., and "O, house of Jacob, come, let us walk by the light of the Lord" [Isa. 2:5]; and again, "The glory of the Lord shall appear, and all flesh, as one, shall behold" [Isa. 40:5], etc.[54]

Shneur Zalman evokes the relation between the Giving of the Torah and the final redemption. The Israelites first experienced the resurrection at Sinai, when, according to tradition, every divine utterance caused them to expire. They died because they achieved complete self-nullification, but God resurrected them with the dew of the Torah, suffusing their existence with his will, which allowed them to live as individual beings and yet to be at one with him through the Torah. Thus, the Giving of the Torah was an experience of God's union with his creation, while the sin of idolatry, committed soon afterward, was its ultimate negation.[55] Idolatry brought the Israelites back to the state in which they considered themselves separate beings and were again becoming engrossed in materiality. This situation will persist until the resurrection, when corporeality and materiality will be purified, and they will no longer limit or obscure the intensity of the divine illumination suffusing the entire world. As a consequence, the world will no longer be experienced as being nondivine. This will inevitably impact the gentile nations, as the light permeating the transformed world will be so intense that at least some of it will reach them, and they will, therefore, also be affected by the final redemption.

Still, the manner of their participation in the redemption remains problematic. The transformation of the world will change the relation between Israel and the nations, although—as Shneur Zalman seems to suggest—Isaiah's prophecy in which "all flesh" shall see the glory of God "together" will not efface the difference between Jew and gentile. For not only will the messianic advent reverse the relations between the nations as rulers and the Jews as their subjects, but the nations will also learn the divine wisdom of Torah from the Messiah, which means that while casting off the burden of foreign rule, the Jews will become spiritual leaders to all other nations. Notably, Shneur Zalman's use of the verse calling on the "House of Jacob" to "walk by the light of the Lord" (Isa. 2:5) is understood in the Habad tradition as referring to the voice of the gentiles as they address the house of Jacob with the words, "You go first, and by dint of this we, too, will follow in the light of God."[56] Moreover, "the house of Jacob" is understood as a reference to the lowest of the Jewish souls, since the name Jacob (*Ya'akov*) derives from the word heel (*'akev*), namely, the lowest part of the body;[57] and if this is the level of the Jewish souls, then the gentile souls, although admitted to the world-to-come, must constitute a class of souls that is lower still.[58]

The new political balance of power in the redeemed world will result not from any shift in the direction or quality of the divine light itself, but rather from the eradication of the husks that obscure it and cause the Jews to be exiled among the gentile nations. The confusion to which the world is subject in its present exilic state allows the gentiles to dominate Israel and thus creates the illusion that they are the primary recipients of the divine vitality, while in fact they are driven to access it indirectly, through Israel's "hind side" (*ahorayim*). In other words, the light that the gentiles receive during the exile reaches them only as a consequence of Israel's sins. But in the messianic era, after the resurrection, the evil husks will be annihilated, and the divine light will shine on Israel with full force. Moreover, since Israel will not commit any more sins, the only channel through which the divine light could reach the gentiles will be obliterated. Yet even then, they will not be illuminated directly; the light reaching them will be an incidental by-product of the overflow intended for Israel. This excess will overflow indiscriminately, reaching them thanks to God's unbound mercy. In short, the gentiles will not be annihilated, but their access to the life-giving energy of the divine will remain inferior.

Not all the gentile nations, however, will deserve redemption. While most of them will be purified and saved, some will have to be completely destroyed to achieve purification. According to Shneur Zalman, one-third of the nations will be destroyed as a punishment for the sin of Noah's son, Ham, father of Canaan (Gen. 9:22–27).[59] Canaan, who had seen the nakedness of his father, Noah, and allowed him to remain exposed, will be restored to purity only by total annihilation. But the descendants of Ham's two brothers, Shem and Japheth, who "took a cloth, placed it against both their backs and, walking backward, they covered their father's nakedness; their faces were turned the other way" (Gen. 9:23), will be saved. Shneur Zalman finds an allusion to this in the biblical emphasis on the withdrawal of the two brothers from the scene with their faces "turned back" (*ahoranit*), a term that links them to the "hind-side" (*ahorayim*), that is, to the source of the divine vitality that is available to the gentile nations during the exile and which will be purified at the redemption, when its "external aspect is nullified in relation to the internal."[60]

There is another reason for the anticipated change in the status of gentiles, which stems from the prospect of a shift in the perception of space. Following the purification of the world in the messianic future, the intensity of the divine light will be such that it will raise the lands of the non-Jews and idolaters to the level of the Land of Israel, so that "the Land of Israel will spread all over the entire world," while at the same time itself being elevated to the level of Jerusalem, which in turn will spread throughout the Land.[61] One can speculate that Shneur Zalman's implicit position is that these new boundaries of the Land of Israel, which would stretch to the extent of incorporating even the impure lands of the idolaters, would grant their gentile inhabitants the right to acquire the protected status of *ger toshav*, and thus to become the mixed multitude who participate in the redemption, as discussed above.

Messianic Age: Now and Then

Shneur Zalman's numerous references to messianic times and Israel's task of bringing them closer raises the question of his view on the imminence of redemption. Some statements suggest that he believed the end of days to be near. He even tried to calculate the precise date, although it should be noted that statements of this nature occupy only a marginal place in his writings.[62] Nevertheless, some scholars have taken them to be representative of his messianic enthusiasm. According to Tishby, for example, Shneur Zalman's definition of his own times as the era of "the footsteps of the Messiah" (*'ikveta di-meshiha*) attests to the presence of messianic tension in early Habad.[63] "The footsteps of the Messiah," a common concept in Lurianic kabbalah, stands for the time of the purification of the sparks entrapped in the feet of either *Adam Beliya'al* or *Adam kadmon*.[64] It originates in the Bible (see Ps.

89:51), and is used in the Mishnah[65] to depict the calamities that will immediately precede the advent of the Messiah, following the continuous erosion of man's spirit, morality, and wisdom over numerous generations. Echoes of, on the one hand, the sense that the task of purification is nearing completion, and on the other hand, the notion that the decline of the generations is reaching its lowest point, can be heard in Shneur Zalman's teachings associated with the time of *'ikveta di-meshikha*. In line with his grasp of history, Shneur Zalman posits the period of "the footsteps of the Messiah" within the framework of the emendation of the *sefirotic* structure; a process that takes place in the soul of each and every Jew.

At the beginning of *Tanya*, Shneur Zalman explains that, despite the fact that all Jews possess a divine soul that is equally a part of God, there are some souls that stem from a higher aspect of the Godhead and others from a lower. This creates a hierarchy of souls, which has both synchronic and diachronic dimensions. From the synchronic perspective, the souls of the leaders of the Jewish people derive from the highest, intellectual *sefirot*, for they are the brain of the nation, whereas the souls of the common folk derive from the lower *sefirot*. Most importantly, however, the souls vary from the diachronic perspective as well: those of earlier generations stem from the higher *sefirot*, but with the passing of time, the souls come into the world from an increasingly lower source within the Godhead until the generation of *'ikveta di-meshiha*, whose souls are as low in relation to the generation of the Patriarchs as feet are in relation to the head.[66]

The time of the footsteps of the Messiah is devoted to the purification of the lowest levels of the *sefirotic* structure. According to an early Habad tradition originating from the Great Maggid and the Ba'al Shem Tov, this final stage in the process of purification is a time of utter confusion and disorder. In earlier generations, Jewish society was divided into various classes, and the class affiliation of every Jew was determined by the origin of the root of his soul within the *sefirotic* hierarchy. The souls originating in the World of Creation were incarnated as scholars; those originating in the World of Formation became businesspeople who supported the scholars financially; and the souls originating in the World of Making formed the lowest caste of ignoramuses. Different types of souls were located in appropriate sectors of the community with an appropriate type of worship designed for each of them. But in the times of Shneur Zalman, which he identified as the time of *'ikveta di-meshiha*, all these distinctions have broken down: lofty souls may incarnate as common folk and educated people may possess lowly souls. In this state of confusion, which according to the Mishnah reflects the chaotic conditions that mark the final stage of the exile, people often worship inappropriately as they do not conform to the mode of worship that is compatible with their social status and the root of their soul.[67] As we see, this confusion does not carry signs of a violent chaos, as the Talmudic Sages imagined it.[68]

This is not to suggest that the generation of the footsteps of the Messiah is morally inferior to other generations; it is characterized by confusion, which does not necessarily reflect its moral fiber. However, previous generations were unequivocally either righteous or wicked because their souls were loftier and thus capable of the complete eradication of the evil that had contaminated them. As a result, there were none in whom both good and evil blended: those who wanted to worship God did so selflessly, and those who sinned must have been entirely wicked to have done so in the first place. By contrast, the souls of the Shneur Zalman's generation are of a lower stature, and much greater effort is required to eradicate the evil that resides within them.[69] This prompts the question concerning the appropriate mode of worship for them. In most cases, Shneur Zalman identifies the time of the footsteps of the Messiah with practical commandments, with charity occupying pride of place.[70] He reevaluates the time of the footsteps by describing it as a necessary and distinct part of the process of redemption, rather than simply a time of chaos and disarray. It may even be argued that associating the footsteps of the Messiah with practical commandments elevates this generation to a higher level than that of the Giving of the Torah.[71] Indeed, the generation of the footsteps of the Messiah has sunk to the lowest step of the *sefirotic* ladder, but it also stands out for being able to bring God down to the lowest spheres of reality more effectively than any of the preceding generations. In line with the general tendency present in his teachings, Shneur Zalman allows for the possibility that the lowest place to which humanity may fall can still be redeemed.[72]

The generation that precedes the advent of the Messiah is thus required to purify the last remaining denigrated sparks. Surprisingly, however, Shneur Zalman defines this generation as extending from the Ge'onic period to the present. Rather than constituting an abrupt rupture in history on the verge of the redemption, the last generation endures for almost a millennium—much longer than the preceding generations of *tana'im* and *amora'im*. This observation takes away much of the urgency of the matter, although there is no denying that redemption is a tangible reality for Shneur Zalman. It depends on the collective effort of the community of Israel, he claims, recalling the Talmudic story in which the Messiah replies to Rabbi Yehoshua's question about the date of his anticipated advent with the single word "today," on which Elijah comments: "Today, if you will hear his voice" (Ps. 95:7).[73] In other words, no matter how long he has been delayed, a collective act of religious improvement can bring the Messiah in an instant. This story also has a kabbalistic underpinning.[74] The word *today* (*ha-yom*) brackets the entire reality, as it refers both to the first day before the emanation of the worlds associated with *Keter*[75] and to the fulfillment of creation in the day of the redemption, the "day that is completely a day" (*yom she-kulo yom*).[76] The redemption will come only if the voice of the Messiah is obeyed, that is, through repentance (*teshuvah*), which also originates in *Keter* and was created on the first day, just before the creation of the world.[77] As such, repentance is located above the order of emanations and is, therefore, free from all temporal restrictions (time develops only once the order of emanations has begun to unfold). In other words, repentance grants the individual direct access to a transcendent reality that comprises both the world's beginning and its end.[78] Accordingly, in the present generation, the redemption is in fact always about to take place: by repenting, the community can leap directly into a redeemed world. The redemption is available on both the collective and the personal level, as Shneur Zalman demonstrates through the classic example of Eleazar ben Durdaya, who repented and acquired his share in the world-to-come in an instant.[79] Shneur Zalman's messianism is therefore not acute, in the sense that he does not anticipate an imminent end of days, constantly calculate its precise date, or attach to it a particular historical event or messianic figure. Nevertheless, he holds a deep conviction that the redemption can instantly be brought about by Israel as a whole, or at least by each and every individual Jew who can reach a personally redeemed state of existence.[80]

The individual's desire to achieve redemption irrespective of time and place, according to which everyone can redeem him- or herself through daily worship, is based on an interpretation of the Exodus as an ongoing event.

> "In every generation and every day a person is obliged to regard himself as if he had that day come out of Egypt."[81] This refers to the release of the divine soul from the confinement of the body, the "serpent's hide,"[82] in order to be absorbed into the Unity of the light of the blessed *Ein Sof*, through occupation in the Torah and commandments in general, and in particular through accepting the

Kingdom of Heaven during the recital of the *Shema'*, wherein the person explicitly accepts and draws over himself his blessed Unity, when he says: "The Lord is our God, the Lord is One."[83]

The representation of corporeality as the "serpent's hide" is a rather common motif in Shneur Zalman's teachings. According to the epistle discussed in chapter 2, the divine soul incarnates in the "serpent's hide" to subjugate the domain of husks and transform it into divinity, thus bringing the collective redemption closer. The above excerpt of the *Tanya* evokes the same idea to show that there is a way out of the confinement of corporeality even before the final redemption.[84] The personal experience of the Exodus, defined here as an act of union with the perfect unity of God's infinite light, takes places on a daily basis within and in spite of the unredeemed world's corporeality and materiality, which creates the impression that the individual is separate from the divine. Moreover, the experience of personal redemption from the confinement of physicality is achievable by no other means than the normative rituals of daily life. While the final redemption will come about only once good and evil have been completely separated, the experience of redemption during the exile is achievable "in the microcosm ['*olam katan*], i.e. [in] man, at every 'time when you [God] may be found' [Ps. 32:6]—namely [during] prayer."[85] And, in addition to prayer, other standard elements of worship such as Torah study and the performance of commandments (in particular of charity) make it possible for the individual to experience the redemption. The rituals provide a practical way of separating good from evil and clinging to the former and, as such, constitute an internalization of the redemption. It is important to note that, for Shneur Zalman, time-bound rituals such as prayer, which is the "time when thou mayest be found," or Torah study at set times, have the power to effect a personal Exodus, to which he refers as the experience of transcending the limitations of time and space.[86]

Shneur Zalman ascribes great significance to the proclamation of faith in the *Shema'*, which in his view is not a purely declarative statement but a performative utterance: it bestows the unity on the person who proclaims it. The proclamation of God's unity is thus an ecstatic experience of ultimate freedom in God. After explaining that Egypt stands for the physical world, Shneur Zalman adds that the cry of the *Shema'* makes it possible to transcend spatiotemporality. It expresses an approach that is not discursive and does not attempt to grasp the world as an object of intellectual comprehension. Discursive thinking inevitably leads to a state of separation between the subject and the object of cognition, which is incompatible with the absolute unity of God as proclaimed in the *Shema'*. Unconstrained by the boundaries of cognition,[87] the individual proclaiming the *Shema'* reaches the essence of God, and most importantly, reaches it from within the world—this is the personal Exodus.[88]

Shneur Zalman uses the deliverance of the Jews by the miracle of Purim as yet another example of how the expression of faith in God's ultimate unity transcends cognition, conceptualization, and even articulation. According to a midrashic interpretation of the Purim story, God decided to save the Jews when he heard their inarticulate outcry, which sounded like the bleating of a goat.[89] This highlights the absence of discursive knowledge (*da'at*) in their plea: they cried out to God out of sheer despair, as a kid crying out to its mother. But this lack of *da'at* actually bridged the gap between Israel below and God above: just as God is beyond *da'at*, so the Jews on that occasion transcended *da'at* through their desperate cry of absolute faith.[90] Such faith comes from the "depth of the heart, from the truly innermost point,"[91] which is beyond *da'at*: the divine spark possessed by every Jew. Its concealment through engagement in worldly affairs constitutes the state of exile, while its full exposure amounts to a state of redemption.[92] This is why, according to a classical rabbinic dictum, the Messiah will come inadvertently, "when *da'at* is diverted" (*be-heseah da'at*).[93]

The focus on speech is notable, as it casts an interesting light on Habad's alleged intellectualism.[94] The route to personal redemption is not study for the sake of intellectual accomplishment, but rather prayer uttered inarticulately in despair. The petition is more powerful than comprehension. That is not to say that Shneur Zalman was anti-intellectual, but that by highlighting the power of speech, he incorporates in the redemptive experience even his less intellectually gifted followers. It is important to clarify, however, that his notion of overcoming *da'at* does not invalidate the importance of cognition in principle. The act of transcending *da'at*, through the recitation of the *Shema'*, is destined to evolve into a redemptive state of total cognition in the messianic future. From this perspective, the redemption constitutes mainly an "epistemological shift" and an "expansion of knowledge [*da'at*]."[95]

The declaration of faith in the *Shema'* bridges the gap between God and the world as it makes it possible to uncover the redeemed, divine reality from within itself without the mediation of discursive knowledge, which by its nature obfuscates the unity of God. This possibility arises from Shneur Zalman's paradoxical view of the creation of the world. On the one hand, it is the product of the divine will, filled with the godliness that is revealed throughout it. On the other, the creation veils the presence of the divine in the world, concealing it behind the facade of separate beings; the world (*'olam*) is "concealment" (*he'lem*).[96] Bearing in mind the delicate balance between concealment and revelation on which, according to Shneur Zalman, the world's very existence depends,[97] it follows that only the redemption resulting from the purification of materiality will allow for a clear perception of the divinity.

> In the days of the Messiah and the resurrection of the dead, when the materiality of this world is purified, [people] will be able to bear exposure to an infinitely stronger radiance, by way of a revelation that is perceived and grasped by everyone, so that each person according to his own ability to grasp [it] will point with his finger, so to speak, and say: "This is our God; we have waited for him" [Isa. 25:9], etc.[98]

In the redeemed world, in contrast to the exilic reality, each person will enjoy immediate cognitive access to God according to his or her own level. The presence of God will be so concretely obvious that one will simply be able to point one's finger at him.[99] Elsewhere, the difference between exile and the redeemed world is defined in terms of knowledge (*yedi'ah*) and vision (*re'iyah*) of God. Moreover, the tangible, sensual experience of God in the redeemed future is the promised reward for the labor of striving to know God during the exile.[100]

The totality of cognition in the redeemed world is sometimes presented as a synesthetic experience that overcomes the distinction between the senses, which is itself an exilic phenomenon. Shneur Zalman hints at this in the account of the Giving of the Torah at Sinai (a prefiguration of the future redemption), where "all the people saw the [audible] thunderings" (Exod. 20:15). He takes the phrasing of the biblical narrative literally and concludes that the Sinaitic experience transcended the division between the senses of sight and audition. "They saw what is heard and heard what is seen,"[101] which means that the Israelites enjoyed the Giving of the Torah as a total experience. This was due to the fact that, at that moment, they overcame corporeality and their souls "took flight with every utterance of the Law,"[102] liberating them from the "confinement of the body."[103] Such an experience, however, is not limited to the one-time Giving of the Torah or to the future redemption: it is also the experience of the penitent in the act of *teshuvah*.[104]

The redemption is also marked by a shift to greater clarity of language. As mentioned above, Shneur Zalman sees faith in the exile figuratively as an inarticulate cry to heaven out of Babylonia, the land of linguistic confusion.[105] The redemption, by contrast, will be the era of "pure language" (Zeph. 3:9). Transparency of language is associated with the idea of redemption as the ultimate disclosure, referred to as the "circumcision from above"[106] or "circumcision of hearts," which reveals the innermost part of the heart[107] and allows for the direct experience of the divinity, without any mediation. It points, on the one hand, to the purification and preparation of the Jewish body for entering the covenant with God while still inhabiting the world in a state of exile, and on the other, to the act of revelation and exposure as inextricably tied to the experience of redemption. In Shneur Zalman's interpretation, circumcision (*milah*) also alludes to the cognate word for the power of speech (*ruah memalela*),[108] which brings "the divine Wisdom out of potentiality into actuality, out of concealment into disclosure."[109] The exile is defined by the confusion of languages and the impossibility of expressing the unity of God in a discursive manner, whereas the redemption liberates language, transforming it into a suitable means for divine revelation.[110]

The redemption, therefore, has an epistemological dimension. In the redeemed state, the individual is released from his or her corporeality and can perceive Godliness intuitively, totally, and directly, in a manner unmediated by discursive thought or the division between the senses. Still, this liberation from corporeality does not entail the rejection of the body: just as at the Giving of the Torah the senses absorbed Godliness freely as a synesthetic experience, so in the state of personal ecstasy and in the future-to-come, the body will exist in its subtle, sublimated form, enabling everyone to experience God sensually.

The definition of redemption as synonymous with *teshuvah* raises the question of the role of the messianic figure in the redemptive process. Regardless of the final redemption, everyone can reach a redeemed state even while still in exile. If redemption comes about through Israel's repentance and results in the entire world being filled with the overflowing light of the Infinite, then the messianic figure, whose task it is to redeem either just the Jewish people, or the entire world, becomes seemingly irrelevant. Indeed, in light of the redemptive significance of repentance, the Messiah plays only a marginal role by prompting the righteous to repent.[111] As explained above, repentance is a means of transcending the boundaries of the emanated worlds, to enter the redeemed reality of an "everlasting day" filled with divine light. While penitents (*ba'ale teshuvah*) are, therefore, both the instruments of redemption and its beneficiaries, the righteous, who technically do not need to repent, appear to be excluded from the process.[112] The Messiah is therefore given the task of concluding the redemptive process by elevating the righteous to the redeemed state, which the penitents have already achieved.[113]

Even though the messianic figure plays only a marginal role in the process of redemption, its significance grows in the postexilic world. As mentioned above, while the Messiah reigns primarily over Israel, his authority spreads to the gentile nations who flock to his court in order to learn wisdom from him. The task of revealing wisdom can be linked to one of the distinctive features of the messianic times: the gentiles will be permitted to study the revealed layers of the Torah, while the Jews will freely explore its inner mystical meanings. In this context, the Messiah's task reflects that of Moses, through whom the Torah was first given to the Israelites: just as Moses at Sinai drew down the revealed aspect of Torah, so the Messiah will draw down its inner aspect.[114]

Finally, one other question should be raised about the messianic figure in Shneur Zalman's teachings: can the Hasidic *tsadik* fulfill this role? There is no indication that Habad Hasidim associated Shneur Zalman with the Messiah,[115] and yet some of the *tsadik*'s functions may be interpreted as messianic.[116] In his sermons, Shneur Zalman distinguishes between two types of *tsadikim*.[117] The first is the hidden *tsadik*, such as Rabbi Shimon Bar Yohai.[118] His soul is so lofty that he is detached from the material world, worshiping God spiritually by performing unifications and ascensions of the soul. The second is the revealed *tsadik*, who worships through materiality. The two types are likened respectively to the Leviathan and the wild ox (*shor ha-bar*)—the two creatures that will be served up at the feast of the righteous in the future-to-come.[119] The hidden *tsadik* is called Leviathan because, like the sea monster, he is concealed, and his lofty mode of worship links him directly to *Ein Sof*.[120] The revealed *tsadik*, on the other hand, is called "wild ox" because he labors within materiality and has the strength required to carry the yoke of Torah and the commandments. Even though, in the present, the Leviathan-type *tsadik* seems loftier due to his otherworldliness, in the future-to-come, the Behemoth-type *tsadik* will be elevated by dint of his transformative work within materiality. Moreover, while the former forges an individualistic connection to God, the latter is engaged with the world and is connected to other people. The former's detachment from the lower worlds brings him "close to the level of prophecy," while the latter, by virtue of his involvement therein, draws down the light of *Ein Sof* and its vitality, and thus transforms not only himself, but also his surroundings.[121]

The category of the "wild ox" is thus applicable to the Hasidic rebbe who functions as leader to his community. The divine attributes are contained within the *tsadik*'s soul without being distorted by his corporeality,[122] and they are achievable by his followers through his "thoughts, speech and deeds."[123] The *tsadik* "heals the souls of those who are of his 'root,' [. . .] imparts 'understanding of the divine' and arouses the depths of the ears of those in his generation."[124] Just as Plato's philosopher, who emerged from the cave to see the light of day and to grasp the true nature of things, returns to help other people share his insight, so the redeemed *tsadik* shares his own grasp of the divine with his followers. The social role of the rebbe as leader and teacher to his Hasidim therefore has a deeper, mystical meaning: he can help an ignoramus who is not capable of cleaving to God by himself, but who can cleave to the *tsadik* and scholar, and through him be united with God himself.[125] The rebbe's death also has a redemptive value. As the ultimate display of self-sacrifice (*mesirat nefesh*), death is related to Torah study and prayer in total devotion.[126] When a *tsadik* passes away, all the "light" that he accumulated through his divine service is fully revealed and grants atonement to his generation in much the same way as the sacrifice of the red heifer.[127] The death of the *tsadik*, just like the ritual of the red heifer, therefore carries messianic significance.[128] For Shneur Zalman, the experience of redemption was sustained over time initially not by their allegiance to the same dynasty of *tsadikim*, but rather by cleaving to the rebbe even after his death, since "when the *tsadik* departs he is present in the world more than during his life-time."[129] Ironically, while there is no indication that Shneur Zalman ever intended to found a dynasty, eventually the dynastic model prevailed in Habad.

While Shneur Zalman did not identify the *tsadik* as the Messiah, despite ascribing him certain messianic functions, his contemporary Nahman of Bratslav claimed the opposite: the true *tsadik*, modeled after Nahman himself, was to bring the redemption. Despite this rudimentary difference, there are many commonalities between Nahman's and Shneur Zalman's messianic visions. Nahman, too, envisioned a total, encompassing redemption that would include non-Jews. While he is credited with saying that "in the future the entire world would be Bratslav Hasidim,"[130] he did not mean that this would be achieved through erasing the boundary separating Jews from gentiles or by tearing down social hierarchies. Using the same Maimonidean trope as Shneur

Zalman, he envisioned the *tsadik*-Messiah as a king and teacher who will impart wisdom to the entire world and bring the gentile nations closer to God and Judaism until "all turn to one pure language."[131]

While both Shneur Zalman's and Nahman's biographies testify to the importance they attached to the Land of Israel (Shneur Zalman turned back from his journey to Palestine in 1777 but kept supporting the Hasidic settlement there; Nahman visited Palestine in 1798–1799),[132] this attachment is not central for their messianic idea. Both subscribed to the same idea that the holiness of the Land of Israel will expand over other lands in the messianic days, as the intermediary forces ruling other lands will be removed and God's providence will directly govern everywhere, just as it does currently in the Land of Israel. In his cryptic *Scroll of Secrets*, Nahman also introduces an idea, absent from Shneur Zalman's teachings, according to which in the course of the redemptive process the *tsadik*-Messiah will take in possession the Land of Israel; the process itself, however, will be peaceful and harmonious as the Messiah will acquire the Land of Israel through barter exchange.[133] In sum, a brief examination of these two takes on messianism shows that both Hasidic masters shared the idea of all-encompassing, harmonistic, and nonapocalyptic redemption. At the same time, they offer different recipes for bringing the messianic advent closer—the difference, seemingly, resulting from their disparate understanding of the character of a Hasidic community. In Nahman's community, the followers' spiritual lives were centered on the *tsadik*, to whom they were obliged to devote fully. In Shneur Zalman's community, the focus was on *beinoni*—the everyman—and his worship. While the *tsadik* was a spiritual guide and communal leader, Shneur Zalman rarely delved into the characteristic of his and his worship's role. His teachings were directed to, and focused on, *beinonim*; the spiritual change was to come from the rank-and-file, with a little help from their rebbe.

Beyond the Messianic Era: The Afterlife and the World-to-Come

In Shneur Zalman's teachings, as in the classical rabbinic sources, the "world-to-come" (*ha-'olam ha-ba*) is often contrasted with "this world" (*ha-'olam ha-zeh*).[134] The assumption is that we can infer the features of the world-to-come from what we know about this world. If this world is marked by confusion, then the world-to-come will have a fixed order.

> When Scripture says "Today to do them" [Deut. 7:11], [it means today] and not tomorrow,[135] stressing that this world is the world of

doing [*'olam ha-ma'aseh*], in which man was given free will [*behirah*] to choose [to do] good. Moreover, even if he has already transgressed, he can repent and [then] resume his divine service. But this is not the case in the world-to-come, where man has no free will; rather, once he is in the world-to-come, he remains the same as he was in this world. [...] The reason for the difference between this world and the world-to-come is that everything in the world-to-come has its own set place, and the levels are all separate from one another: angels and souls are segregated within their own holy quarters, and evil has nothing whatsoever to do with good. For this reason, where there is evil, there is no trace of good. But this is not the case in this world, where good occurs even where there is evil. Therefore, even if a person has committed a transgression, he can perform a commandment and change his demeanor from evil to good.[136]

There are two crucial differences between this world and the world-to-come, one cosmic and the other personal. From the cosmic perspective, this world is a place in which good and evil are intermingled. Good can be drawn to evil entities and evil can reach places that are intrinsically good. The hierarchical structure of this world is fluid and constantly liable to be disturbed: what is high may become low, and what is low can rise up. This results from the two types of divine light that illuminate our world: the immanent and the transcendent. The immanent light of *memale*, which "fills all the worlds," varies according to the order of emanations and determines the hierarchy of beings by shining on each and every one according to its place. This light can be compared to the powers of the soul that animate all the body parts, each according to its place and function.[137] The transcendent light of *sovev*, which "surrounds all the worlds," shines equally everywhere, so that the lower entities in the hierarchy of concatenation receive it in equal measure to the higher entities. Effectively, the lower entities can rise above the level determined by their status, as the surplus of transcendent light makes up for, and supplements, the lesser radiance of the immanent light.

The state of confusion in the lower worlds is closely related to the concept of the breaking of the vessels, after which the creative divine sparks were scattered throughout this world, trapped in the material broken shards of the vessels. The world-to-come, by contrast, is "the world of purification, which has already been purified, where everything is in its proper place: a head is a head and a foot is a foot."[138] It is thus the world of the reinstated order of creation, with clear-cut borders between different levels within its hierarchy. The difference between the transcendent and the immanent light is annihilated, and the light shines only by way of *memale*.¹³⁹ Effectively, what is fixed at the bottom of the hierarchy of the world-to-come can no longer move upward. Paradoxically, then, owing to its fixed order, the world-to-come is associated with the restricting powers of *Gevurot*, a motif that Shneur Zalman links to the classical rabbinic notion whereby God created the world-to-come with the letter *yud* of the Tetragrammaton.¹⁴⁰

The idea that this world is distinguished from the world-to-come by the absence of a fixed hierarchy of beings, however, can also be approached from a personal perspective. For the individual who inhabits this world rather than the next, both sin and redemption are possible. In this world, good and evil are intermingled, and people tainted with evil are able to veer toward the good, thus lifting themselves to a higher position in the hierarchy of beings. Here, too, the illumination of this world by both types of divine light plays a key role: if the sinner was sustained in this world by the immanent light alone, he would receive only the precise measure of vitality required for his lowly position, and this would never allow him to change his demeanor from evil to good. But since he also receives the transcendent light, which is bestowed on everyone in equal measures of intensity, he is just as able to do good as the righteous individual, and this means that he has the opportunity to fully repent. The scope for individual redemption in this world is therefore practically unlimited, as one can swerve at any time from one extreme to another, rising from the lowly status of the wholly wicked to the lofty one of the wholly righteous.¹⁴¹

This scope for redemption is further associated with the existence of free will in this world against its absence in the world-to-come. The concept of free will seemingly clashes with that of God's omniscience (this is the so-called paradox of *yedi'ah u-veḥirah*).¹⁴² Shneur Zalman here connects free will with the equal access to the transcendent light that is granted to everyone,¹⁴³ while in other contexts, he links it to the immanent light and associates divine omniscience with the transcendent light.¹⁴⁴ There is no contradiction between these two positions, however, since one can always transcend oneself in this world, reach out to the aspect of *sovev*, and become a better person, whereas in the world-to-come, the two types of light will no longer be distinguishable from one another and individuals will thus no longer be able to access any distinctly transcendent divine force to improve and rise up in the hierarchy of beings. Rather, they will remain fixed permanently at the level determined by the immanent light they occupied while inhabiting this world.

At times, Shneur Zalman's narrative zooms in from the abstract world-to-come to more concrete images of the afterlife: *Gehinom* (a place for the souls of the wicked) and the Garden of Eden (the paradise for the righteous). In some cases, he speaks figuratively about living in this world as clothing the soul in garments, whether the pure garments of Torah and commandments or the impure garments of worldly existence. The soul then enters the afterlife, where it can no longer change them on its own. This frames Shneur Zalman's notion of the afterlife in the rabbinic context of reward and punishment. The afterworld preserves the pure garments of Torah and commandments as the reward of the righteous, and those of worldly pleasures as punishment for the wicked, thereby keeping every individual "separate, each in his place, with every righteous person having his own section."[145]

When discussing the punishment of the wicked, Shneur Zalman refers to the rabbinic depiction of the sinner's soul being cast off in the afterlife from the hollow of a sling—an image based on Abigail's cursing of David's enemies (1 Sam. 25:29).[146] The rabbis envisaged the angels casting the souls of the sinners from one corner of the earth to another, or God shaking them out of the redeemed Land of Israel "as a man who shakes his garment."[147] According to the *Zohar*, the image refers to the banishment of sinful souls to this world, where they are doomed to suffer endless wanderings through countless incarnations, even as demons.[148] In one place, the *Zohar* explains that the cord of the sling is formed out of all of the deeds that have not been entirely devoted to divine service.[149]

Shneur Zalman clearly draws on this idea. Even though he sees a person's mundane actions as his garments rather than the cord of the sling, he still considers them a yoke he must carry over to the afterworlds, where it attracts appropriate punishment. In his interpretation, the hollow of the sling is a procedure that shakes off the impure, worldly garments rather than the punishment of transmigration.[150] He considers the zoharic understanding of the punishment of the hollow of the sling as the expulsion of the soul back to its mundane, impure frame of mind.

> This is the meaning of the hollow of the sling: he [i.e., the soul of the departed] is slung, cast out and thrown down into those thoughts that—while he was still alive in this world—drew him to the vanities of the world; and he is ridiculed and made to believe that he still exists in this world, thinking, speaking and acting in his usual manner.[151]

After death, the wicked are made to suffer, not by undergoing a chain of incarnations but rather by entertaining the illusion that they are still alive in this world. This lasts only until they have been stripped of the unclean garments of mundane thoughts, words, and deeds. The purpose of the hollow of the sling, therefore, is not to punish the soul for the misdeeds it committed in this world, but rather to purify and prepare it for entering the Garden of Eden. Following Rabbi Meir's pronouncement on the death of Elisha ben Avuya that it would have been better to judge him first and then allow him to enter the afterworld,[152] Shneur Zalman sees the suffering of the sinner's soul as a transitory stage that the soul must pass through on its way to the redeemed world. As such, it is a process whose true purpose is to grant, as he states explicitly, "kindness, not retribution."[153]

Still, the hollow of a sling is not always sufficient for the purification of the soul. In some cases, the tribulation of the "*Gehinom* of snow" or the "*Gehinom* of fire" may be necessary, depending on the severity of the transgressions.[154] In several instances, however, the punitive role of *Gehinom* is downplayed against its purifying and transformative function, and it is presented as a stage that the soul must go through on its ascent to the highest level—the Upper Garden of Eden. For this reason, all of the souls that do not merit immediate elevation to the Upper Garden of Eden may ascend gradually after death, from the hollow of a sling, through *Gehinom*, to the Lower Garden of Eden, the River of Fire, right up to the Upper Garden of Eden.[155] The sufferings of the hollow of a sling, *Gehinom*, and the River of Fire thus prepare the soul for its final ascension. In a beautiful metaphor, Shneur Zalman compares the fire of *Gehinom* to the fire of the crucible: just as the latter, in the process of smelting ore, separates silver from waste matter and slag, so the former separates good from evil, thus enabling the soul to ascend to the Garden of Eden.[156] The sufferings of *Gehinom* are worth enduring as they lead to the ultimate delight,[157] although since they are much more painful than any suffering experienced in this world, it is much better to suffer for one's sins in this world (through self-mortification such as fasts, for example) than in the world-to-come.[158]

Gehinom and the River of Fire play similar but distinct roles. Just as passing through the fire of *Gehinom* purifies the soul before it enters the Lower Garden of Eden, so immersion in the River of Fire is necessary before ascending to the Upper Garden of Eden.[159] In some places, Shneur Zalman even goes on to claim the existence of more than two Gardens of Eden, which are distinguished from one another by the level of delight they generate.[160] In contrast to the static image presented above, in which the hierarchy of beings in the world-to-come is fixed once and for all, here the afterlife is in permanent motion, with the righteous constantly ascending from the lower to the higher levels of the Garden of Eden.[161] This is in line with the classical rabbinic statement that the righteous "have no rest in the world-to-come, as Scripture says: 'They go from strength to strength'" (Ps. 84:7).[162] However, these ascensions, and the delights related to them, most likely refer to life after death rather than to the redeemed world at the end of days.

The River of Fire, therefore, can be seen as a transitory stage, either between the Lower and the Upper Gardens of Eden, or between countless other levels of the Garden. The image is not uncommon in Jewish sources; it originates in the vision of Daniel (Dan. 7:10) and was reinterpreted time and again in the mystical tradition. It is said to issue from the perspiration of the four living creatures (*hayot*) of the vision of Ezekiel (Ezek. 1:5–14)[163] and surrounds the Throne of Glory, investing it with extra splendor and regulating access to the divine presence. It also has both a punitive and a restorative function: it pours fire over the heads of the wicked, and yet the angels bathe in it to be renewed every day.[164] In the *Zohar*, the River of Fire has one effect on the souls of the wicked and another on those of the righteous: "The souls of the righteous immerse and are purified in it, [while] the souls of the wicked are judged in it, and they burn before it like straw before fire."[165] Shneur Zalman also underlies the *Zohar*'s idea that the River of Fire constitutes the second stage of purification, because even in the Lower Garden of Eden, the soul has not yet been fully cleansed of its worldly appearance.[166]

In some of Shneur Zalman's sermons, the stage of being cleansed in the River of Fire acquires special significance: the pure souls who have arrived in the lower levels of the Garden of Eden do not need to shed any trace of worldly impurity. Rather, they must leave behind the worldly delights that they experienced there, so as not to be confused when they experience those of the Upper Garden of Eden. The crossing of the River of Fire effectively erases their memory and prepares them for the new delights awaiting them at the higher level of the garden. It is worth noting that the River of Fire's function here resembles that of the River Lethe, which flows through Hades, whose waters the dead drank in order to forget their earthly lives.[167]

Time and space emerge from Shneur Zalman's teachings as the two factors that shape the condition of metaphysical exile in which the world has endured since its creation. Inevitably, therefore, the world's transformation into God's dwelling place, the overthrowing of material limitations, and the sublimation of corporeality will all impact time. Time will not cease to exist in the future-to-come. Like other elements of God's creation, it appears to exist in its own right only from the perspective of the created beings, while in fact it is part of the divine.[168] For the time being, in exile, God reveals his infinite will to the world by means of the Torah and commandments, as well as certain ritual objects. But in the future-to-come, he will reveal himself in his transcendent mode (the light of *sovev*) throughout all the worlds, by "the sense of vision," at which point both time and space, without being annihilated, will no longer appear to contradict the divine infinity and transcendence.[169]

The status of time in the redeemed world thus conforms to the pattern wherein mundane reality continues to exist in a manner that does not obfuscate the absolute unity of God. In order to understand the change that will affect time after the resurrection, one has to return to Shneur Zalman's functional definition of time as primarily a measure of the back and forth (*ratso va-shov*) flow of the life-giving energy, and of history as the process of gradual purification of worlds in preparation for the overflow of divinity. In the future-to-come, when the process of purification is complete, the limitation of materiality will be overturned and there will be no further need for the mode of *ratso*. The redeemed world will be overflowing with divine abundance in the mode of *shov*, from above to below.[170] If the rhythm of time in exile has been regulated by the constant pulse of divine energy that annihilates all existence only to re-create it, then in the future-to-come, due to the abundance of the divine life-giving energy, the world will cease to vanish at every single moment.

Without the *ratso* mode that pushes it forward, time will effectively stop. The resurrection of the dead will mark the end and the fulfillment of cosmic history, and the world will enter "the day that is entirely Sabbath" or "the day that is entirely long and entirely good."

The Sabbath is a rupture in the course of the week, a transcendent moment that is separate from mundane time.[171] It interrupts the sequence of the six working days and elevates the sparks that have been purified during the week to their supernal source. The influx of divine energy flowing to the worlds returns to its infinite source, and all the lower worlds experience a moment of eternity by being elevated to the *sefirah* of *Keter*, which lies above time.[172] But when the Sabbath ends, the energy descends and time is created anew.[173] Now, the supernal Sabbath, or "the day that is entirely Sabbath," follows the same pattern as it marks the conclusion of the work of purification performed during the exile. The supernal delight of the upper Sabbath is the source of the delight experienced on each and every Sabbath day throughout history.[174] In the era of redemption, the world will return to its source within *Keter*—the transcendent attribute of God's will and his delight.[175]

In some texts, the day of circumcision serves as an alternative paradigm of redemption, "the day that is entirely long and entirely good." Shneur Zalman interprets circumcision, which marks the covenant between Abraham and God, as the act in which Israel reveals itself in preparation for the full receipt of the divine revelation in the world. He also sees it as a more important rite than the Sabbath, for according to the Sages, "circumcision and all its preliminaries take precedence over the Sabbath,"[176] since the delight of the Sabbath, which comes from above, is still somehow dependent on the preparatory work done during the six days of the week. Circumcision, in contrast, is a free gift "from above," a process that takes place within the divine realm.[177] The fact that circumcision is performed on the eighth day is also highly symbolic, as the eighth day supersedes the Sabbath (the seventh).[178] The number eight also symbolizes the Messiah inasmuch as it is the sum of seven, the Sabbath day representing holiness, and one, representing the freedom it brings.[179]

The eschatological circumcision "from above" will come to pass only after the fulfillment of the whole Torah and the ingathering of the exiles.[180] Its description is based on the biblical account of Abraham's circumcision.

> Abraham merited the disclosure of the mode of "then the Lord your God will circumcise your heart" [Deut. 30:6], and therefore Scripture said: "was Abraham circumcised" [Gen. 17:26], etc. And this is the meaning of [the beginning of the same verse], "in the selfsame day was [Abraham] circumcised," that is to say, in the essence of that day, and that day is the day that is entirely long and entirely good, etc. And the essence of that day is the disclosure that will come to pass in the future-to-come, the disclosure of "your abundant goodness" [Ps. 31:20, 145:7].[181]

The passive voice used by the biblical author in the verse "Thus Abraham circumcised on that very day" (Gen. 17:26) indicates to Shneur Zalman that Abraham's circumcision was not merely a rite that he performed on himself, but rather an act initiated entirely by God and conducted "from above to below," as a result of which his heart was circumcised.[182] The emphasis in the verse on "the selfsame day" (*be-'etsem ha-yom ha-zeh*) alludes, in Shneur Zalman's view, to the essence (be-'atsmiyut) of the final redemption, which was revealed to Abraham on that occasion. His circumcision and its theosophic consequences thus prefigured the final redemption. On the eighth day, at the time of the redemption, the divine abundance and all its goodness will be revealed in full and equal measure (hence, "entirely good"), with no hindrances above or below.[183] Here, too, Shneur Zalman's concept of time gives away its functional character of a measure of the flow of the divine light, which at the end of days will radiate universally, filling the entire cosmos and turning it into the everlasting divine day.

Conclusion

This chapter explored the eschatological ideas that feature in Shneur Zalman's teachings. Not unlike earlier rabbinic sources, Shneur Zalman often fails to distinguish clearly between various traditional eschatological concepts. However, some of his teachings that deal with practical issues related to the redeemed future make it possible to distinguish the messianic era from the subsequent era of the resurrection. The former is a transitional stage between exile and redemption in which the world moves along its customary lines, and Jewish law is as much in force as in the time of exile, but the Jews are no longer subjugated to the power of other nations and are free to perform all the commandments and to study the deepest layers of the Torah. Following the resurrection, the sublimated, revived bodies receive the full revelation of the divine light and experience the supernal divine delight. The sublimation of bodies is part of the transformation and purification of the world, as a result of which materiality is sublimated and no longer obfuscates the divine light as it did during the exile. Rather, it becomes a perfect vehicle for the full revelation of the light. Shneur Zalman's concept of the redemption also involves non-Jews, who—purified by Israel in the time of exile—will be resurrected thanks to the surplus of the divine light.

Unlike the teachings of twentieth-century Habad leaders, Shneur Zalman's teachings do not convey a sense of acute messianism. Neither do they display any urgent expectation of the imminent, abrupt, and apocalyptic end of the world or of the immediate advent of the Messiah. On the contrary, the Messiah seems to play no part in the process that culminates in the redemption but acquires a significant role only as leader of the liberated Jewish people in the redeemed Land of Israel. And yet the redemption is a tangible reality for Shneur Zalman. He is convinced that the world stands on the threshold of redemption, a situation to which he refers as being the generation of the "footsteps of the Messiah." This generation has already lasted for hundreds of years, but it may nevertheless complete the task of purifying the world at any moment, and thus may finally bring about the messianic era. Moreover, even in exile, the individual can reach the divine by way of personal redemption. Because repentance is above temporal limitations in the opinion of Shneur Zalman, it can redeem the individual and, indeed, the whole world, at any time. "The footsteps of the Messiah" marks a peculiar and prolonged moment of messianic immediacy which binds together a teleological notion of time as leading to a particular eschatological moment versus eternal re-creation and personal moments of redemption even in the present. The redemptive state is, indeed, within the reach of every Jewish person at any given time, as they may transcend the exilic conditions of spatiotemporal reality and ascent to the transcendent source of everything. By doing so, they bring down additional divine energy to the constantly re-created world and push it forward to the ultimate redemption at the end of days, to the "day that is entirely good," in which this process of constant re-creation and improvement can, finally, seize.

The exilic world is one of confusion as opposed to the redeemed world, in which the hierarchy of beings is fixed. Present-day confusion has both negative and positive aspects, for example, the enslavement of the Jews by the nations, on the one hand, and the possibility of repentance and self-improvement, on the other. The process of the soul's purification continues after death, with the purifying torments of *Gehinom* or the "hollow of the sling." Only after that does the soul ascend through the numerous Gardens of Eden, constantly uncovering new aspects of the light of the *Shekhinah*. In the redeemed world, however, after the resurrection of the sublimated bodies, the whole divine light of *Ein Sof* (rather than merely the radiance of the *Shekhinah*) will be fully revealed, marking the end of the process of the soul's ascension. The constant rhythm of the divine light's descent and withdrawal will cease, as the overflow of light will never end. Time, which measures the pulse of the divine light, will come to a complete halt in the everlasting Sabbath—the holy day that transcends mundane time, or on the eighth day of circumcision, which is "entirely good."

The double-ending eschatology that emerges from Shneur Zalman's messianic teachings is particularly significant in light of the scholars' quest for the messianic idea in Judaism. In his highly influential essay "The Messianic Idea in Judaism," Gershom Scholem strove to draw a line between Jewish and Christian types of messianism. In order to do so, Scholem insisted on associating the former with a public, social, historical, and national redemption that comes about as a result of an apocalypse, as opposed to the latter that could take place in each person's soul and lead to a personal transformation.[184] Shneur Zalman removes the tension between these two ideas by introducing a model of redemption in two stages, featuring the days of the Messiah followed by the era of the resurrection of the dead. The process leading to the Messianic era unfolds gradually and depends on the inner transformation of the Jewish people rather than on historical events. Even the time of the "footsteps of the Messiah" is presented in utterly noncatastrophic terms as a state that has been experiencing the imminence of redemption for one hundred years. Only the second stage of redemption, namely the days that follow the resurrection, contains catastrophic elements, with the world undergoing a radical transformation. As a result, Shneur Zalman's messianism is mystical and historical, spiritual and activist, individual and collective, all at the same time.[185]

Shneur Zalman's inclusive vision of the messianic days, in which all nations return to God, gained a fascinating twist in the radical messianism of the last Habad rebbe. Menahem Mendel Schneerson did not stop at theorizing about the participation of the gentiles in the future redemption. Believing that the Messianic advent was imminent, and enjoying new opportunities in the postwar United States, Schneerson turned the idea into a coordinated activity. In 1983, Schneerson announced a new "campaign" directed specifically to non-Jews. The goal of the new campaign was to encourage the gentiles to accept the Seven Noahide Commandments (the only God-given commandments that non-Jews should keep) as their contribution to the advancement of the redemption.[186]

While Shneur Zalman's concept of redemption has provided the conceptual framework for the Noahide campaign, the campaign itself is a novel contribution of Menahem Mendel Schneerson. In Shneur Zalman's teachings, the Noahide commandments play only a marginal role. They appear in his *Shulhan 'arukh* in the context of the prohibition on theft that is also applicable to non-Jews, which is one of the seven Noahide laws, and again, in a discussion about the prohibition on hiring a *ger toshav* (a non-Jew who took on himself the seven Noahide laws) as a slave.[187] There has been no attempt on the part of Shneur Zalman to incorporate the Noahide commandments and the gentiles into the redemptive ethos of early Habad.[188]

The Noahide campaign has been something of a curiosity within the orthodox community, being perhaps the first and only attempt at an orthodox Jewish outreach to non-Jews. While it admittedly broadened the margin of non-Jewish partnership in the process of redemption, the campaign did not blur the boundary between Jews and non-Jews, nor did it change the balance of power between the Jews and the nations. While it may seem that the main goal of the Noahide campaign is to empower the non-Jews to assume an active role in redeeming the world, the opposite is true. The real objects of the campaign are the Jews themselves, who—thanks to that very campaign—may fulfill their obligation to be the "light unto the nations" (Isa. 49:6).[189] By engaging in this form of outreach and bringing non-Jews to a limited form of observance, the Hasidim collectively assume the role, which Shneur Zalman, following Maimonides, attributed to the Messiah: they, as the community, become the teacher of the Torah to the nations.

These tangible examples of engagement in global redemption indicate the continuity of the Habad perception of the role of the Land of Israel in the messianic process as peripheral. Certainly, the question of the Land of Israel became much more palpable and complex in the twentieth century, with the growth in significance of the Zionist movement and the establishment of the State of Israel in 1948. Menahem Mendel Schneerson adopted the anti-Zionist stance of his two predecessors, albeit he maintained relationships with Israeli politicians and military figures and occasionally tried to influence Israeli politics. Habad has maintained a visible presence in Israel. The movement established a separate village of Kfar Chabad in 1949 and attracted many new followers from the whole spectrum of the Israeli society, who brought their respective cultural backgrounds with them. Nonetheless, the rebbe Schneerson maintained that settling the land does not negate the exile; indeed, Jews living in Israel are all the more so in a state of deeper spiritual exile than their brethren outside of it. Revealing the esoterics brings about the redemption, and this should be done indiscriminately around the entire world. The impure, non-Jewish lands require a Jewish presence and emendation (*tikun*) even more so than the pure and holy Land of Israel; to paraphrase the expression attributed to the Tsemah Tsedek, the task of the Jews is to turn the diaspora into the Land of Israel, not to move there.[190] For this purpose, the Habad headquarters in Brooklyn can be more effective than Jerusalem, and, in fact, in Habad imagination, the central Habad synagogue at 770 Eastern Parkway Avenue in Brooklyn has, to some extent, replaced the Jerusalem Temple.[191] The role of sacred and profane space in contemporary Habad still awaits its researcher.

✧ 4 ✧

TIME AND RELIGIOUS PRAXIS

Torah Study: Between *Halakhah* and Mysticism

There seems to be a scholarly consensus that Rabbi Shneur Zalman broke new ground by making esoteric lore meaningful and inspirational to a broad circle of followers. In both *Tanya* and the sermons, he introduced his followers to kabbalistic ideas, which many of his contemporaries considered irrelevant and perhaps even harmful for people outside of scholarly and mystical elites. Despite the controversies that accompanied his leadership, Shneur Zalman continued putting the rank-and-files at the center of his Hasidic project, ascribing them the main role in the drawing down of divinity into the material world and bringing the redemption closer. Additionally, in his teachings he invested common experiences and precepts of normative Judaism with mystical meanings, and thus proposed a new, inclusive concept of mystical experience. This was possible, by and large, thanks to the emphasis he put on the temporal aspect of worship, which allows transcending temporal limitations on the personal, the national, and the cosmic level. He also presented routine rituals, characteristic of the everyday life of common people, as quintessential modes of worship. The reinterpretation of the precept of setting times for Torah study (*kevi'at 'itim la-Torah*) in Shneur Zalman's teachings was one factor that greatly contributed to the reevaluation of the role ordinary people played in religious life, and to shaping Habad's inclusivist vision of mysticism.

The precept of setting times for Torah study is not Shneur Zalman's innovation in and of itself. Its origins can be traced back to a Talmudic saying attributed to Rava, concerning the proceedings of the heavenly court after someone's death. When people are judged in the next world, the second question the heavenly court asks them is whether they set time aside for studying Torah.[1] Commenting on this passage, Rashi observes that the basis of setting times for Torah is practical. People ought to divide their time between Torah and mundane occupations (*derekh erets*). Fixing times for study is intended to establish a balance between the two: one should neither entirely neglect worldly responsibilities, nor be so engrossed in worldly matters as to shun religious precepts. Accordingly, allotting a certain time of the day solely for that purpose is regarded as a simple way of integrating Torah learning into one's daily routine and refraining from neglecting the commandment of Torah study.[2]

Medieval commentators followed Rashi's view on fixing time for Torah study as a means of fulfilling a *mitsvah* rather than as a *mitsvah* in its own right and so did not count it as one of the 613 commandments. Both the author of *Sefer ha-hinukh* and Maimonides considered it a procedure that makes the commandment of Torah study accessible to everyone, including the less gifted and the busiest of men. Although the commentators did not dwell on the technicalities of the issue, they did consider it an obligation to study Torah day and night in order to fulfill the biblical injunction: "Let not this book of the law cease from your lips, but meditate therein day and night" (Josh. 1:8).[3] Some of the rabbis attached particular significance to the fact that the Talmud uses the plural form of the noun "time" (*'itim*), and perceived it as an implicit order to set at least two times for study, one during the day and one at night.[4] Additionally, the main codes of Jewish law determined the time just after morning prayers to be appropriate for the daily fixed time of study.[5]

Shneur Zalman fosters the ideas outlined by the medieval halakhists in his *Hilkhot talmud Torah*. Just like them, he juxtaposes setting times for study with full-time learning. In his view, one should strive to learn the whole of the Oral Torah—a task that requires one's full attention. If this is not possible, however, one must nonetheless allot "a significant portion of time to Torah learning," defined here as at least half a day, in addition to night-time study. In order to fulfill the biblical command "And you shall recite them [God's words]" (Deut. 6:7), one should "Make his Torah [study] perpetual and his occupation casual." The opposite situation—occasional study and permanent work—is futile: one ends up forgetting what one has learned before memorizing the entire Oral Torah.[6]

Shneur Zalman was aware of the fact that to devote most of one's day and night to study was an ideal that only few could fulfill. He maintained, rather pragmatically, that only a scholar (*talmid ḥakham*) who has prior experience of study, or someone who has a "fine mind'" which makes him capable of becoming a scholar, could aspire to such behavior. For others to sacrifice all their time to learning would be pointless, as their natural disposition prevents them from grasping the entire Torah, no matter how long they invest in study. Shneur Zalman therefore restricts full-time Torah study to the intellectual elite.

This elitist approach to full-time study should not be read as a relegation of Torah learning to a secondary role in divine worship.[7] Rather, Shneur Zalman's approach should be viewed as pragmatic: even though the religious ideal dictates that everyone should master the entire Torah, reality shows that only a few gifted individuals are predestined to do so, while the vast majority are doomed to remain "ignoramuses" (*burim*) as a result of their limited intellectual disposition.[8] The term *bur*, used here to denote the unscholarly class, may be misleading. It refers to people who study the Torah yet do not reach the very high standards of Talmudic scholars (*talmid ḥakham*). These standards include the ability to memorize the entire Oral Torah[9] and to master the "rationales and sources of the commandments."[10] As a result of setting such high standards, Shneur Zalman sometimes counted among the *burim* even people who had mastered the study of the Pentateuch and the Mishnah but had not been trained in the Talmud.[11] *Bur* in this context should therefore not be understood as a pejorative reference to people who are literally ignorant, but rather as a term that covers a broad range of individuals who do not fall into the category of scholars.[12] Study still plays a highly important role in religious life for those people, but not on a full-time basis, and with an emphasis on practical laws as opposed to aiming at a comprehensive knowledge of the entire Torah.[13] Consequently, Shneur Zalman's *halakhah* delineates a community of Torah students divided into two groups: scholars and ordinary people.[14] Both groups have certain obligations that are determined by different criteria.[15] The scholars are obliged to study full-time at all costs, even if this compels them to live in poverty and destitution, whereas laypeople should not risk poverty but should rather earn a living. They should set times for study every day and night as a way of fulfilling the commandment of *Talmud Torah*.[16] In particularly difficult circumstances, their study may even be further limited to one chapter in the morning and one in the evening.

The distinction and different obligations that follow are based on Shneur Zalman's understanding of the commandment of Torah study. He points to two strands of the commandment: one for knowing the

Torah (*mitsvat yedi'at ha-Torah*) and one for "Meditat[ing upon it] therein day and night" (*ve-hagita bo yomam va-lailah*, Josh. 1:8).[17] These two components are interrelated. Despite the apparent superiority of the former over the latter,[18] one is not mutually exclusive from the other. Moreover, the inability to fulfill the former does not amount to transgressing the commandment of Torah study. The focal point merely shifts to the second commandment (to meditate therein), which is fulfilled by setting special times for Torah study. The criterion for fulfilling the commandment of knowing the Torah is thereby relativized to adjust to particular intellectual dispositions. Therefore, a laypersonn still ought to fulfill the obligation of knowing the Torah, but in his case, this means that person should "grasp and comprehend as much as it is possible for his soul to grasp."[19] Moreover, the commandment of "Thou shalt meditate therein day and night" obliges the unscholarly to invest every free moment in Torah study, as anything else is "idle chatter" (*devarim betelim*).[20] Similarly, Shneur Zalman prohibits studying gentile wisdom on the grounds of the sin of neglecting the Torah, permitting only the scholars to learn it occasionally, for the sake of divine service.[21]

Shneur Zalman's pragmatism is conspicuous in the additional concessions he granted to those who were particularly troubled. Perhaps in response to the social and economic hardships experienced by his followers, he limited study to two chapters a day, or even merely to the recitation of the *Shema'*, the minimal obligation incumbent on the less learned.[22] He even allowed scholars to set particular times for study instead of dedicating themselves to it full-time, so that they could secure their livelihood.[23] This leniency, however, refers only to unplanned situations and does not stand in contradiction to the earlier obligation to suffer deprivation rather than give up one's commitment to full-time study. Interestingly, Shneur Zalman imposes the obligation of full-time study on everyone who is sustained by others or lives off charity, regardless of his intellectual skills.[24] One's obligation to study full-time does not fall under the commandment of knowing the Torah, but rather under that of "Thou shalt meditate therein day and night literally."[25] In addition to obligating individuals to study at set times, Shneur Zalman obligates entire communities to study the whole of the Talmud every year, by apportioning the tractates among the congregants.[26] This way the individual becomes inherently connected to the communal.

The distinction between the commandments of "knowing the Torah" and "meditating therein" effectively identifies two parallel modes of Torah study: elitist and egalitarian. The former, available to the few, requires continuous study for the purpose of memorizing the entire Torah. The latter, intended for the majority, demands only limited study sessions, focused on the laws that govern proper conduct.[27] The majority is not obliged to comprehend the entire Torah; the criterion for determining whether they have fulfilled the commandment of knowing the Torah depends on their particular intellectual disposition. Their obligation derives from the second part of the commandment, "Meditate therein day and night," which means reciting the Torah twice a day at fixed times.[28] Following the main codices of the Law, Shneur Zalman identified the time immediately after prayer as being the most appropriate for a fixed period of study.[29]

The importance of set-time study goes beyond *halakhah* into the realm of mysticism. This nexus of law and mysticism underscores the worldly aspect of Shneur Zalman's doctrine. Shneur Zalman was the leader of a broad community of Hasidim who were fully engaged in worldly matters rather than a secluded group of mystics. His Hasidic leadership was not limited to the delivery of mystical sermons but comprised a good deal of halakhic teachings as well. It is not surprising, therefore, that his effort to incorporate ordinary householders in the Hasidic experience constituted an important aspect of his project. For the majority of his followers, the opportunity to find God within their mundane existence must have been much more compelling than a highly abstract and sophisticated quest for transcendence. Placing the routine of Torah study at set times within a mystical framework was an expression of the worldly and practical dimension of the early Habad doctrine, and one of the ways by which Shneur Zalman injected Hasidic spirituality into the everyday religious experience of his followers.

Halakhists requested that Jews set time aside for study to prevent them from neglecting the commandment to study twice a day because of the pressures of everyday life.[30] In one of his discourses, however, Shneur Zalman presents this ostensibly commonsensical idea as underlying his mystical concept of repentance (*teshuvah*). Habad tradition relates Torah study to repentance in a nonmystical way, as a practice that keeps people away from sin.[31] Here, however, Shneur Zalman explores the literal meaning of the Hebrew word for repentance (*teshuvah*, literally "return") in order to present setting times for study as an actual act of return to God from profanity and mundaneness.

> When tradesmen, who are not always for God but only sets [*sic*] times for Torah study, returns from dealing with mundane affairs to learning, then this is called repentance [*teshuvah*], for he returns

[*shav*] from what he was dealing with at first, etc. In this way ecstasy becomes more intensive than if he had not been dealing with worldly matters at first [. . .] for ecstasy is an essential change. [. . .]. Ecstasy comes about because his essence has changed, from dealing with worldly matters to being a Torah student. [. . .] Scripture says: "I will show him wondrous deeds as in the days when you sallied forth from the land of Egypt" [Mic. 7:15], namely, like at the Giving of the Torah, as Scripture says: "Face to face the Lord spoke" [Deut. 5:4]. The disclosure of God below is in the aspect of "face," for the prior concealment of the face [*hester panim*] during the 212 years of the exile in Egypt was necessary so that later, "face to face" would be possible.[32]

This excerpt encapsulates several ideas that recur throughout Shneur Zalman's writings. They are intertwined here with the practice of setting times for Torah study and the concept of repentance (albeit with no indication of sin).[33] Here, the tradesmen are not sinners; they do not transgress Jewish law, and yet everyday matters separate them from God. For them, the setting of times for Torah study, defined by the *halakhah* as the absolute minimum required for observing the law of Torah study, becomes both a vehicle for the return to the divine and an inner transformation[34] of the individual's attributes (*midot*) through redirecting them from the mundane to God. This process, which entails a pivotal change of self, demands the eradication of one's interests in this world by way of complete self-nullification. Setting time aside for Torah study, a routine ritual demanding no special intellectual or spiritual abilities, proves to have an advantage over permanent studies, as it allows one to reach higher aspects of the divine realms.[35]

By setting times for Torah study, one prepares oneself for the experience of a personal Exodus and the Giving of the Torah. This echoes the commandment to remember the Exodus every day[36] and the Talmudic dictum according to which all Jews should see themselves as if they had come out of Egypt (*b*Pesahim 116b). In Shneur Zalman's teachings, however, the ritual of remembrance becomes an act of personal redemption from the limits of materiality and finitude, therefore reconnecting the individual to the divine.[37] Indeed, a study routine becomes a personal experience of the Giving of the Torah, during which God reveals himself to the learner "face to face," as with Moses on Mount Sinai. Consequently, Shneur Zalman reevaluates the seemingly ordinary ritual and endows it with profound mystical import by linking it to the concept of repentance.

The excerpt above reveals an ostensibly paradoxical feature of Shneur Zalman's thought: he seems to value the occasional study of ordinary people more than full-time study by scholars. This paradoxical approach is based on an appreciation of the transformative value of setting times for Torah studies, and of the far greater effort simpletons must make to direct themselves toward God than the Torah scholar.[38] According to Shneur Zalman, a merchant who returns to the Torah at fixed times attains a higher level of ecstasy than someone who has been studying continuously. The meaning of ecstasy (*hitpa'alut*), a prevalent and prominent concept in Shneur Zalman's writings, remains a matter of dispute in later generations of Habad.[39] In this context, it is defined in ontological rather than psychological terms as an essential change (*shinui ha-mahut*) in a person, which need not be accompanied by an emotional outburst.[40] The transformative aspect of Torah study is emphasized elsewhere, although without reference to the psychological factors mentioned above:

> This is the advantage of setting times for Torah study by a tradesman, that it is more in the nature of subjugation [of the evil side] than is [the case of] those who dwell in tents [i.e., full-time scholars].[41]

Ordinary people, subject to an ongoing struggle with materiality, seem to be of greater importance than the scholars and mystics who dwell permanently on a lofty spiritual plane. Laypeople who give up some of their worldly interests in order to set time for Torah study subjugate profanity to holiness (in Habad terminology, "the subjugation of the evil side [*itkafya de-sitra ahra*]"). This is not the case of the full-time scholar, who is constantly joined with the divine and therefore needs no effort to subjugate the evil side and reconnect with God.

Repentance also has theurgical significance: it restitutes order in the divine realm by restoring the sequence of letters forming the Tetragrammaton.[42] The personal and the theurgical aspects of repentance converge in the commandment of setting times for Torah study. According to *Tanya*, one must overcome one's nature and join one's emotional and intellectual attributes to their counterparts in the Godhead. In particular, one's mind and speech should cleave to "God's word, namely to *halakhah*."[43] Overcoming one's nature also means achieving more than one usually achieves in study, as the midrash states: "If he was accustomed to study one page [of Written Law], let him study two; if he was accustomed to study one chapter [of Oral Law], let him study two."[44]

What *Tanya* presents in general terms as the obligation to increase the regular measure of Torah study acquires a much more concrete shape in one of Shneur Zalman's discourses, where the "two chapters" are understood as referring to the two times that one must set for studying Torah: "'If one was accustomed to study one chapter, let him study two': this stands for setting times for Torah study: [two] times indeed."[45] Given the identification of halakhic material with the divine word, its study and recitation brings about the reunification of the soul, which is the "part of God above,"[46] with the divine life force. This is identified as a theurgical mode of repentance qua return, through the reconnection of the letter *heh* with the rest of the divine name. The theurgical process of restoring order in the divine name is available to, and indeed incumbent on, practically all Jews. Thus, an activity previously reserved for scholars immersed in mysticism appears here to be open to any literate person through the routine study of normative halakhic literature.[47]

This reevaluation of the layperson's study at fixed times may seem paradoxical, given the prevalent portrayal of Habad as an intellectualist Hasidic school, yet it is compatible with Shneur Zalman's broader enterprise, intended to empower the ordinary folk and supposedly lower members of Jewish society. In numerous places throughout his writings, Shneur Zalman cites or refers to the Talmudic saying, "Where penitents [*ba'ale teshuvah*] stand, not even the perfectly righteous can stand" (*b*Berakhot 34b), and it is clear that he saw in fixing times for Torah study a mode of repentance. It similarly serves as a means of elevating the ordinary person above the righteous and the scholarly, and of drawing attention to the more intense ecstasy and greater subjugation of the evil side that the layperson can achieve.

Two Modes of Torah Study: Scholars and Laymen

Shneur Zalman acknowledges that laypeople will always constitute a substantial proportion of the Jewish community, be it because of socioeconomic conditions, the intellectual limitations of common folk, or because of their place in the hierarchy of souls. Moreover, in the *Tanya*, he states explicitly that there are only a handful of true *tsadikim*,[48] separated from the *beinonim* by a clear-cut border.[49] He does not perceive as problematic the existence of tradespeople engrossed in materiality and immersed in the troubles of everyday life. On the contrary, their inferior position presents them with opportunities and tasks beyond the reach of full-time scholars.[50] Setting times for Torah study can thus serve different, yet complementary purposes from full-time Torah study.

In one of his late discourses, Shneur Zalman resorts to kabbalistic imagery to express the interdependence of scholars and laypeople.[51] He starts with a verse from Song of Songs: "You have captured my heart, my sister, my bride; you have captured my heart with one of your eyes, with one bead of your necklace" (Song 4:9). In his interpretation, this refers to two separate groups among the Jewish people: the "eye" denotes leaders of the community, namely, the scholarly elite, whereas the "bead of your necklace" represents the layperson. This reading shows that the biblical author considered both these groups as equal in status. In spite of the fact that "Ostensibly there cannot be any comparison between them at all,"[52] they both capture the heart of the Song's groom—or in other words, God cherishes them equally. Shneur Zalman then branches out to concepts from the kabbalah of Moses Cordovero, explaining that both groups are assigned different, yet complementary roles. The scholars, as "the eyes of the congregation" (an allusion to *Shir ha-shirim rabah* 1:15), bring Wisdom down from its source in direct light (*or yashar*), while the laypeople respond by elevating the Torah in refracted light (*or hozer*).[53] He stresses not only two different modes of study ("drawing down" in full-time study and "elevation" when it is pursued at set times), but also two different dispositions: the scholars' study is intellectual, since they bring down the wisdom of the Torah, whereas the power of the laypeople's Torah lies in their voice, and derives from their deeds. Shneur Zalman explains that laypeople purge the husks of *nogah* by means of conducting faithful business transactions and achieve the state of "polished precious stones"—hence the "bead of your necklace"—which are capable of reflecting the divine light.[54] For these reasons, ordinary people participate alongside scholars in a theurgical act, bringing the flow of divine light and the Torah's wisdom into the world. Through their effort to study Torah at fixed times, they enable the reunification of the light of the Torah with its supernal source, once it has been drawn down to the world by the scholars' study. Their Torah study at set times is thus perceived as a necessary element of the dynamics of the divine light and serves as a kind of counterbalance to the leaders' scholarship. This vision in which ordinary people purify the material world around them, acting as a mirror that reflects the divine light encapsulated in the sound of the Torah they recite, demonstrates not only the interdependence of scholars and laypeople, but also that of Torah study and deeds.

The excerpt cited above states that purification through good deeds paves the way for the reunification of the Torah with its supernal source in the reflected light. In another discourse, however, the relation between good deeds and Torah study appears to be reversed: setting times for study actually provides strength to purify the sparks of holiness that fell into the husks during the cosmic process of the breaking of vessels.[55] At this point, mystical imagination intertwines with halakhic pragmatics. According to Shneur Zalman's halakhic works, those who fix times for study should concentrate on practical laws that regulate their everyday lives and determine the way they act. It is precisely their *halakhah*-abiding deeds that purify the sparks of holiness entrapped in material reality. He anchors this idea in the Talmudic saying, "Study is greater [than practice] for it leads to practice" (*b*Kidushin 40b), and explains that "A deed without study cannot prevail; however, study without a deed is not the essential thing [*ha-'ikar*] either, for 'The essential thing is not study [*midrash*], etc. [but deed] [*m*Avot 1:17]'."[56] This saying has evolved with time into one of the most popular slogans of Habad-Lubavitch, "Deed is the main thing" (*ma'aseh hu ha-'ikar*), while the attitude that underlies it has led Norman Lamm to present Shneur Zalman's doctrine as relegating Torah study to a secondary place.[57] Both excerpts from MAHZ 5571, however, seem to prove the opposite, for they show that he meant to reveal the hidden significance of fixed times of study—both mystical, as "reflected light," and magical, as the strength necessary to achieve the purification of the sparks.[58] The passage discloses a broader function of Torah study than mere intellectual cognition, and through the idea of study at fixed times it finds a way to incorporate the nonscholars' study into the Hasidic mystical project. As a result, even apparently futile study at fixed times by ignorant men who are nevertheless devoted to the halakhic lifestyle complements the Torah study of scholars.

In certain cases, the laypeople's punctual study gains a dimension previously reserved for the scholars. This is expressed, for example, in the idea that the person is a substitute temple for the divine presence.[59] The Hasidic authors based the idea of a human temple on the biblical verse, "Let them make me a sanctuary that I may dwell in them" (Exod. 25:8). The fact that God said "in them"—in the people of Israel—instead of using the seemingly more suitable "in it"—in the sanctuary—led Safedian kabbalists and the Hasidic masters who followed in their footsteps to believe that Scripture actually meant that humans are God's sanctuary in the world.[60] In their view, the commandment of building the sanctuary is detached from its biblical setting and refers to people, at any time, "It is not written 'in it,' but 'in them,' to say that each and every Jew must build the tabernacle in his soul," that is, draw down God's presence through prayer,[61] fulfilling the commandments, and Torah study.[62] The latter occupies a distinguished place in this list, and the Talmudic saying that "Since the destruction of the temple, the Holy One blessed be he has nothing in the world but four cubits of *halakhah* alone" (*b*Berakhot 8a), prompted Shneur Zalman to declare that the Torah is "verily the tabernacle of the Holy One, blessed be he."[63] In short, drawing down the divine presence into the human temple is achievable not only by lengthy studies but also by setting times for studying *halakhah*.

The process of building a human sanctuary is detailed in *Tanya*.[64] It follows the pattern of the biblical narrative, albeit in a decontextualized manner. In the Bible, the Israelites were commanded to build the sanctuary when it became clear that they could not witness the divine revelation and remain alive. Indeed, the Talmud states that during the revelation at Mount Sinai, "at every utterance their soul took flight" (*b*Shabat 88b). Shneur Zalman interprets this to mean that they could not handle the ultimate nullification of existence that revelation entailed.[65] Accordingly, only the creation of the sanctuary—a suitable vessel for the divine presence—made a union with God in the world possible without the annihilation of existence.

The creation of the human temple follows the very same pattern. Full disclosure of the Torah is to come about only in the future.[66] Yet, even before this happens, it is possible to draw the divine down to into one's personal temple through Torah study. Admittedly, in terms of the position of the *Shekhinah* in the order of concatenation, there is a difference between both types of revelation. In contrast to Temple times, the *Shekhinah* in exile descends to the lowest *sefirah* within the lowest of the four worlds: *Malkhut* of *'Asiyah*. Nonetheless, what might seem like a downgrade is characterized rather positively in Shneur Zalman's writings. In the Temple, only the high priest was permitted to enter the Holy of Holies in order to commune with the divine, yet in exile, where a person's heart is the Holy of Holies,[67] this experience is open to every *halakhah*-abiding Jew able to recite words of Torah.[68] Elsewhere, he states explicitly:

> Therefore, after one has meditated deeply, according to his abilities, on the subject of this above-mentioned nullification of existence, let him reflect in his heart as follows: "The capacity of my intelligence and of my soul's root is too limited to constitute a chariot and

a sanctuary for God's unity in perfect truth, for my thought cannot grasp or apprehend his unity at all with any degree of comprehension in the world, not an iota, in fact, of that which was grasped by the patriarchs and prophets. This being so, I will make him a sanctuary and an abode by studying Torah at fixed times by day and by night, to the extent of my free time, as stipulated by the law governing each individual's situation, set forth in *Hilkhot talmud Torah*, as our Sages say, 'Even one chapter in the morning [and one at night; (*b*Menahot 99b].'"[69]

It is not the scholarly or mystically oriented elite who bring about God's abode on earth, but rather, anyone who sets time for Torah study, even only the halakhic minimum of reciting one chapter during the morning prayers and one during the evening service. Obviously, a scholar differs from the ordinary person in the way in which he grasps the divine, yet God effectively dwells in both of them, according to their degree of comprehension. This difference is illustrated by the verse "How fair are your tents, o Jacob, your dwellings, o Israel!" (Num. 24:5), where tent, or casual abode (*dirat 'ara'i*), stands for study at fixed times, and dwelling, or permanent abode (*dirat keva'*), for study by the scholar.[70]

But study at set times, in some contexts, can be valued even more highly than full-time study. Shneur Zalman's persistent effort to reinstate a balance between scholars and laymen, full-time and part-time Torah study, as well as Torah and deeds, derives from his understanding of human beings as intermediaries who carry down the divine light into the world. This idea is rendered in different configurations throughout Hasidic lore, especially in reference to the role of the *tsadik* as a link between heaven and earth.[71] In several areas of his teachings, Shneur Zalman indicates that ordinary people are bound to play an analogous role.[72] This follows the more general tendency of his teachings to reevaluate the layperson's immersion in the material aspect of reality. The particular place that the layperson occupies in the world impacts his or her task as transmitter of the divine vitality.

> Also, a tradesman must fix times for Torah, for every drawing down [of divine influx] needs to go by degrees, through a transmitter. Even though the essence of drawing down is performed here by a deed, the first stage must be performed by thought and speech, and only later by deed. Therefore, one needs to set times for Torah study, which is thought and speech.[73]

The passage follows a description of the process by which the divine light, divine will, and by association, divine delight, are drawn down through Torah study for its own sake (*Torah li-shmah*).[74] Shneur Zalman explains that the Oral Torah surpassed the Written Torah in drawing down and disclosing the divine light, for through elucidation of the laws that are mentioned only in the Written Torah, the Oral Torah spread the divine will in the world and made it comprehensible.[75] He adds that even the regular study of ordinary men can bring down the divine light. Indeed, an ordinary person draws down the influx mainly through his deeds, yet the deeds must be preceded by thought and speech as these three dispositions amount to the "three garments of the soul" that a person should direct to God.[76] Drawing down by means of deeds takes place when someone obeys practical commandments; drawing down by means of thought and speech is achieved by studying Torah at fixed times.[77] Another reference elsewhere to the delight derived from Torah study justifies studying twice a day rather than continuously. Shneur Zalman refers to a Hasidic maxim, whereby "constant delight is no delight," neither for the donor nor the recipient.[78] Continuous study would thus turn delight into affliction.[79]

This discourse effectively juxtaposes Torah study for its own sake with the injunction to fix times for study. Here, *li-shmah* means "drawing down the light of the Infinite [or *Ein Sof*] into *Hokhmah* and *Binah*," a goal achievable not only through detailed intellectual studies or mystical practices, but also by the repetition of the words of Torah at set times by an ordinary, *halakhah*-abiding Jew.[80] Moreover, Torah study at set times, described in some sources as "spiced wine," acquires greater value than "plain wine," the continuous study by scholars, even when the latter delve into the secrets of Torah. This is because the Torah of ordinary people crosses the boundaries of intellect and is brought into the material world.

> This is the case of tradesmen who occupy themselves with the Torah and commandments by means of their palate and tongue, as Scripture says: "And your mouth (of the congregation of Israel, etc.) like the choicest wine" [Song 7:10], in the manner of scent that is above the delight limited to wisdom and understanding, which are the vessels.[81]

In this passage, Shneur Zalman presents the intellectual deficiency of nonscholars as an advantage. Indeed, their study is restricted to short sessions twice a day, and they do not enter the secret, inner pathways of the Torah; nonetheless, they bring the Torah out of the ivory tower of intellectual cognition. In other words, they do not comprehend the Torah fully, be it because of lack of time or because of their deficient intellects, but they can experience it sensually, or, as he puts it, with their "palate and tongue," and can therefore disclose the Torah on the sensual, material levels that are beyond the reach of scholars. Greater delight results from such revelation of the Torah than from its disclosure on higher, intellectual levels, for the former transcends the "vessels" of the Torah—wisdom and understanding—and reaches down to the lower, sensual attributes.[82]

Torah Study within the Daily Worship Cycle

Halakhah encourages individuals to study immediately following prayer on the assumption that one might otherwise get caught up in mundane responsibilities and forget about learning. The pragmatic considerations that underlie the halakhic regulations acquire a variety of other explanations in Shneur Zalman's mystical teachings, connected to the theurgical purposes of Torah study. These include the idea that prayer is a necessary preparation for study by way of the *ratso* that precedes *shov*, and that the Torah is a factor that perpetuates the self-nullification and union with God that are achieved during prayer.[83]

The assumption that prayer is an appropriate preparation for Torah study is compatible with the halakhic call to set times for study immediately after prayer on pragmatic grounds. Torah study and other religious obligations are interdependent: the former cannot function on its own; it should constitute one form of an individual's divine service. Moreover, Torah study *li-shmah* demands self-nullification: "The Holy One, blessed be he, does not come to rest on someone who is an existent being [*yesh ve-davar*], for I and he cannot dwell [together] in the world."[84] Nullification of the self (the "I" in this example), equivalent on the spiritual level to martyrdom in sanctification of the divine name (*kidush ha-Shem*), is achievable through the recitation of the *Shema'* and, more generally, through prayer.[85] The believer substitutes his will with God's, which is embodied in the words of the Torah, thus achieving a level similar to that of Moses when "the *Shekhinah* was speaking from his throat."[86] According to *Tanya*, the blessings in the prayer service reenact the process by which one's soul returns to God and reunites with him; they function as a necessary preparation for the *beinonim* to attain the intention *li-shmah*. Only after such a preparation can one begin one's regular course of study. This preparation should be repeated whenever one sits down to learn the Torah.[87]

The interdependence of Torah and prayer appears in numerous places across Shneur Zalman's lore, as the relation between ascending and descending, or the lower and upper "arousal" (*it'aruta dile-tata* and *it'aruta dile-'ila*). The soul ascends to God in ecstatic love during prayer, and through this earns the power to bring the divine light down to earth in the Torah.[88] Thus, prayer and Torah emulate the *ratso va-shov*, the continuous dynamics of ascent and descent, of nullification and of drawing down the divine. *Ratso* is achieved through the desire to leave the body and erase one's subjectivity in ecstatic prayer; only when there is no subjectivity left to function as a barrier separating one from God can the divine light descend, clothed in Torah and commandments.[89]

What is expressed here in technical kabbalistic terms as *ratso va-shov*, lower and upper arousal, is elsewhere directly applied to the routine stages of everyday worship. Praises of God recited out loud in *Pesuke de-zimra* serve as a means of attaining ecstasy, which reaches its peak when the word *one* of the *Shema'* is uttered. Following his teacher the Maggid, Shneur Zalman considers the *Shema'* as more than a declaration of God's oneness; it is inherently bound with experiencing its awareness.[90] The silent prayer of the '*Amidah* that follows symbolizes the eradication of the self.[91] The Hasidic masters, in a manner recalling the Aristotelian definition of a human being as *zoon logon echon*, defined the faculty of speech as that which elevates human beings above other creatures.[92] To stand in silence during the '*Amidah* therefore equals giving up one's uppermost faculty and substituting God's speech for it, since it is not the individual who recites the words of Torah, but rather "the *Shekhinah* speaking from his throat" with "the words which I have placed in your mouth" (Isa. 59:21). It should be noted that although he stressed the importance of preparatory prayer,[93] Shneur Zalman still believed that Torah study without it could impact the divine reality.

Discussion of ecstatic prayer leads to another significant aspect of the obligation to study directly after prayer. Whereas the self-nullification and unity with the divine achieved by means of prayer are only temporary, the spiritual achievements attained through Torah study are eternal. Contemplation of the words of *Pesuke de-zimra* and the *Shema'* stands for accepting the yoke of Heaven. Therefore, whoever does so

> Will always be bound in contemplation, i.e. nullification of the worlds, to the one who brings them to life and constitutes them, and it is only in his corporeal body he will not be able to achieve true nullification, so during the recitation of the *Shema'*, he shall direct his mind to Torah study in the words "you shall recite them" [Deut.6:7].

Namely, through Torah study his divine soul will become truly unified with the Torah, and the Torah and the Holy One blessed be he are verily one.[94]

According to the Hasidic worldview, corporeality separates human beings from the divine and prevents them from true unity with God. One possible way of breaking this barrier is through prayer. Such nullification, however, is only temporary, for the ecstatic state achieved during prayer ceases when the recitation of the *Shema'* is over, and the ecstatic love of God is transformed into its opposite: the love of corporeality.[95] In Shneur Zalman's writings, the Torah is the third way to transcend the duality of divinity and materiality, and bestow lasting unity with God in the material world.[96] Only by studying Torah immediately after prayer can one maintain the ecstatic state for longer.[97] The principle that Israel, Torah, and God are a unity is used to present the way to perpetuate self-nullification through Torah study. However, the unity is understood as an aspiration rather than a description of the actual state of things. People who study Torah and put its laws into practice nullify their wills before God's,[98] and even when they are busy with daily concerns, do not break their communion with God.[99] Substituting one's will with the divine's requires ordinary people to transcend their nature, which prayer can achieve since it arouses the hidden love concealed in the heart of all Jews—a love that surmounts their nature.[100] Obviously, one may choose not to study immediately after prayer and return to it later in the day, but in that case, one loses the state of love achieved in prayer and moves away from God.[101]

Shneur Zalman continued to elucidate the essential difference between Torah study and prayer that determines whether *devekut* (cleaving to God) is temporary or perpetual. According to one explanation, the union with the divine can be perpetuated by memorizing the words of the Torah. Since "Torah and the Holy One, blessed be he, are one," when a person has the words of the Torah "carved in the mind of his memory which is in his soul," it is as if that person is united with God himself, even if engaged in mundane occupations.[102]

According to another explanation, the difference between these two modes of worship lies in their different ontological features. The love engendered by prayer dissipates since prayer is time-bound, whereas the Torah is above the dimension of time.[103] After all, the words of Torah recited by a student are the very same that were spoken to Moses on Mount Sinai. A dichotomy of the corporeal and the spiritual is inscribed into the Hasidic metaphysics of light: Torah study is bound to the light of *Ein Sof*, the surrounding light that shines equally everywhere and stands above time, as opposed to the light that fills all the worlds and is bound to time. For this reason, the words of Torah are not subject to the passage of time but are always perceived as new.[104] Every time someone recites the words of Torah it is as if he has just received them from God.[105] Consequently, Torah study brings eternity and unity down into the world of temporality and multiplicity, whereas prayer makes one reach out of temporality into the moment of infinity in an ecstatic gesture of unity with the oneness of the divine.[106]

The relation between prayer and study is described either in terms of the mutual relation between two types of divine light (*sovev* and *memale*),[107] or in *sefirotic* terminology as a correlation of *Malkhut* and *Ze'ir anpin*.[108]

> Contemplation in prayer [...] is in the nature of *ratso*, the elevation of *Nukba*, and is called "temporal life" [*haye sha'ah*], for time is in *Malkhut*, and when one elevates it from the state of being it is called "temporal life." The main thing, however, is "eternal life" [*haye 'olam*], namely that *Ze'ir anpin* should become specifically world [*'olam*]. This is *shov*, the disclosure of the [light] surrounding all the worlds and which comes to dwell specifically in the lower worlds, which is called "eternal life": drawing down the divine actually and specifically into the world.[109]

The above excerpt, charged with kabbalistic concepts, requires unpacking. Shneur Zalman describes prayer in terms of the elevation of *Nukba* (the feminine aspect of the Godhead, a term used interchangeably with *Malkhut*)[110] above the sphere of being. Furthermore, since *Malkhut* is identified as the source of time in the *sefirotic* structure,[111] prayer appears as an ecstatic moment that restores time back to its source, where all three tenses unite.[112] "Temporal life," a phrase coined by the Talmud in reference to prayer (*b*Shabat 10a),[113] emphasizes here the momentariness of this experience: it ceases immediately after the service ends.[114] In fact, in prayer one transcends the differentiation between past, present, and future; yet one does not transcend time as such. Prayer is a transcendental experience that reaches the borderline between divine nothingness and worldly being—the *sefirah* of *Malkhut*, the point comprising the past, the present, and the future—without going beyond it.

Torah study, in contrast, is called "eternal life," for it draws that which is beyond time into temporal reality. The passage is based on the double meaning of the word *'olam* as both "world" and "eternity." Here, *Ze'ir anpin*, an aspect of the divinity above *Malkhut*, which is not subject to temporality, is drawn down into the world (*'olam*) to give it eternal life (*haye 'olam*),[115] which amounts to transforming it into "the dwelling place [of the divine] in the lower worlds," a conspicuously eschatological idea in the Habad tradition. Torah study allows for ascent above the source of time, at the level of *Ze'ir anpin*, of the "source of the coming-to-be of time that is in *Malkhut*," as described by Shneur Zalman's son, Dov Ber.[116] "Eternal life" in Shneur Zalman's discourses also denotes "articulation of words of *halakhah*,"[117] meaning that the study of *halakhah* has an eschatological value too. In their days, Shneur Zalman explains, the Sages could forsake temporal life (prayer) and focus solely on eternal life (Torah),[118] but now, at a time of "the footsteps of Messiah," to enable the articulation of *halakhah* in order to draw down the divinity into the world, one has to sacrifice one's soul in prayer.[119]

There emerges from these observations a paradoxical relationship between worship by means of prayer, on the one hand, and Torah study, on the other. Although prayer liberates the individual from the limits of existence and corporeality, it fails to consistently fulfill its essential purpose—the attainment of ecstatic experience. First, since the rhythm and time of prayer are externally determined by Jewish law, the ecstatic experience one strives to attain is framed by *halakhah*; second, ecstasy in prayer is the product of love and fear of God. As such, it is subject from its inception to the limitation of corporeality. Consequently, it does not reach beyond temporality and is followed immediately by a return to the domain of time and matter.[120]

Nonetheless, permanent release from time is attainable by means of Torah study at set times. Through it, one draws down onto oneself and into the world the eternity enclosed in the letters of the Torah. In contrast to prayer, the precise time of Torah study is determined not by Jewish law but rather by the individual (even though preferred times are suggested in the halakhic texts). The act of setting times for study triggers the process of release from the bounds of time, achievable within the material world rather than beyond it, by adhering to an entity (Torah) that originates above and beyond the source of time.

To recap, for Shneur Zalman, self-effacement in ecstatic worship is a path to further and fuller engagement in the world, and in that respect, he follows his teacher, the Maggid of Mezrich. Ariel Mayse summarized the latter's outlook in the following words:

The mystic ventures into the ineffable realm, moving beyond his personal identify and transcending his sense of self. The true purpose of this journey, however, lies not in the experience of the *ayin* [divine nothingness], but in the return to the world that brings about an increase in blessing within the physical. The trajectory of mystical self-nullification leads one back to corporeal world, and does not end with the moment of rapture itself.[121]

Shneur Zalman transposes this concept onto the framework of nomian religious routine and shows that this journey is not restricted to mystics, but can be taken by an average member of the Jewish community.

Habad: Hasidism for Householders and Tradespeople

The teachings of Shneur Zalman demonstrate that adherence to the Torah, which entails the transformation of the self and the sanctification of the world, can be achieved through the seemingly trivial ritual of Torah study at set times. Framed in halakhic literature as a means of motivating even the unscholarly classes to a routine of daily study, he endows it in his sermons with mystical and magical significance. This reinterpretation of the precept should be considered not only in the framework of his conception of time but also in the wider context of his unique style of leadership, marked by his effort to empower ordinary men to reevaluate their religious service, and to create a more inclusive Judaism, which was eventually to become the emblem of the Habad movement.[122] This has been underscored by the later generations of Habad too. The sixth rebbe of Habad-Lubavitch, Yosef Yitshak Schneersohn, delivered a speech in Riga in 1932 for Simhat Torah describing Shneur Zalman's concept of setting time for Torah study as one of the novelties introduced by Hasidism. According to Schneersohn, when asked about the difference between the ways Hasidim and *mitnagedim* apply the precept, Shneur Zalman allegedly replied that Hasids not only set time for Torah study, but in doing so, also set their souls for the Torah. A Hasidic tradesperson who sets times for study, adds Schneersohn, is like a young groom supported by his father-in-law: he can pursue his studies without having to worry about bringing bread to the table.[123]

The emphasis placed on the precept of setting time aside for Torah study exemplifies some conspicuous trends in Shneur Zalman's style of leadership and in the early Habad community. It shows the level of spiritual independence enjoyed by Habad Hasidim under his leadership: although he was eager to provide guidance, he nonetheless held each and every Hasid responsible for his own spiritual achievements.[124] The "Liozna Ordinances" bear witness to Shneur Zalman's continuous efforts to set limits on access to his court for the growing number of his followers.[125] It is therefore plausible that the reevaluation of the value of routine Torah study at set times was aimed at enhancing the spiritual involvement of his disciples without the need to be present at the rebbe's court.

One can surmise that Shneur Zalman's style of leadership was, to a great extent, determined by the fact that his followers were predominantly middle-class tradespeople and householders—people whose everyday duties allowed only limited time for study, prayer, or visits to the rebbe's court.[126] Reevaluating their limited daily Torah study was one of the means by which Shneur Zalman included them in his spiritual project. Other means were the reevaluation of their prayer and, in connection to this, a direct instruction for *shelihe tsibur* neither to rush through the service, nor to overly prolong it (to accommodate the needs of many congregants, who "had to rise early and go to work,"[127] and who therefore could not afford to stay in synagogue for longer services). Finally, frequent visits to the rebbe's court were replaced with guidance through pastoral letters and emissaries, as well as with the transfer to local leaders of some of the functions usually performed by the rebbe during the private audiences he granted his Hasidim on an individual basis.[128]

One can only speculate about the factors that shaped Shneur Zalman's unique style of leadership. The Habad tradition has preserved an image of him as a reluctant rebbe, who even considered immigration to the Land of Israel in order to avoid taking on the mantle of leadership.[129] It may have been this reluctance that prompted him to construct his ideal of the distant Hasidic leader, who guides a decentralized network of autonomous congregations of followers by means of letters and emissaries rather than direct involvement with a central court. The personal example of Shneur Zalman's mentor, Menahem Mendel of Vitebsk, who led his followers in a similar way over many years following his immigration to the Land of Israel, must have had an impact on him.[130] During the years preceding his ascent to leadership, Shneur Zalman was responsible for maintaining a network of fund-raisers for Hasidic settlement in the Land of Israel.[131] After his rise as an independent Hasidic leader, this network was further used to spread and enforce his teachings and lifestyle.[132] It therefore comes as no surprise that in Shneur Zalman's Hasidism, so much attention is paid to the spirituality of middle-class, independent, and relatively well-educated householders and tradesmen; these people were at the center of his successful fund-raising network, and when he became a rebbe in his own right, they formed the core of his following.

Conclusion

The precept of setting time for Torah study constitutes an integral part of Shneur Zalman's project of making Hasidic spirituality accessible to "intermediate" individuals, a project that attracted many people to Habad during his lifetime and beyond. This precept, which only occupied a secondary place in the halakhic tradition as a means of preserving study within the daily schedule of working people, he employed to form a new spiritual paradigm in which routine religious praxis was invested with mystical meaning. Shneur Zalman saw it as an ideal for the majority of his community, and restricted full-time study to a presumably narrow scholarly elite. The many comments in his mystical sermons touching on the requirement to set times for study show that not only did he ascribe equal value to it as to full-time study, but also that he invested study at set times with particular importance because of its perceived role in both the individual and the cosmic dimensions of repentance.

In some sermons, the masses and the elite take on complementary roles: while the latter draw down the divine light by fulfilling the ideal of full-time study, ordinary people reflect this light by purifying the lower world when they comply with the halakhic requirement to study at set times. In other sermons, Shneur Zalman makes study at set times an alternative means of achieving comparable effects to those achieved by the elite, as through it both scholars and ordinary people play a part in the construction of God's sanctuary. Even simpletons can do so by fulfilling the minimum halakhic requirement of reciting one chapter of the Torah during the morning and the evening prayers. In some places, Shneur Zalman underscores the value of this method of study by presenting Torah study at set times as superior to full-time study, because it brings the wisdom of Torah out of the intellectual ivory tower of the elite and into the sphere of materiality and corporeality. This mode of study, which enables the ordinary person to detach himself from mundane affairs and to turn instead toward the divine words of Torah, generates more divine delight and produces a more intense state of ecstasy than the static study of the full-time scholar who is permanently engrossed in holiness.

The instruction that Torah study at set times should follow after prayer is of paramount importance. What was traditionally seen as a means of encouraging ordinary people to study before leaving the synagogue after prayer in order to resume work is incorporated by Shneur Zalman into the dynamics of *ratso va-shov*: while prayer is identified with the *ratso* mode of worship at the preparatory stage in which one effaces one's subjectivity in ecstatic prayer, study is identified with the *shov* mode, where the divine light clothed in the Torah descends into the world.

These two sequential modes of worship have special significance in the personal quest for eternity. Although prayer, whose timing is determined arbitrarily by Jewish law, grants the worshiper an instantaneous release from the bonds of past, present, and future, the transcendental experience it offers is ephemeral, as it depends on the corporeal powers of love and fear. Paradoxically, it is Torah study—the times of which are set by the worshipers—that ultimately allows them to transcend temporality by drawing down the eternal Torah into the temporal world.

Shneur Zalman's concept of setting times for Torah study allows for a better understanding of the ideology that lay behind his unique style of Hasidic leadership. It highlights one of the tools that helped him build and sustain a decentralized network of Habad communities, whose members could remain his Hasidim in the fullest sense of the word even without frequent visits to his court, engagement in lengthy ecstatic prayer, or full-time dedication to study. It freed his Hasidim from the need to resort to activities that put their livelihood at risk. The mystical reinterpretation of the halakhic precept helped Shneur Zalman reinvent Hasidism as a movement open to broad circles of independent tradespeople and householders. This ideology may well have played a part in shaping Habad's inclusivist vision of mysticism in the twentieth century, but the question of doctrinal continuity and change in the history and ideology of Habad still awaits further research.

✧ 5 ✧

TIME'S GENDER TWIST

So far, I have discussed Shneur Zalman's concept of time and, in particular, its practical implications for the divine service from the vantage point of a hypothetical male audience. Both the symbolism used to describe the flow of time and its overcoming on the everlasting eighth day of circumcision, as well as the practices of prayer and Torah study aimed at transcending temporal limitations, pointed to male Hasidim as both subjects and recipients of Shneur Zalman's teachings. A twist occurs, however, signaling the striking possibility of a reversal of the gender hierarchy at the end of days and the full inclusion of women in Habad spirituality. This chapter will explore female symbolism in Shneur Zalman's theosophical discourse on time and examine its impact on the life and praxis of Habad women in Shneur Zalman's times and for the future-to-come.

The discussion of the gender dynamics in time is not purely theoretical. The implications of this discussion are important for two main reasons. First, some scholars claim that Hasidism brought about full equality of Jewish men and women in the field of spirituality. While historians have rejected this conceit on the grounds that Hasidism neither improved women's position in the community nor included them in the ethos of Torah scholarship, nor even enabled them to ascend to leadership positions, the romanticizing perspective that sees Hasidism as a movement that created an inclusive spiritual space within traditional Judaism still resurfaces in scholarship.[1] Second, the change envisaged by Hasidism in its formative years in relation to the communal role of women began to take shape in the twentieth century when the challenges posed by modernity encouraged some Hasidic leaders to consider attracting women to their cause. In particular, the last two leaders of the Habad-Lubavitch movement, Yosef Yitshak Schneersohn and Menahem Mendel Schneerson, pioneered the development of spaces for women in the Hasidic model of spirituality.[2] The radical reshaping of women's participation in Hasidism in twentieth-century Habad and, more broadly speaking, the feminist turn in Judaism in the twentieth century, prompted research on continuity and change in the Habad teachings on gender.[3] The following discussion will bring to light the feminine symbolism in Shneur Zalman's teachings. It will respond to attempts to read contemporary notions of inclusivism into writings and demonstrate how these texts provided an ideological basis for the development of feminine spirituality in twentieth-century Habad.[4]

The main difficulty for a historian looking into Shneur Zalman's ideas on women's participation in Hasidism arises from the fact that his writings provide little indication of the role he envisaged for them. This might partially be a result of the fact that his teachings, sermons, and letters were intended for a male audience, and as such dealt predominantly with matters relevant to men's welfare. Indeed, his *Hilkhot talmud Torah* did advocate that women learn Torah, albeit within a very limited scope, yet neither was this innovative nor did it result in any organized framework for women's Torah education.[5] An additional difficulty results from the extensive editing of Shneur Zalman's teachings, which often involved removing topical references in their transcription and translation from Yiddish into Hebrew.[6] One can therefore assume that direct references to women that may have been made verbally would have been edited out as being of little significance to their male readers. In general, early Habad material is much more abstract and detached from the social reality of its time than that left by the last Lubavitcher Rebbe.[7]

Nonetheless, there is more on early Habad than mystical sermons and halakhic books. To compensate for the lack of direct evidence on Shneur Zalman's notion of the role of women in Hasidic society, scholars have sought to extract his view from indirect references. Notable is the belief, explicitly expressed by Rivka Dvir-Goldberg, that in Hasidic literature "woman [. . .] is a subterranean spring, which greatly influences life and people, though not publicly but rather silently and beneath the surface."[8] Habad tales seemingly support this claim by ascribing extraordinary intellectual and spiritual achievements to some female members of Shneur Zalman's family, but the evidence they provide is questionable.[9] Not only may one argue that this characteristic is yet another link in the long chain of tradition that "acknowledged certain women's capacity to acquire scholarly or spiritual accomplishments by virtue of their intimate association with distinguished men,"[10] but there are other hagiographic traditions that claim that Shneur Zalman denied the existence of any such strong, spiritual bond between him and his wife.

> Once our Rebbe overheard the *rabbanit* [Shterna] sitting and talking with her [female] friends, and in the middle of the conversation she said: "and mine [that is: my husband] says such and such." When he heard it he called out to her, saying: "what makes me yours? One single commandment! No, I am not entirely yours!"[11]

Contrary to the image of the close relations between Shneur Zalman and Shterna presented by Heilman, this tradition shows him rebuking his wife for speaking out in his name, as if the marital bond gave her special access to her husband's spirituality and wisdom. He responds that this bond is in fact restricted to one commandment only, presumably to "be fruitful and multiply," or the commandments of *'onah* (regular conjugal relations).

An expanded version of this story appears in *Ha-yom yom*, a collection of Habad sayings and thoughts published in the early 1940s by Menahem Mendel Schneerson.

> Once, as the Alter Rebbe [Shneur Zalman] stepped out of his room, he overheard his wife remarking to several women, "Mine says . . ." The Rebbe said: "With one commandment I am yours; with how many are we G-d's!" With these words he fell onto the doorpost in [the ecstatic state of] *devekut*. On "awakening" from the *devekut* he said: "Go forth and gaze" [Song 3:11]—to step out of self and perceive the divine comes from [the following words in the verse] "daughters of Zion," *Malkhut* arousing *Ze'ir anpin*. The Future will bring the fulfillment of "A virtuous woman is a crown to her husband" [Prov. 12:4].[12]

This version of the story introduces the mystical dimension, absent from the version cited above, whereby Shneur Zalman ecstatically loses consciousness as he experiences *devekut* after hearing his wife talking to other women. Still in front of the female crowd, he utters kabbalistic exegetical comments about the feminine and masculine aspects of the Godhead (respectively, *Malkhut* and *Ze'ir anpin*), alluding to the former's future supremacy. At the center of this version of the story stands the tension between the marital (or romantic) bond between spouses and the spiritual bond with God. The transition to the mystical state of *devekut* echoes the concept of elevating strange thoughts in early Hasidism, which according to some Hasidic masters may be achieved by gazing at women. A Hasid begins by contemplating her carnal beauty and then proceeds by cleaving to abstract divine attributes, which bestow beauty on women of flesh-and-blood.[13]

Indeed, this version turns the message of the story from *Migdal 'oz* on its head, showcasing women as playing an important part in triggering the mystical experience and as recipients of mystical teaching. But it can't reasonably be taken at face value as a historical source. It stands to reason that the *Ha-yom yom* story is a more recent elaboration of that from *Migdal 'oz* and expresses the stance of Habad's later leaders, rather than that of its founder.[14] Furthermore, *Migdal 'oz*, unlike *Ha-yom yom*, actually provides us with the names of the transmitters of this tradition.[15] The way the story has been retold resembles other attempts by Yosef Yitshak Schneersohn to revise and rewrite the history of Habad so as to adjust it to his vision of the movement in the twentieth century.[16]

Still, the *Ha-yom yom* story points at important theoretical Hasidic concepts. The story itself is a compilation of three layers of tradition. The first is the anecdote about the exchange between Shneur Zalman and his wife. The second is from a homily by Shneur Zalman's mentor, Dov Ber of Mezrich, in which the verse "Go out and see, daughters of Zion" refers to the act of going forth out of corporeality, which is triggered by gazing at women.[17] In *Ha-yom yom*, the mystical experience is no longer prompted by looking at women but by hearing them, perhaps because the notion of gazing at women seemed to clash with the standards of modesty maintained by Habad in the twentieth century.[18] Finally, the third layer of this story, which is absent from its Maggidic source, introduces the idea of a dynamic relation between the feminine and masculine *sefirotic* constellations in the present and in the future-to-come—a recurrent motif in Shneur Zalman's mystical teachings.

Female Imagery in Shneur Zalman's Theosophy

Before delving into the details of the gendered dynamics of time, a few words of introduction on gender imagery in Shneur Zalman's Hasidism are called for. In his summary of the Hasidic attitudes to women, Moshe Rosman lists materiality, corporeality, incompleteness, the evil inclination, and irrationality.[19] Indeed, Shneur Zalman endorses all of the above, although he generally replaces flesh-and-blood women with the abstract "female." Nonetheless, in some cases, he blurs the border between the categories of gender and sex, and between women and the abstract category "female." For example, he sometimes employs kabbalistic ideas to justify certain halakhic rulings regarding women, or conversely, a saying of the Sages or a principle of Jewish law to provide an insight into the gendered aspect of the Godhead.

The most important gender qualification concerns the construction of the sefirotic structure, which consists of both male and female aspects. The source of this division lies in the image of the androgynal primordial man (*Adam kadmon*), whose upper body is linked with the male, and the lower body with the female, mirroring a common association of upper body parts with spirituality and lower body parts with sexuality and corporeality, an association that has been enforced in Hasidism by the custom of wearing a sash during prayer.[20] The attribution of a gender to the upper and lower parts of the divine body has two major consequences. First, it suggests the lower status of the female on the axiological scale; second, it portrays the female aspect as more remote than the male from the infinite divine source in the theosophical scheme. In this connection Shneur Zalman offers an interpretation of the verse "Let us make man in our image, after our likeness" (Gen. 1:26).

> It is written in the *Zohar*: "Image [*tselem*] [refers to] the man, likeness [*demut*]—to the woman" [Ziii, 35b]; "image" is when it is drawn from an image of the face itself, as in the case of the letters of a stamp [impressed] in wax, or similarly in the appearance of the face itself in water and in a mirror, whereas "likeness" of the female is when it is drawn from a separate object that received the essence of the form; and this is the meaning of [1 Sam. 2:2]: "There is no rock [*tsur*] like our God" who "forms a form within a form [*tsar tsurah be-tokh tsurah*]" [bBerakhot 10a, Megilah 14a], for he derives it from the form which had been drawn from the essence of the attribute, called the primary form [*tsurah ha-rishonah*], etc.[21]

This excerpt leans on a zoharic interpretation of the pleonasm in Genesis 1:26, whereby God creates the first human according to his "image" and "likeness." The *Zohar* unpacks this expression by referring to male and female as, respectively, close and direct (image), and remote and mediated (likeness) impressions of the divine. This interpretation integrates two distinct descriptions of creation—Genesis 1:26–27 and Genesis 2:7, 18–22—the former having Adam and Eve created simultaneously, while the latter has Eve molded out of Adam's rib. Shneur Zalman's discourse draws on philosophical terminology; in his view, the male is formed out of the primary form, which makes him a direct reflection, or impression, of the divine, whereas the female is only the reflection of a reflection, or a divine form mediated through the male form. In a sophisticated wordplay based on the multiplicity of meanings associated with the root *tsade vav resh*, God-rock (*tsur*) becomes a demiurge who formed (*tsar*) or drew (*tsiyer*) both male and female forms (*tsurot*), with the female form being merely secondary to the male, primary form. The phrase is a direct quote from the Talmud (*Berakhot* 10a; *Megilah* 14a), but Shneur Zalman invests it with a new meaning. In the Talmud, it is a vivid description of God's creative powers as radically distinct from those of a human: the latter is compared to an artist drawing two-dimensional figures (*tsurot*) on a wall; God, in contrast, "shapes one form in the midst of another, and invests it with breath and spirit, bowels and intestines." In other words, God creates three-dimensional, living creatures. Shneur Zalman, however, uses this expression to illustrate God's creation as a process of emanation of divine attributes, a process that, by its nature, is necessarily gendered and the sequence of which determines the hierarchy of genders in the created reality.

The linking of the male with the upper, loftier intellectual sphere in contrast to the female, who is associated with the lower, material, corporeal one, implies the latter's inferiority and dependence on the former. A hint of this valorization appears in a notorious Talmudic saying (*bShabat* 33b) according to which "all women are light-minded" (*nashim da'atan kalah*) while men are reasoning people (*bar da'at*). Equipped with *da'at*, men always strive to achieve their goal, whereas women tend to mistake derivative achievements for the primary purpose, as is evident in the difference between male and female love: the former strives for God himself, whereas the latter is self-interested and seeks a reward (the above story about Shneur Zalman's wife can also be read as a parable for this distinction).[22] This juxtaposition could represent an ontological justification for marriage: women need a halakhically sanctioned union with a man to achieve completeness. By superimposing the Talmudic masculine "mind" (*da'at*) onto a *sefirotic* structure, however, Shneur Zalman constructs a parallel between the Sages' view of the nature of men and women and the order of the divine realms. The light-minded female (or, on the theosophical level, the feminine *sefirah* of *Malkhut*) needs to be complemented by the male knowledge (or by the influx drawn down from the male *sefirah* of *Da'at*).[23]

The drawing down of *da'at* to the female underscores femaleness as receptivity. While the male is characterized by his overflowing capacity of giving, the female is a passive vessel for the influx bestowed on her by the male. The male is constructed as the donor and the female as the recipient (*mashpi'a* and *mekabel*).[24] Moreover, the female's inherent weakness[25] manifests itself in the fact that the influx she receives is drawn from the backside and external aspect of the male, rather than from its innermost parts.[26]

The limiting and constricting role of the female is also brought forward in the Hasidic concept of creation by means of the divine word. The female (*nekevah*) is identified with divine speech;[27] her name is explicated as *nekev he*,[28] a wordplay that alludes to the unlimited voice emerging from the unbounded divine attributes through an aperture (*nekev*), and subsequently being dispersed and formed into separate words of divine speech, uttered by the five (represented by the Hebrew letter *he*) organs of verbal expression.[29] These are subsequently identified with the limiting forces in the Godhead, the five "Judgments," symbolized by the five letters in the Hebrew alphabet that have a special final form: *kaf, mem, nun, pe, tsade*.[30] As a result, the female is envisioned as the recipient of the male divine voice and as the vessel, which limits and transforms the unlimited voice into finite, articulated words of divine speech. The process of drawing down *da'at* from the male to the female, while being an important component of Shneur Zalman's theosophy, also has an experiential dimension that goes beyond a reciprocation of the divine male-female dynamics within marriage. It has a direct correlate in religious ritual, being an interesting example for the Hasidic "displacement of desire" discussed by David Biale.[31] In this case, one draws down the *da'at* in the ritual of waving the four species during the festival of Sukkot, where the palm tree stands for the six attributes constituting the male constellation of *Ze'ir anpin*, while the *etrog* stands for the feminine *sefirah* of *Malkhut*.[32]

As in the kabbalistic writings from which Shneur Zalman drew inspiration, one can discern in his teachings a need for balance between the masculine and feminine aspects. Masculinity and femininity are presented as mutually dependent, as in the Talmudic saying: "If the man first emits seed, the child will be a girl; if the woman first emits seed, the child will be a boy" (*b*Berakhot 60a). A phrase that seemingly serves as an encouragement for men to pleasure their wives in order to get sons illustrates here the idea that the male, which stands higher than the female, was actually feminine at its source.[33] Moreover, just as the genders are mutually related and cannot function in isolation, so

Adam must be complemented by his female partner Eve, for "without Eve he is not called Adam at all."[34]

But the need for balance does not only concern husband and wife; it must be reinstated in reality as a whole. In a sophisticated interpretation, Shneur Zalman explains the biblical sin of the spies (Num. 13:1–14:9) as the distortion of the balance between feminine and masculine in the world. Being all men, the spies who rejected the Land of Israel represented the world of the masculine (*'alma di-dekhura*)[35] and did not find it necessary to embrace the feminine Upper Land (an alternative term for *Malkhut* of the World of Emanation).[36] On the practical level, they did not want to move on from performing the commandments spiritually (in thought) to actually performing them materially (by means of speech and deeds).[37]

In order to demonstrate the vital role of the feminine element in a well-balanced world, Shneur Zalman revisits the negative characterizations of the female as lowly and impure. First, there is no place void of God, which means that there is room for Godliness in even the lowest domains of reality.[38] Second, and more importantly from the perspective of the temporal discourse, Shneur Zalman refers in multiple places to such principles as "Their [the *sefirot*] end is fixed in their beginning,"[39] and "what descends lower ascends higher."[40] These principles indicate two important things: that the lowly material status of the female paradoxically points at her lofty source in the divine prior to creation and that the telos of history is to uncover Godliness in reality as a whole. The greatness of the female therefore lies in her ability to reveal and uplift Godliness from its lowliest and crudest aspects. Placing the focus on worship in corporeality and materiality, as we have seen earlier in his descriptions of the worship of the common man in the era of the "footsteps of the Messiah," allows Shneur Zalman to bring the female to the center of the divine drama as it evolves in time and to break down the hierarchy in which the female is subjugated to the male.[41]

It is important to stress here that the gender categories in Shneur Zalman's teachings, as in the kabbalah and Hasidism in general, are fluid.[42] Defining the male as donor and the female as recipient not only detaches gender from sexual categories, but in fact makes all gender attributes relative since, depending on circumstances, the same entity can be seen as both feminine and masculine.[43] In certain contexts, male and female can therefore stand for God and the people of Israel, for God injects life into Israel, and Israel longs for God as the wife longs for her husband.[44] Conversely, the people of Israel may represent the male, and the Torah the female.[45] The Torah itself can also be divided into the masculine Written Torah and the feminine Oral Torah.[46]

The identification of the bride with both the Torah and Israel creates a problem that Shneur Zalman tries to resolve by ascribing the Torah-bride and Israel-bride to two different types of divine service, namely, to worship through recitation of the Torah by learned men, and to worship through performance of commandments—charity in particular—by uneducated men who cannot recite the whole Torah.[47] Elsewhere, the letters in the liturgy are described as feminine, as opposed to those in the Torah.[48] In some cases, gender characteristics can be ascribed to different stages of worship. For example, humility, described as descending to the level of a woman, is a condition necessary to achieve the state of cleaving to God, accessible to every Jewish soul.[49] Furthermore, gender categories are used to draw borders between different modes of Hasidic worship and between a Hasidic *tsadik* and his flock. On the grounds of the distinction between the active male and the passive female, Shneur Zalman distinguishes between feminine and masculine modes of Hasidic worship, where the former concentrates on receiving spiritual power from the *tsadik*, and the latter on individual spiritual effort. Even though the "feminine" Hasidim excel in the attribute of awe, it is more limited than the "masculine" attribute, since by dint of being feminine it lacks understanding (*da'at*). By contrast, one whose worship is based on individual spiritual powers is equipped as a "male" with *da'at*—the attribute that comprises two opposite aspects simultaneously.[50] Thanks to this he may serve God even when he is struck by "alien" thoughts and reach a loftier level than one who stays on the "feminine" level of worship.[51] Additionally, in a manuscript text by a Habad follower, the relation between *tsadik* and Hasid is compared to that of man and wife; just as a man acquires his wife by money, document, and intercourse,[52] so the *tsadik* acquires followers by drawing down love of God[53] (or alternatively, by the money the Hasid gives to the tsadik),[54] through his teachings,[55] and through one-on-one encounters (*yehidut*).[56] The separation of gender from sex and the feminization of various aspects of male worship therefore further complicate the application of Shneur Zalman's theosophical musings to actual women's worship.

The Temporal Female

The special connection between the female and time comes from her place in the *sefirotic* structure, represented as the androgynal macroanthropos. According to Shneur Zalman, the feminine part of the macroanthropos, *Malkhut* or *binyan ha-nukba* ("constitution of feminine"), which begins from the chest of the macroanthropos downward, is where finitude and time come about. Not only does he hint at the position of the female in the *sefirotic* tree, he connects it with temporality by showing the correlation between the feminine and time, and in particular at the function of the feminine in two temporal settings: the time of creation and the time of redemption. The subjugation of the temporal feminine *Malkhut* to the eternal male *Ze'ir anpin* prevails only as long as the world is not redeemed. In the future-to-come, however, the female shall rise above *Ze'ir anpin* to receive the influx from the higher *sefirot* of *Hokhmah* and *Binah*, and will therefore transcend the boundaries of time. The material world of revelation, linked with femininity, will be elevated and transformed to the level of the loftier world of concealment. The future transition from temporality to eternity in the created world is unequivocally related to the dynamic of the feminine.[57]

This exposition of the female is deliberately ambiguous and may be seen as an expression of a general tendency in Shneur Zalman's teachings to view evil as an epistemological rather than an ontological problem, which vanishes if looked upon from the proper perspective. Accordingly, he views the female as the negative factor that brings about separation from God, impurity, and enhances the power of the external forces only when looked upon from the perspective of Habad soteriology.

As shown in the previous chapters, Shneur Zalman's soteriology is rooted in his doctrine of creation: the contraction and apparent withdrawal of God from the world in the process of creation constitutes part of the divine plan to bring into existence separate beings opposed to the divine unity, which in time will carry out the task of reinstating cosmic unity and bringing about the redemption. Relying on the idea that "last in deed comes first in thought" (*sof ma'aseh 'alah be-mahashavah tehilah*), Shneur Zalman explains that the creative thought of God above, from which everything began, would be completed through Israel's actions below—a power bestowed on the congregation of Israel by virtue of its origin in the primordial divine thought.[58] The eschatological state discussed above, described as "[God's] dwelling place in the lower worlds," acquires a gendered characterization. The task to establish "God's dwelling" is laid on the shoulders of the congregation of Israel, identified as the female, who is to be elevated to the level of its male counterpart.

> As Scripture says [Prov. 12:4]: "A virtuous woman is a crown to her husband"; the aspect of *Malkhut* of the World of Emanation, [which is] the source of the congregation of Israel, is the "crown to her

husband," [that is, to] the aspect of *Ze'ir anpin*, which is the end of the world of *Ein Sof*, for "their end is fixed in their beginning" [*Sefer yetsirah* 1:7].[59]

This passage describes the elevation of the female *sefirah* of *Malkhut* from her lowly state to the crown of her husband, the male constellation of *Ze'ir anpin*, at the time of redemption. The female, identified here with the congregation of Israel, is lifted out of her state of separateness to be reinstated within the unity of *Ein Sof*, rising above the constellation of *Ze'ir anpin*, which somewhat paradoxically marks the limit of the world of limitlessness—*Ein Sof*.

The characterization of the female as the limiting force to the divine overabundant influx, as the entire description of creation, is dialectical. The ostensibly negative limitation of God's force has positive outcomes in the emergence of new beings; in other words, the concealment of God's light results in the disclosure of God's world. This feminine quality is revealed to us in the verse, "I will make a fitting helper for him" ('*ezer ke-negdo*, Gen. 2:18).[60] In Shneur Zalman's exegesis, Adam and Eve allegorically represent God and the *Shekhinah*, hence, he interprets the first half of the same verse, "It is not good for man to be alone," as referring to God. In other words, the Bible explains that it is not desirable for there to be nothing other than God. Therefore, God created woman as a helper ('*ezer*) who would be opposed to him (*ke-negdo*), that is, her limiting force would constrict the unbounded expansion of the divine light and, in this way, would help God to create the material world.[61]

The process of creation, however, is not complete with the emergence of nondivine beings, and consequently the role of the feminine is not limited to it. Unlike the commentators on whom Shneur Zalman bases his exegesis, who considered '*ezer* and *ke-negdo* to refer to two mutually exclusive possibilities of what woman can become for man,[62] he sees these two terms as complementary. Not only has the female helped in the process of creation, she has also brought out of concealment the reflected light that "returns and ascends to a far higher level than that of the source of the illumination."[63] In other words, it is precisely the materiality and limitedness of the feminine that intensifies the flow of divine light, to the point of its full revelation in the future-to-come, when it will be brighter than its source. So, while the first, limiting aspect of a female, necessary for the emergence of any separate and ostensibly nondivine entities, is illustrated by Eve's formation from Adam's rib, so the fulfillment of her task, which is the enhancement of the light hidden to the level above the source of the illumination in the redeemed future, is manifested in marriage, when man and wife are united again. Shneur Zalman points out the peculiar difference in the wording of the penultimate and ultimate blessings of the seven (*sheva' berakhot*) recited during a marriage ceremony. The sixth ends with the words, "Blessed art Thou, Lord, who gladdens the bridegroom *and* the bride" (*hatan ve-kalah*), whereas the seventh blessing has, "gladdens the bridegroom *with* the bride" (*hatan 'im ha-kalah*). The shift in the formulation symbolizes the change that will happen in the world-to-come.

> In the beginning she [*Malkhut*] receives the light from the bridegroom, drawn from the world of the masculine into the world of the feminine. And this is [the meaning of] "bridegroom and bride." However, later he "gladdens the bridegroom with the bride," because by means of the bride he gladdens the bridegroom, for she is verily made a helper [*'ezer*] for him and an addition of light from the aspect of "opposite him" [*ke-negdo*]. [. . .] And this is what is meant by: she becomes a crown to her husband.[64]

Shneur Zalman expounds the different wording of the two blessings in eschatological terms as the reversal of gender roles at the time of redemption.[65] The first blessing refers to the present time, when the male facet of reality draws down the divine light to its female counterpart. Its primacy is inscribed in the wording of the blessing, where the female follows and is thus secondary to the male. But in the future time of redemption, this relationship will be reversed: the female will become the donor, and the male the receiver of divine influx, as in the wording of the final blessing, according to which the bridegroom is to be gladdened with, or *by means of* the bride.

Remarkably, Shneur Zalman interprets the reconfiguration of divine powers at the end of time as an act that exceeds the completion of the process that took its course at the beginning of time. The elevation of the female above the male marks the completion of the creation of woman, for by becoming the donor who brings an additional influx of light to the male, she fulfills her task of being his "helper." Her opposition to the male is not effaced; on the contrary, while the genders are transfigured in the future-to-come, woman retains her otherness in relation to man. She achieves, however, the perfected state, in which her opposition to the male does not limit him but complements and enriches him. In the words of Shneur Zalman's allegory, the woman who opposes the male (*ke-negdo*) simultaneously becomes his helper (*'ezer*). Indeed, at the time of redemption the female is elevated to a state in which the two gender opposites coincide, and while the female retains her separateness from the male, she is rid of her negativity.

The idea of the empowerment of the female in the future-to-come is further reinforced by the idea that while, in the time of exile, the bride remains silent during the rite of marriage, in the redeemed world "the voice of the bride will be heard, for in the future the bride will have a voice."[66] This idea is remarkable given Shneur Zalman's association of speech with self, discussed in chapter 4 in the context of the silent prayer of the *'Amidah* as an example of utmost humility and eradication of self. The voice, in contrast,

> [S]tands for drawing down and revelation, as in the case of the material voice that is drawn down and revealed from the breath of the heart to the trachea. In the future, when "a virtuous woman is a crown to her husband" [Prov. 12:4], the bride will have the voice of drawing down and revelation.[67]

The female acquires a voice at the time of the transfiguration of genders in the future to come, which is the fulfillment of the verse from Proverbs whereby the "virtuous woman" (*Malkhut*) ascends to be a crown to her husband (*Ze'ir anpin*). That is to say, the female will turn from passive to active. References to activity versus passivity in terms of silence versus voice or effacement versus the drawing down of the divine influx recur in Shneur Zalman's sermons.[68] Analogously, when *Malkhut* is elevated in the future-to-come, it will be transformed from a receptive vessel of the influx into its transmitter to the *sefirot*.

The disclosure of divinity in the future-to-come turns the negative feminine force into good. The female, material and impure, is compared to a beautiful captive gentile woman (Deut. 21:11–13) who can be redeemed by marriage with an Israelite soldier. Although the reference to a gentile woman only enhances the otherness of the female, Shneur Zalman emphasizes the male's ability to release her from captivity (undoubtedly a reference to the exile of the Jewish nation, which can be brought to an end by God), to uncover her hidden beauty, and to unite with her in a halakhically sanctioned marriage. Moreover, the *rite de passage* from captivity to freedom prescribed by Scripture includes the paring of nails. Nails, like hair, stand for the divine vitality when it is drawn by the external forces; therefore, in the future-to-come, by paring the excess of the nails, the female will cut off the flow of divine vitality to the external forces, and her carnal beauty will be revealed for the exclusive enjoyment of the male. While in the present time of exile, the female, and particularly feminine carnality, is linked to the *sitra ahra*, in the future-to-come it will be tempered and directed solely to holiness, and evil will be transformed into good.[69]

The elevation of the female in the end of days is an outcome of the continuous process of emendation of the world by dint of purification of the divine sparks that fell into the realm of husks, in which the gender dichotomy plays an important role. Although the final redemption is to come at the end of days, there are special times in the as yet unredeemed world that temporarily bring closer, or anticipate, the time of the redemption. This temporal gender dynamic is illustrated, again, with the image of a wedding.

> And behold, in the future-to-come there will be [Isa. 62:5] "as a bridegroom rejoices over his bride," [. . .] there will be [Jer. 31:22] "a woman shall compass a man [*nekevah tesovev gaver*]," the bride will ascend with her vessels to the aspect of canopy surrounding all the worlds, and then there will be "he gladdens the bridegroom with the bride"—by means of the bride; [. . .] whereas now there is [bKetubot 16b] "how does one dance before the bride."[70]

Here, the image of a wedding ceremony conveys the idea of ultimate redemption in which the female—*Malkhut*, the congregation of Israel—ascends to the wedding canopy. Since the image of the canopy spread over the bride and groom represents the transcendent aspect of God ("surrounding all worlds"), and the bride (*Malkhut*) stands for the immanent aspect of the divine ("filling all worlds"),[71] the ritual of the ascent of the bride to the canopy symbolizes the unification of transcendence and immanence at the end of days. In addition, the verse from Jeremiah proclaiming that "Woman shall compass a man," which the bride traditionally enacts by turning around the groom seven times, acquires here an eschatological meaning. It is understood to refer to the elevation of the female above the male which is the state envisioned by the final wedding blessing, "gladdens the bridegroom with the bride."[72]

We can have a foretaste, even in exile, of the future delight derived from the union between God and Israel. This is not permanent, however, as they constantly draw near and then separate from each other, a dynamic reflected in Shneur Zalman's homily on the *mitsvah tants*, which is the customary Hasidic dance where the groom dances in front of his bride, drawing near and withdrawing from her again and again, until they finally hold hands.[73] Similarly, the male and the female aspects of the Godhead draw near to each other only to be subsequently separated, until finally, in the end of days, their union becomes permanent.

> [It is] as in the example of the dance, during which one draws near [to one's partner] and then moves away, and this is the essence of delight, as in the case of two lovers who have not seen each other for a long time, but who later draw near [to each other], which gives rise to great delight. Similarly, since she [the bride] has descended and clothed herself below by way of distance, when later she draws closer to her groom and rises up, great delight arises from it, and [Eccl. 2:13] "a light is superior to darkness," for she [Lev. 22:13] "is back in her father's house."

The reference to Ecclesiastes points to the idea that evil turned into good holds greater power than good itself, which appears to be one of Shneur Zalman's favorite motifs.[74] It provides justification for the distance between the male and the female in the present: the bride's final return to the house of her father, namely, the reunification of the female and the male facets of the Godhead at the end of days, will bring about greater light and more intense delight than when both of these aspects were one, before creation. Moreover, the verse from Jeremiah, "The woman will compass the man," may also be read as meaning that "The woman will court the man."[75] Considering that Shneur Zalman refers to the present as the times when "It is the way of man to go in search of [or 'to woo'] a woman, but it is not the way of a woman to go in search of [or, 'to woo'] a man" (*b*Kidushin 2b), and "It is the nature of man to conquer, but it is not the nature of woman to conquer" (*b*Yevamot 65b), his use of this passage to depict the future-to-come suggests a forthcoming reversal in which the male is passive and the female active. Nonetheless, in the present time, the active role decidedly belongs to the man. During the lengthy process of purification that still lies ahead, as in the image of *mitsvah tants*, the masculine and feminine aspects draw near to each other at certain times, only to be separated again, until the process is finally complete at the end of days and they are permanently united as bride and groom under the canopy.

The process of purification of the sparks that fell into the world of husks engages the female facet of the Godhead and is compared to the night. The completion of the process marks the advent of the time of redemption, which corresponds to "the day that is entirely Sabbath" (*b*Sanhedrin 97a), an ultimate, everlasting day that transcends the division between day and night.[76] The process of purification is overtly gendered and sexual, although it acquires different forms in various discourses. The underlying principle, nonetheless, remains the same: the feminine aspect carries out the process while being empowered by its male partner. So, for instance, Shneur Zalman integrates in his teachings the Lurianic discourse on the four divine names derived from the Tetragrammaton: the name of 72 letters corresponding to the constellation of *Aba*, the name of 63 to *Ima*, of 45 to *Ze'ir anpin*, and of 52 to *Malkhut*.[77] The process of purification takes place between the lower two names, which are subsequently depicted as masculine and feminine: 45 corresponds to Adam (its numerical value) and 52 to Eve and *Malkhut*. As Eve was taken out of Adam's flesh, the feminine name of 52 is derived from the masculine name of 45.[78] The female name, corresponding to *Malkhut* of the World of Emanation, fell down during the breaking of the vessels and is responsible for the purification of the lower worlds (Creation, Formation, and Making), that is, for the separation of good from evil. The male name, which stands higher in the hierarchy and transcends the reality in which evil can occur, subsequently purifies the female name, transforming it to good.[79]

The purification is described in overtly sexual terms as the elevation of female waters (*mayin nukbin*) and the drawing down of male waters (*mayin dukhrin*),[80] which correspond to two types of nullification: the nullification of being (*bitul ha-yesh*) and the uppermost nullification (*bitul 'elyon*).[81] In the former, independent existence is nullified;[82] in the latter, the female waters are elevated and reunited with the divinity in the World of Emanation, that is, in the part of the *sefirotic* domain in which the *sefirot* are in the state of unity with God, or, to use the expression borrowed by Shneur Zalman from *Tikune Zohar*, in the world where "He and his life forces and his causations are one."[83]

The lower purification is attributed to Aaron and the upper one to Moses.[84] They are attributed feminine and masculine qualities, respectively, and appropriate temporal configurations. The upper purification, linked to the figure of Moses, is described as being beyond the limits of time, for Moses's candle burns indefinitely. Moses's bynames, such as "man of God," or "the king's best man,"[85] point to his relation with the male aspect of the Godhead.[86] Aaron, in contrast, is "the best man" of Matrona (i.e., *Shekhinah*, *Malkhut*), and as such remains under the governance of time, which is why his lamp burns "from evening to morning" only.

The expression "from evening to morning" suggests a link between the purification of the lower worlds and nocturnal time, which in turn corresponds to the well attested connection in the kabbalah between night and *Malkhut*.⁸⁷ In Shneur Zalman's writings, *Malkhut* descends at night to purify the lower worlds, while during the day it returns to its position within the Godhead.⁸⁸ One of the reasons for the bond that ties *Malkhut* to the night may be found in the idea, expressed above, that the twenty-four hours of day and night are governed by different combinations of the divine name: twelve combinations of the Tetragrammaton governing the twelve hours of day, and twelve combinations of the name Adonai (corresponding to *Malkhut*) governing the twelve hours of night.⁸⁹ The transition between day and night therefore reflects processes that take place in the upper worlds.

Malkhut, the tenth *sefirah*, mediates between the divine and the created worlds, and binds together the external aspects (the sparks of holiness trapped in the world since the breaking of the vessels, which represent the state of separation from the divine unity and correspond to bodily functions, such as digestion) and the internal aspects (the intellectual attributes—*Hokhmah, Binah,* and *Da'at*—described collectively as the brains [*mohin*], as well as the lower *sefirot*, which correspond to the emotional attributes) of the divine. During the daytime, she transmits the internal influx into the worlds. At night, in the absence of the internal influx,⁹⁰ the overflow of the divine vitality is transmitted from the external aspect of *Malkhut* of the World of Emanation toward the lower worlds, and it purifies the 288 sparks trapped there. This is how Shneur Zalman interprets Prov. 31:15, which in its original context refers to the woman of valor's deeds: "She rises while it is still night and supplies provisions for her household." To him, the woman of valor is *Malkhut*, and the "food" (*teref*) she brings, the numerical value of which is 288 plus 1, points to the 288 holy sparks.⁹¹

Malkhut's nocturnal activity should not necessarily be read, however, as an indication of its independence. On the contrary, the image of *Malkhut* as a housewife, on whose shoulders rests the responsibility for sustaining the entire household, stresses her dependence and subordination to the male. Shneur Zalman compares the nocturnal descent of *Malkhut* to purify the lower worlds to the wife who is adorning herself with beautiful clothes at night to please her husband.⁹² He also quotes the Sages' statement that "it is not in her [the woman's] nature to conquer" (*bYevamot* 65b); all her active pursuits are for her husband's sake.

Moreover, as the gender perspective is imposed on the weekly cycle, the female's role is diminished even more, as the purifications of the lower worlds associated with her nocturnal activity in fact derive from the powers bestowed on her by her male partner every day.⁹³ In terms of the inner dynamic within the Godhead, this means that the six working days of the week correspond to the influx from one of the six *sefirot* constituting the male constellation of *Ze'ir anpin*, whereas the seventh day—the Sabbath—corresponds to the feminine *Malkhut*.[94] Shneur Zalman even reiterates the view of the female as weak and passive by claiming that the process of purification that takes place on the six days of the week must cease on the Sabbath. He applies the halakhic prohibition on the work of "sorting" (*borer*)[95] to the purification of the sparks by way of separating them from the "husks," and concludes that just as sorting is prohibited, so the purification of sparks cannot take place on the seventh day. This arises from the fact that, according to the Sages, "it is not woman's nature to conquer." It is the male (*Ze'ir anpin*) who carries out this work through her during the week so that she can later carry the sparks up with the female aspect of the Godhead as she rises on the Sabbath.[96]

The elevation of the female on the Sabbath enables a union of the male and female, expressed in the Sabbath hymn *Lekhah dodi* by the words "'observe' and 'remember' [*shamor ve-zakhor*] in one utterance," where *shamor* corresponds to the female and the Sabbath's eve, and *zakhor* to the male (*zakhar*) and the Sabbath day.[97] Moreover, the commandment to sanctify (*le-kadesh*, which also means "to betroth") the Sabbath carries overtly sexual connotations: not only does Shneur Zalman explain the function of this commandment as drawing down delight—a notion packed with sexual undertones[98]—but he also often interprets the verb "to sanctify" as denoting sexual union.[99]

The distinction between the masculine days of the week and the feminine Sabbath distinguishes between the time of exile and that of redemption. Referring to the *Zohar*, Shneur Zalman presents the former allegorically as the time when the groom, moved by his love for his bride, spends the night with her in a tanners' market, and, as the *Zohar* continues: "Since she is there, it is for him as a market of spices, where all the good smells of the world are."[100] The image of a tanners' market, a smelly, dirty, and despicable place, stands for the world of nature, while the bride who lives there is the *Shekhinah—Malkhut*—the feminine divine presence who enclothes herself in the husk of *nogah* in order to give life to this world. Finally, the bridegroom who comes down every night to his bride's humble residence represents the masculine facet of the Godhead that is beyond the world of nature, yet which bestows its attributes on the female.[101]

In its original context, this allegory explains the incidence of miracles in exile and, in particular, God's miraculous acts described in the Scroll of Esther, in spite of the fact that God's name doesn't appear within it. It shows very well, however, the parallel between the male's descent to the female during the six days of the week and the Exile, and the promised elevation of the female in the future-to-come. This analogy is further corroborated by the correspondence between, on the one hand, the six *sefirot* of *Ze'ir anpin* (or the six supernal days), the six thousand years of the exilic world, and *Malkhut*, and on the other hand, the six attributes of *Ze'ir anpin*, the six working days of the week and the Sabbath.[102] Therefore the Sabbath functions, for Shneur Zalman, as for many others before him,[103] as a prolepsis of the redemption, a foretaste of the future-to-come, which is indeed described as a day that is "entirely Sabbath"[104] or as the supernal Sabbath. The process of purification will by then be complete, there will be no need for the days of work, and *Malkhut* will transcend the level of the lower Sabbath, which she currently occupies that occurs every seven days.[105]

At the same time, however, Shneur Zalman points to an utterly masculine ritual that surpasses the feminine Sabbath, that of circumcision. In kabbalah, circumcision derives from a source that lies above the polarity of weekdays and Sabbath. The Sages emphasize its supremacy over the Sabbath by stating that "circumcision and all its preliminaries takes precedence over the Sabbath" (*b*Shabat 131b). It is performed on the eighth day in order to ensure that the newborn baby experiences the Sabbath before being circumcised.[106] Shneur Zalman weaves these classical rabbinic notions into a theosophical system. According to him, circumcision is located in *Yesod* of *Adam kadmon*, above the division between the worlds of Emanation, Creation, Formation, and Making, whereas the Sabbath ascends from the lower worlds to Emanation but not beyond it. Since *Adam kadmon* is above the four cosmic worlds, he also transcends the distinction between weekdays and Sabbath.[107] The ritual of circumcision therefore releases the radiance of a brighter light that has not yet materialized to "encloth" in the four cosmic worlds. It must be preceded by the Sabbath, as the release of light from beyond the four worlds must be preceded by the release of light in the World of Emanation.[108]

Circumcision ultimately transcends time. Following traditions that have been traced to the medieval Ashkenazi Pietists,[109] Shneur Zalman decodes the Hebrew word for circumcision (*milah*) as an acronym of the verse "Who among us can go up to the heavens?" (*mi ya'ale lanu ha-shamaymah*, Deut. 30:12), the final letters of which constitute the Tetragrammaton,[110] representing supratemporal reality.[111] This is made even clearer in the emphasis he places on the symbolic significance of the eighth day and the messianic connotation of the number eight.[112] This in turn links the ritual of circumcision to Hadar, the eighth

Edomite king, and the only king whose death is not mentioned in the Bible and whose spouse is named in the Torah—facts that represent, according to Shneur Zalman, the rectification of the breaking of the vessels and the reconnection of the male to the female.[113]

Although this restoration is achieved by means of a ritual, which seems to be exclusively masculine, there is a Talmudic tradition that counts women among the circumcised (*b'Avodah zarah* 27a), and Shneur Zalman incorporates it in his teachings that play on the fluidity of gender categories.[114] Since gender relates to the qualities of donor and recipient, it may change when a certain *sefirah* changes from one to the other. Furthermore, the same *sefirah* can be considered both female and male, depending on the perspective from which it is being viewed. The feminine *sefirah* of *Malkhut* can be perceived as masculine when it bestows the divine life force on the lower worlds. Consequently, it, too, is subject to circumcision. Yet the covenant of the circumcision of the female (*Malkhut*) differs from that of the male (*Ze'ir anpin*).

> This clarifies the statement of the Sages, of blessed memory, that the woman: "concludes the covenant only with him who transforms her into a vessel" [*b*Sanhedrin 22b], for the covenant of the female [*brit de-nukba*] is made out of the overflowing *Yesod* of the male, who is the one who transforms her into a vessel, as Scripture says [Isa. 54:5], "for your maker is your husband." This refers to the conclusion of her covenant [*keritat ha-berit*] with him who transforms her into a vessel [. . .] (and the meaning of [the words]: "who transforms her into a vessel" is that she becomes an aspect of the male to beget, etc., and this should suffice for one who understands), [. . .] for the covenant of the female is actually called a covenant of the aspect of the masculine donor after it has become a vessel for the covenant of the male [*brit di-dekhura*]. [. . .]. Therefore, it was said that: "the woman is considered as though she is circumcised" [*b'Avodah zarah* 27a], for she is called an aspect of the male, yet she is not such on account of herself, but rather on account of having received from the donor.[115]

It appears that gender fluidity is, in fact, fluid: even though the female acquires a masculine character, she does not do so by herself but through the male. The female enters the covenant (and is thereafter referred to "as one who is circumcised") during her first marital intercourse, or to be more precise, she is brought into the covenant by her husband's phallus (*yesod di-dekhura*) which makes her a "vessel." It enables her to take upon herself the maternal role, which, because of its active character, is described specifically in masculine terms.[116] Therefore, this concept of women as being subject to circumcision seems to serve the purpose of their masculinization rather than their empowerment as women. In other words, the elevation of the female results with the confirmation, rather than the subversion, of the gender hierarchy in the Godhead, which remains, ultimately, a male androgyny.[117]

Between Theosophy and Life Praxis

The above examples of Shneur Zalman's homilies demonstrate that the gender discourse of the Godhead touches on *halakhah* and the custom of his community. The laws of ritual purity pertaining to women, the obligation to cover their hair, or even the opinion whereby women are light-minded all reflect in the material world certain aspects of the sefirotic reality. The liminal function of the feminine *Malkhut* in creation, where it is associated with the forces of "Judgments" that restrain the unbounded influx of the divine life force in the process of creation, puts her in proximity to evil, death, and, consequently, impurity. After all, the contractions of the divine life force that nourish the lower worlds are so intense that they enable nondivine beings to emerge and the external (evil) forces to draw their vitality from it.[118] Here, cosmology and halakhic praxis intertwine: Shneur Zalman points at the proximity of the abstract "female" to death as the reason for the exclusion of women from performing the ritual of the Red Heifer (which purifies a person from defilement caused by contact with a corpse).[119]

The crossovers between theosophy and *halakhah* in descriptions of women and femaleness recur throughout Shneur Zalman's lore. The notorious expression of the Sages according to which, "The hair of woman is a naked thing" (*b*Berakhot 24a),[120] which eventually led to instituting a halakhic obligation for married women to wear a head covering, is also explained symbolically. Hair, as a body part that contains such little vitality that cutting it off causes no pain, symbolizes the division, diminishment, and the enclothment of the divine life force in an entity radically remote from its source: the external (evil) force.[121] In a similar vein, Shneur Zalman links menstrual blood with the external forces. By extending impurity from the halakhic domain to metaphysics, he thus exacerbates the perception of women as impure.[122] This in turn is echoed in the instructions on behavior that appear in *Tanya*, where the description of woman as "a vessel full of filth" (*b*Shabat 152a) is used in reference to evil and decay embodied in worldly delights, which one should learn to abhor.[123]

It is not different with regards to the genders' temporal dynamics, which can be divided into three main questions that I now wish to discuss: how the temporal characterization of the abstract categories of male and female impacts the divine service of men and women; how the anticipated elevation of the female in the future-to-come will impact women's worship; and, finally, whether the concept of the overturning of gender hierarchy in the future-to-come might impact the position of women in Habad communities.

One of the most tangible areas in Judaism in which gender and time correlate is the halakhic exclusion of women from the obligation to observe positive time-bound commandments. This rule, which originates in classical rabbinical literature, supposedly grants women the freedom they need to take care of their families.[124] Shneur Zalman, however, does not allude to this medieval rationale for the Talmudic precept. He refers instead to the juxtaposition of the temporal female (*Nukba, Malkhut*) and the eternal male (*Ze'ir anpin*) in the Godhead in order to justify the exemption of women from time-bound commandments.

An elaborate interpretation of the halakhic principle that excludes women from positive time-bound commandments appears in one of his later sermons.[125] It is at variance with numerous blunt references which occur throughout his teachings to the aforementioned precept, where he simply takes the exemption to be a self-evident consequence of the association of the feminine with the source of time, as testified in the Lurianic corpus.[126] In this particular sermon, however, Shneur Zalman demonstrates in detail how theosophy determines *halakhah*. *Malkhut*, the feminine source of time, is dependent on *Ze'ir anpin*, its higher masculine aspect which transcends time. For its own fulfillment, *Malkhut* needs an influx from the male mind (*da'at*, a concept reminiscent of the Talmudic dictum on women's light-mindedness), which is why the feminine aspect in the Godhead nests within the lower part of the male aspect. Now, *da'at*'s function is to bind opposites together[127]—in this case, the forces of Judgments and Kindnesses, which are the roots of, respectively, the negative and positive commandments. Consequently, the male, equipped with *da'at*, possesses both attributes and is obliged to perform both types of commandments.[128] The light-minded female, in contrast, is predominantly associated with the constricting Judgments and is thus obliged to perform only the negative commandments. To fulfill positive commandments, she is dependent on the flow of Kindnesses from the male.

Now, there are two types of positive commandments: those that are time-bound and those that are not. The female, incorporated within the male, receives Kindnesses from the lower part of the male's body which Shneur Zalman identifies as the male's feminine, and, consequently, time-bound aspect. This has practical consequences: a woman does not need to perform positive time-bound commandments, for she receives the influx of Kindnesses flowing from the time-bound commandments performed by her husband. She is obliged, however, to fulfill positive commandments that are not time-bound, for her union with the male does not guarantee her the Kindnesses that lie in the upper part of *Ze'ir anpin*'s body. The female's observance therefore depends on legitimate sexual union. While on the theosophical level the female category is incorporated in the male body (an incorporation underscored by *da'at*'s sexual connotations), on the practical level, a woman's divine service needs to be complemented by her husband's.

Notably, Shneur Zalman assumes the possibility that, in the messianic future, women will also be obliged to perform time-bound commandments. This will happen within the eternity of redeemed reality when the difference between time and what-transcends-time ceases to exist, and the consequent distinction between men and women regarding the commandments no longer stands. As we know, temporality will have no impact on this redeemed reality and will therefore not impede women's observance of time-bound commandments. In this regard, women and men will be equal in the world-to-come.[129]

Because women are exempted from positive time-bound commandments, the modern Habad movement has designated certain tasks as being specifically feminine and put emphasis on their immense spiritual potency, turning them into a crucial part of its twentieth-century Jewish renewal project. These tasks are the three commandments traditionally considered as pertaining particularly to women: ritual purity, lighting the Sabbath candles, and separating a portion of dough when baking bread (the commandment of *halah*).[130] This emphasis on women's participation in the spiritual enterprise of the Jewish people is absent from the writings of Shneur Zalman, where the actions performed by women are generally presented as merely enhancing men's spirituality rather than being spiritually significant in their own right.

Such a change between early and late Habad can be seen in their attitude toward the commandment of lighting the Sabbath candles, which in recent years has been propagated by Habad Hasidim as the quintessential feminine commandment, even though Shneur Zalman did not seem to attribute any special significance to it. Following early rabbinic tradition, he states in his *Shulhan 'arukh* that women light the Sabbath candles to atone for the fact that Eve "extinguished the candle of the world and was given the commandment of lighting the Sabbath candle in order to make good the damage she had caused."[131] Yet, a woman still performs this commandment only as "an agent of her husband's."[132] It was the last Lubavitcher Rebbe, Menahem Mendel Schneerson, who viewed his own lifetime as a moment of unprecedented darkness, and therefore encouraged not only married women but also young girls to light the Sabbath candles and bring radiance into the world, even though they were not halakhically obliged to do so. Even children were recruited to help disperse the darkness of "alien thoughts" and the "thoughts of the street." In Menahem Mendel's spiritual project, a girl who lights the Sabbath candles becomes God's agent, whereas in Shneur Zalman's writings, this function is reserved for the married woman, who acts as her husband's agent.[133]

Shneur Zalman adopts a similar approach with regard to the role of women in marital life. Despite the fact that he attributes a great deal of significance to sexual union both in this world and in the upper world,[134] it seems that he views the role of women as extending no further than facilitating the spiritual development of their husbands. He invokes the figure of the defiantly unmarried Shimon ben Azzai, of whom the Talmud says that he entered paradise, "cast a look and died" (*bHagigah* 14b), in order to stress the value of marriage in a man's life. In Shneur Zalman's opinion, ben Azzai failed because he did not find the right balance between the spiritual and the earthly dimensions of life.

Ben Azzai was in the aspect of *ratso*, of "great love," [. . .] in the nature of the expiration of the soul [*kelot ha-nefesh*], and he did not want to be reduced to the aspect of *shov*. For this reason, he refused to marry, saying that the world could be preserved by others, and this is why he "cast a look and died" [*bHagigah* 14b], for he completely withdrew from the vessel.[135]

Ben Azzai's example demonstrates that marital relations are necessary even for the most pious and devoted Jew. The passage also reiterates the characterization of women as material "vessels" for their husband. In his halakhic work, however, Shneur Zalman states that a man should postpone marriage until he has learned the entire Oral Torah, although he may go ahead if the sexual urge distracts him from his studies.[136] Indeed, even though ben Azzai's approach is discouraged,[137] marital union is seen either as a means to the end of performing the commandment of "be fruitful and multiply," or else as the lesser transgression that a young man may commit to study in a state of purity.

Following earlier sources, Shneur Zalman attributes significance to the timing of sexual union, pointing to Friday night as the appropriate time for it in terms of the role of the Sabbath in the dynamic of genders within the Godhead. The Talmudic Sages had already singled out Friday night as the appropriate time for Torah scholars to engage in marital intercourse, and the idea was reinforced in the halakhic codices, including Shneur Zalman's *Shulkhan 'arukh*.[138] In the *Zohar*, and later in Eliyahu de Vidas's *Reshit hokhmah*, the same idea is linked to the commandment of sanctifying the Sabbath. In addition, the Zohar presented Torah scholars as wanderers, studying away from their home and family all week long, and returning only for the Sabbath. They were said to believe that sexual union with their wives on Friday night would cause the *Shekhinah* to descend on them and stay with them during the following week, when they returned to Torah study (considered as sexual union with the *Shekhinah*). They therefore remained permanently in the state of union between male and female.[139]

Shneur Zalman, on the other hand, stresses the importance of sexual union in the process of restoration: the phallus (*yesod di-dekhura*) brings down the divine overflowing Kindnesses to sweeten the female's constricting Judgments. These Kindnesses can be drawn down only at specific times (during the Sabbath and the three pilgrimage festivals),[140] because "the corporeal kindness, if drawn down in an inappropriate combination and at an improper time, is not a kindness at all."[141]

Contrary to twentieth-century Habad, Shneur Zalman neither considers the envisioned elevation of the female to the top of the theosophical structure in the future-to-come to have any significant implications for the role of women in the redeemed world, nor ascribes any redemptive significance to the commandments they perform.[142] As Ada Rapoport-Albert points out, Shneur Zalman's presentation of the transposition of the gender hierarchy as a result of the redemption has the effect of neutralizing the subversive message of his teachings regarding the female; it reaffirms the status quo rather than challenges it.[143] Even his scant comments on women's fate in the redeemed world do not indicate any change in their roles. An example of this is his elaboration on the status of the commandments in messianic times.

> It will be further necessary to know the laws governing the impurity of a woman who has given birth; as Scripture says: "those with child and those in labor, together" [Jer. 31:8]. Even if a woman gives birth every day as a result of one marital union, nonetheless, the law with respect to restrictions resulting from her impurity will not change.[144]

Even though women are only of marginal concern in this passage, one may learn from it that Shneur Zalman subscribes to the view that women will continue giving birth in messianic times, albeit unconstrained in their ability to do so.[145] To avoid the contradiction implicit in the notion that the laws of ritual purity will persist even though women conceive every day, he adds that these daily deliveries will result from the same marital union.[146]

Subsequent Habad thinkers who noted that Shneur Zalman mentioned explicitly the impurity of a woman who gives birth but made no reference to the issue of menstrual impurity took this to be a hint of the annulment of menstrual impurity in the world-to-come. The Tsemah Tsedek, for example, explains that the deep meaning of female impurity (*nidah*) is that the *Shekhinah* has wandered away from God during the exile. In the redeemed world, when the exile comes to an end, the state of impurity caused by distance from God will cease, and the laws of impurity will become redundant.[147] This seems to conform to Shneur Zalman's grasp of menstrual impurity as a connection to the external forces, which will not prevail in the future-to-come.[148]

Be that as it may, according to Shneur Zalman, the future ability of women to give birth every day will arise from the eradication of the barriers between the spiritual and the material spheres of reality.

> "In the future a woman will give birth every day" [*b*Shabat 30b], that is to say, the sowing and growing [conception and pregnancy] will occur every day in full disclosure, so that it will not be necessary for them to take as long as nine months.[149]

While in this world the limitations of materiality account for the lapse of time between the "sowing" of the divine life force and its disclosure, these will be removed in the future-to-come, when the sowing will yield immediate fruit and women will give birth immediately after conception. It is worth noting that this exemplifies Shneur Zalman's vision of the elevation of the female to—or above—the male: both man and woman are primarily donors. Yet even this comes to reinforce rather than overturn the conservative notion of woman as defined primarily by her ability to give birth.

Conclusion

Although Shneur Zalman's teachings may seem to reiterate the traditional and generally negative characterization of the female, his temporal discourse enables him to underscore its positive features, which also pervade the kabbalistic sources he draws on. Thus, the female facet of the Godhead, with all her apparently negative traits, carries a crucial role by facilitating the emergence of separate beings in the process of creation. In the future-to-come, through the process of purification, she will ascend to (or above) the male facet of the Godhead in order to bring him the creative light that is intensified precisely because it is reflected in her materiality.

While referring to the elevation of the female in messianic times, however, Shneur Zalman seems neither to anticipate the overturning of the patriarchal order, nor to attempt to empower women in his own time. The role of the female in facilitating the redemption remains dependent on the strength she draws from the male, while her ascent in the future-to-come is imagined in terms of her reunification with the male in the rite of marriage. It is hard to speak of the empowerment of the female in this context; even though she casts off her negative traits during the transition from exilic to redemptive times, she does so only by virtue of her union with the male and by fulfilling her duties toward him. By the same token, in the image of circumcision as a prolepsis of redemption, the female enters the redemptive event only through the male.

The elevation of the female in the future-to-come can be seen, on the one hand, as the integration of the female in a male-dominated structure. On the other hand, it can be perceived as her masculinization, where, defined as the receiver, she takes on the male function of donor, ascends from the world of the feminine to the world of the masculine, and is transformed from "female" (*nukba*) to "mother" (*ima*), who in turn is described in overtly masculine terms. While Menahem Mendel Schneerson has been led, as Wolfson states, "to affirm a notion of unity that [. . .] does not entail the androcentric restoration of the female to the male,"[150] Shneur Zalman holds on to a more conservative belief.

His theosophical concepts have an impact on practical issues, as there seems to be no indication of significant changes in the status of flesh-and-blood women in the future-to-come. From the scant remarks on this theme scattered throughout Shneur Zalman's lore, one can deduce at most that the nullification of the barriers between the material and the spiritual realms, followed by the transformation of the female from recipient to donor, will reverberate in the life of women, freeing them from certain limitations in their role as life-giving mothers.

Analogously, the special role attributed to the gender category of "female" in Shneur Zalman's theosophy does not seem to have an impact on the position of women in the present. He makes use of the theosophical nexus of time and the female when he interprets women's participation in religious life, which is particularly conspicuous in his explanation of the halakhic principle that exempts women from positive time-bound commandments. This example, however, further reinforces the notion of women's inferiority to men, since it mandates that the spiritual task of performing some of the commandments is entrusted to their husbands. Similarly, Shneur Zalman holds a rather conservative view of the commandment of lighting the Sabbath candles, seeing in it an element of masculine spirituality that women perform as proxy. He disregards the possibility of linking the commandment's apparent feminine character with the particular time at which it is performed, which is at the start of the Sabbath, defined as the time of elevation for the female aspect of reality. In a similar vein, although he recognizes the Sabbath as the propitious time for conjugal relations, he does not seem to invest the act with any particular spiritual meaning for women. Quite the contrary, his perception of women's role remains solely to facilitate their husbands' spiritual fulfillment. It appears, therefore, that although Shneur Zalman created the conceptual framework for the reevaluation of women's spiritual capacity, he refrained from drawing any conclusions from it. This was to be done only by his most recent successors in the leadership of Habad.

CONCLUSION

Temporality has been one of Shneur Zalman's main concerns on all fronts—as a mystic, as a thinker, and as a fully engaged leader to a large community of Hasidim. Contrary to the common depiction of his teachings as a mystical doctrine focused primarily on transcendent realities, this study shows Shneur Zalman to have been equally concerned with the concepts of worldly time, temporality, and history. His engagement with the idea of time had tangible implications for the everyday religious experience of his followers and enabled him to transform Habad into a large and broad-based movement. Moreover, while Shneur Zalman's teachings have been portrayed as devoid of messianic tension (so prominent in contemporary Habad), this book shows some form of messianic awareness to be inherent in his concept of both individual and communal divine service.

It cannot be stressed enough that Shneur Zalman's rich corpus of writings does not represent a self-contained, harmonious philosophical system. The sources of his teachings differ in genre, purpose, and target group; the process of their edition and publication may in many cases span two centuries, and the editor may often have had a significant impact on their final shape. There is, therefore, no systematic exposition of Shneur Zalman's concept of time. Throughout his teachings, he tackles such questions as the nature of time-flow, its relation to the supratemporal God, and its role in the lives of the ordinary Hasidim who are all subject to temporality and yet aim at uniting with the infinite and timeless God. First, Shneur Zalman integrates in his teachings the kabbalistic concept of *ratso va-shov* with the philosophical definition of time as a measure of movement, resulting in the notion that time is a rhythm of the constantly alternating descent and ascent of the divine life-giving energy, which amounts to a continuous cycle of creation, annihilation, and re-creation. Locating the source of time in the *sefirah Malkhut*, Shneur Zalman proceeded to explore the various means by which temporality connects with the supratemporal God so as to solve the enigma of the apparent flow of time prior to the creation of the world and of time itself.

Having set the theoretical framework of time and its origin in Shneur Zalman's work, this book proceeded to consider his understanding of history as the period that has elapsed since the beginning of time at the very moment of creation, and its progress toward its end in the final redemption. Shneur Zalman's teachings testify to his deep interest in instances of exile and deliverance throughout Jewish history, which he uses to highlight his sense of the current exile, and to add gravity to both individual and communal worship as the path leading toward the messianic future. Messianic redemption, albeit fragmented as a project to be accomplished by all Jews and suspended in the protracted transitional period of the "footsteps of the Messiah," underpins Shneur Zalman's grasp of worship in the era of exile. Admittedly, there is no evidence of acute messianic tension among his followers, yet his teachings clearly convey the message that not only does every righteous act bring us closer to redemption, but the fulfillment of the specific commandments of prayer and study of the Torah enables everyone to attain the state of redemption, even within the unredeemed world.

The final redemption is unveiled when the world is transformed in the messianic era, as well as in the subsequent time of the resurrection of the dead. This is the time when the Jews, having purified their bodies during the exile and become capable of receiving the full revelation of God, will delve into the secret layers of the Torah and be sustained by direct exposure to the divine light. Moreover, the divine illumination, due to God's unbound mercies, will be so abundant that even the gentile nations will be resurrected and sustained by it.

It is important to note that, for Shneur Zalman, time and timelessness or exile and redemption are not abstract ideas but tangible realities woven into the fabric of his own everyday life and the lives of his followers. Shneur Zalman's interest in time helps him make his model of spirituality accessible and meaningful to a broad mass of followers, whose occupations did not leave them the time required for total commitment to study. He encourages them to set special times for Torah study as a means of drawing the supratemporal divinity down to their temporal reality. He shows that not only could everyone subjugate temporality to the Torah through this relatively simple and undemanding halakhic precept, but also that study at set times was equally, if not even more important to his Hasidic project than the full-time study of the scholarly elite. This awareness of time, and the control exercised over it by means of nomian ritual, allows him to include in his quest for the infinite God even ordinary people who are engrossed in worldly affairs. It also binds together personal moments of redemption even in the present in the cycles of continuous re-creation and annihilation, with the collective, cumulative effort leading toward the eschatological end of history.

Finally, temporal teachings display gendered characteristics. Following in the footsteps of kabbalists, Shneur Zalman associates the source of time, *Malkhut*, with the feminine aspect of divinity, and foresees the elevation of the female at the end of days—an idea that served his twentieth-century successors as a doctrinal basis for rethinking the role of women in the Habad movement of their day. Unlike them, however, Shneur Zalman does not translate the overturning of the gender hierarchy at the end of days into any actual change in the role or status of women within his own community. He employs the nexus of femininity and time to explain the exclusion of women from some commandments in the unredeemed world, and comments occasionally on women's elevation to a higher status than men in the future-to-come. But his ideas of the messianic future only reinforce the traditional role of women in the present, where their spiritual capacities are entirely subordinate to their husbands'.

Study of Shneur Zalman's concept of time enables us to look at his teachings as a whole from a new perspective. It shows early Habad doctrine to have recognized the path to God above all in temporal, worldly action rather than in pursuit of timeless transcendence by means of an acosmistic doctrine that is completely detached from worldly concerns. Certain elements of this doctrine, such as the messianic idea or the nexus of women and time, are echoed in the acute messianism of twentieth-century Habad. We still await a thorough analysis that would trace the development of these ideas in Habad teaching from their inception in the eighteenth century to the present. Yet a close reading of Shneur Zalman's teachings yields precious insights into the worldview of early Habad in particular, and Hasidism in general, and a greater understanding of the Hasidic conception and experience of temporality.

NOTES

Introduction

1. See Shapiro, *The Limits*, in particular, 139–56.
2. See, for example, Jacobs, *Hasidic Prayer*, 48–53; Wilensky, "Hasidic-Mitnaggedic Polemics," 247–51; Wertheim, *Law and Custom*, 134–43. On the "Orthodox turn" in the nineteenth-century's Hasidism, see Brown, "Substitutes for Mysticism," 247–58; on the Hasidic-*mitnagedic* conflict and its eventual end, see Wodziński, *Historical Atlas*, 26–32, and Biale, *Hasidism*, 83–99.
3. See Scholem, *Major Trends*, 328–31; Scholem, *The Messianic Idea*, 176–202.
4. See Idel, *Messianic Mystics*, 212–13, 223, 237–38; *Hasidism*, 16–17; "Mystical Redemption," 12–19; "Multiple Forms," 58–69.
5. As M. Avrum Ehrlich dubbed him in the title of his book, *The Messiah of Brooklyn*, the last leader of Habad, Menahem Mendel Schneerson.
6. See Biale, *Hasidism*, 17–74; Rosman, *Founder of Hasidism*.
7. For an academic biography of Shneur Zalman, see Etkes, *Rabbi Shneur Zalman*. In the Habad circles, Shneur Zalman's status as the founder of the movement is underscored by his popular moniker "der Alter Rebbe" in Yiddish or "ha-Admor ha-Zaken" in Hebrew, both meaning "the Old Rebbe." He is also identified with his literary works as "Ba'al ha-Tanya" and "Ba'al Shulhan 'arukh," namely the author of *Tanya* and *Shulhan 'arukh*.
8. Of note is a Habad Hasid who would later significantly contribute to the creation of the myth of Ba'al Shem Tov as the founder of Hasidism by publishing *Shivhe ha-Besht*, a collection of hagiographic stories on the Ba'al Shem Tov in 1814. See Biale, *Hasidism*, 70; Rosman, *Founder of Hasidism*, 187–212.
9. According to the Habad tradition, Shneur Zalman was attracted by the Maggid because he put emphasis on prayer, as opposed to the Vilna Gaon

(Eliyahu ben Shlomo Zalman, 1720–1797), who emphasized Torah study. See Heilman, *Bet rabi*, folio 2a, note 2.
10. Etkes devotes half a page to this stage of Shneur Zalman's biography; see Etkes, *Rabbi Shneur Zalman*, 1. Foxbrunner is slightly more generous (see his *Habad*, 46–48), but his account is based entirely on Hasidic hagiography produced by the last two Habad rebbes, Yosef Yitshak Schneersohn and Menahem Mendel Schneerson. For partisan accounts based on Hasidic stories, see Mindel, *Rabbi Schneur Zalman*, i, 35–43; Glitzenstein, *Sefer ha-toldot*, 21–46.
11. See Rapoport-Albert, "Hasidism after 1772"; Biale, *Hasidism*, 76–155.
12. Mayse, "Beyond the Letters," 121–34, discusses problems with defining the Maggid's circle and describes some personalities involved in it. See also Green, "Around the Maggid's Table."
13. See Rapoport-Albert, "Hasidism after 1772," 42–43. For a survey of the Maggid's students, see Green, "Around the Maggid's Table."
14. See T4, 28:147b-148a and Heilman, *Bet rabi*, 62a–67a, 103a, which lists several other personalities from within and without of the Maggid's circle. See also Sagiv, *Ha-shoshelet*, 64. Levi Yitshak later supported him in his conflict with another Maggid's disciple, Avraham of Kalisk (see Etkes, *Rabbi Shneur Zalman*, 244–46). On the significance of pedigree (*yihus*) and the use of arranged marriages for forging alliances and spreading influence among Polish *tsadikim*, see Dynner, *Men of Silk*, 117–35 and 231–39.
15. See Rapoport-Albert, "Hasidism after 1772," 65–68; Rapoport-Albert, "Hagiography with Footnotes," 217–19.
16. This stage of Shneur Zalman's biography is discussed in detail in Etkes, *Rabbi Shneur Zalman*, 9–21.
17. See Etkes, *Rabbi Shneur Zalman*, 28–31.
18. See Hillman, *Igerot Ba'al ha-Tanya*, 58-70 (Levine, *Igerot kodesh*, i, 53–59, 65–68, 75–79, 103–5), discussed in Etkes, *Rabbi Shneur Zalman*, 41–49; Etkes, "Darko shel R. Shneur Zalman," 334–41.
19. See Loewenthal, *Communicating*, 1–6.
20. See Etkes, *Rabbi Shneur Zalman*, 129–31.
21. See Loewenthal, *Communicating*, 76; Hillman, *Igerot Ba'al ha-Tanya*, 176; Levine, *Igerot kodesh*, i, 127.
22. Etkes (*Rabbi Shneur Zalman*, 64) points at the growing role of the *gaba'im* (collectors) in Shneur Zalman's community, but he comes short of noticing the influence of the social structure of the *kollel* on the leadership and teachings of Shneur Zalman as a Hasidic leader.
23. Mondshine, "Ha-ma'asar ha-sheni," 79; Etkes, *Rabbi Shneur Zalman*, 189–90.
24. See *Avaneha barzel*, 34 par. 46; Rapoport-Albert, "Hasidism after 1772," 60; Etkes, *Rabbi Shneur Zalman*, 2; Perl, *Uiber das Wesen der Sekte Chassidim*, 122. This, and other matters concerning the imagined and factual demography of Hasidism, is discussed in Wodziński, *Hasidism: Key Questions*, 133–64.

25. See Etkes, *Rabbi Shneur Zalman*, 54–55.
26. See Hillman, *Igerot Ba'al ha-Tanya*, 105–7, discussed in Loewenthal, *Communicating*, 51–52; Elior, *Paradoxical Ascent*, 21; Elior, "Vikuah Minsk," 193–96; Etkes, *Rabbi Shneur Zalman*, 208–58. According to Habad hagiography, the conflict between Shneur Zalman and other Hasidic masters about the idea of communicating the esoterics to the masses can be traced back to the time when Shneur Zalman was still a student of the Great Maggid. One should keep in mind, however, that Habad stories transmitted by the sixth leader of the movement, Yosef Yitshak Schneersohn, in which Shneur Zalman defends the idea of teaching the esoteric against the criticism of Pinhas of Korets, were aimed to present the Habad communication ethos as the genuine teachings of Dov Ber of Mezrich and the Ba'al Shem Tov, and can hardly be seen as a historical source. See *Ha-tamim* 2 (1936): 49 [143], and 8 (1938): 50–51 [802–3], and Glitzenstein, *Sefer ha-toldot*, 29–30. On Habad historiography originating in Yosef Yitshak Schneersohn, see Rapoport-Albert, "Hagiography."
27. See Etkes, *Rabbi Shneur Zalman*, 151–207; for documents concerning Shneur Zalman's arrests, see Mondshine, *Ha-ma'asar ha-rishon*; Mondshine, "Ha-ma'asar ha-rishon"; Mondshine, "Ha-ma'asar ha-sheni." 19 Kislev, which is the anniversary of Shneur Zalman's release from prison in 1798, became a festival celebrated throughout Habad communities. For the use of 19 Kislev as a community-building tool in interwar Habad, see my forthcoming article, "The Scroll of 19 Kislev."
28. See Mondshine, *Ha-masa' ha-aharon*.
29. For Habad's history in the eighteenth and nineteenth centuries, see Loewenthal, *Communicating*; Lurie, *'Edah u-medinah*; Lurie, *Milhamot Lyubavich*. For the partisan accounts of Habad history, see Levine's series *Toldot Habad*.
30. On *Sefer ha-hakirah*, first published in 1912 in Poltava, see: Gotlieb, *Sekhatlanut*, 71–88; Loewenthal, "'Reason' and 'Beyond Reason,'" 123–26; Loewenthal, "The Image of Maimonides," 290–92; and Stamler, "Sekhel," 203–10, who argues against considering *Sefer ha-hakirah* and its interest in philosophy as in any way representative for Habad, in general, or the Tsemah Tsedek, in particular.
31. See Balakirsky Katz, *The Visual Culture*. On the apparently first Hasidic journal for children *Ha-ah*, see Mondshine, "Ha-shavu'on la-yeladim."
32. See Brawer, "Resistance and Response to Change," 184–286; Brawer, "'Yisudah shel yeshivat 'Tomkhe Temimim,'" 357–68; Lurie, "Ben dat le-politikah," 201–21; Lurie, "Hinukh ve-ide'ologyah," 185–221; Lurie, *Milhamot Lyubavich*, 60–126.
33. A thorough research on this issue remains a desideratum. For the time being consider Balakirsky Katz, *The Visual Culture*, 19–90; a short excursus on the imagery technique deployed by Yosef Yitshak Schneersohn in his stories in Daniel Reiser, *ha-Mar'eh ka-mar'ah*, 277–79. On the

nexus of ritual and new media, see my forthcoming article, "The Scroll of 19 Kislev." The new categories, such as *penimi* (an inward person) and *'atsmi* (a person in touch with his essence), introduced by, respectively, Shalom Dovber and Yosef Yitshak Schneersohn, may also have been influenced by the development of psychology. See Loewenthal, "The Thickening of the Light," 26–27; for the discussion of these terms in the Habad context and on the impact of psychology on Hasidism in the late-nineteenth century and early-twentieth century, see Reiser, "The Encounter in Vienna." On the contacts between Shalom Dovber and a Viennese psychoanalyst, Wilhelm Stekel, see Balakirsky Katz, "An Occupational Neurosis"; Balakirsky Katz, "A Rabbi, a Priest, and a Psychoanalyst."

34. On Schneerson's Berlin and Paris years, see Heilman and Friedman, *The Rebbe*, 103–29; Miller, *Turning Judaism Outward*, 83–121. For some affinities between Habad and German philosophy, see Wolfson, "Achronic Time." For a short summary of Schneerson's critical approach to sciences and philosophy, see Wolfson, *Open Secret*, 310–12n3.

35. For a survey of Habad activity in the first years of the Soviet Union, see Fishman, "Preserving Tradition." The transformation of Habad in interwar Poland is a topic of my current research. For the time being, see my "The Scroll of 19 Kislev" and "Between Hagiography and Historiography," as well as Rapoport-Albert and Sagiv, "Habad ke-neged Hasidut Polin."

36. The academic and partisan literature on twentieth-century Habad is immense and growing. For the Habad emissaries and their place in Habad messianism, see, for example, Heilman and Friedman, *The Rebbe*, 1–12, 23–28, 163–96, 254–74; Kraus, *Ha-shevi'i*, 92–131; Dahan, "Dirah ba-tahtonim," 163–72; Roth, *Ketsad li-kero*, 164–66; Wodziński, "Historical Atlas," Map 8.5. See also Fishkoff, *The Rebbe's Army*, which is a journalistic account of Habad activities in the US. For the impact of Habad activities on non-Hasidic orthodox outreach, see Ferziger, *Beyond Sectarianism*, 175–94.

37. For comprehensive discussions of messianism in the doctrine of twentieth-century Habad, see Dahan, *Dirah ba-tahtonim*; Elior, "The Lubavitch Messianic Resurgence"; Schwartz, *Dilug el ha-or*, 227–78; Schwartz, *Mahashevet Habad*, 271–318; Wolfson, *Open Secret*. There are several biographies of the rebbe Schneerson. The most important are the controversial academic biography by Heilman and Friedman, *The Rebbe*, and the more comprehensive, but not unproblematic work by a Habad Hasid Chaim Miller, *Turning Judaism Outward*. For the discussion of the twenty-first century Habad biographies, see Tworek, "Beyond Hagiography."

38. On the impact of major twentieth-century historical events on Habad doctrine, see Elior, "The Lubavitch Messianic Resurgence"; Greenberg, "Menahem Mendel Schneerson"; Loewenthal, "Contemporary Habad," 385–90.

39. On Habad messianism as a state of consciousness, see Wolfson, *Open Secret*, 164–65. Wolfson's view is particularly noteworthy in light of Joseph Dan's claim that while messianism was always an important component of Hasidism, the experience of messianic redemption was confined to the spatial boundaries of the Hasidic court and perpetuated over time by the duration of each court's particular dynastic leadership; in other words, the redemption was at hand for the Hasidim only as long as their particular dynasty endured (see Dan, "Kefel ha-panim," 306–9). Habad's overtly messianist factions have managed to break these temporal and spatial limitations in two ways: first, they have immortalized their last leader by propagating the belief that he did not die and by introducing rituals perpetuating his virtual presence within the community, and, second, they have taken his message out to the non-Habad, non-Hasidic, and even non-Jewish audiences. It is important to note, however, that some of these practices (for example, the use of video recordings of the rebbe's speeches, the dispatch of Habad emissaries to Jewish communities over the world, or the printing of Hasidic material for the purely magical purpose of "purification of the air") are not considered controversial at all within the nonmessianist Habad mainstream. See Bilu, *Itanu yoter mi-tamid*; Dein, *Lubavitcher Messianism*, 113–21; Foxbrunner, *Habad*, 52; Heilman and Friedman, *The Rebbe*; 24–27; Wolfson, *Open Secret*, 356n67; Shandler, *Jews, God and Videotape*, 230–74. This only illustrates how difficult it is to draw a clear-cut distinction between different factions within contemporary Habad.
40. See Loewenthal, *Communicating*.
41. For criticism of Eliade's approach to Jewish time, see Idel, "Some Concepts of Time."
42. See Rubenstein, "Mythic Time," 181.
43. Stern, "The Rabbinic Concept," 130.
44. See Stern, "The Rabbinic Concept," 138.
45. Stern, "The Rabbinic Concept," 137–38.
46. Stern, "The Rabbinic Concept," 144. Wolfson, *Crescas' Critique*, 93–98, 282–91.
47. Stern, "The Rabbinic Concept," 144, names Sa'adya Gaon (tenth century) as the earlier source of the concept of time in Jewish philosophy.
48. See Rudavsky, *Time Matters*, 35.
49. See Aristotle, *Physics*, 4, 11, 219b2, 4, 12, 221b8; see also Rudavsky, *Time Matters*, 14.
50. See, for example, the recent intellectual biography of Maimonides: Halbertal, *Maimonides*, 202–8 and 313–21.
51. See Wolfson, *Crescas' Critique*, 93–98; Rudavsky, *Time Matters*, 46–49.
52. See Dauber, *Knowledge of God*.
53. See Idel, "Some Concepts of Time"; "Higher than Time," 180–81.
54. See also Afterman, "Time, Eternity and Mystical Experience," 168–71; Idel, "Higher than Time," 185–97.

55. See Rudavsky, *Time Matters*, 54–55.
56. See Idel, "Some Concepts of Time," 162–63; "Higher than Time," 180–83; Wolfson, *Aleph, Mem, Tau*, 84–86, 88; Shuchat, *'Olam nistar*, 116. The kabbalists appropriated the phrase *"seder ha-zemanim"* from the midrash *Bereshit rabah*, 3:7.
57. On the diverse kabbalistic literature, which influenced Hasidic teachings, see Idel, *Hasidism*, 9–17.
58. See Idel, "Higher than Time," 198; *Kabbalah*, 58.
59. See Idel, "Higher than Time," 201–8.
60. See Green, "Around the Maggid's Table"; Haran, "Mishnato," in particular 527–29; Loewenthal, *Communicating*, 45–54, 69–77.
61. See Menahem Mendel of Vitebsk, *Peri ha-'ets*, Ki tetse 14a. Elsewhere, however, Menahem Mendel softens the spiritualist overtones of his teachings; see Hallamish, "The Teachings," 279–83. The role of the body in Shneur Zalman teachings will be further discussed in chapter 2.
62. Nahman of Bratslav's messianism has been discussed in Green, *Tormented Master*, 182–220 and in Mark, *The Scroll*. For a comparison between Nahman's and Shneur Zalman's messianism, see chapter 3, below. For a comparison of Bratslav and Habad messianism in current times, see Bilu, *Itanu yoter mi-tamid*, 317–33.
63. See Garb, *Yearning of the Soul*, 52–53. For the two souls, see T1, 1–2:5b–7a. For man as the microcosm, see T4, 12:118b.
64. On the use of the terms *derush* and *ma'amar* in Habad, see Roth, *Ketsad li-kero*, 63–85.
65. On problems arising from the fact that Hasidic homilies, spoken primarily in Yiddish, were transmitted in Hebrew translation, see Etkes, *Rabbi Shneur Zalman*, 52–53; Gries, "The Hasidic Managing Editor," 141–42; Loewenthal, *Communicating*, 66–68, Reiser, "Ha-derashah ha-hasidit"; Mayse and Reiser, "Derashato ha-aharonah"; Mayse and Reiser, "Sefer Sefat Emet"; Mayse and Reiser, "Territories and Textures."
66. Shneur Zalman's *Hilkhot talmud Torah* was the first attempt since Maimonides's *Mishneh Torah* to provide an extensive and original treatment of the subject of Torah study; see Foxbrunner, *Habad*, 137. On the publication of Shneur Zalman's halakhic works, see Mondshine, *Sifre ha-halakhah*; see also Cooper, "Mysteries of the Paratext," which revisits the history of the book and analyzes the role of Shneur Zalman's sons in the shaping of his manuscripts into a code of law. Shneur Zalman's activity as a legal thinker and jurist still awaits thorough research. For the time being, consider Cooper, "Towards a Judicial Biography"; Cooper, "Mysteries of the Paratext"; Hallamish, "Shulhan 'arukh ha-rav." For a more general overview of Hasidic Halakhah, see Kahana and Mayse, "Hasidic Halakhah."
67. On the history of the publication of the *Tanya* see Mondshine, *Likute amarim*. Additionally, in 1981, *Likute Amarim—Mahadura kama*, containing manuscript variations of the *Tanya*, was published by Kehot.

68. See T1, Introduction, 4a, discussed in Loewenthal, *Communicating the Infinite*, 47–48, and, with a slightly stronger stress on *yehidut* in *Likute amarim: mahadura kama*, 4–6, discussed in Roth, *Ketsad li-kero*, 155–56.
69. For the distinction on Shneur Zalman's esoteric and exoteric teachings, see Tishby and Dan, *Torat ha-hasidut*, and Foxbrunner's criticism in his *Habad*, 39. For recent echoes of this distinction, see Dov Schwartz's *Dilug el ha-or*, which devotes a chapter to the distinction between Shneur Zalman's sermons and discourses, on the one hand, and his monographic writings (*kuntresim*), on the other. Schwartz, additionally, distinguishes between *derushim* (sermons, published in the nineteenth century) and *ma'amarim* (discourses, published in the twentieth century); see 279–315.
70. See T1, Hakdamah, 4a-b, where Shneur Zalman presents the dissemination of unsupervised manuscripts that misrepresent his teachings as one of the reasons for the publication of *Tanya*. See also "The Liozna Ordinances" in Hillman, *Igerot Ba'al ha-Tanya*, 58–59; Levine, *Igerot kodesh*, i, 104. For Shneur Zalman's instructions regarding the supervision of manuscript copies of his sermons, see "The Liozna Ordinances," where his brother, Yehuda Leib of Yanovitch, referred to as transcriber of his sermons, is charged with the responsibility for checking and correcting the transcripts that are held by Shneur Zalman's other Hasidim. His transcripts were later used by Shneur Zalman's grandson, the Tsemah Tsedek, as the basis for the publication of Shneur Zalman's *Torah or*. He is also known as the editor of *Shulhan 'arukh ha-rav*, and as the author in his own right of the collection of responsa *She'erit Yehuda*. See Heilman, *Bet rabi*, 55a-b; Loewenthal, *Communicating*, 67–68 and 256n8.
71. See Heilman, *Bet rabi*, 55a, where, even though he testifies that Yehuda Leib's transcripts are "very accurate, truly as they [the sermons] were said," he also recalls a Habad tradition, according to which Yehuda Leib added some of his own ideas to Shneur Zalman's writings against the latter's will. Shneur Zalman's son, Dov Ber, was another important editor of his father's teachings. However, even the editors of the twentieth-century editions of Shneur Zalman's sermons admit that in the case of Dov Ber's transcripts, it is often difficult to determine whether they transmit his own discourses or those of his father. See "Sekirah kelalit 'al devar ha-Ma'amarim ha-Ketsarim" in MAHZ *Ketsarim*, 602. In addition, Foxbrunner (*Habad*, 52 and 243n385) gives examples of variant versions of Shneur Zalman's discourses and points out that the Tsemah Tsedek was often unable to draw the line between his grandfather's words and editorial additions.
72. See Foxbrunner, *Habad*, 243n363, where he criticizes Hallamish who "for some unfathomable reason feels [that Dov Ber's *Be'ure ha-Zohar*] is more attributable to R. Dov Ber than M[AHZ] 5568, a transcription by the latter that he does use," and for not mentioning *Shene ha-me'orot* at all in his dissertation.

Chapter 1

1. Kabbalists varied in their approach to philosophical knowledge. Boaz Huss provides an overview of three dominating models of kabbalists' attitudes toward philosophy: the first considers philosophy and kabbalah to be two different paths leading to the same truth; the second views kabbalah as superior to philosophy; the third rejects philosophy as false and demonic. The latter was a common attitude among the postexilic Spanish kabbalists; see Huss, "Mysticism versus Philosophy," 125–33. Shneur Zalman oscillated between a qualified acknowledgment of the validity of philosophy and outright animosity toward it.
2. See TI, 8:13b. The three intellectual attributes of a person correlate with the three upper *sefirot* in the Habad *sefirotic* realm, namely, *hokhmah*, *binah*, and *da'at*. On the psychological understanding of *sefirot* in kabbalah, see Idel, *Kabbalah*, 146–53.
3. See TI, 8:13b, and HTT, 3:7, 848a, where he also allows outstanding scholars to study philosophy in order to support "words of Torah and fear of God, and the ways of proper conduct [*derekh erets*]."
4. *Seder tefilot*, 133a.
5. See *Seder tefilot*, 133a. For a detailed discussion of the status of non-Jewish philosophy in Shneur Zalman's teachings, see Stamler, "Sekhel," 107–62. This is an interesting deviation from the medieval philosophical and kabbalistic ethos, which has professed investigating and understanding God as the core element of the normative Jewish life (see Dauber, *Knowledge of God*, 61–96 and 138–89). In Shneur Zalman, the affirmation of the unity of God is possible through faith and worship, it is irrespective of knowledge, and it depends solely on the unique status of the Jewish soul. I will discuss the outstanding value of the worship of nonscholars in Shneur Zalman's Habad in chapter 4.
6. See Stamler, "Sekhel," 163–94.
7. See HTT, 3:7, 848b. Shneur Zalman justifies the use of philosophy in the past by claiming that only a limited number of rabbis devoted themselves to it; study of philosophy was relevant only to their times; it was necessary as a tool in dispute with non-Jewish philosophers. See also Stamler ("Sekhel," 174–76), who evaluates this threefold argumentation of Shneur Zalman and sums it up as being of apologetic rather than of historical character.
8. For a characterization of the *sefirot* and the four kabbalistic worlds, see Scholem, *Kabbalah*, 96–122; Idel, *Kabbalah*, 136–53. For the doctrine of the *sefirot* in the teachings of Shneur Zalman, see Hallamish, "Mishnato ha-'iyunit," 61–69.
9. See Hallamish, "Mishnato ha-'iyunit," 70–74; Schwartz, *Mahashevet Habad*, 64–65n142.
10. See TI, 2:6a, and Stamler, "Sekhel," 169.
11. For the statistic sample of Shneur Zalman's references to Maimonides, see

Stamler, "Sekhel," 187. For the use of Maimonides in *Tanya*, see Stamler, "Sekhel," 167–68.
12. See Aristotle, *Physics*, 4, 11, 219b2, 4, 12, 221b8; see also Rudavsky, *Time Matters*, 14, 46–47.
13. LT *Ba-midbar*, 7d.
14. MAHZ *'Inyanim*, 49.
15. See TI, 48:67b. Referring to this passage in *Tanya*, Shneur Zalman's grandson and third Habad leader, Menahem Mendel Schneerson (*Derekh mitsvotekha*, 57a), formulates the general principle that "the infinite may not come into being out of the finite."
16. For relevant examples in Jewish philosophy, see Maimonides, *Moreh nevukhim*, 2:13, discussed in Davidson, *Moses Maimonides*, 366–67; Wolfson, *Crescas' critique*, 663–64; Gersonides, *Milhamot ha-Shem*, 6, 1:11, 55a–57a. In kabbalah, see, for example, Vital, *'Ets hayim*, Gate 1, Section 1, 25, where the infinite and supratemporal *Ein Sof* is juxtaposed with *Adam kadmon* and the created worlds, which have a beginning and an end, are therefore subject to time. For the discussion of the Hasidic view regarding the divine realm, which is higher than time, see Idel, "Higher than Time," 197–210.
17. For the origins and history of the term *Ein Sof* see Scholem, *Kabbalah*, 131. For the use of this term and the difference between *Ein Sof* and the light of *Ein Sof* in Shneur Zalman's teachings, see Schwartz, *Mahashevet Habad*, 28–29; Jacobson, "Torat ha-beri'ah," 308–10.
18. This is an allusion to the Tetragrammaton, which is interpreted as comprising three temporal forms of the Hebrew verb "to be"; Stern (*Time and Process*, 33n21) names the piyut *Ha-ohez be-yad midat ha-mishpat* as the first occurrence of this idea.
19. TO 9a. See also TI, 20:25b–26a; MAHZ *Ketsarim* 25–26. This represents another illustration of his conviction that traditional sources offer lofty truths otherwise inaccessible to philosophers.
20. Schneersohn, *Derekh mitsvotekha*, 57a.
21. *Bereshit rabah* 9:2. See also Rudavsky, *Time Matters*, 6.
22. See *b*Rosh ha-shanah 10b–11a. See also *Tosafot* Rosh ha-shanah, 27a, which reconciles the two opinions of the Sages by stating that "in the month of Tishri [God] thought about creating [the world], but it was not created until Nissan."
23. Vital, *'Ets hayim*, Gate 1, Section 1, 25.
24. This particular teaching is not attested in any of the Maggid's published works. In the Habad edition of his sermons it has been added in the supplement with "Teachings and sayings of the Rav Maggid of Mezrich, collected from the books of our holy rabbis and leaders and their disciples." See Dov Ber of Mezrich, *Magid devarav le-Ya'akov*, Teachings and sayings of the Rav Maggid, 14b–15a.
25. See *Seder tefilot* 75d–76a. See also TO 37a. In another sermon, Shneur Zalman combines Vital's and the Maggid's arguments. On the one hand,

following the Maggidic concept, he underscores the fact that "the world is in the nature of time, and the influx of worlds [hashpa'at ha-'olamot] is in the nature of time" (MAHZ Parshiyot, i, 126). As such, temporality is a product of the creation. On the other hand, he points out that creation followed a cosmic stage of unity and concealment, after which division was introduced by the powers of Judgments (Gevurot)—an observation which resembles Vital's argument on the duration of the emanation that preceded creation. Dov Ber Shneuri, Shneur Zalman's son and successor, further refines his father's refutation of Vital's argument in Imre binah, in the section "The Gate of Keri'at shema'," 39d–40c. See also Gotlieb (Sekhaltanut, 63), who discusses this issue in the writings of the Tsemah Tsedek. This resolution of the question of the timing of the creation had already been formulated by Sa'adyah Ga'on: "If, again, that individual was to ask, 'Then why did he not create them [the beings] before this time?' Our reply would be: 'There was no time in existence as yet that one could ask about, and furthermore it is of the very nature of him that acts by free choice to do what he wants when he wants.'" Emunot ve-de'ot, Ma'amar 1, 22b.

26. See Schwartz, Mahashevet Habad, 15, where he presents the creation as the main topic of Habad thought. However, Shneur Zalman delves occasionally into the issues related to the transcendent and infinite God. See Schwartz, Mahashevet Habad, 46–57. Shneur Zalman's discussion on the time of the creation also belongs to this aspect of his thought, since 'Ets hayim, to which he refers, presents this issue as being "close to the question of what is above and what is beneath, what was before, and what will be after [mHagigah 2:1] [. . .] and since the question is very profound, so much so that one comes close to danger when one looks deeply into it. We reply as the Sages had said in the above mentioned mishnah: 'whoever looks into these four things, it is better for him not to have come into the world.'" (Vital, 'Ets hayim, Gate 1, Section 1, 25).

27. On the view of Shneur Zalman and his immediate followers on the unknowability of any aspect of the essence of the divine and its manifestations, see Elior, Paradoxical Ascent, 73–77. The transformation of human cognitive powers in the messianic future will be discussed in chapter 3.

28. See Maimonides, Moreh nevukhim, 1:54, and the discussion in Davidson, Moses Maimonides, 338, of Maimonides's interpretation of the denial of Moses's request to see God's face (Exod. 33:20–23), whereby "Moses' cryptic request at Sinai and the cryptic replies he received hence teach that the aim of human life is knowledge of God, that man cannot attain knowledge of the divine essence, yet that man can know God indirectly, through his ways and through what he created."

29. See Maimonides, Mishneh Torah, Laws of the Foundations of the Torah, 1:1.

30. See MAHZ Parshiyot, i, 94–96. On the Tetragrammaton, see note 18 above.

31. MAHZ Parshiyot, ii, 865.

32. *Sefer yetsirah*, 3:3–8, 4:4–12, 6:1–2. On the triad of *'olam, shanah, nefesh* in *Sefer yetsirah*, see Stern, *Time and Process*, 35–37, where he dismisses the later interpretations of these terms as abstract notions of space, time, and person, showing instead that they originally referred to the twelve signs of the Zodiac, seven planets, and human organs. The importance of these notions in their later, abstract sense in Habad tradition is evidenced by the Tsemah Tsedek's statement (*Or ha-Torah*, Shemot, iii, 823) that they constitute the very basis of *Sefer yetsirah*.
33. On the "secret of smoke" (*sod 'ashan*) in the teachings of Ya'akov Yosef of Polnoye and Maggid of Mezrich, see Margolin, *Mikdash adam*, 325n143, 404. The interpretation of the Hebrew word for smoke (*'ashan*) as an acronym for *'olam, shanah, nefesh*, comes from the Ra'avad's commentary on *Sefer yetsirah*. See *Sefer yetsirah*, 2b. For the overt images of the Sinaitic revelation as the moment of the convergence of heaven and earth, see, for example, *Midrash Tanhuma*, 2, 2:15; Rashi to Exodus 20:19.
34. LT *Shir ha-shirim* 7b. For the history of the formula "He reigned, he reigns, and he will reign," traced back to the seventh-century liturgy attributed to Eleazar ha-Kalir, see Stern, *Time and Process*, 33n21. For the concept of space in the sermons of Shneur Zalman, see Schwartz, *Dilug el ha-or*, 299–306.
35. See TO 116d.
36. On the difference between the Maggid and Shneur Zalman regarding the temporal relation between God and the world, see Schwartz, *Mahashevet Habad*, 37n33.
37. For the idea of the Torah, which preceded the world, see *Bereshit rabah* 8:2; bPesahim 54a; for the Torah as the blueprint for creation, see *Bereshit rabah* 1:1.
38. For the Maggid's view on eternal Torah clothed in the temporal garments of narratives and laws, see Mayse, "Eternity in Hasidism," 232–33.
39. On the identity of *Keter* and the divine will, see, for example, LT *Shelah* 38c, *Balak* 68a, *Shir ha-shirim* 26d; *Seder tefilot* 161c. See also Hallamish, *Introduction*, 129.
40. MAHZ *'Inyanim*, 93.
41. The idea of the Torah as the link between God and the world is reinforced elsewhere in Shneur Zalman's sermons: "[The Torah] binds two opposites: the [transcendent] aspect of [God] Surrounding All Worlds [*sovev kol 'almin*], which is above time and space, with the aspect of time and space"; See MAHZ *'Inyanim*, 265. This reading is supported by an invented etymological association, whereby the Hebrew word for "command" in "I command thee" (*anokhi metsavekha*, Deut. 66) derives from the root *tsade-vav-tav* (to join) rather than *tsade-vav-he* (to command); see, for example, TO 6b, 18b, 82a; LT *Be-hukotai* 45c, 47b, *Hukat* 57c–d, 58c, *Pinhas* 76a, 77a–b, *Mas'e* 92c, *Va-ethanan* 8c, *Nitsavim* 85d, *Shemini 'atseret* 83c. Wordplays based on invented etymologies can be found throughout the traditional Jewish sources. See Greenstein, "Wordplay, Hebrew"; Heinemann, *Darkhe*

ha-agadah, 110–12, 117; Barr, *Comparative Philology*, 44–50. On the two modes of the divine lights, surrounding [*sovev kol 'almin*] and filling all worlds [*memale kol 'almin*], corresponding to divine transcendence and immanence, see Elior, "HaBaD," 171–72; Foxbrunner, *Habad*, 65–66, Hallamish, "Mishnato ha-'iyunit," 50–55, Schwartz, *Mahashevet Habad*, 62–63 and 68–75.

42. MAHZ 5570, 10.
43. See *Bereshit rabah* 8:2.
44. See Idel, "Higher than Time," 197.
45. Nigal (*Ledat ha-hasidut*, 24n8) points to Yosef Gikatilla's *Ginat egoz* as a source of this gematria.
46. T2, 4:78b–79a.
47. MAHZ *'Inyanim*, 265. Shneur Zalman often intentionally misspells the Tetragrammaton as HVYH in order to avoid writing God's holy name.
48. For the Lurianic model of creation and the divine contraction, see Scholem, *Kabbalah*, 129–35; Scholem, *Major Trends*, 260–64.
49. Shneur Zalman explains the role of the Tetragrammaton in the process of creation *ex-nihilo* by referring to its etymology, where YHVH is understood as the imperfect form of the verb "to cause to exist." See, for example, T2, 4:79a: "The meaning of the name HVYH is that which brings everything into existence [*mehaveh et ha-kol*] *ex-nihilo*. The letter *yud* [modifies the verb] indicating that the action is present and continuous."
50. This idea will be further discussed below in relation to the *sefirah* of *Malkhut*.
51. See, for example, T2, 6:80a-b. On the two contractions in Shneur Zalman's teachings, see Schwartz, *Mahashevet Habad*, 86–114.
52. MAHZ *'Inyanim*, 92.
53. MAHZ *'Inyanim*, 92.
54. See, for example, Elior, *Paradoxical Ascent*, 27–29; Foxbrunner, *Habad*, 111.
55. See, for example, T2, 7:81b, based on Zii, 134a.
56. See T2, 7:81b, based on Zii, 134a.
57. See T2, 7:81b, MAHZ *Ketuvim*, ii, 20. The idea of the interchangeability of these two words comes from Zii, 135a, and is based on the fact that letters that belong to the same group of vowel-letters (*matres lectonis*), such as the *alef* of *ehad* and the *vav* of *va-'ed*, are interchangeable. The *het* of *ehad* and the *'ayin* of *va-'ed* are similarly interchangeable since they are both gutturals. See on this Wineberg, *Lessons in Tanya*, iii, 908–9.
58. See T2, 7:81b; MAHZ *'Inyanim*, 92; Elior, *Paradoxical Ascent*, 202.
59. See T2, 7:81b.
60. On *Malkhut* as a liminal *sefirah* in Shneur Zalman's teachings, see, for example, T2, 7:81a-b; TO 37a. For a discussion of this concept in his doctrine of creation, see Jacobson, "Torat ha-beri'ah," 340–43; Schwartz, *Mahashevet Habad*, 67. The concept itself occurs in older sources. See the discussions of *Malkhut/Shekhinah* in Scholem, *On the Mystical Shape*,

157–82; Hallamish, *Introduction*, 138; Tishby, *Wisdom of the Zohar*, 373–76. On the role of *Malkhut* as an intermediary, see Schwartz, *Mahashevet Habad*, 55–56n107.
61. T2, 7:82a.
62. LT *Ahare* 27b. See also TO 37a-b; LT *Be-ha'alotekha* 30a; MAHZ *Ketuvim*, i, 21.
63. Wolfson, *Alef, Mem, Tau*, 108–9.
64. T2, 7:82a.
65. MAHZ 5564, 199.
66. See Wolfson, *Alef, Mem, Tau*, 111; see also Wolfson, *Open Secret*, 105–6.
67. On the use of this wordplay in Habad thought, see Wolfson, *Open Secret*, 103–14.
68. Wolfson, *Open Secret*, 105.
69. See MAHZ 5571, 168. See also MAHZ 5564, 199; LT *Ha'azinu* 74d. On the symbolism of *Ze'ir anpin* in Lurianic kabbalah, see Scholem, *Kabbalah*, 141–42.
70. See, for example, T1, 39:52b, 40:55a, 42:59a, 51:72b; T2, 5:80a; T4, 6:110a; TO 64d. See also Schwartz, *Mahashevet Habad*, 50.
71. T2, 7:82a.
72. LT *Shir ha-shirim* 8b.
73. The notion of *'Atik* or *'Atik yomin* ("the ancient of days") denotes a higher aspect of *Keter*, as opposed to *Arikh anpin*, which denotes its lower aspect. See Foxbrunner, *Habad*, 71–72. Both these terms come from the *Idrot* of the *Zohar* where they are used interchangeably as names of the first *partsuf* (see, for example, Giller, *Reading the Zohar*, 105; Hellner-Eshed, *A River Flows from Eden*, 272); a clear distinction between *'Atik* and *Arikh* in Shneur Zalman's teachings is influenced by the Lurianic kabbalah, see Giller, *Reading the Zohar*, 109–10; Vital, *'Ets hayim*, Gate 12, chapter 1, 167; Schwartz, *Mahashevet Habad*, 53–54n99, 55n107.
74. LT *Shabat shuvah*, 67c.
75. For the Aristotelian concept of eternity, see Wolfson, *The Philosophy of Spinoza*, i, 358–69.
76. On the relation between the Tetragrammaton and the order of time, see, for example, *Seder tefilot* 76b; MAHZ *Nevi'im*, 116.
77. Wolfson presents a similar Habad model of time's coming-into-being based on his analysis of the writings of Dov Ber. In his book on time in kabbalah (*Alef, Mem, Tau*, 109), Wolfson distinguishes between three levels: *Malkhut* as the origin of time, YHVH as the "compresence of the three temporal modalities—what was, what is, and what will be," and the light of *Ein Sof* "that is utterly beyond time." The fragment of Shneur Zalman's teachings quoted above presents, however, a slightly different picture: *Ein Sof* is entirely above any temporal or quasi-temporal characterization; the Tetragrammaton transcends temporality, yet comprises *modi* of priority and posteriority; eternal *Malkhut* is the source of time, as it comprises all three tenses; and finally, the lower worlds are subject to

temporality. The discrepancies between this model and that of Wolfson have their source in Dov Ber's text, wherein he transposes the source of time into the Tetragrammaton, and states that contrary to his father's words, it "comprises past, present and future as one, but [...] does not belong to that which is entirely above time." See Dov Ber Shneuri, *Imre binah*, Gate of *keri'at shema'*, 40c.

78. On the notion of *Adam kadmon* in the Lurianic kabbalah, see: Scholem, *Kabbalah*, 137; Fine, *Physician*, 133–34.
79. See MAHZ 5565, i, 323.
80. See Idel, "Higher than Time," 182–83; Idel, "Time and History," 162–63.
81. *Bereshit rabah*, 3:7. The midrash does not conceive of *seder ha-zemanim* in the same way as Shneur Zalman, as a quasi-temporal entity.
82. On the rabbinic time, see Stern, "The Rabbinic Concept."
83. LT *Balak* 70c.
84. See Vital, *'Ets hayim*, Gate 1, Section 1, 25, and see *Seder tefilot* 75d–76a.
85. Arama, *'Akedat Yitshak*, Be-reshit, 40a-b.
86. Schneersohn, *Sefer ha-hakirah*, 114a.
87. See Wolfson, *Crescas' Critique*, 93–98, 290–91, 657–58; Harvey, *Physics and Metaphysics*, 4–8.
88. See Wolfson, *Crescas' Critique*, 290–91. This contradicts Maimonides in *Moreh nevukhim*, 1:30. See also Wolfson (*Crescas' Critique*, 663) and Rudavsky (*Time Matters*, 46–49) on the disassociation of time from creation in Crescas and its consequences for his doctrine of creation.
89. Arama, *'Akedat Yitshak*, Be-reshit, 40a-b.
90. LT *Balak* 70c.
91. See Schneersohn, *Derekh mitsvotekha*, 57b.
92. This idea is attested in various kabbalistic sources. See, for example, Wolfson, *Alef, Mem, Tau*, 73, on the order of time as the root of time in Cordovero's *Pardes rimonim*; see also Idel, "Time and History," 162.
93. *Seder tefilot*, 76b. Dov Ber Shneuri further develops this idea in *Imre binah*, Gate of *Keri'at Shema'*, 42c-d.
94. On the model of continuous creation in Shneur Zalman's thought, see Schwartz, *Mahashevet Habad*, 35–36. For a brief discussion of the theme in the teachings of Levi Yitshak of Berdichev, see Mayse, "Eternity in Hasidism," 231–32.
95. One of the morning blessings before the prayer *Shema'*.
96. See his *Kedushat Levi*, Bereshit, 1, translated in Green, *Speaking Torah*, i, 80; discussed in Mayse, "Eternity in Hasidism," 232.
97. See Hillman, *Igerot Ba'al ha-Tanya*, 23, and ibid., 228–29 (Levine, *Igerot kodesh*, i, 184-6), for Shneur Zalman's Yiddish letter taking a similar stance.
98. See LT *Yom ha-kipurim*, 68c; see also LT *Be-ha'alotekha* 33a. This is related to the traditional belief that a person surrenders his soul to God at dusk and receives a new soul the next morning, when "he is made as a new creation" (*Shulhan 'arukh Rabenu ha-Zaken*, Orah hayim, 1:4). A brief

comparison between Shneur Zalman and Menahem Mendel of Vitebsk can be found in Hallamish, "The Teachings."
99. See LT *Yom ha-kipurim*, 68c. On *ratso* and *shov* see Elior, "HaBaD," 178–81; Elior, *Paradoxical Ascent*, 30 and 127–34; Idel, *Hasidism*, 123; Schwartz, *Mahashevet Habad*, 58n109; Wolfson, *Open Secret*, 145.
100. See, for example, TO 2c-d; MAHZ 5565, i, 126; 5566, i, 61; 5568, 543. See also Schwartz, *Mahashevet Habad*, 58.
101. For gentiles, see *Seder tefilot*, 303a-b. See also Foxbrunner, *Habad*, 108, and the sources listed there. For heretics, see T2, 2:77a-b. See also Schneersohn, *Sefer ha-hakirah*, 3b.
102. LT *Ba-midbar* 1a.
103. On the occasionalist features of Shneur Zalman's teachings and their sources in the Maggid of Mezrich, see Schwartz, *Mahashevet Habad*, 58 and 35n27. Shneur Zalman may also have been influenced by the occasionalism of the Kalam school of thought as mediated by Maimonides's *Moreh nevukhim*, 1:73–74, particularly propositions 6 and 7, whereby God is responsible for every change that occurs in the world, as he creates all accidents at will constantly. Using an example provided by Maimonides, when one dyes white cloth red, it is not the color that penetrates the white cloth when it comes into contact with the red pigment, but God who creates the attribute of redness in the cloth (proposition 6). Even life and death are accidents according to Kalam; God constantly destroys and renews life during the whole existence of a living being (proposition 7). Although Maimonides dismisses this view as mockery of God, Shneur Zalman seems to accept it in his concept of existence that is repeatedly annihilated and re-created by the flow of divine energy.
104. See *Seder tefilot*, 303b.
105. See T1, 1:6a.
106. Job 31:2. On the soul as part of God, see, for example, T1, 2:6a, 35:44a; TO 16a; LT *Va-yikra* 2d.
107. Dov Ber of Mezrich, *Or ha-emet*, 8a, quoted and discussed in Idel, "Higher than Time," 205–6.
108. See bBerakhot 6a.
109. The relation between *ratso va-shov* and time in Shneur Zalman's teachings has been noted by Foxbrunner. See his *Habad*, 71 and 249n71 for the list of sources.
110. See, for example, LT *Hukat* 65a.
111. See, for example, T1, 41:58b; T4, 6:110a; LT *Rosh ha-shanah*, 61a; MAHZ 5567, 347; 'Inyanim, 127; *Ketsarim*, 329.
112. LT *Rosh ha-shanah* 61a. Similar etymology appears in the teachings of Shneur Zalman's teacher, the Maggid, who derives the word *sha'ah* from the verse "do not turn [*al yish'u*] to deceitful promises" (Exod. 5:9). See his *Magid devarav le-Ya'akov, Or Torah*, 71a, par. 231.
113. *Zeman mah* in the Hebrew text. Inverted commas appear between the letters *mem* and *he* of the word *mah*, possibly alluding to a link between

the atomic unit of time and the divine name 45 (the numerical value of the word *mah* is 45), which in turn is associated with *Ze'ir anpin*, the supra-temporal source of time. The author, however, does not elaborate on it in the text that follows, and it is possible that the inverted commas were added either by the transcriber of the oral *ma'amar* or by the editors of the printed edition.

114. MAHZ 5566, i, 61. See also MAHZ 5568, i, 542–43 and 5563, ii, 753 where the *ratso va-shov* of a time unit is compared to the cycle of exhalation and inhalation: "The meaning of the division of an hour into the number of exactly 1080 moments [See Maimonides, *Mishneh Torah*, Laws of the Sanctification of the Moon, 6:2], comes from the measure of 1080 breaths in every hour, and each and every breath consists of [two] aspects of *ratso* and *shov* [. . .] and it is called a heartbeat, for the heart beats in [the rhythm of] *ratso va-shov*, because it beats in double beats: the first one is the withdrawal of the life force, and the second one is the drawing down of it [. . .]. And similarly, this is the case of the material breath in man's nostrils, as it is written: 'All in whose nostrils was the breath of life' [Gen. 7:22], etc., as in the example of a sleeping man's breath, as it is known, that the measure of the duration of a breath that consists of the above mentioned *ratso va-shov* is one moment out of 1080 moments of an hour." MAHZ 5568, i, 543.
115. See also Schwartz, *Mahashevet Habad*, 37n33; Foxbrunner, *Habad*, 71.
116. For the correspondence between the days of the week and the attributes, see, for example, LT *Pekude* 5b; *Seder tefilot* 26d-27a; MAHZ 5566, i, 60. For the sources of this concept in kabbalah, see Scholem, *Kabbalah*, 100; Tishby, *Wisdom of the Zohar*, 283 (where he discusses the zoharic tradition, according to which *Yesod*, rather than *Malkhut*, corresponds to the Sabbath). See also Cordovero, *Pardes*, 333–34.
117. See, for example, MAHZ 5566, i, 61; TO 7d.
118. See Cordovero, *Tefilah le-Moshe*, discussed in Idel, "Sabbath," 80–81.
119. MAHZ 5566, 60.
120. Musaf prayer for Rosh ha-shanah.
121. See, for example, MAHZ *Nevi'im*, 9; *Parshiyot*, i, 409.
122. See Barayta de-rabi Yishma'el in *Sifra*, 1a-b.
123. See MAHZ 5565, 320–21.
124. Wolfson, *Alef, Mem, Tau*, 83.
125. On the role of the divine speech in Shneur Zalman's doctrine of creation and its sources in the teachings of the Besht, see Idel, "Le-'olam ha-Shem," 239–43. See also Foxbrunner, *Habad*, 105. On the role of speech in the manifestation of the divine in kabbalah, see Scholem, *Kabbalah*, 99.
126. See Zii, 155b.
127. See *b*Berakhot 32a.
128. MAHZ 5564, 205.
129. See Zi, 116b, 194a; Ziii, 58a-b.
130. On *Shekhinah* as *et*, see Zi, 15b, 247a; Zii, 81b, 90a, 135b; Ziii, 190b. See

also T2, 2:77a-b, where Shneur Zalman, following Zi, 1:15b, interprets the verse, "You keep them all alive" (*atah mehayeh et kulam*, Neh. 9:6) as referring to the totality of the Hebrew alphabet (*alef* and *tav* of the word *atah*) and the five organs of verbal articulation (the letter *he* of the word *atah*, whose numerical value is five). The notion of *Malkhut* as the source of speech is further emphasized by reference to *Sefer yetsirah* (2:3), where the twenty-two letters of the alphabet are said to be situated within the mouth in the five organs of verbal articulation. This, in turn, corroborates the description of *Malkhut* as a mouth in *Tikune zohar*, Introduction, 17a, which is also adopted by Shneur Zalman, for example, in T4, 26:144a.

131. See MAHZ *Ketsarim*, 43–44.
132. MAHZ 5563, ii, 747.
133. Since every supernal day contains one thousand earthly years.
134. MAHZ 5563, ii, 748. See also MAHZ 5567, 211; TO 7d.
135. MAHZ *Ketuvim*, i, 30–31.
136. On *Hokhmah* and *Binah* as intuitive thought and its conceptualisation, see T1, 3:7b.
137. Wolfson, *Alef, Mem, Tau*, 229n266.
138. See, for example, MAHZ 5567, 340 and LT *Hukat* 64d, where Shneur Zalman explains that the light and divine life force are renewed every day in the act of continuous creation. See also MAHZ 5569, 286 and *Seder tefilot*, 234a, where he describes Rosh ha-shanah and the New Moon as days that contain the totality of the divine light and life force, usually fragmented, respectively, in the rest of the days of the year and the month. See also T4, 14:120a-b, where he writes that, every Rosh ha-shanah, the divine life force comes into the world afresh, drawn from a higher level than in the preceding year.
139. LT *Hukat* 64d–65a.
140. See, for example, T1, 43:61b, 48:67a; T2, 7:84a, 10:88a; TO 64a-c; LT *Nitsavim* 47b, based on *b*Hagigah 13a. See also Wolfson, *Alef, Mem, Tau*, 56, where he quotes Judah Loew ben Bezalel's (the Maharal of Prague, d. 1609) statement that "time and place are one matter."

Chapter 2

1. See Idel, "Some Concepts of Time," 153–54; "Higher than Time," 180–81. See also my Introduction above.
2. See, for example, Hillman, *Igerot Ba'al ha-Tanya*, 111, 231 (Levine, *Igerot kodesh*, i, 115–19, 183–84); Etkes, *Rabbi Shneur Zalman*, 132–50.
3. See Hillman, *Igerot Ba'al ha-Tanya*, 74; Levine, *Igerot kodesh*, i, 186–87.
4. On the espionage conducted by Habad Hasidim during Napoleon's Russian campaign, see Etkes, *Rabbi Shneur Zalman*, 261–64 and 270–73. For the famous letter in which Shneur Zalman allegedly states that Napoleon's victory would enhance the Jews' wealth and social position but

estrange them from God, and concluding that they should support the Russians, see Heilman, *Bet rabi*, 47a-b; Rodkinson, *Toldot 'amude Habad*, 83; Hillman, *Igerot Ba'al ha-Tanya*, 238; Levine, *Igerot kodesh*, i, 150–51. For discussion of this letter, see Loewenthal, *Communicating*, 209–10; Teitelbaum, *Ha-rav mi-Ladi*, 156. However, Etkes (*Rabbi Shneur Zalman*, 279–80) argues that Shneur Zalman was not the author of the letter.

5. On the attitude of rabbinic literature to history, see Yerushalmi, *Zakhor*, 21–24.
6. See also Jacobson, "Torat ha-beri'ah," 308–68; Schwartz, *Mahashevet Habad*, 23–137; Hallamish, "Mishnato ha-'iyunit," 112–35.
7. T2, 7:81b.
8. See Rashi on Judg. 5:14. Rashi sees in verse 14 ("After thee, Benjamin, among thy people ['amamekha]") the prophecy of Barak and Deborah foretelling the rise of King Saul from the tribe of Benjamin, who will "stone and slacken [ya'amim] him [Amalek] like dying ['omemot] embers."
9. On God as king reigning over people in Shneur Zalman's concept of creation, see Jacobson, "Torat ha-beri'ah," 340–45.
10. See also *Seder tefilot* 47b, according to which the multitude of contractions results in a multitude of generations in time and space, which form the nation for God to reign over. The multitude of contractions increases God's glory, as "A numerous people is the glory of a king" (Prov. 14:28). This interpretation of *tsimtsum* complicates the dichotomy according to which Hasidim applied *tsimtsum* to the soul, as opposed to Moshe Hayim Luzzatto and, influenced by him, the Vilna Gaon, who applied it to the realm of historiosophy (see Shuchat, *'Olam nistar*, 122–25). For Shneur Zalman, the spiritual (or psychological) and the historiosophical are two intertwined realms. See also note 184 to chapter 3 below.
11. For the concepts of the breaking of the vessels and the emendation, see Scholem, *Kabbalah*, 138–39; *Major Trends*, 266–68; Fine, *Physician*, 134–38. For a comparison of Shneur Zalman's and Isaac Luria's models of creation, see Hallamish, "Mishnato ha-'iyunit," 105–111, and Schatz Uffenheimer, *Hasidism as Mysticism*, 270–71.
12. TO 27c. See also Wolfson, *Open Secret*, 335n95, where he describes the breaking of the vessels in Shneur Zalman's teachings as "The metaphoric trope to mark the transition from the aspect of boundlessness [*bilti ba'al gevul*] to the aspect of boundary [*gevul*]," and points to the elucidation of this approach in the book of Shneur Zalman's student, Aharon ha-Levi of Starosielce, *Sha'are ha-yihud veha-emunah*, iii, 20b–21a.
13. *Seder tefilot*, 237a.
14. See *Midrash Tanhuma*, Naso, 16.
15. See, for example, *Seder tefilot*, 109b-d, where Shneur Zalman states explicitly that God's dwelling place in the lower worlds is the reason for the contraction, following the maxim that "last in deed, first in thought" (*sof ma'aseh be-mahashavah tehilah*). The actual redemption in the end of days was part of the initial divine plan of creation (on the source of the maxim,

see Wolfson, *Language, Eros, Being*, 506n207). To this interpretation of the maxim Shneur Zalman adds yet another layer: the establishment of God's dwelling place depends specifically on the deeds of Jews, as the Jews also "originated in the beginning of thought," and "the last in production, that is, the dwelling place in the lower worlds, is achieved through purification by means of the fulfillment of the Torah and its commandments."

16. TI, 36:46a.
17. See TI, 36:46a.
18. See also Shneur Zalman's commentary on Psalm 145 in the morning prayer in *Seder tefilot*, 53d–54a, which further underscores the transposition of particular motifs from Jewish history onto the larger framework of cosmic history. In the commentary, Shneur Zalman explains the verse from Amos 9:11, "the fallen booth of David" (standing in its original context for the disintegration of the Davidic dynasty), as referring to the divine presence, which falls into the lower worlds in order to enliven them. As a result, the active, overflowing and limitless life-giving force (the *Hesed* aspect of *Malkhut*) becomes confined within the boundaries of the material world, which effectively render it a limited entity. Yet, according to the Psalmist, God also "supports all who fall" (Ps. 145:14), a verse interpreted as the promise of the emendation and redemption, and a process that takes place throughout the duration of the exile, leading to restoring "the fallen booth of David."
19. See *b*Megilah 29a: "R. Shimon ben Yohai says: come and see how beloved the children of Israel are before the Holy One, blessed is he! For wherever they were exiled, the *Shekhinah* was with them. When they were exiled to Egypt, the *Shekhinah* was with them [. . .]. When they were exiled to Babylonia, the *Shekhinah* was with them." For the use of this expression in Shneur Zalman's lore, see, for example, TI, 17:23a; T4, 4:105b, 21:133b, 25:140a; TO 5a, 11a, 38a, 51a, 100b 119a; LT *Matot*, 83d, *Mas'e* 88b, *Tetse* 35d, *Shabat shuvah* 67c, *Shir ha-shirim* 35b.
20. This is, most likely, a trace of Lurianic kabbalah, in which one can find examples that conflate the emendation with messianic redemption and define it as the a priori purpose of creation rather than an a posteriori salvaging world following a cosmic catastrophe. See, for example, Idel, *Messianic Mystics*, 172, quoting Vital's *'Ets hayim*. However, this idea occurs in earlier kabbalists, too. See, for example, Idel's discussion of Meir ibn Gabbai (1480–c.1540), a Spanish-born kabbalist, in his "Multiple Forms," 54–55.
21. See TI, 6:10b.
22. TI, 6:10b.
23. See TI, 6:10b–11a. Even the worldly entities that are not outwardly impure belong to the "other side" and the husks. Nonetheless, Shneur Zalman divides the husks into two categories. The higher one, *nogah* (radiance), consists of a mixture of good and evil, and comprises all the entities that may or may not be purified by means of divine service. This includes the

animal soul and the body. The lower category consists of three impure husks: *ruah se'arah*, *'anan gadol*, and *esh mitlakahat* (stormy wind, huge cloud, and flashing fire; the names of the four husks are borrowed from Ezek. 1:4), and it is a domain of complete impurity, associated with gentile bodies and souls, with unclean food, and with the forbidden parts and mixtures of clean food. These three husks will be purified at the end of days.

24. See, for example, TO 100b, where the exiled *Shekhinah* is presented allegorically as the bride waiting for her groom in the tanners' market; the tanners' market, a despicable place exuding an unpleasant odor, represents the realm of nature (*levush ha-teva'*).
25. T1, 19:24b–25a.
26. See, for example, T1, 2:6a, 35:44a, 41:65b; T4, 15:123a; TO 24a, 84b; LT *Va-yikra* 2d, 6a, 39d, *Va-yikra hosafot* 51c, *Ba-midbar* 1b, *Hukat* 61d, *Mas'e* 91, 28c, 34a, c, *'Ekev* 13d, *Tetse* 37d, *Rosh ha-shanah* 62c, *Ha'azinu* 74c, 77c, *Shir ha-shirim* 2b, 5c. On body as "the exile of the soul," see, for example, TO 64d; LT *Shabat shuvah* 67c, *Matot* 83d.
27. See, for example, T1, 1–13:5a-19b; MAHZ *Parshiyot*, i, 140–41. For the three garments of the soul in Habad thought, see Hallamish, "Mishnato ha-'iyunit, 227–32.
28. See T3, 6:96a. In some places, Shneur Zalman refers to the agents of the evil side as the "Ten crowns of impurity" (*ketarim di-mesa'avuta*), which parallel the ten *sefirot* of holiness according to the oft-quoted statement that "God set the one over against the other one" (Eccl. 7:14). See, for example, T1, 6:10a.
29. See, for example, T3, 6:96b.
30. T4, 25:139b–140a.
31. See also T3, 6:96b.
32. See *Bereshit rabah* 16:4; *Vayikra rabah* 13:5. Shneur Zalman occasionally changes the list of the four kingdoms that enslaved Israel by substituting Media with Egypt. See, for example, MAHZ 5566, i, 232.
33. See MAHZ 5568, ii, 655, 694; TO 41c; LT *Be-ha'alotekha* 35d. Each refer to the vision of the metal statute from the book of Daniel and sees in Babylonia, as the "head of gold" (see Dan. 2:38), the crown (*Keter*) at the top of the world of husks; Media and Persia, the silver arms, stand for the *sefirot* of *Hesed* and *Gevurah*; and Greece, the brass, for *Hokhmah*. Shneur Zalman manifestly takes Greece to symbolize non-Jewish wisdom and philosophy, which is why he identifies it as the *sefirah* of *Hokhmah*'s counterpart in the world of husks. See, for example, TO 41a. In MAHZ *Ethalekh*, 63–64, however, Shneur Zalman changes the order of the exiles and presents Egypt as the *Keter* of the world of husks, the Egyptian wisdom as *Hokhmah* and *Binah*, Babylonia and Media as *Hesed* and *Gevurah*, while Greece is the "middle line" of the world of husks, namely *Da'at*, *Tif'eret* and *Yesod*.
34. T4, 4:105b. Symptomatically, given Shneur Zalman's lack of consistent historiosophical outlook regarding subsequent developments of Jewish

history, he elsewhere ascribes similar features to the exile of Edom. See, for example, TO 24a.
35. Similar motifs can be found throughout the exegetic and the kabbalistic tradition. See, for example, David Kimhi on Isa. 43:19: "'If thou turn unto the Lord thy God with all thine heart and with all thy souls' (Deut. 30:10): those returning to Babylonia [*Bavel*] did not turn unto the Lord with all their hearts [*be-khol levavam*]"; see also Luzzatto, *Adir ba-marom ha-shalem*, 379, were *Bavel* becomes *levav* by dint of Moses's emendation.
36. Based on the verse "God set the one over against the other one" (Eccl. 7:14).
37. See MAHZ *Razal*, 204; based on Rashi to *b*Ta'anit 10a; see also *b*Shabat 113b and *b*Zevahim 113b.
38. See T4, 4:105a. See also Zii, 63b.
39. See Zii, 63b, where prayer "out of the depths" refers to the prayer that draws from the "depth of all": the *sefirah* of *Hokhmah*.
40. *Shemot rabah*, 35:5.
41. LT *Be-ha'alotekha* 35d.
42. See TO 118b; MAHZ 5568, i, 96; T1, 4:8a–5:10a.
43. "The Hellenizers did not want to spill the blood of Israel, but to make them forget God's Torah," as it is phrased in the prayer *'Al ha-nisim*.
44. TO 41a. See also TO 30a, 34a, 41a; MAHZ 5568, ii, 655. This is slightly modified in another *ma'amar*, where the Greeks' opposition to the Torah locates them in the "middle line" of *da'at*, *tif'eret*, and *yesod* within the hierarchy of the evil *sefirot*, in juxtaposition to the Torah, which forms the middle line within the Godhead's scheme of emanations; see MAHZ *Ethalekh*, 64.
45. *b*Megilah 29a.
46. T1, 17:23a.
47. See T1, 17:23a. See also T1, 26:32b; T4, 18:126b. Moreover, in TO 83a, the iron barrier that separates Israel from "their father in heaven" rose after the destruction of the Temple and is thus explicitly linked to the exile.
48. See *Midrash Tanhuma*, Terumah 7.
49. For the rabbinical discussion of the sins which brought the destruction of the Temples, see *b*Yoma 9a-b.
50. Shneur Zalman uses here the term "attributes" (*midot*) in order to link the wickedness of the Canaanite nations and the sins of Israel with the construction of the lower and impure world. In kabbalistic symbolism, the three upper *sefirot* are referred to as the brains (*mohin*), and the seven lower *sefirot* as emotional attributes (*midot*) (see, for example, T1, 3:7a-b). In kabbalistic literature, the terms *sefirot* and *midot* are often used interchangeably. See Hallamish, *Introduction*, 125; Scholem, *Kabbalah*, 100. See also *Seder tefilot*, 189b, where the purification of the seven lower *sefirot* of the world of husks is not associated explicitly with the Babylonian exile. Rather, the seven evil *sefirot* derive from the death of the seven primordial kings and the breaking of the vessels. See, for example, MAHZ 5565, ii,

774. On the death of the kings in kabbalah, see Wolfson, "Min u-minut," 254n109, and the literature listed there.
51. LT *Matot* 85d–86a; see also Foxbrunner, *Habad*, 90.
52. Based on Hab. 1:3.
53. *b*Shabat 31a.
54. See LT *Matot* 85d–86a.
55. *b*Pesahim 116b, "In every generation a person in obliged to look at himself as though he departed from Egypt."
56. TO 51a.
57. TO 64d.
58. See, for example, T1, 39:52b, 40:55a, 42:59a, 51:72b; T2, 5:80a; T4, 6:110a; TO 64d. See also Schwartz, *Mahashevet Habad*, 50.
59. See, for example, TO 64a–c. Elsewhere, Shneur Zalman attributes the creation of limits and borders in the lower worlds to the influx from the vessels (*kelim*) of the attributes of the World of Emanation. See TO 102a. It is worth noting that, for this reason, the World of Making is explicitly referred to by the name "Egypt" (see LT *Shelah* 47c. See also LT *Shir ha-shirim* 14d).
60. TO 103c–104c; see also TO 64d; MAHZ 5562, 148; 5565, 394, 444; 5566, 242.
61. See, for example, TO 49d, 58b, 71d.
62. TO 51a; see also TO 105a; *Seder tefilot* 8d.
63. See TO 51a, 58c–d; LT *Ba-midbar* 11d. See also Ornet, *Ratso va-shov*, 127–28, which discusses the role of the throat as a transition point between intellect and emotions in the context of worship through love of God.
64. TO 22c.
65. TO 22c. Shneur Zalman associates the name Haran with Ps 69:3 ("My throat is dried"), as Haran is the anagram of *nihar* ("is dried"). See, for example, TO 21c–d; Vital, *'Ets hayim*, Gate 28, chapter 5, 68.
66. On the role of divine speech in Shneur Zalman's doctrine of creation and its sources in the teachings of the Besht, see Idel, "Le-'olam ha-Shem," 239–43. See also Foxbrunner, *Habad*, 105. On the role of speech in the manifestation of the divine in kabbalah, see Scholem, *Kabbalah*, 99.
67. See TO 57.
68. TO 22b–c.
69. See, for example, LT *Ba-midbar* 10c.
70. See T1, 47:66b; TO 35b, 67a; LT *Ba-midbar* 2b–c, 10c. On the body as the confinement of the soul, see Wolfson, *Open Secret*, 139–41.
71. See LT *Emor* 35c, where the Exodus beyond the limitation of physicality is transposed onto the discourse of the divine names, whereby Elohim represents the exile (by its numerical value), and the Tetragrammaton (comprising all three tenses) represents the divine reality that transcends temporal limitations. Shneur Zalman refers here to Pharaoh's words, "I do not know the Lord [YHVH]" (Exod. 5:2), as evidence that

the Tetragrammaton was not known in the Egyptian exile but was only revealed later. Elsewhere (TO 56d), he quotes Exod. 6:4, where God explains that he revealed himself to the Patriarchs by the name of Elohim and to Moses by the name YHVH. This distinction between Elohim and YHVH as referring, respectively, to the natural and the supranatural resonates with the Nachmanides's comment on Exod. 6:4, where he interprets the verse as related to the miracles that God performed for the Patriarchs, which were confined to the natural framework, in contrast to the miracles he performed for the Israelites on their way out of Egypt, which changed the course of nature.
72. TO 58b.
73. *Malkhut* is therefore referred to as the Upper Land (*erets 'elyonah*) in the theosophic structure, which parallels the Land of Israel (*erets tahtonah*) in the physical world.
74. See LT *Shir ha-shirim* 45c. It mirrors the idea presented above, whereby the throat prevents the revelation of the light originating in the brain within the heart.
75. See LT *Shir ha-shirim* 28d.
76. Hebr. *hester panim*, an expression borrowed from Deut. 31:17.
77. See, for example, MAHZ 5565, i, 495.
78. Or, alternatively, to pregnancy and birth. See, for example, TO 58d.
79. TO 61a.
80. LT *Pekude* 4d. On the broken heart (*lev nishbar* or *tsebrokhenkeyt*) in Habad, see Loewenthal, *Communicating*, 195–98; Etkes, *Rabbi Shneur Zalman*, 112–14.
81. TO 56d; see also MAHZ *Parshiyot*, i, 235.
82. TO 64d. On the notions of "arousal from below" and "arousal from above" in kabbalah and in Hasidism, see Idel, *Kabbalah and Eros*, 84.
83. See TO 98d, based on *b*Shabat 88a.
84. See TO 98d.
85. TO 65b.
86. On the traditional claim that the Patriarchs kept the Torah, see Urbach, *The Sages*, 335–36.
87. See LT *Mas'e* 88c–89a.
88. Because the Bible describes it as the place of "fiery serpents and scorpions" (Deut. 8:15).
89. Based on Ezekiel's reference to the wilderness as the "wilderness of the peoples" (Ezek. 20:35).
90. Shneur Zalman compares the Congregation of Israel (*keneset Yisra'el*, also identified with *Malkhut*) to a sheep, and reads the verse, "Like a ewe, dumb before those who shear her" (Isa. 53:7) as a hint at the husks that draw the life-giving energy from the hair of *Malkhut*, namely, from its external part, which has no connection to its essence (since haircuts are not painful). The silence of the sheep at the shearing symbolizes the absence of the creative divine speech in the realm of husks: the wilderness

(see LT *Mas'e* 88c). The link between the wilderness and the (divine) speech, based on the fact that these two Hebrew words are derived from the same root (*dalet, bet, resh*), appears throughout Shneur Zalman's teachings, for example, in TO 23b, where the generation of the desert is blamed for not being willing to perform the commandments by means of both speech and deed but only by means of thought, that is, exclusively by way of spirituality. Interestingly, a similar attitude is described (see LT *Shelah* 38b) as the sin of the spies (Num. 13:1–14:9).

91. See also LT *Re'eh* 32b-c, where Shneur Zalman plays on the proximity of the terms wilderness (*midbar*) and speech (*davar*). The wilderness, that is fallow land, stands for thoughts, speech, and deeds that are not directed at God and do not function as worship. *Midbar* is also the place into which the sparks of holiness have fallen. In this allegory, the dispersion of the sparks of holiness is compared to the loss of precious objects, and they can be recovered from the wilderness, that is, from the "words of the letters that make up prayer" and through the study of Torah. One should therefore look deeply into one's thoughts and words, searching for any wrongdoing, in order to trigger the flow of God's mercy and thus elevate the sparks.

92. TO 49a.

93. See TO 54a. The distinction between the audible revelation on Sinai and the visual revelation at the end of days is based, on the one hand, on the emphasis on hearing in "we will do" and "we will hear," and on seeing in Isaiah's prophecy, "For every eye shall behold" (Isa. 52:8), on the other hand. I will discuss it in detail in the next chapter.

94. TO 54a; see also TO 15a.

95. TO 49a.

96. On the purification of sparks in kabbalah and Hasidism, see Jacobs, "The Uplifting of Sparks," 106–26.

97. See, for example, MAHZ 5566, i, 232, where the sin of the Tree of Knowledge and the biblical description of the expulsion from the Garden of Eden are used as a metaphor of the exile of *Shekhinah* and the dispersion of holy sparks. The four rivers flowing out of Eden are identified with the four exiles (see *Bereshit rabah* 16:4; *Vayikra rabah* 13:5), which represent the four ways by which the sparks and the souls of Israel fell under the power of husks and the seventy gentile nations.

98. See *Seder tefilot*, 53d-54a. On the traditional belief that the world will last for six thousand years, see bA'vodah zarah 9a.

99. On the 288 sparks in kabbalah, see Jacobs, "The Uplifting of Sparks," 106–7; Scholem, *Major Trends*, 268.

100. TO 27d. On the Lurianic notion of the Messiah, who appears only in order to bring the process of *tikun* to conclusion, see Scholem, *The Messianic Idea*, 47–48.

101. From the Rosh Hashanah liturgy. See TO 5d.

102. TO 5d-6a.

103. Hebrew: *hakamat Shekhinta me-'afra*, based on Zi, 203a. Hillman, *Igerot Ba'al ha-Tanya*, 18. See also Hallamish, "The Teaching," 273–74.
104. See LT *Hukat* 59d–60a.
105. See *Tikune zohar* xxi, 48b.
106. T4, 26:144b–145a.
107. See, for example, TI, 37:48b, 49:69a. See also Ornet, *Ratso va*-shov, 136; Wolfson, *Open Secret*, 140.
108. MAHZ *Ketsarim*, 119. See Loewenthal, *Communication*, 69 and 243n32.
109. MAHZ *Ketsarim*, 119.
110. On worship through corporeality in Hasidism, see Kauffmann, *Be-khol derakhekha*. On Shneur Zalman's doctrinal innovations aimed at making the Hasidic spirituality available to nonscholarly layers of the community, see chapter 4.
111. See *m*Avot 4:2.
112. TI, 37:46b.
113. See Green, "Around the Maggid's Table," 164–65n102; Idel, *Messianic Mystics*, 222–27 and 405n39. See, however, Sagiv (*Ha-shoshelet*, 378–32), who downplays the significance of the messianic motifs, seeing in them part of rhetoric and an expression of a vague messianic hope rather than a call for collective redemptive action.
114. See Mark, *The Scroll*, 65–128; Green, *Tormented Master*, 182–220.
115. See Mark, *Megilat setarim*.
116. See Mark, *The Scroll*.
117. On a brief overlook of *beinoni* and his place and tasks in the world, see Etkes, *Rabbi Shneur Zalman*, 103–31. See also chapter 4.
118. *m*Avot 4:2.
119. Maimonides, *Mishneh Torah*, Laws of the Red Heifer, 3:9.
120. LT *Hukat* 56a-c. This is based on the phrasing of the biblical verse "This is the ordinance of the law [*zot hukat ha-Torah*] which the Lord hath commanded, saying, Speak unto the children of Israel, that they bring thee a red heifer without spot, wherein is no blemish, and upon which never came yoke" (Num. 19:2), which may suggest that the law of the red heifer is the quintessential law of the Torah.
121. LT *Hukat* 56d.
122. Shneur Zalman refers here to a verse from *Sefer yetsirah* 1:8, "If thy heart fail thee ['im rats libekha] return to thy place," which originally refers to *ratso va-shov* in Ezek 1:14.
123. The letters are called vessels as they contain the light of *Ein Sof*. See LT *Hukat* 57a.
124. *b*Makot 23b. See also Urbach, *The Sages*, 342–43.
125. The development of this concept in the teachings of the last Habad rebbe, Menahem Mendel Schneerson, is discussed in detail by Wolfson (*Open Secret*, 130–60).
126. See TI, 37:47b–48a
127. TI, 37:47a.

128. See T1, 37:47b–48a.
129. See LT *Ahare* 25d–26a.
130. Garb, *Yearning of the Soul*, 52.
131. See T5, 162a-b. On the "hidden love" possessed by every Jewish person regardless of merit, see Foxbrunner, *Habad*, 99–103; Hallamish, "Mishnato ha-'iyunit," 320–23; Etkes, *Rabbi Shneur Zalman*, 118–24.
132. This is related to the idea that the word *barukh*, which opens the standard blessing formula, is etymologically related to kneeling (and in the *'Amidah*, it translates into the practice of bending the knee when saying the word *barukh*), and as such symbolizes movement from up downward, not only in this world but also in the world of the *sefirot*. See, for example, TO 20a, 53b; LT *Be-hukotai* 48b, *Seder tefilot* 142b. In TO 37c, Shneur Zalman derives the word *barukh* from the word *bending* (*mavrikh*—see *m*Kilayim 7:1: "He who bends the vine shoot into the ground").
133. See TO 37b-c, where the blessing recited before fulfilling a *mitsvah* connects the material with the spiritual dimension of the Torah and all its commandments. The Torah, as well as the ritual object employed in the performance of a commandment, is described as a material "sign" signifying the spiritual dimension of reality; by reciting an appropriate benediction prior to performing a *mitsvah*, one connects these two dimensions of reality. Consequently, by drawing down vitality from the supratemporal reality of the divine, the spatiotemporal Torah and its *mitsvot* become, for Shneur Zalman, the "source of time and space." See also LT *Be-hukotai* 48b, where he associates the benediction (from the Passover *Hagadah*) "Blessed is the Omnipresent [*ha-Makom*], blessed is he!" with drawing divine vitality into space (*makom*), and the ninth benediction of the *'Amidah* prayer, pleading for "good years," with drawing this vitality into time.
134. On self-sacrifice (*mesirut nefesh*) at the time of uttering the *ehad* of *Keri'at Shema'*, see, for example, T1, 25:32b, 46:65a; T4, 128:148a; TO 29b. On the role of *mesirat nefesh* in Habad, see Loewenthal, "Self-sacrifice," 463–78.
135. LT *Ahare* 26a, based on *b*Sukah 45b.
136. LT *Ahare* 26a. The creative role of blessings is associated with the blessings of the morning prayer, supposedly fixed by the Sages in order to ensure that the divine vitality would be drawn into the world every morning, namely, at the time when God creates the world anew according to the wording of the morning prayer, whereby he "renews each day the work of creation."
137. For the seven principles of rabbinic hermeneutics attributed to Hillel the Elder, see *Avot de-rabi Natan*, chapter 37, 69a. For the thirteen hermeneutical principles of Rabbi Ishmael, see *Sifra* 1a–3a.
138. One of the meanings of *bar* in Aramaic is "field." *Baraita* means a tannaitic tradition that is "external" to the Mishnah and is therefore associated here with work carried out outside, namely in the field.

139. TO 49a.
140. See Ziii, 153a.
141. TO 49c–d. The idea of the clarification of the law as purification (*berur*) of sparks resonates with Shneur Zalman's diagnosis (TO 49a) of the current exile as a time when there is "no clear [*berurah*] *halakhah* and no clear [*barur*] judgment." See also T4, 12:117b, where a person studying Torah *li-shmah* makes peace in both the upper and the lower worlds, namely, separates good from evil, the mingling of which characterizes the exile, and the separation between them—the redemption at the end of days.
142. On the nexus of mystical doctrine and social ideology in Shneur Zalman's teachings on charity, see Hallamish, "Torat ha-tsedakah."
143. See, for example, *Seder tefilot* 16a; TO 29c; LT *Shelah* 43d, *Re'eh* 23c. See also TO 63c, where all the commandments are called "charity," as all of them bring divine vitality and light into the corresponding body parts through an act of goodness and mercy.
144. See, for example, T1, 37:48b; TO 27c, 29c; LT *Shelah* 43d, *Balak* 68b, *Re'eh* 23c.
145. T4, 17:125a
146. See, for example, T1, 37:48b; T4, 30:151a; *Seder tefilot* 19b. Based on *b*Bava Batra 9a. See the discussion of this aspect of charity in Hallamish, *Torat ha-tsedakah*, 128.
147. See *Seder tefilot* 19b.
148. See TO 29c and T4, 3:104a.
149. *Seder tefilot* 19b
150. Zi, 249b.
151. See, for example, *Seder tefilot* 17a (where the attribute of Mercy below triggers an influx of Upper Kindness), and 19b; T4, 21:133b.
152. Literally, "the light of seven days [of creation]" (see Isa 30:26), which according to the Sages will shine also in the messianic days. See *b*Pesahim 68a.
153. *Seder tefilot* 19b.
154. See *Seder tefilot* 4a. See also T4, 17:125a, where charity is described as the Lord's commandment, for God causes the worlds to exist by an act of charity, and T1, 34:43b, where charity is recognized as "one of the attributes of the Holy One, blessed be he, who is merciful."
155. See T4, 4:105a–106b and TO 38c, discussed in Hallamish, "Torat ha-tsedakah," 133–34.
156. See, for example, T4, 9:114a, and Hallamish, "Torat ha-tsedakah," 129–31.
157. *Seder tefilot* 19b.
158. See Etkes, *Rabbi Shneur Zalman*, 81–92; Hallamish, "Torat ha-tsedakah," 125–27.
159. See T4, 4:105a, 9:114a, 10:116a, based on Maimonides, *Mishneh Torah*, Laws of Gifts to the Poor, 10:1.
160. T1, 37:48b–49a; T4, 21:134a.

161. See, for example, T4, 5:106b. On the significance of the Land of Israel in Shneur Zalman's teachings, see Hallamish, "Ha-hasidut ve-Erets Yisra'el," 240–55.
162. See T4, 9:114a. The generation of the "footsteps of Messiah" is the last generation before the coming of the Messiah. This concept will be discussed in the next chapter.
163. On the basis of this particular passage in *Tanya*, Norman Lamm claims that Shneur Zalman, unlike his *mitnagedic* contemporary, Hayim of Volozhin, holds charity rather than Torah study as the main religious value (*Torah Lishmah*, 151–52). Admittedly, in some instances (e.g., HTT 3:4, 847a) Shneur Zalman does indeed suggest that charity can complement the divine service of a person who cannot study Torah in depth. Such statements show, on the one hand, that he considered Torah study an imperative that had to be made up for in cases where, for objective reasons, it could not be fulfilled. On the other hand, it demonstrates his pragmatism as a leader for a broad community consisting of people with a variety of professions, talents, and skills, rather than an elitist circle of scholars. Shneur Zalman's strategy of making spiritual experience accessible by attaching mystical or magical significance to the practical commandments that are obligatory and—unlike full-time Torah study—attainable by all, should not be understood as a relegation of Torah study in his hierarchy of values. I shall return to this issue in chapter 4, devoted to the mystical meaning that he invested in the precept of setting time for Torah study. See also Foxbrunner, *Habad*, 148–49 on the interdependence of Torah study and other types of worship in Shneur Zalman's teachings.
164. See Rashi to Gen. 1:1.
165. T1, 37:48a.
166. See T1, 37:46b–47a. See also LT *Be-har* 42b: "Now, the purpose of and the reason for all the commandments is to turn being [*yesh*] into naught [*ayin*], so that the nullification of being [*bitul ha-yesh*] would be accomplished. And this is why, according to the Sages, 'the entire Torah was compared to the phylacteries' [bKidushin 35a], for with regard to the phylacteries, when one writes 'One' [*ehad*] on a material parchment that derives from the husk of *nogah* and is a being unto itself, it is incorporated in the category of naught [*ayin*], as it becomes a vessel for the divinity that rests upon it by way of 'One' etc. And this applies to all the commandments of the Torah."
167. See T1, 37:47a–b; TO 16c, 55d, 65b–c, 66a, 117c; LT *Tsav* 13b–c, *Tazri'a* 20d, *Sukot* 78d.
168. See LT *Emor* 38c. Shneur Zalman establishes four categories of beings: inanimate (*domem*), vegetative (*tsomeah*), animate (*hai*), and speaking (*medaber*). Only human beings fall into all four. See T1, 38:50b; TO 3d. See also *Seder tefilot* 69c, 203a, and 101a–c, discussed in Jacobs, "Eating as an Act of Worship," 163–64, where every meal is considered a war between the holy and the unholy, an idea based on the fact that the Hebrew words

for "bread" (*lehem*) and "war" (*milhamah*) share the same root. Shneur Zalman also associates the Talmudic prohibition on the eating of meat by an ignoramus (*b*Pesahim 49b) with purifications: red meat that stems from *Gevurot* (for the association of the color red with *Gevurah*, see Hallamish, *Introduction*, 146) is too closely related to the external forces to be purified by an ignoramus; according to the saying that ascribes purifying powers to the attribute of *Wisdom* ("through *Hokhmah* they are purified" based on Zii, 254b]) only a scholar equipped with wisdom is fit to purify it. See LT *Be-ha'alotekha* 31c–33b. A variation on this motif can be found in LT *Berakhah* 97d, where the inability of the ignoramus to elevate the meat results from the fact that he possesses only the lower level of "hidden love" to God, as opposed to the scholar, whose love to God is ecstatic and powerful "like coals of fire." Elsewhere (LT *Tsav* 8a, *Balak* 72b, *Pinhas* 79d), the prohibition on eating before prayer is explained in terms of the obligation to let the soul spread throughout the entire body during prayer, as only then would the food consumed by the body provide energy for the soul rather than the *sitra ahra*. Finally, Shneur Zalman identifies eating with a blessing as a realization of God's "dwelling place in the lower worlds," for it enables the light of the *Ein Sof* contained in the vitality of food to dwell in man. See LT *Naso* 26b. For a general discussion of the mystical dimension of eating in Hasidism, see Jacobs, "Eating as an Act of Worship"; Jacobs, "The Uplifting of Sparks," 117–21.

169. This idea resembles the concept, present in early Hasidic teachings, that the 600,000 souls of Israel combine to form the full stature of the Messiah, each responsible for restoring to its source the part it constitutes of the messianic stature, and thus ultimately for bringing on the final redemption. See on this Idel's discussion ("Mystical Redemption," 50–54) of two passages from Menahem Nahum of Chernobyl's *Me'or 'enayim*, 166–67. In the above passage from *Tanya*, however, there is no reference either to these 600,000 souls or to the Jews of Shneur Zalman's own time as being their incarnations. Shneur Zalman is aware that the total number of Jews living in his own day far exceeds that of the Jews who left Egypt at the time of the Exodus. He therefore considers the souls of his contemporaries to be splinters or offshoots rather than incarnations of the original 600,000 souls that took part in the Exodus. See TO 27d.

170. Based on Ps. 90:10.

171. See also TO 53d, where an individual life span is associated with the halakhic precept of saying one hundred blessings every day. A seventy-year life span divided into 365 days, during each one of which one says one hundred blessings, is apportioned so that every person would say enough blessings to bring about the disclosure of the light of *sovev* in *memale*, in other words, the disclosure of transcendence within immanence.

172. See TO 27d.

173. See *Seder tefilot*, 53d–54a.

174. See TO 5d–6a. Thus, Shneur Zalman's concept of collective redemption differs from the messianic concept in Menahem Nahum of Chernobyl's *Me'or enayim*, discussed in Idel, *Messianic Mystics*, 221–34.
175. See Wolfson, *Open Secret*; Schwartz, *Mahashevet Habad*, 271–318.
176. Regardless of partisan traditions dating the institution of the *sheluhim* all the way back to the times of Shneur Zalman, it is indeed a novel contribution of the twentieth-century Habad. Yosef Yitshak Schneersohn was seemingly the first leader of Habad who would send his Hasidim to non-Habad synagogues and yeshivas to promote Habad teachings and ways of life. See Rapoport-Albert and Sagiv, "Habad ke-neged Hasidut Polin," 250–56. Clearly aware of the novelty of his invention, Yosef Yitshak Schneersohn produced stories supporting the alleged long history of the outreach carried out by the *sheluhim*; see Roth (*Ketsad li-kero*, 164–65), who seems to accept these stories as historically accurate. Still, the *sheluhim* gained a new impetus in the post-Holocaust United States, when the last Habad leader, Menahem Mendel, dispatched them en masse to proselytize among nonaffiliated Jews. On the institution of *sheluhim* see note 29 in my Introduction, above.
177. See Kraus, *Ha-shevi'i*, 132–76; Fishkoff, *The Rebbe's Army*, 46–65; Heilman and Friedman, *The Rebbe*, 166–90.
178. One particular campaign has been addressed to non-Jews. I will discuss it in the next chapter.
179. For the criticism of the *mitsvah camp* by the rebbe of Satmar, Yoel Teitelbaum (1887–1979), see Kraus, *Ha-shevi'i*, 161–76.
180. On *tsadik* as Moses in Menahem Mendel's Habad, see Wolfson, *Open Secret*, 7–12. The communal responsibility in the face of the imminent messianic advent found its radical expression in Menahem Mendel Schneerson's notorious speech from 11 April (28 Nissan) 1991, when he declared in front of astonished Hasidim: "What more I can do, I don't know. Because everything I've done until now has been futile and ineffective. Nothing has come of it (. . .). The only thing I can do is to hand this over to each one of you: do everything you can to bring Messiah!"; see Miller, *Turning Judaism Outward*, 405–6; Heilman and Friedman, *The Rebbe*, 230–32; Dahan, Kraus, *Ha-shevi'i*, 86–91; Dahan, "Dirah ba-tahtonim," 384–88
181. See Loewenthal, *Communicating*, 3–4; see also Elior, *Paradoxical Ascent*, 21–22.
182. See Loewenthal, "The Ba'al Shem Tov's 'Iggeret ha-kodesh'"; Kraus, *Ha-shevi'i*, 34–91. For the discussion of the letter and its messianic component, see Idel, *Messianic Mystics*, 213–20; Rosman, *Founder of Hasidism*, 97–113.
183. See Fishkoff, *The Rebbe's Army*; Kraus, *Ha-shevi'i*; Balakirsky Katz, *The Visual Culture*, 91–224; Shandler, *Jews, God and Videotape*, 230–74. See also Tworek, "Beyond Hagiography with Footnotes," on academic literature as a channel for outreach in contemporary Habad.
184. See Wolfson, *Open Secret*, 28–65; Wolfson, "Revealing and Re/veiling."
185. See Jacobson, "Galut u-ge'ulah"; Jacobson, "Mi-ne'urim," in particular,

435n34, which claims that among Hasidic authors Shneur Zalman had the biggest influence on young Yehudah Aryeh Leib.
186. See Jacobson, "Galut u-ge'ulah," 175–202.
187. See Jacobson, "Galut u-ge'ulah," 203–8; Jacobson, "Kedushat ha-hulin," 242–44.
188. In the times of the Sefat Emet, non-Jews were prohibited from observing the Sabbath. Those who did were punishable by death by the hands of heaven. See bSanhedrin 58b; Maimonides, *Mishneh Torah*, Laws of Kings and their Wars, 10:9.
189. See Jacobson, "Galut u-ge'ulah," 202–3.
190. Some of the features of the redemption discussed here, which have their roots in Shneur Zalman's teachings, will be examined in the next chapter. At this opportunity, however, one correction of Jacobson's evaluation of the Sefat Emet is due. In Jacobson's view, the Sefat Emet's innovation lies in adding a historical dimension to Shneur Zalman's spiritual and eschatological dimensions of the redemption. In this respect, the Gur Hasidim supposedly broke with the earlier tendency in Hasidism of the neutralization of messianism (see Jacobson, "Galut u-ge'ulah," 190–91). However, if one leaves aside the Scholem's thesis on the neutralization of the messianic idea in early Hasidism, as I postulated in the Introduction, then a new perspective unfolds. In light of this chapter, it becomes clear that the historical dimension has been very much part and parcel of Shneur Zalman's redemptive project, and the influence of early Habad thought on the Gur worldview turns out to be even more substantial. See also Wolfson, *Open Secret*, 67, where he argues for the continuity of the messianic element in the Habad thought through its history and claims that "from the inception [of Habad], the cosmological and apocalyptic are intertwined branches that cannot be severed."

Chapter 3

1. Conflicting eschatological notions have been present in the Jewish sources since the time of the Sages. See Ginsburg, *Sabbath*, 145–46n46; Klausner, *The Messianic Idea*, 408–19; Rapoport-Albert, *Women and the Messianic Heresy*, 119n35; Urbach, *The Sages*, 651–52. See also Scholem, *The Messianic Idea*, and its critique in Idel, *Messianic Mystics*, 30–37. For the Talmudic distinction between the days of the Messiah and the resurrection of the dead, see bBerakhot 34b, bShabat 63a, 113b, bPesahim 68a, bSanhedrin 91b, 99a, bZevahim 118b.
2. T1, 36:46a, my emphasis.
3. See bNidah 61b and Ziii, 124b.
4. These include biblical prophecies referring to death and birth at the end of days (Isa. 65:20; Jer. 31:8), and Talmudic speculations on *halakhah* in messianic times in bSanhedrin 51b.

5. *Derasah* refers to a ritual slaughter performed by applying pressure on the knife; *haladah* to a slaughter performed by a cut too deep; *shehiyah* when there is a pause in the cut.
6. T4, 26:143a-b.
7. See Maimonides, *Mishneh Torah*, Laws of Repentance, 8–9; Laws of Kings and Their Wars, 11–12. For a discussion of messianism in Maimonides, see Ravitzky, "To the Utmost Human Capacity," 221–56.
8. Maimonides, *Mishneh Torah*, Laws of Kings and their Wars, 12:1.
9. See also *Seder tefilot* 291a, where Shneur Zalman states that the obligation to remember the Exodus will remain valid in the messianic era.
10. *b*'Eruvin 22a; see also *b*'Avodah zarah 3a.
11. *b*Berakhot 34b and *b*Sanhedrin 91b.
12. TO 46a-b.
13. In *Tanya*, he makes a distinction between worship before and during the messianic days, according to the different purposes it serves at each stage. Worship before the messianic days serves to purify the divine sparks, while in the messianic days, when all the sparks have been purified, it facilitates unifications both with and within the divine realm by way of the inner dimension of Torah. See T4, 26:145a.
14. See, for example, LT *Va-yikra* 4d.
15. See, for example, LT *Hukat* 64c-d. See also *Tsav* 15d–16a, according to which the Jews will deserve the resurrection in the future by virtue of their labor and enslavement to money in the present. The resurrection is compared here to the liberation of Passover.
16. Shneur Zalman's writings contain some statements that suggest the opposite. See, for example, LT *Shabat shuvah* 64b, where the reward is unambiguously associated with the days of the Messiah. In this case, the new way in which the believers will experience the divinity is to be the main distinction between the exile and the redemption in the messianic days.
17. LT *Nitsavim* 50b.
18. This is a reference to the statement of Rabbi Hiya bar Abba (*b*Berakhot 34b), who said in the name of Rabbi Yohanan that the prophets prophesized only with regard to the days of the Messiah, "but as for the world to come, 'no eye has seen, oh God, but you'" (Isa. 64:3).
19. See LT *Nitsavim* 50c and MAHZ 5566, ii, 703–4. In both the *ma'amarim* that deal with the material reward versus the spiritual reward, Shneur Zalman replaces the terms "messianic days" and "resurrection of the dead" with "Lower" and "Upper" Garden of Eden respectively (*gan 'eden tahton* and *'elyon*). See MAHZ 5566, ii, 703 and LT *Nitsavim* 50d. Elsewhere, however, he distinguishes the Garden of Eden from the world-to-come (*'olam ha-ba*) that will follow the resurrection: in the former, the souls of the righteous enjoy the radiance of the *Shekhinah*, whereas all Jews take part in the latter, with both soul and body. See MAHZ 5569, 193.
20. See, for example, *b*Shabat 88b, *b*Hagigah 12b, *b*Ketubot 111b; *y*Berakhot 38b, *y*Ta'anit 2b. See also T1, 36:46a-b, where Shneur Zalman compares

the revelation at Sinai to the resurrection of the dead. At Sinai, each utterance of the Torah, at which the Israelites' souls took flight, was followed by another utterance, which restored their souls to them with the same dew by means of which God will effect the resurrection of the dead (see *bShabat* 88b). However, the Israelites then sinned by worshiping the golden calf, and this dragged them back into materiality. Only in the future-to-come, when materiality and corporeality are purified, will they merit the dew of resurrection and the full light of Torah.

21. See, for example, LT *'Ekev* 13d; MAHZ 5562, 103; 5565, i, 22–24, 33, 37, 39, 412–13, 427; 5566 i, 420, ii, 624; 5567, 282–83, 420.
22. On the subtle body at the time of the resurrection, see Schwartz, *Mahashevet Habad*, 277–80. On the development of this topic in the *ma'amarim* of the fifth Lubavitcher Rebbe, Shalom Dovber Schneersohn, see Wolfson, "Neqqudat ha-Reshimu," 90–91.
23. See MAHZ 5565, i, 412–13.
24. LT *Shelah* 46d. According to Shneur Zalman, the traditional blessing formula recited before performing a commandment ("Blessed are thou, o Lord our God, king of the universe, who sanctified us with his commandments") hints at the delight derived from the commandments, wherein the word *asher* ("who") stems from *ashre* ("happy are those"). For the source of this interpretation, see *Tikune zohar*, xxx, 74b, xxxix, 79a. On the medieval concept of Paradise as the immersion of the soul in the light drawn down by a person in the acts of performing commandments while he or she was still alive, see Idel, "On Paradise in Jewish Mysticism," 10–12.
25. This reversal comes to full realization at the resurrection, yet it can be effected to some extent even in the present, unredeemed world by means of the practical commandments, which bring the higher level of delight to realization through the material objects utilized in their performance; see LT *Shelah* 47c-d. See LT *Shelah* 47c-d.
26. Based on Exod. 33:20: "There shall no man see me, and live."
27. See, for example, T1, 36:46b; TO 22c, 76d; LT *Shabat shuvah* 66a, *Shir ha-shirim* 7b; *Seder tefilot* 19b.
28. See, for example, TO 54c; LT *Re'eh* 28a-b, *Rosh ha-shanah* 90a; MAHZ 5566, i, 382; 5569, 42–45, and Schwartz, *Mahashevet Habad*, 279. See also LT *Shir ha-shirim* 41a, where the unification of *sovev* and *memale*, or *Kudsha Berikh Hu* and his *Shekhinah*, is described as God's dwelling place in the lower worlds (*dirah ba-tahtonim*).
29. See, for example, T1, 7:12a; T4, 25:139b.
30. Based on the interpretation of Isa. 58:11 where God "will make fat thy bones."
31. MAHZ 5566, i, 420–21. See also LT *Re'eh* 28a: "Thus in the future-to-come the body will be infinitely purer than the human body nowadays, for the body will be [made] entirely out of the bone that would remain for the time of the resurrection (see *Bereshit rabah*, 28:3; *Vayikra rabah* 18:1), from which the body will be constructed as leaven in the dough (see Zi,

69a; Zii, 28b; *Pirke de-Rabi Eli'ezer* ch. 34, 34a) by means of the dew that will be drawn from above."

32. See, for example, MAHZ 5563, i, 202; 5569, 42–45; LT *Re'eh* 24a, *Shir ha-shirim* 42b. The belief that the resurrected bodies will not need to eat and drink appears in *b*Berakhot 17a. See also MAHZ 5564, 138, discussed in Schwartz, *Mahashevet Habad*, 278, where Shneur Zalman states that bodies after the resurrection will not be sustained by food but by hunger and thirst, namely hunger and thirst for God.

33. Based on Job 31:2. See, for example, T1, 2:6a, 35:44a, 41:65b; T4, 15:123a; TO 24a, 84b; LT *Va-yikra* 2d, 6a, 39d, *Va-yikra hosafot* 51c, *Ba-midbar* 1b, *Hukat* 61d, *Mas'e* 91, 28c, 34a c, *'Ekev* 13d, *Tetse* 37d, *Rosh ha-shanah* 62c, *Ha'azinu* 74c, 77c, *Shir ha-shirim* 2b, 5c.

34. See MAHZ 5569, 42–45.

35. See *b*Sanhedrin 90a. Shneur Zalman generally excludes from the resurrection all those whom the Sages had excluded from the future-to-come. See TO 73c; MAHZ 5569, 192. He refers specifically to heretics who deny the resurrection, and who will be punished by way of "measure for measure." See LT *Shelah* 46d. Elsewhere, following the *Zohar* (Zii, 100a; Ziii, 164a, based on *b*Bava kama 16a), he excludes from the resurrection "a person who does not bow at the [recitation of] *Modim*," as the thanksgiving in *Modim* is an expression of the complete nullification of the self, necessary for both the transformation of evil into good and the unification of the transcendent and immanent aspects of the divinity. See, for example, LT *Be-har* 42c, *Balak* 71a, *Pinhas* 75d, 76d, *Re'eh* 23d–24a; MAHZ 5566, i, 382, ii, 650–51; 5568, 420.

36. TO 73c; MAHZ 5569, 148, 192–93.

37. See T1, 50:70b; LT *Korah* 54b, *Berakhah* 96c. See also Vital, *Likute Torah*, *Sefer Yehezkel*, 323.

38. See, for example, *Seder tefilot* 67d; MAHZ *Ketsarim*, 438–40; *Razal*, 316. See also MAHZ *Ketsarim*, 256, where Shneur Zalman quotes a tradition in the name of the Ba'al Shem Tov, according to which the Jews have been dispersed to the most remote parts of the world in order to "purify the land of the nations and its impure air," and by this means to prepare God's dwelling place in the lower worlds. The concept of "purifying the air" as a means of bringing on the redemption by performing rituals all over the world became a trademark of the Habad movement in the twentieth century. See my Conclusion to chapter 2, above.

39. Poles are identified here with Esau, whom Isaac blessed with the words, "By thy sword shall thy live" (Gen. 27:40). See MAHZ *Ketsarim*, 438–40, and Mondshine, *Migdal 'oz*, 454–57, discussed in Foxbrunner, *Habad*, 91–92. See also MAHZ 5570, 30, discussed by Mondshine, *Masa' Berditshov*, 56–57, according to which Jews redeem the sparks from the nations by paying them off (*she-notnin la-hem damim*); this way they give a part of themselves to the *sitra ahara* in order to stop the flow of the divine vitality to it, and thus they act as a scapegoat for Azazel (see Lev. 16:7–10). The

association of paying off the gentiles with self-sacrifice is underscored by the use of the Hebrew word *damim*, which means both money and blood.
40. T1, 1:6a. See also Wolfson, *Open Secret*, 231–32, 235.
41. T1, 1:6a.
42. See TO 99a, discussed in Wolfson, *Open Secret*, 233. In *Tanya*, the capability of self-nullification is described as the readiness of every Jew for martyrdom expressed in the hidden love of God (*ahavah mesuteret*). See T1, 14:19b, and Elior, *Paradoxical Ascent*, 216; Foxbrunner, *Habad*, 100, 180–81; Hallamish, "Mishnato ha-'iyunit," 320–23; Loewenthal, "Self-Sacrifice," 463–65. I discuss the Hasidic attitudes to non-Jews in a forthcoming joint article with Marcin Wodziński, "Hasidism and the Gentile World." See also Turov, *Rannyi khasidizm*, 125–58.
43. See TO 6a; Maimonides, *Mishneh Torah*, Laws of Kings and their Wars, 11:4.
44. The original has the zoharic Aramaic phrase: *le-mat'am me-ilana de-haye* Ziii, 124b.
45. T4, 26:145b. See also bPesahim 68a; Zi, 114b.
46. See also Onkelos to Exod. 12:28, where '*erev rav* is translated as "many gentiles."
47. Rashi to Exod. 32:4. On the responsibility of the '*erev rav* for the sin of the golden calf, see also *Shemot rabah* 42:6. See MAHZ 5572, 69–72.
48. Since '*erev rav* is contrasted here with "every Jew," subsequent Habad commentators have suggested that in this chapter of *Tanya* it should be emended to the unequivocal "nations of the world." See *Likute hagahot le-Sefer ha-Tanya*; Wineberg, *Lessons in Tanya*, v, 144. For a different interpretation see Ornet, *Ratso va-shov*, 277, where she interprets '*erev rav* as referring to ignoramuses, who need to carry on their inner struggle with evil in the messianic era, as opposed to scholars, who by then will have subjugated evil and have become free to study the secrets of the Torah. However, she does not provide any source to support her understanding of '*erev rav* in this way.
49. See T4, 26:144b.
50. This also conforms to Maimonides's notion that, in the messianic days, all Jews will reach the intellectual level of the Sages and will know "hidden matter," for "the earth shall be full of the knowledge of the Lord" (Isa. 11:9). See Maimonides, *Mishneh Torah*, Laws of Kings and their Wars, 12:5.
51. See LT *Shelah* 43a.
52. The passivity of the gentiles in the process of redemption also testifies to the fact that Shneur Zalman constructs the gentiles as being feminine. On associating of passivity with femininity and on the female aspect of the Godhead and its role in the redemptive process see chapter 5 below.
53. Shneur Zalman does not state this explicitly, but the idea concurs with his view whereby the gentile nations will acquire the status of *gerim* in the messianic future. As *gerim* in the biblical times gained protected status

by virtue of living among Israelites, and they took it upon themselves to observe some of the precepts of the Torah (see b'Avodah zarah 64b) in exchange, so the gentiles will be included in the days of Messiah and will need to study and follow the *halakhah*. The emphasis on the partial participation of gentiles in the life of Torah and *mitsvot* suggests that they will achieve the status of *ger toshav* (resident alien) rather than that of *ger tsedek* (a full convert to Judaism). It should also be noted that the idea that the duration of the exile has been granted to Israel as an opportunity to save *gerim* from the nations recurs in Shneur Zalman's writings (see, for example, TO 6a, 11a-b, 26c; MAHZ 5566, i, 231, based on bPesahim 87b). Nevertheless, in most of these instances, *gerim* symbolize the divine sparks, and their salvation in the hands of Israel stands for the purification and refinement of the sparks. In TO 20c, however, the term *gerim* appears in the same context in its literal meaning, with the examples of such proselytes as Rabbi Meir, Onkelos, Shema'ya and Ovadiah, whose souls were sparks confined within the soul of Esau. But in this case, the conversion to Judaism of certain non-Jews is not seen as part of the wider transformation of the gentile world but rather as the recovery of the particular sparks of certain Jewish souls that fell into gentile bodies. On a similar motif in the thought of the seventh Lubavitcher Rebbe, see Wolfson, *Open Secret*, 261–62.

54. TI, 36:46b.
55. Shneur Zalman extends in *Tanya* the meaning of idolatry from idol worship or service of other gods to the negation—in thought or conduct—of God's oneness, his uniqueness, and his unity with the world. Pride is the root of idolatry because proud individuals see themselves as independent beings in their own right rather than a part of the pleroma. See TI, 22:28a.
56. Korf, *Likute be'urim*, i, 221; based on Rashi to Isa. 2:5.
57. See Shalom Dovber Shneersohn, *Be-sha'ah she-hikdimu*, ii, 992. On this collection of *ma'amarim* see Wolfson, "Nequddat ha-Reshimu."
58. Also, "the house of Jacob" is traditionally understood as referring to women of Israel (see *Mekhilta de-Rabi Yishma'el*, Yitro, 19:3; Rashi to Exod. 19:3), so perhaps Shneur Zalman means here that it will be the women (who have a very passive and limited role in the early Habad spirituality) who lead the gentiles toward the messianic era.
59. In rabbinic literature, Canaan is identified with the Slavic nations (see Jakobson and Halle, "The Term 'Canaan'"). It is likely, therefore, that Shneur Zalman refers in this *ma'amar* to the Slavs. Still, he himself does not provide any clues that would help anchor the concept in his immediate surroundings. He may be drawing here on the zoharic take on Noah's curse of Canaan in Gen. 9:25, which associates Canaan with filth, evil, and death (see ZI, 73a), without supplying any topographical reference.
60. TO 102b. See also MAHZ 5563, 81, and an elaboration on the same motif by the Tsemah Tsedek in *Or ha-Torah*, Bereshit, vi, 1127a. The status in the

redeemed world of Amalek, Israel's traditional archenemy, is not easy to determine. In contrast to the biblical call for his total annihilation (see Deut. 25:17–19; 1 Sam. 15:3) and the rabbinic tradition whereby God's name and his throne will remain incomplete until the name of Amalek is obliterated (see *Midrash Tanhuma*, Tetse, 11), Shneur Zalman seems to assume the possibility that even Amalek will be redeemed after the resurrection. See MAHZ 5572, 169. He explains in this *ma'amar* that because Amalek is rooted in the metaphysical domain that lies above the breaking of the vessels, where the purification of sparks does not apply, it will not be rectified by way of purification, but will be included in the redemption when its name is completely blotted out. Wolfson reads this *ma'amar* as an example of Shneur Zalman's inconsistency, arising from the clash between his notion of a universal redemption that would include even Israel's arch-enemy, and the "scriptural mandate [. . .] to erase [Amalek's] name to the point of 'complete extermination'" (Wolfson, *Open Secret*, 254). I am inclined to read the Hebrew expression *bitul le-gamre* ("complete extermination"), not as a reference to actual extermination but rather as a technical term denoting complete self-nullification, which is comparable to the transformation of "being" (*yesh*) into "naught" (*'ayin*). This reading is reinforced by Shneur Zalman's description of Amalek's *bitul* as "hearkening," which is preferable to "sacrifice" (based on 1 Sam. 15:15 and 22: "Behold, to obey is better than sacrifice, and to hearken than the fat of rams"), where the sacrifices symbolize purification of sparks while hearkening to God's voice is compared to the Israelites' *bitul* at Sinai (when they said *na'aseh ve-nishma'*). Rather than finding an inconsistency in Shneur Zalman's view of Amalek's redemptive prospects, I read this *ma'amar* as an elaborate interpretation that draws on the tradition of erasing Amalek's name but transforms it into Amalek's redemption by playing on the meanings of *bitul* as both concrete eradication and self-nullification.

61. LT *Mas'e* 89b-c; based on *Pesikta rabati*, pis. 1, 2a.
62. See Mondshine, *Migdal 'oz*, 483–88. Moreover, one of the texts published there and attributed to Shneur Zalman suggests the futility of any attempts to calculate the time of the end of days. See Mondshine, *Migdal 'oz*, 509.
63. Tishby, "Ha-ra'ayon ha-meshihi," 512–13.
64. Wolfson, "Walking as a Sacred Duty," 194.
65. mSotah 9:15.
66. See TI, 2:6a-b and MAHZ 5566, i, 423, ii, 685; *Parshiyot*, i, 39. On the idea of the decline of the generations in Hasidism, see Jacobs, "Hasidism and the Dogma," 208–13. The souls of the generation of *tana'im* originated in Hokhmah, Binah, and Da'at of the World of Creation; those of the generation of *amora'im* in Hesed, Gevurah, and Tif'eret of the World of Formation; and the souls that have come into the world since the era of *ge'onim* originate in Netsah, Hod, and Yesod of the World of Making; see MAHZ 5566, ii, 556–57; 5569, 151–52; LT *Hukat* 63b. The decline of the generations in *Tanya* has a functional dimension. The descent of the generations down

the *sefirotic* tree refers to the different levels of souls that incarnate with the purpose of undergoing purification, a process that will end with the advent of the Messiah. Based on *b*Yevamot 62a, 63b, "The son of David will not arrive until all the souls are vacated from the *guf*," and according to Rashi, until all the souls created in the six days of creation are born. See also Zii, 258a, where Zechariah's prophecy regarding God, who "On that day, [. . .] will set his feet [*raglav*] on the mount of Olives" (Zech. 14:4) refers to the day of the end of exile, on which all impurity will be removed from the world.

67. See Aharon ha-Levi, *Sha'are ha-yihud*, Petah u-mevo she'arim, 5a-b. See also Tishby, "Ha-ra'ayon ha-meshihi," 513. Tishby explains this passage in terms of the Hasidic tendency to renounce traditional class divisions within the Jewish community, and to follow the imperative of "In all your ways acknowledge him" (Prov. 3:6). Contrary to Tishby, I do not see this confusion as a positive state, but rather as a negative aspect of the premessianic generation's tribulations. Although Shneur Zalman certainly subscribed to the idea of knowing God in all his ways, he nevertheless divided his Hasidim into separate groups according to the roots of their soul and their social status, prescribing different paths of worship to each of them. This will be further discussed in the next chapter. See also T4, 26:142a, where the confusion of the present time is said to result in scholars being left at the mercy of ignoramuses who support them financially, while in the redeemed world this will be reversed and the ignoramuses will be sustained by what they receive from the scholars. Aharon ha-Levi also sees in the confusion a challenge to overcome rather than an opportunity, and he asks his readers to find, through introspection, their own appropriate mode of worship that would correspond to the root of their soul rather than to their current status in the material world.

68. We find literal reading of the tribulations in the period of the footsteps of Messiah in the Vilna Gaon's circle; see Shuchat, *'Olam nistar*, 199–202; 220–24.

69. See TO 41a.

70. See T4, 9:114a, *Seder tefilot*, 23a. Conversely, in T5, 162a, prayer is identified as the mode of worship appropriate for the time of the footsteps, as opposed to Torah study, which was appropriate for the time of the Sages. This should, however, be seen in the context of this particular section of *Tanya*, which focuses on the value of prolonged prayer, aiming to empower Hasidim who wanted to spend more time on prayer than their fellow congregants.

71. See Shneur Zalman *ma'amar* "Va-yikhu li terumah," reedited by his son and published in *Ma'amre Admor ha-Emtsa'i*, Shemot i, 305. An extract from this *ma'amar*, published by Mondshine in *Masa' Berditshov*, 55, states that the "crown of the Messiah's good name" will be created out of the "yoke of the commandments that are truly in praxis."

72. See also Foxbrunner, *Habad*, 92–93.

73. *b*Sanhedrin 98a.

74. See LT *Shemini 'atseret* 85d.
75. *Keter*, according to the Habad tradition, stands above the ten *sefirot* and is their source (see Hallamish, "Mishnato ha-'iyunit," 70–74; Schwartz, *Mahashevet Habad*, 64–65n142). It also stands for God's will to create the world on the first day of creation (*Keter* and *ba-yom ha-rishon* [on the first day] share the same numerical value of 620).
76. On the redemption as the everlasting day, see Wolfson, *Alef, Mem, Tau*, 113–14.
77. Following the midrashic idea that repentance preceded the creation of the world, on which see *Midrash Tanhuma*, Naso, 11.
78. See Wolfson, "Eternal Duration," 229–30; Idel, "Higher than Time," 207.
79. See *b'Avodah zarah* 17a.
80. See Wolfson, *Open Secret*, 278–84, where he discusses the immediacy of the messianic advent in the teachings of the last Lubavitcher Rebbe, Menahem Mendel Schneerson, as expressed in the often repeated slogan: the Messiah shall arrive "immediately and truly without delay." Wolfson points out that Shneur Zalman, takes the concept of immediacy to mean that the time of the redemption is not bound to any sequence of historical events, as the redemption transcends worldly time and is a "timeless moment, which cannot transpire temporally and therefore must always be capable of occurring (in)temporally" (281). Admittedly, the acute messianism of twentieth-century Habad was a response to certain historical events, yet the concept that redemption may come at any time, because, by its very nature, it transcends all temporal limitations, and can already be found in the teachings of the movement's founder. Also, recognizing repentance (regardless of its definition) as a precondition of redemption is a point of difference between Shneur Zalman and his older contemporary, the Vilna Gaon. The Vilna Gaon attributed greater significance to the order of the seven millennia of cosmic history (corresponding to the seven lower *sefirot*) than Shneur Zalman and did not allow much room for achieving the final redemption before time by means of repentance. Following the Talmud (*b*Sanhedrin 98b), the Gaon declares that the Messiah will arrive in the "generation that is entirely guilty." See Shuchat, *'Olam nistar*, 171–79. The question concerning the role of repentance in redemption was raised already by the Talmudic Sages; see *b*Sanhedrin 97b.
81. *b*Pesahim 116b.
82. See *Tikune zohar* xxi, 48b.
83. T1, 47:66b. On the relation between personal and collective redemption in Habad, see Lowenthal, "Habad Messianism." On a variety of modes of redemption in Hasidism in general, see Idel, "Multiple Forms of Redemption," 61, where he presents the collective redemption that results from many individual redemptions as one of the ways in which messianism manifests itself in the teachings of the Besht. One of the sources to which Idel refers is Gedalyah of Lynitz's *Sefer teshu'ot hen*, in which the Besht

is said to have described the collective mode of redemption (followed by the advent of the Messiah) as the sum total of numerous individual redemptions. For a discussion of personal redemption in other schools of Hasidism, see Faierstein, "Personal Redemption," 214–24. See also Idel, *Messianic Mystics*, 244; Wolfson, "Walking as a Secret Duty," 183–84n10.

84. As stated elsewhere, "Egypt exists in every person and at all times," TO 62b.
85. T4, 12:118b.
86. See, for example, TO 64a. This will be discussed in detail in the next chapter.
87. Shneur Zalman commonly interprets the *Shema*'s "with all thy might" as meaning "without limit." See, for example, TO 18b, 33b, 35d, 64a, 64d; LT *Shemini* 18b, 19d, *Emor* 33d, 35b, *Shelah* 47a, 50d, *Hukat* 64c, *Balak* 67d, *Mas'e* 92b, *Va-ethanan* 9b, *Re'eh* 25b, *Shir ha-shirim* 20c, 25d, 30d, 40a, 43a, 45b.
88. TO 64a.
89. See Grossfeld, *Two Targums of Esther*, Targum rishon to Esther, 6:1, 69.
90. See TO 94d–95a. Despite the fact that the Purim miracle belongs in an account of the Persian exile, Shneur Zalman refers to it here as if it happened in Babylonia, perhaps drawing on Esth. 2:6, where Mordecai is said to have been exiled from Jerusalem by a Babylonian king. By doing so, he emphasizes the inarticulate manner by which the Jews expressed their trust in God: "And this was the Purim miracle, which was like Babylonia, for 'there the Lord confounded the speech' [Gen. 11:9]" (TO 95a). For a discussion of Shneur Zalman's teachings on Purim in relation to contemporary events, see Loewenthal, *Communicating*, 90–97. For faith that is beyond reason, see Loewenthal's "'Reason' and 'Beyond Reason,'" 118*–120*.
91. T4, 4:105b.
92. See T4, 4:105a.
93. T4, 4:105b, based on bSanhedrin 96a. See also Wolfson, *Open Secret*, 51. In LT *Hukat* 61b-c Shneur Zalman describes faith as complete trust in the Creator without any reason or understanding (*be-lo ta'am ve-da'at*), by dint of which one takes oneself out of Egypt.
94. For Habad's "intellectualism," see the discussion in my Introduction. For the significance of voice and orality in Hasidism, see Idel, *Hasidism*, 160–70.
95. Wolfson, *Open Secret*, 164–65, 273–74. Wolfson describes Menahem Mendel Schneerson's messianism as contingent not on historical, national redemption or on personal, spiritual redemption, but rather on the expanding consciousness that apprehends the world as being redeemed and filled with godliness. While Wolfson focuses on Menahem Mendel's millenarian enthusiasm, which impacted his messianic teaching, I argue that the idea of the expanding consciousness of messianic times features already in the teachings of Shneur Zalman, albeit less prominently. Idel

has singled out a "noetic" model of the redemption, which he claims to be ever present, in a variety of forms, in the Jewish mystical tradition as a whole. See his *Messianic Mystics*, 51–53, and "Multiple forms of redemption."
96. See note 68 to chapter 1.
97. See chapter 2; LT *Balak* 68d.
98. *Seder tefilot* 19b.
99. Based on *b*Ta'anit 31a.
100. See LT *Shabat shuvah* 64b. Notably, the word used here to describe the nature of comprehension in the conditions of exile is *knowledge*, which shares its root with the word *da'at*. Although Shneur Zalman does not say so explicitly in this particular passage, the visual perception that transcends exilic knowledge is beyond *da'at* as well. See a LT *Va-ethanan* 3c on the superiority of vision, which is understood as complete and intuitive cognition as opposed to discursive knowledge, and its relation to the future redemption.
101. LT *Ha'azinu* 77c, based on Vital, *Likute Torah*, 'Ekev, 246, and *Mekhilta de-Rabi Yishma'el*, Yitro, 20:15, See also T1, 36:46a
102. *b*Shabbat 88b.
103. LT *Ba-midbar* 10c.
104. See *Seder tefilot* 308d. See also LT *'Ekev* 13d–14a, where God's great mercy rests on every person who performs repentance and brings him back to life, which constitutes a personal experience of the future resurrection of the dead. On the relation between the Sinaitic experience and the resurrection of the dead, see note 20 of this chapter, above.
105. See note 93 of this chapter, above.
106. See Wolfson, *Alef, Mem, Tau*, 113–15.
107. See T4, 4:105b. On the nexus of circumcision, theophany, and the divine word in kabbalah, see Wolfson, *Circle in the Square*, 41–47.
108. See Onkelos to Gen. 2:7.
109. TO 12b.
110. Elsewhere, Shneur Zalman describes circumcision as a revelation of God's voice to the mute congregation of Israel. See LT *Pinhas* 79c.
111. Following the description of the redeemer's mission in Ziii, 153b.
112. This follows on from Shneur Zalman's valorization and empowerment of ordinary people's mode of worship, which will be further discussed in the next chapter.
113. See, for example, LT *Rosh ha-shanah* 58d, *Ha'azinu* 75b, *Shemini 'atseret* 92b, *Shir ha-shirim* 45a, 50a–c; MAHZ 5562, 274, 542. This concept is based on the Talmudic dictum "In the place where penitents stand, the completely righteous cannot stand" (*b*Berakhot 34b). See also Tishby, "Ha-ra'ayon ha-meshihi," 38; Tishby and Dan, "Torat ha-hasidut," 794–95.
114. See LT *Tsav* 17c. Thus, Moses is the first and the Messiah the last redeemer. See, for example, *Seder tefilot*, 307a.
115. This is the case of the seventh Habad rebbe, Menahem Mendel

Schneerson, who to this day is believed by some to be the Messiah. On the messianic ferment in Habad of the twentieth and twenty-first centuries, see Bilu and Kravel-Tovi, "The work of the present"; Dahan, "Dirah ba-tahtonim"; Dein, *Lubavitcher Messianism*; Elior, "The Lubavitch Messianic Resurgence"; Heilman and Friedman, *The Rebbe*, 197–247; Loewenthal, "Habad Messianism."

116. This was the claim of Joseph Dan, who saw the idea of cleaving to the *tsadik* as the way in which Hasidism in general neutralized apocalyptic messianism by transforming it into redemption through affiliation to a certain Hasidic court. In Dan's view, the *tsadik*'s court is a redeemed space and its dynastic character guarantees the continuity of redemption over time. See Dan, "Kefel ha-panim," 300–10; Margolin, *Mikdash adam*, 406–8.
117. See LT *Shemini* 18a–19d; MAHZ 5571, 163–69.
118. Rabbi Shimon Bar Yohai studied in seclusion for twelve years. See *b*Shabbat 33b. Shneur Zalman includes in this category also the Patriarchs, who fulfilled the Torah spiritually before it was handed down on Sinai, as well as Isaac Luria and the Ba'al Shem Tov.
119. See *Vayikra rabah*, 13:3.
120. This is based on the deriving Leviathan etymologically from the root *lamed vav yud* (or *he*), which means to accompany or to connect.
121. The distinction between the *tsadikim* engaged in the material world and those detached from it is present in the teachings of the Maggid of Mezrich; in contrast to the Maggid, Shneur Zalman seems to be more decisively pointing toward the advantage of the *tsadik*'s engagement in the world. See Mayse, "Beyond the Letters," 193–95.
122. See T1, 29:36a, where Hillel treats his own body as if it were a strange object, which is based on *Vayikra rabah*, Be-har 34:3.
123. See T4, 27:146b.
124. See Loewenthal, "Self-sacrifice," 460.
125. See T1, 2:6b–7a. This resembles Dan's idea of Hasidic redemption *qua* cleaving to the *tsadik* and joining his court. See Dan, "Kefel ha-panim," 300–310.
126. Loewenthal, "Self-Sacrifice," 463–65.
127. See Shneur Zalman's epistle to Levi Yitshak of Berdichev, on the occasion of the passing of the latter's son, T4, 28:148b.
128. See Maimonides, *Mishneh Torah*, Laws of the Red Heifer, 3:9.
129. Ziii, 71b. See Shneur Zalman's epistle sent to the Hasidim in the Land of Israel, following Menahem Mendel of Vitebsk's passing away, T4, 27:146a–b.
130. See Sternharts, *Haye moharan*, ii, Ma'alat ha-mitkarevim elav, par. 49, 30. On the gentiles in Nahman's messianic concept, see Mark, *The Scroll*, 73, 80–85; Green, *Tormented Master*, 205–6.
131. See Mark, *The Scroll*, 81. Nahman refers explicitly to the prophecy of Zephaniah (3:9). For a similar concept in Shneur Zalman, see above.

132. See Green, *Tormented Master*, 63–93.
133. See Mark, *The Scroll*, 165–70 and 77–79; Mark, *Mysticism and Madness*, 173–84.
134. See Klausner, *The Messianic Idea*, 409.
135. "Doing" refers to the performance of the commandments. See *b'Eruvin* 22a and *b'Avodah zarah* 3a, on the verse "Therefore, observe faithfully the commandments, and the statutes, and the judgments, which I command you today, to do them" (Deut. 7:11). According to Rashi, "today" refers to this world and "tomorrow" to the world-to-come, where after death, there will no longer be any point in performing the commandments, because (*b'Avodah zarah* 3a) "[only] he who has toiled on the eve of the Sabbath will eat on the Sabbath."
136. LT *Pinhas* 75b–c.
137. See, for example, LT *Pinhas* 75c.
138. LT *Pinhas* 75c; see also LT *Va-ethanan* 4d, *Yom ha-kipurim* 70a.
139. See also LT *Re'eh* 33c.
140. "This world was created with [the letter] *he*, and the world to come with [the letter] *yud*" (*bMenahot* 29b). See LT *Re'eh* 33c. In numerous places (e.g., LT *Pinhas* 76c, *Shemini 'atseret* 83d), the *yud* is associated with the contraction and with the restricting powers of *Gevurot*.
141. See LT *Devarim* 1b. In LT *Shemini 'atseret* 85d–86a, Rabbi Eleazar ben Durdaya is presented as a paragon of radical transformation through repentance (see *b'Avodah zarah* 17a). This apparently contradicts the definition in *Tanya* of the complete *tsadik* as one who has never even harbored a sinful thought (see T1, 10:14b–15). However, repentance transcends time and can therefore undo whatever has been done within time's boundaries. On Shneur Zalman's concept of *tsadik* see Hallamish, "Mishnato ha-'iyunit," 352–63; Loewenthal, "Self-Sacrifice," 458–60. The confusion between divine and ostensibly nondivine elements in exilic reality prompts a comparison to a dream, which is characterized by the "withdrawal of consciousness." According to this analogy, the wakeful mind perceives reality as a divine whole, whereas the imagination, which is active in a dream, tends to divide its object into separate and independent entities (see TO 28c–d). However, a dream can also combine "two opposites in one subject": *sacrum* and *profanum*, Godliness and materiality, and so on (see MAHZ 5565, i, 184–85). While the imagination generating the dream-like reality of the individual in exile does not provide the sharp and explicit cognition of the divine reality that is available to the wakeful consciousness of the redeemed individual, nevertheless, it makes it possible to overcome the chaos of exile by finding Godliness within the separate beings that inhabit the lower worlds (see Wolfson, *A Dream*, 203–17). The states of sleeping and dreaming also evoke other associations with the exile: the dream is the debris of materiality that remains in the body after the divine vitality has departed from it while the person is asleep. Analogously, the state of confusion in the exilic world constitutes the material

waste that is being purified over the course of the exile; see MAHZ *Razal* 315–16. It is also worth noting that, for some Hasidic masters, dreams may give access to a realm that transcends the boundaries of time and space ("is higher than time"). See Idel, "Higher than Time," 203–4.

142. On the paradox of *yedi'ah u-vehirah*, literally, "knowledge and choice," see Jacobs, "Divine Foreknowledge."
143. LT *Pinhas* 75b-c.
144. See Foxbrunner, *Habad*, 265n75.
145. LT *Shemini 'atseret* 86a.
146. LT *Re'eh* 33b-c.
147. See bShabat 152b and *Pirke de-Rabi Eli'ezer*, chapter 34, 33b.
148. See Zii 142a-b and Ziii 25a.
149. See Zii 59a.
150. See LT *Re'eh* 33b and *Va-ethanan* 4d, where it is compared to the cutting of the cord that keeps the soul clothed in the sackcloth of mundane deeds, words, and thoughts.
151. LT *Pinhas* 75c.
152. Here referred to as the world-to-come (*'alma de-ate*); see bHagigah 15b.
153. LT *Korah* 53d. It is often difficult to ascertain whether Shneur Zalman regards the hollow of a sling as something that happens to individual souls in the unredeemed world immediately following their death, or as a transitory period preceding the resurrection and the collective redemption. Such confusion between the realm of the souls after death and the redeemed world (either in the messianic era or at the resurrection of the dead) is common in rabbinic literature.
154. See T1, 8:13a; see also Zi, 62b, 237b; Zii 150a-b; Vital, *Likute Torah*, Shemot, 122.
155. See, for example, LT *Devarim* 1b, *Yom ha-kipurim* 70a. See also LT *Re'eh* 23c, where Shneur Zalman states that three things were given to Israel by God through sufferings: the world-to-come, Torah, and the Land of Israel (see bBerakhot 5a).
156. See TO 49a.
157. See, for example, TO 49a-b; LT *Be-shalah* 1d, *Be-ha'alotekha* 33b, *Va-yikra hosafot* 52b, *Hukat* 62b, *Shir ha-shirim* 4b.
158. See LT *Re'eh* 23d. See also T3, 12:101a, where Shneur Zalman links this to the idea that this world was built with the attribute of Kindness (*Hesed*), while the world-to-come was built with the attribute of Judgment (*Din*). See also LT *Pinhas* 76c. On the significance of fasts and other mortifications, see T3, 1–12:91a–93a, 7:97a. In some places, Shneur Zalman states that to confront all the obstacles, sufferings, and labors of this world would result in a higher elevation in the world-to-come. This is also the reason why, according to Shneur Zalman, Abraham preferred the enslavement of Israel by other nations to the sufferings of *Gehinom* (see *Bereshit rabah* 44:21): from the lowest level of exile one can ascend to the highest levels of the world-to-come. See TO 8b

159. See, for example, TO 31a, 69c, 96a; LT *Be-shalah* 1d *Be-ha'alotekha* 33d, *Va-yikra hosafot* 52b, *Shemini 'atseret* 84d-85a; *Seder tefilot*, 10; MAHZ *Ethalekh*, 168. See also Zii 211b.
160. See TO 49a, 98b, and LT *Be-har* 41b, where Shneur Zalman reasons that the sources only wished to reveal these two to us, and therefore did not mention the other Gardens of Eden.
161. See, for example, TO 32d, 49a, 81d, 98b; LT *Ba-midbar* 18a, *Be-ha'alotekha*, 33d.
162. bBerakhot 64a; bMo'ed katan 29a. Note, however, that in both of these instances, the Talmud refers to "scholars" (*talmide hakhamim*) rather than to "the righteous" (*tsadikim*), as Shneur Zalman does in most cases.
163. See bHagigah 13b; *Bereshit rabah* 78:11; Zii 221b; LT *Shelah* 41a, *Matot* 86b.
164. See, for example, 3 Enoch 18:19, 33:5, and the notes provided there; bHagigah 13b; *Eikhah rabah* 3:8; *Tikune zohar*, Hakdamah, 4a.
165. Ziii 16b; see also Zi, 201a; Zii, 247a; Ziii, 159b.
166. Zii 211b. See also de Vidas, *Reshit hokhmah*, Gate of Fear, chapter 33.
167. See TO 69c, where Shneur Zalman directly refers to the River of Fire as the river of oblivion: "This is like the level of the Lower Garden of Eden, that comes after this world, which requires immersion in the River of Fire that separates between them, in order to forget the disposition of material memory; for as long as one remembers materiality, one is not able of delight in the Garden of Eden."
168. See MAHZ *'Inyanim*, 92.
169. See MAHZ *'Inyanim*, 93–94.
170. See TO 2b-d.
171. See, for example, MAHZ *Nevi'im* 252–54, or MAHZ *Parshiyot*, i, 296–97, where Shneur Zalman defines the Sabbath and the delight associated with it as originating above time and above the order of concatenation. He reads the following verse literally, "then [on the Sabbath] shalt thou delight thyself above the Lord ['*al YHVH*]" (Isa 58:14), taking it to mean that the delight of the Sabbath lies above the Tetragrammaton, which comprises all three dimensions of time in the, past, present, and future tense of the Hebrew verb "to be."
172. See, for example, TO 10a; LT *Shir ha-shirim* 32a; *Seder tefilot* 169a–174a. See also Idel, "Sabbath," 86–88 for a similar concept of the Sabbath in Kalonimus Kalman Epstein's *Ma'or va-shemesh*, Va-yeshev 28a. According to *Ma'or va-shemesh*, the righteous ones cause the *sefirah* of *Malkhut* to ascent to *'Atika kadisha* in each and every Sabbath, and then draw down the influx on the congregation of Israel, a process that resembles the anticipated redemption at the end of days.
173. See, for example, LT *Shir ha-shirim* 25a,
174. See *Seder tefilot* 139c; TO 8c.
175. On the idea of delight, see Idel, "Ta'anug."
176. bShabat 131b; see *Seder tefilot* 139a, 141b.
177. On "circumcision from above" as "arousal from above" without prior arousal from below, see LT *Tazri'a* 21a.

178. See *Seder tefilot*, 139a.
179. See LT *Tazri'a* 21d, based on Bahya bar Asher *Midrash Rabenu Bahya*, Naso, 4:47; *Bamidbar rabah* 15:11.
180. See TO 13c.
181. TO 13d, discussed in Wolfson, *Alef Mem Tau*, 113–15.
182. See also T4, 4:105a-b, where Shneur Zalman compares the two stages of circumcision, *milah* and *peri'ah*, respectively, to circumcision as performed by man (from below) and by God in the messianic era (from above). *Milah* stands for contemplation, in which the individual casts off all of his worldly concerns and strives to understand and know God; *peri'ah* stands for God's response to man's contemplation, whereby he uncovers the innermost part of man's heart, ceases to be an object of man's contemplation, and becomes "literally your whole life" beyond discursive comprehension. This spiritual transformation achieved by the individual's worship of God will become a collective experience in the messianic era, "when *da'at* is diverted" (T4, 4:105b). On individual worship that transcends *da'at*, see above.
183. See TO 18d.
184. See Scholem, *The Messianic Idea*, 4.
185. See also Garb, "Rabbi Kook," 82–83, which presents Hasidic messianism as a spiritual process that aims at removing the psychological barriers that separate God from the world, as opposed to the messianism of M. H. Luzzatto and the Vilna Gaon, which seeks to remove the historical obstacle to the revelation of God's absolute oneness. Shneur Zalman's messianic idea, however, defies this dichotomy, and Garb's description of the *mitnagedic* messianism, according to which "the entire course of history is designed to enable the formation of a power seemingly opposing God, and then to annul this semblance" (Garb, "Rabbi Kook," 82) could serve as an apt summary of Shneur Zalman's messianic concept of *dirah ba-tahtonim*. As we have seen, the *psychological* is closely connected in his teachings with the *historical*, and the transformation of one's personal "four cubits of *halakhah*" in the present has far-reaching consequences for the future redemption of the nation.
186. On the Noahide laws, see Novak, *The Image*. On the Habad Noahide campaign, see Wolfson, *Open Secret*, 229–31; Heilman and Friedman, *The Rebbe*, 214; Dahan, "Dirah ba-tahtonim," 369–73; Kraus, *Ha-shevi'i*, 224–49.
187. See *Shulhan 'arukh Rabenu ha-Zaken*, Hoshen mishpat, Hilkhot gezelah u-genevah, par. 23, 881 and *Orah hayim*, Mahadura batra, 411a.
188. Shneur Zalman indeed authored a text, addressed to non-Jews, which included explanations of some kabbalistic and Hasidic concepts. He wrote it in 1800 while in prison, and the text in question is a refutation to a list of allegations raised against the Hasidim by their opponents. Therefore, while a doubtlessly fascinating and unique document, it can hardly be seen as an example of outreach. See Mondshine, "Ha-ma'asar ha-sheni,"

88–105. See also Loewenthal, *Communicating*, 205–11 on a similar document penned in similar circumstances by Shneur Zalman's son and successor, Dov Ber Shneuri.
189. See Dahan, "Dirah ba-tahtonim," 371; Wolfson, *Open Secret*, 229–31.
190. See Schneersohn, *Igeret ha-kodesh*, i, 485, discussed in Dahan, "Dirah ba-tahtonim," 308–9.
191. For a detailed analysis of the complex attitude of Menahem Mendel Schneerson to the Land of Israel, the state of Israel, and the Zionist project, see Dahan, "Yahaso shel R. Menahem Mendel"; Dahan, "Dirah ba-tahtonim," 295–340.

Chapter 4

1. *b*Shabat 31a. The first question concerns business ethics.
2. "If there is no *derekh erets*, there is no Torah." Rashi to *b*Shabat 31a, quoting *m*Avot 3:17.
3. *Sefer ha-hinukh*, 419; Maimonides, *Mishneh Torah*, Laws of Torah Study, 1:8.
4. Shmuel Eidels (Maharsha), *Hidushe agadot*, 18b to *b*Shabat 31. See also Horovits, *Shene luhot ha-berit*, Masekhet shavu'ot, ner mitsvah, 11: "'Itim in the plural, because one should set as many times as possible, whenever he is free from his occupation."
5. Ya'akov Ben Asher, *Arba'ah turim*: Orah hayim, par. 155; Karo, *Shulhan 'arukh*, Orah hayim, par. 155; for the Talmudic source informing the codices, see *b*Berakhot 64a.
6. HTT 3:2, 846a, based on *b*Yoma 19b. Despite being a highly creative author himself, Shneur Zalman does not include—at least not explicitly—creative skills in his description of the scholarly ideal. This makes him different from his teacher, the Maggid of Mezrich; see Mayse, "Beyond the Letters," 403–45.
7. This has been argued by Norman Lamm, who juxtaposed Shneur Zalman's and Hayim of Volozhin's (1749–1821) ideals of Torah study; see his *Torah Lishmah*, 152. For arguments in favor of the centrality of Torah study in Shneur Zalman's doctrine, see Foxbrunner, *Habad*, 137–39.
8. Shneur Zalman refers to *Kohelet rabah* 7:28 on Ecclesiastes 7:28 to illustrate the relation between these two groups: "'I found only one human being in a thousand.' Usually if a thousand men take up the study of Scripture, a hundred of them proceed to the study of Mishnah, ten to Talmud, and one of them becomes qualified to decide questions of law"; HTT 3:4, 846b–47a.
9. HTT 3:1, 841a.
10. HTT 3:4, 446b.
11. See HTT, *Kuntres aharon*, 3:1, 844a; *Ma'amar* "Perek ehad shaharit," in Ashkenazi, *Hilkhot talmud Torah*, 5:621, and in Mondshine, *Migdal 'oz*, 5.

12. See Ashkenazi, *Hilkhot talmud Torah*, 5:102.
13. Shneur Zalman referred to his Hasidim as "learned" (*yod'e sefer*), a category that covers a wide range of literacy levels falling short of the elitist status of scholar. His Hasidim were conversant with rabbinic literature (see, for example, his epistle on the yearly cycle of Talmud study in congregations of his followers in T4, 1:102a–3a) and capable of following his mystical sermons, transcribing and distributing them in manuscript form, and reading as well as understanding the *Tanya*—either on their own or with the help of prominent Hasidim who functioned as local leaders (see T1, Hakdamah, 4a). The classification of the vast majority of Shneur Zalman's Hasidim as nonscholars certainly does not imply that they were ignorant; it simply aims to distinguish them from the scholarly elite. On the high standard of Torah education among Shneur Zalman's followers, see Etkes, *Rabbi Shneur Zalman*, 114, 129–31; Etkes, "Darko shel R. Shneur Zalman," 349, 352–53.
14. The distinction between the elite and the common people is addressed in Shneur Zalman's writings in various ways. Two such distinctions occur in both his sermons and his halakhic writings. The first one, which is focused on their Torah knowledge and position in society, is between scholars and nonscholars such as tradesmen (*ba'ale 'asakim*), householders (*ba'ale batim*), and those who perform commandments (*ba'ale mitsvot*). The second one distinguishes between penitents (*ba'ale teshuvah*) and righteous men (*tsadikim*) in terms of their relation to God: the latter are permanently united with God, while the former may return to God from their secular activities by means of ritual. Several sources indicate that these two distinctions are synonymous. See, for example, the excerpt from LT *Shir ha-shirim* 44d–45a, discussed on page 231. Finally, in the first part of *Tanya*, Shneur Zalman introduces the distinction between the intermediate and the righteous person (*beinoni* and *tsadik*), namely, between two ethical paradigms. The *beinoni* has the potential to sin, yet always manages to suppress his urge to do so, whereas the *tsadik* never sins, and is also able to transform evil into good. While only a very small group of saintly individuals can reach the level of *tsadik* (if it is attainable at all—see LT *Tazri'a* 22b), the level of *beinoni* seems to correspond to the ethical ideal of the first Habad followers, who were predominantly householders and tradesmen (see Etkes, "Darko shel R. Shneur Zalman," 353; Etkes, *Rabbi Shneur Zalman*, 114). On the problem of transposing the categories of *beinoni* and *tsadik* from *Tanya* to the sermons, see Moshe Hallamish, "Yahase tsadik ve-'edah," 90; Dan and Tishby, "Torat ha-hasidut," 792–93. See also Etkes, *Ba'al ha-Tanya*, 208, where he resolves this problem by defining the categories from *Tanya* as abstract ideals, which the Hasidim should strive to achieve, and the categories prevalent in the sermons as descriptions of real-life people that emerged from Shneur Zalman's direct contact with his followers.
15. The importance of such a stratification of the Jewish community in Habad ideology is evident in a letter written by the sixth Lubavitcher Rebbe, Yosef

Yitshak Schneersohn, in 1932, in which he emphasizes the traditional difference between tradesmen, including those who spend a good deal of time on study, and scholars (*yoshve ohel*), sharply criticizing the modern idea that "everyone should be equal" as wasteful and destructive. See his introduction to Shalom Dovber Schneersohn, *Kuntres 'ets ha-hayim*, 7.

16. See HTT 3:4, 847a.
17. See HTT, *Kuntres aharon*, 3:1, 843; on the novelty of the commandment of knowing the Torah, see Foxbrunner, *Habad*, 138–40. An analogous typology appears in MAHZ 5562, i, 182–83, where Shneur Zalman lists two commandments included in the Torah: reasoning and study (*higayon ve-'iyun*), and reading out loud (*keri'ah be-dibur*); see also Hallamish, "Mishnato ha-'iyunit," 276n7.
18. HTT, *Kuntres aharon*, 3:1, 843c. However, in TO 108d–9a, Shneur Zalman dismisses this view and presents the verbal articulation of Torah as superior to comprehension, for through "speech" of Torah, one draws down *Keter* (divine nothingness and the source of *Hokhmah*) into *Malkhut* (speech) and achieves self-nullification.
19. HTT 1: 4, 831b–32a. Elsewhere, Shneur Zalman presents knowledge of Torah in general as a regulative idea rather than something that anyone could really achieve, given the infinity of the Torah: "No one can reach the end of the Torah, which in itself does not have an end or limit." Even if someone was to memorize the entire corpus of Written and Oral Torah, that person should continue with learning its possible interpretations. See HTT 2:5, 835a.
20. HTT 3:6, 847b–48a; T1, 8:13a.
21. HTT 3: 7, 848a. See also T1, 8:13b. On Shneur Zalman's attitude to non-Jewish philosophy, see chapter 1.
22. In letters sent to his followers, Shneur Zalman acknowledges their worsening economic situation. See, for example, T4, 16:124a-b; Hillman, *Igerot Ba'al ha-Tanya*, 32–33, 70, 94–95, and 217–21, where Dov Ber, Shneur Zalman's son, notes that even the most gifted and intelligent young men are not being spared the toil of trade, and expressed the fear that they would, as a result, forget everything that they had learned (Levine, *Igerot kodesh*, i, 52–53, 59–60, 60–65, 225–33). Similarly, according to the Habad chronicler Hayim Meir Heilman, Shneur Zalman began working on his *Shulhan 'arukh* in order to ensure that his contemporaries would be able to learn all 613 commandments despite the economic situation that deprived them of the time necessary for deep halakhic studies; see Heilman, *Bet rabi*, 3b. For a discussion of the origins of *Shulhan 'arukh*, different from Habad narratives, see Cooper, "Mysteries of the Paratexts." See also Hallamish, "Mishnato ha-'iyunit," 309, where Shneur Zalman's affirmative attitude toward tradesmen among his followers is said to have been motivated by his compassion and understanding of the circumstances in which they lived.
23. HTT 3:4, 847b, based on *b*Menahot, 99b.
24. HTT 3:5, 847b.

25. *Shulḥan 'arukh Rabenu ha-Zaken*, Orah hayim, Seder masa u-matan, par. 156.
26. T1, 4:102a; T5, 163a.
27. HTT 3:4, 847a.
28. The distinction between these two modes of Torah study is rendered in Shneur Zalman's mystical writings as a distinction between two types of souls: those of scholars and those individuals who perform the commandments (*ba'ale mitsvot*). The former are committed to full-time study; the latter devote a limited time to learning, but make up for this by performing other commandments, particularly charity (T4, 5:109a; LT *Ha'azinu* 74b; see also Lamm, *Torah Lishmah*, 149–50). The scholars' souls derive from limitless *Hesed*, whereas the souls of *ba'ale mitsvot* derive from the constraining *Gevurah*, which is the reason for the precept of fixing limited times for study. However, in Shneur Zalman's doctrine, every Jew carries both traits, which in practical terms means that *ba'ale mitsvot* should complement their limited Torah study with generous charity (T4, 13:119a). This charity should facilitate Torah study by scholars and credit the donor "as if he truly studied himself" (HTT 3:4, 847a). See also Ornet, *Ratso va-shov*, 181–82 on the two types of souls—those of scholars and tradesmen—and their respective obligations in relation to the biblical distinction between the tribes of Issachar, predestined to study the Torah, and Zebulun, commanded to support the Issacharites. On Issachar and Zebulun in rabbinic literature and Hasidism, see S. D. Breslauer, "Zebulun and Issachar."
29. *Shulḥan 'arukh Rabenu ha-Zaken*, Orah hayim, Hilkhot talmud Torah, par. 150.
30. *Shulḥan 'arukh Rabenu ha-Zaken*, Orah hayim, Hilkhot talmud Torah, par. 1.
31. See, for example, Dov Ber Shneuri, *Pokeaḥ 'ivrim*, 54.
32. LT *Shir ha-shirim* 44d–45a.
33. LT *Shir ha-shirim* 75a; on repentance which is not related to sins, see TO 74a; LT *Re'eh* 24d, 33a, *Nitsavim* 48d, *Rosh ha-shanah* 60d, *Shabat shuvah* 65c, 66c, *Ha'azinu* 77b, *Shir ha-shirim* 44d; MAHZ 5565, i, 493–94; 5572, 5; Seder tefilot, 226a.
34. Although in several discourses (MAHZ 5571, 84, 92, 106, 119) he mentions people who are completely "unable to study and to fix times," and for that reason their worship is based exclusively on good deeds, one can surmise that they are still obliged to recite the *Shema'*, which in certain circumstances is considered to be Torah study, too.
35. Described in the kabbalistic parlances as "Kindnesses of the Father" (*ḥasadim de-aba*), which lie higher than "Kindnesses of the Mother" (*ḥasadim de-ima*), achievable through full-time studies. MAHZ 5565, ii, 873. "Father" and "Mother" are two constellations of *sefirot* (so-called *partsufim*), which refer to the *sefirot Hokhmah* and *Binah*—the respective sources of unbounded *Hesed* and constricted *Din*. One who is engrossed in worldly affairs and studies at set times needs to dissolve himself in the

unbounded divine Wisdom in order to arouse in himself the love of God, whereas a full-time Torah student is able to find the love of God by means of contemplation (*hitbonenut*—a term deriving from *binah*) of the Godliness within the constrictions of the world. For the Lurianic doctrine of *partsufim*, see Scholem, *Kabbalah*, 140–44. For the source of the notions of "Kindnesses of Father" and "Kindnesses of Mother," see Vital, *'Ets hayim*, Gate of Principles, chapter 10, 15–16.

36. Rashi to *b*Berakhot 21a.
37. LT *Sukot* 81a.
38. Elsewhere, he points at another advantage of Torah studies undertaken by ignoramuses. According to him, Torah study requires that the student's mind should be entirely devoted to the Torah. A wise person preoccupied with numerous worldly matters may find it difficult to disengage in that manner and focus exclusively on the Torah, whereas ignoramuses, whose strengths are not intellectual, are not distracted by worldly matters when they undertake Torah study, and from this perspective, they are paradoxically more successful in their studies than the more intellectually gifted people. See LT *Shir ha-shirim* 25d.
39. Elior, *Paradoxical Ascent*, 191––; Elior, *Torat ha-elohut*, 290–315; Jacobs, *Hasidic Prayer*, 100–3; Etkes, "The War of Lyady Succession."
40. LT *Shir ha-shirim* 44d; see Ornet, *Ratso va-shov*, 182–83. See also: MAHZ 5565, i, 494–95, where the essential change is defined as the cause of ecstasy, and MAHZ 5565, i, 502–3, where the cause of ecstasy is the renewal, inherent in penitence.
41. TO 80c.
42. "Let us begin with the *Zohar*'s esoteric interpretation of *teshuvah*. [*Teshuvah*] is *tashuv heh* ['the *heh* is to be returned']. [The reconnection of] the letter *heh* [to the preceding letter *vav*] is *teshuvah tata'ah* ['lower-level *teshuvah*']; [the reconnection of] the former *heh* [to the precedent letter *yud*] is *teshuvah 'ila'ah* ['upper-level *teshuvah*']." T3, 4:93b, based on Ziii 122a. The letters of the Tetragrammaton refer to different aspects of the sefirotic tree: *yud* to Hokhmah, *heh* to Binah, *vav* to the six lower *sefirot* (Hesed, Gevurah, Tif'eret, Netsah, Hod, and Yesod), and the second *heh* to the lowest *sefirah* Malkhut, identified with the divine speech. See T3, 4:94b. For a scholarly discussion on this, see Foxbrunner, *Habad*, 133–36.
43. T3, 9:98b. See also T3, 8:98b, where Shneur Zalman presents Torah study as the "upper-level" *teshuvah*, following Ziii, 123a.
44. *Vayikra rabah*, 25:1.
45. MAHZ *Ketuvim*, i, 17. In a similar vein, Maharsha interprets the plural of *'itim* as referring to morning and evening study. See Eidels, *Hidushe agadot* 18b, to *b*Shabat 31a.
46. Job 31:2. On the soul as part of God, see, for example, T1, 2:6a, 35:44a; TO 16a; LT *Va-yikra* 2d.
47. On the possibility of achieving mystical union through halakhic study, see Loewenthal, "Finding the Radiance," 301–8.

48. TI, 10:16a
49. See TI, 14:20a, 27:33b–34a, and Polen, "Charismatic Leader," 57–59. Shneur Zalman does not deny the possibility that by means of repentance, the wicked person (*rasha'*) could be transformed into a *beinoni* or even into a *tsadik* in some particular cases, such as that of Eleazar ben Durdaya (*b'Avodah zarah* 17a); see *Seder tefilot*, 226c; LT *Ahare* 26c, *Va-ethanan* 9b, *Nitsavim* 46d, *Shemini 'atseret* 84d–85a; TO 20d; MAHZ *Razal* 106–7.
50. MAHZ *Ketsarim*, 119; see also Loewenthal, *Communicating*, 69.
51. MAHZ 5571, 204–5.
52. MAHZ 5571, 204–5. See also Green, "Around the Maggid's Table," 141–49 for the use of the same midrashic image of "the eyes of the congregation" to define the relationship between the *tsadikim* and their followers in Levi Yitshak of Berdichev, Issakhar Dov of Zlochov, Dov Ber of Mezrich, and Elimelekh of Lizhensk. Notably, Shneur Zalman does not limit the "eyes of the congregation" to singular *tsadikim*, whose status is based on their spiritual stature, but broadens the scope of the term to include the still elitist, yet relatively more inclusive, merit-based class of Torah scholars.
53. On Cordoverian notions of direct and reflected light see Scholem, *Major Trends*, 261–73; Scholem, *Kabbalah*, 131.
54. On extracting the sparks of holiness from the husk of *nogah*, see Foxbrunner, *Habad*, 22.
55. MAHZ 5571, 105. On the breaking of the vessels in Lurianic kabbalah, see Scholem, *Kabbalah*, 135–40; Scholem, *Major Trends*, 265–68.
56. MAHZ 5571, 105.
57. Lamm, *Torah Lishmah*, 152.
58. MAHZ 5571, 105 and 204–5.
59. On the idea of the human temple in the beginnings of Hasidism, see Margolin, *Mikdash adam*, 127–38.
60. See, for example, de Vidas, *Reshit hokhmah*, Gate of Love, chapter 6, 58a; Alshekh, *Torat Mosheh*, Terumah, 148a; Horovits, *Shene luhot ha-berit*, Gate of Letters, ot kuf, 5.
61. LT *Naso* 20b.
62. See TO 87a, where commandments are compared to the curtains that covered the sanctuary on the outside, and Torah study to the instruments of the tabernacle, the inner components of the sanctuary.
63. LT *Be-har* 43a. See also TI, 53:74b; TO 90d; LT *Va-yikra* 1d, *Balak* 74d, *Va-ethanan* 10a.
64. TI, 34:43a-b.
65. On different types of nullification in the Habad tradition, see Wolfson, *Open Secret*, 75–76.
66. On the complete disclosure of the Torah in the future-to-come, see, for example, LT *Matot* 84a-b.
67. Horovits, *Shene luhot ha-berit*, Gate of Letters, ot kuf, 5.
68. TI, 53:74a-b.

69. TI, 34:43a-b.
70. LT *Balak* 74d–75a; *Va-ethanan* 11a.
71. Idel, *Hasidism*, 198–207.
72. See, for example, LT *Tetse* 40c.
73. MAHZ 5571, 83.
74. On Shneur Zalman's understanding of *Torah li-shmah*, see Foxbrunner, *Habad*, 152–54. See also Idel, *Hasidism*, 176–85, who compares it with other Hasidic masters; and Lamm, *Torah Lishmah*, 191–92, who proposes functional, devotional, and cognitive definitions of *li-shmah*.
75. MAHZ 5571, 81–82.
76. TI, 4:8a.
77. See also TO 47c on set times for study as disclosure of the divine will in thought and speech.
78. See, for example, *Keter shem tov*, par. 121, and Dov Ber of Mezrich, *Or Torah*, 1:84d. For a discussion of this issue see Idel, "Ta'anug," 132–35, where he places this dictum in the context of avoiding routine worship. Notably, in his discourse Shneur Zalman uses the same dictum precisely in order to empower religious routine.
79. MAHZ *Parshiyot*, i, Hosafot, Va-yetse, 7; 5572, 102–3.
80. See also LT *Ha'azinu* 76a, discussed in Hallamish, "Mishnato ha-'iyunit," 274, where it is explicitly stated that a tradesman can draw down the divine light by *li-shmah* study at set times. In this case, the difference between a full-time student (*she-torato omanuto*) and a tradesman who studies at set times is annulled, for they both allow the Torah to speak through them. Tradesmen, however, must complement their study with charity. Notably, some passages in Shneur Zalman's *ma'amarim* (MAHZ 5571, 84, 92, 106, 119) seem to exempt those "who cannot set times for study at all" and are "empty of Torah," but nevertheless draw down the influx through their *mitsvot*.
81. MAHZ 5571, 119.
82. MAHZ 5571, 119; see an alternative version of the discourse in TO 80c. This differs from the Maggid's approach, who is said to refer to study *li-shemah* as a domain specifically of scholars, and who interprets the verse "Let not this book of the law cease from your lips, but meditate therein day and night" (Josh. 1:8) as referring to contemplating the Torah thoughts rather than reciting its text, as in the average man's study, according to Shneur Zalman. See Heller, *Yosher divre emet*, 11–12, par. 10, discussed in Mayse, "Beyond the letters," 385–87.
83. On the ideological implication of setting study sessions immediately after prayer, see Hallamish, "Mishnato ha-'iyunit," 257–58, where he presents Torah study at set times as the final stage of the process that begins with prayer and effects the spiritualization of the self.
84. LT *Va-yikra* 4d; see also TI, 6:10b. On the interdependence of Torah and other types of worship in the context of *bitul*, see Foxbrunner, *Habad*, 148–49.

85. On *mesirat nefesh* and *kidush ha-Shem* in the Habad school, see Loewenthal, "Self-Sacrifice," 457–94; Elior, *Paradoxical Ascent*, 185–89.
86. LT *Shir ha-shirim* 22a. On the development of the idea of the *Shekhinah*, which overtakes man's vocal apparatus in prayer and study, see Idel, "'Adonai Sefatai Tiftah,'" 34–49; Idel, *Enchanted Chains*, 196–202.
87. TI, 41:58b; LT *Be-har* 40c-d, *Ha'azinu* 74a, *Tazri'a*, 22d–23a, *Va-yikra* 5a.
88. See, for example, LT *Ha'azinu* 74a, *Shir ha-shirim* 17a, 49a-b.
89. See, for example, TO 25b; LT *Shir ha-shirim* 46a; MAHZ *Ethalekh*, 17–18.
90. See Mayse, "Beyond the Letters," 491. See also chapter 3 above.
91. See, for example, TO 45c; LT *Tsav* 15c, *Shir ha-shirim* 5c-d; MAHZ 5564, 238; *Seder tefilot*, 116a, 132c, 237d. See Ornet, *Ratso va-shov*, 229–31. The custom of praying *'Amidah* quietly is already attested in the Talmud (*b*Berakhot 24b). However, see Garb, *Shamanic Trance*, 80–81, which discusses the rite of *Nefilat apayim* as the culmination of prayer, in which a person reaches the state of absolute unification with God. In this case, the *'Amidah* is considered a preparatory stage that transforms the self into a perfect vessel for the divine influx. See also *Seder tefilot*, 26a. For a brief survey of the use of silence in kabbalah and Hasidism, including examples of use in Habad, see Hallamish, "'Al ha-shetikah."
92. Based on the typology, which classifies four types of beings: inanimate (*domem*), vegetative (*tsomeah*), animate (*hai*), and speaking (*medaber*).
93. For various discourses arguing in favor of study following prayer, see LT *Shir ha-shirim* 20d, LT *Berakhah* 96b-c, *Va-ethanan* 4a. On self-sacrifice in prayer as the condition for Torah study, see also LT *Shir ha-shirim* 41a, *Emor* 33c, *Be-har* 40d, *Ba-midbar* 19d; MAHZ 5570, 8; *Ethalekh*, 90.
94. TO 16b. On the unity of the Torah and God, see Tishby, *Wisdom of the Zohar*, 3.1085–86. See also Tishby's *Hikre kabalah*, 3.941–53, where he corrects the common erroneous attribution of this expression to the *Zohar* by pointing out its origin in Moshe Hayim Luzzatto's writings. See also LT *Sukot* 79c, "A man can have the impression of the nullification of 18 blessings ['*Amidah*] set and affixed, so it will never be shaken, every day in his Torah studies," and the discussion of this passage in Hallamish, "Mishnato ha-'iyunit," 257–58.
95. TO 28d; see also TI, 12:16b–17a.
96. On Habad worship through corporeality, see Wolfson, *Open Secret*, 138–40.
97. On twofold ecstasy in Shneur Zalman, see Wolfson, *Open Secret*, 145; Wolfson, "Oneiric Imagination," 141.
98. Based on *m*Avot 2:4.
99. LT *Shir ha-shirim* 25d–26a; on the mystical role of ritual routine, see Wolfson, *Open Secret*, 74: "Indeed, even the minimal halakhic routine should and can be endowed with this mystical valence predicated on the consubstantiality of God and the Jewish soul."
100. LT *Ba-midbar* 13d.

101. See LT *Tavo* 43a.
102. LT *Kedoshim* 30d. Ideally, everyone ought to memorize the entire Written and Oral Torah. However, because of the "affliction of the times, shortness of the comprehending consciousness and the deepness of the subject," it is enough for a scholar to memorize merely the Pentateuch and the *Seder kodashim* from the Talmud.
103. LT *Re'eh* 23b. On eternal Torah, see, for example, LT *Ba-midbar* 13a-b, *Balak* 68b.
104. Based on the midrash to Exod. 34:11: "What I am command you this day"—"Every day [these words of Torah] will be in your eyes as new"; see *Pesikta zutarta* Va-ethanan, 69; Rashi to Deut. 26:16; Bahya bar Asher, *Midrash Rabenu Bahya*, Deut. 6:10; see also *Pesikta de-Rav Kahana*, Ba-hodesh ha-shelishi, pis. 12:138–39, 107a.
105. Wolfson notes that in Torah study, "Each interpretative gesture is a re-enactment of the revelatory experience, albeit from its unique vantage point, each moment a novel replication of the past" (*Alef, Mem, Tau*, 64–65).
106. See MAHZ 5570, 10, and LT *Shir ha-shirim* 42a-b, *Matot* 82a-b.
107. See MAHZ 5570, 10.
108. On the symbolism of *Ze'ir anpin* and *Nukba* in Lurianic kabbalah, see Scholem, *Kabbalah*, 141–42.
109. MAHZ *Ketuvim*, i, 233; *Boneh Yerushalayim*, 80 (77); MAHZ *Ketsarim*, 251.
110. Scholem, *Kabbalah*, 141.
111. See chapter 1.
112. See also *Seder tefilot* 75a-b, where *sha'ah* is identified as the unity of past, present, and future. An instructive passage on *Malkhut* as *haye sha'ah*, in the sense of an ecstatic moment encapsulating all three tenses, can be found in Tsemah Tsedek's *Derekh mitsvotekha*, 1:151a-b, and is discussed in Wolfson, *Open Secret*, 277–78. On the relation between contemplation and ecstasy in Habad worship, see Elior, *Paradoxical Ascent*, 162.
113. The comparison of prayer to "temporal life" and of Torah to "eternal life" is used by Shneur Zalman to justify exempting professional scholars from praying the 'Amidah, see HTT 3:5, 85la, *Shulhan 'arukh Rabenu ha-Zaken*, Orah hayim, par. 106, discussed in Foxbrunner, *Habad*, 139.
114. *Seder tefilot* 28a.
115. See also T5, 155b. The connection between the temporal life of prayer with *Malkhut* and the eternal life of Torah study with *Ze'ir anpin* appears in Mosheh Hayim Luzzatto, *Sefer adir ba-marom ha-shalem*, 109–10, see also Liwer, "Torah shebe-'al peh," 329.
116. Dov Ber Shneuri, *Perush ha-milot*, 59b.
117. MAHZ *Ethalekh*, 90.
118. *b*Shabat 10a.
119. MAHZ *Ethalekh*, 91.
120. One of the characteristics of Hasidism that occasioned fierce criticism by its opponents was its flexible attitude to the halakhically set times of prayer.

Indeed, in many Hasidic courts, proper preparations for prayer were considered more important than adherence to the halakhically prescribed times for each of the three daily services, and the desire to attain ecstasy and *devekut* led to unusually prolonged prayer. See Jacobs, *Hasidic Prayer*, 48–53; Schatz Uffenheimer, *Hasidism as Mysticism*, 245–46; Wertheim, *Law and Custom*, 134–43. Shneur Zalman addressed this issue in his teachings. In some of his epistles, sent to various communities, he encouraged *shelihe tsibur* to lead the morning prayer on regular days for an hour or an hour and a half (T4, 1:103a, and see Etkes, *Rabbi Shneur Zalman*, 67), but also sympathized with those who could not invest too much time in prayer because of their professional obligations (T5, 161b–62a, and see Etkes, *Rabbi Shneur Zalman*, 67). He related the deferred time of prayer to the status of different classes of souls: the souls that originate in the world of *Atsilut* pray according to the time of prayer set specifically for that supernal world, while the souls that originate in the lower worlds of *Beri'ah* and *Yetsirah*, which are more remote from God, need to wait until the souls of *Atsilut* have finished praying before commencing their own prayers, at which point they can gather the particles of the innermost light of *Ein Sof* left over from the prayer of the souls in the world of *Atsilut*; the souls of *'Asiyah*, however, owing to their engrossment in materiality, do not have any access to this aspect of the light of *Ein Sof*, and are therefore forbidden to delay their prayers but must comply with the normative set times. In practical terms, this means that while the most distinguished righteous men (*tsadikim muflagim*) are allowed to delay their prayers, simple men and ignoramuses are forbidden to do so. See Mondshine, *Migdal 'oz*, 378–80. According to Heilman, (*Bet rabi*, 89a), Shneur Zalman himself used to prolong the morning prayers until 2:00 p.m.
121. Mayse, "Beyond the Letters," 11–12.
122. See also Hallamish, "Mishnato ha-'iyunit," 309, where he suggests that Shneur Zalman's positive attitude to the nonscholarly folk, exceptional when compared to the elitist ethos of Lithuanian Jewry, contributed to the growing popularity of Hasidism in general and Habad in particular. Hallamish's opinion is based on Shneur Zalman's instruction to allow tradesmen to be called to the pulpit as *shelihe tsibur* on Sabbaths and festivals (T4, 1:103a) and not on his egalitarian approach to Torah study. What Hallamish reads as an "explicit instruction," however, is merely a suggestion to consider them on an equal basis with other members of the congregation for leading services. Be that as it may, the Vilna Gaon, for example, according to a tradition transmitted by his student and cousin Avraham Ragoler (for information on him see Fishman, *Russia's First Modern Jews*, 102–3), compared a man who studies Torah intermittently (*ha-lomed Torah li-ferakim*) to an adulterer (see bSanhedrin 99b), for one who approaches the Torah only occasionally treats it as a harlot, not as a wife (Ragoler, *Ma'alot ha-Torah*, 8). Habad tradition refers to the same Talmudic passage in quite a different way: "The Tsemah Tsedek said: This world is a world of falsity. Therefore, even good is adulterated with chaff

and must be purified 'from below upward' as well as from 'above downward.' The Coming World is the world of truth. In Torah there are discussions of matters which may appear negative, yet the same matters, as they are studied in the Garden of Eden—are actually positive qualities [...]. In This World the statement 'He who studies Torah li-ferakim,' refers to one who studies Torah intermittently; in the Garden of Eden they interpret the statement to mean that he studies Torah and the Torah 'takes him apart,' [namely,] the words of Torah possess him" (Schneerson, Ha-yom yom, entry for 11 Elul, 86).

123. See Schneersohn, *Likute diburim*, 7a–10b. It is also plausible that Shneur Zalman's reevaluation of Torah study at set times laid the conceptual basis for the rejection of the so-called *kolel*-culture by the seventh leader of Habad-Lubavitch, Menahem Mendel Schneerson (see his *Igerot kodesh* [xiv, 30–31] and *Likute sihot* [xxiii, 443]).
124. See Etkes, *Rabbi Shneur Zalman*, 27.
125. See Etkes, *Rabbi Shneur Zalman*, 41–49, and my Introduction above.
126. See Etkes, *Rabbi Shneur Zalman*, 114.
127. Etkes, *Rabbi Shneur Zalman*, 67.
128. Etkes, *Rabbi Shneur Zalman*, 64.
129. Etkes, *Rabbi Shneur Zalman*, 15.
130. On Menahem Mendel as one of the three most important sources of inspiration for Shneur Zalman, see Etkes, *Rabbi Shneur Zalman*, 22.
131. On Shneur Zalman's role in collecting donations for the Hasidim in the Land of Israel, see Etkes, *Rabbi Shneur Zalman*, 81–92.
132. On the role of the "collectors for the sake of the Land of Israel" in enforcing the "Liozna Ordinances" in Habad communities, see Etkes, *Rabbi Shneur Zalman*, 64.

Chapter 5

1. See, most prominently, Horodecky, *Ha-hasidut*, iv, 65–71. For the critique of his approach, see Rapoport-Albert's "On Women in Hasidism" and "The Emergence." See also Wodziński's "Women and Hasidism" and *Hasidism: Key Questions*, 43–86. Hasidic texts using gender imagery, including those discussed below, have experienced a certain resurgence both within the scholarship and across the wide spectrum of Jewish revivalist theologies. See, for example, Polen, "Miriam's Dance," and Rapoport-Albert's rejoinder in her "The Emergence," 404n12. See also Schwartzmann, "From Mystical Visions," a critique of feminist theologies built on kabbalistic and Habad readings of gendered biblical verses; Schwartzmann, "Rabbi Yitzchak Ginsburgh," which points out that the same Hasidic ideas of femininity may serve an ultraorthodox theopolitical agenda, as in the case of Yitshak Ginsburgh, who puts the feminine in the center of his redemptive process in order to counter the masculine narrative of Zionism.

2. See Rapoport-Albert, "On Women in Hasidism," 333–34 and 364–67nn83–84; Rapoport-Albert, "From Woman as Hasid," and "The Emergence"; Loewenthal, "Daughter/Wife"; Loewenthal, "Women and the Dialectic." Loewenthal ("Women and the Dialectic," 8*) argues that the development of the role of Habad women in the twentieth century was motivated by the spiritual concept of "Lower Unity," which was present in Habad thought from its inception. Rapoport-Albert ("From Woman as Hasid"), however, argues that while kabbalistically informed teachings on the female had always been part of Habad's teachings, they were only applied to women within the Habad community in the twentieth century.
3. For a very brief recap of the impact of feminism on Jewish studies and Judaism, see Tirosh-Samuelson, "Gender in Jewish Mysticism," 199–205. For its impact on Habad women, see Morris, *Lubavitcher Women*, in particular 100–22.
4. In form and method, I am indebted to the historical studies of Habad practices by Ada Rapoport-Albert and Tali Loewenthal, as well as to Elliot Wolfson's Lacanian reading of the kabbalistic symbolic system's androcentrism, according to which the female aspects achieve fulfillment only when they perform inherently masculine functions and are included in the male realm. See Wolfson, *Language, Eros, Being*; Wolfson, *Aleph, Mem, Tau*; Wolfson, *Circle in the Square*; and the literature listed in note 2 of this chapter, above.
5. HTT 3:2, 835a-b; see Loewenthal, "Women and the Dialectic," 20*–21*. Organized networks for religious education for Hasidic women emerged only in the twentieth century. For examples in Habad, see Rapoport-Albert, "The Emergence," 387–91; Loewenthal, "Communicating Jewish Spirituality." For the major interwar Hasidic (non-Habad) project of girls' education, Beit Ya'akov, see Naomi Seidman, *Sarah Schenirer*.
6. See Saperstein's "The Sermon" and his *Jewish Preaching*, 22–23, where he discusses this problem in the history of Jewish homiletics in general. See also literature cited in my Introduction, note 65.
7. In addition to his formal *ma'amarim*, a large number of his *sihot* (talks) circulate in unedited form, thus giving us access to the immediate circumstances and topical issues that concerned him, including his perspective on women in Hasidism. On the sources for the doctrines of Menahem Mendel Schneerson, see Roth, *Ketsad li-kero*, 131–32; Dahan, *Dirah ba-tahtonim*, 35–39; Wolfson, *Open Secret*, 15–16.
8. Dvir-Goldberg, "Kolo shel ma'ayan," 28.
9. Habad chronicler, Hayim Meir Heilman, ascribed such qualities and powers to, respectively, Shneur Zalman's daughter, Freida, and wife, Shterna. See his *Bet rabi*, 57b, 92an2 and *Bet rabi*, 54a. On the letter, wrongly attributed to Freida, on which Heilman based his opinion, see Mondshine, "Igeret mi-bat Rabenu marat Freyda(?)." On women in Bet rabi, see Dvir-Goldberg, "Ha-Besht u-'mahbarto ha-tehorah,'" 59–61. See also Loewenthal, "Women and the Dialectic," 21*–22*; Rapoport-Albert,

"The Emergence," 371; Rapoport-Albert "On Women in Hasidism," 354n41. For a discussion of Shterna's personality, see Loewenthal, "Women and the Dialectic," 21*–22*; Rapoport-Albert, "The Emergence," 399. For an analysis of similar storytelling traditions concerning the women in the Belz dynasty, see Lewis, *Imagining Holiness*, 183–206.
10. Rapoport-Albert, "The Emergence," 317, and 395; Rapoport-Albert, "From Woman as Hasid," 428.
11. Mondshine, *Migdal 'oz*, 174. The tale was apparently transmitted by a certain Avraham Abba Person, a follower of the third Habad rebbe, the Tsemah Tsedek. The tale is told in the name of Ze'ev Volf Vilenker, a follower of Shneur Zalman.
12. Schneerson, *Ha-yom yom*, entry for 23 Shevat, 22.
13. See Dov Ber of Mezrich, *Magid devarav le-Ya'akov*, 7c-d, par. 19, discussed in Rapoport-Albert, *Women and the Messianic Heresy*, 269–70. On gazing at women as a route to mystical experience in kabbalah and Hasidism, see Idel, *Kabbalah and Eros*, 153–78; Idel, "Female Beauty," 317–34; Idel, *Hasidism*, 61–64. Shneur Zalman in *Tanya* limits this practice only to the righteous (*tsadikim*); common "intermediate men" (*beinonim*) should try to chase away the temptation rather than attempt to elevate it. See TI, 28:35a-b.
14. This discrepancy between earlier and later versions also occurs with other stories, with the earlier occurrence often portraying Habad masters refraining from dealing with women. See Rapoport-Albert, "The Emergence," 372–81.
15. The editors of later editions of *Ha-yom yom* claim that the version presented in *Migdal 'oz* is of lesser credibility: "It is however known that there [in *Migdal 'oz*] it is only an oral tradition [*mi-pi ha-shemu'ah*], and this suffices for him who understands" (*Ha-yom yom*, 251n1). In other words, they favor their own leader's version. For yet another version of the story, see Menahem Mendel Schneerson, *Sihot kodesh 5713*, 137.
16. See Rapoport-Albert, "Hagiography with Footnotes." In this context it is worth mentioning the memoirs of Yosef Yitshak Schneersohn, which also enhanced anachronistically the notion of the special attitude to women in early Habad. The memoirs were first published in Yiddish in installments in the *Morgen zhurnal* from October 7, 1940 to February 23, 1942, and subsequently appeared as a book in 1947 as *Lyubavitcher Rebens zikhroynes*. An English translation by Nissan Mindel was published as *Lubavitcher Rabbi's Memoirs*, Brooklyn, Kehot, 1949. On the nonhistorical character of these memoirs, see Rapoport-Albert, "Hagiography with Footnotes," 236–37.
17. See Dov Ber of Mezrich, *Magid devarav le-Ya'akov*, 7c-d, par. 19. See also Weiss, *Studies*, 197.
18. The interpretation of Song 3:11 allowing the avoidance of direct sexual connotation may be found already in the writings of the Maggid and his disciples; see Dov Ber of Mezrich, *Magid devarav le-Ya'akov*, *Or Torah*,

63a, par. 136; Ze'ev Volf of Zhitomir's *Or ha-meir* 37b. In this interpretation, the expression "The daughters of Zion [*tsiyon*]" refers to the fact that all material things are signs (*tsiyunim*) pointing at the divinity that brings them to existence.

19. See Rosman, "'Al nashim va-hasidut," 157; see also Rapoport-Albert, *Women and the Heresy*, 271–76.
20. LT *Ba-midbar* 7d. On the custom of wearing the sash (*gartl* in Yiddish or *avnet* in Hebrew), see Wertheim, *Law and Custom*, 113–14, and Biale, *Eros and the Jews*, 134. On the idea of the divine androgyne in Jewish mysticism, see Idel, *Kabbalah and Eros*, 53–103.
21. *Seder tefilot*, 113d.
22. LT *Tazri'a* 20b.
23. Imparting knowledge (*da'at*) is associated with sexual intercourse, since *da'at* bears sexual connotations in biblical terminology, for example, "Now Adam knew his wife Eve" (Gen. 4:1). In Shneur Zalman's writings, see, for example, T1, 3:7b; LT *Ba-midbar* 9a; MAHZ 5572, 46. This idea of sexual intercourse as an act of bestowing knowledge on a woman also occurs in the description of sperm in T1, 2:6b (based on *b*Nidah 31a) as the derivative of man's brain and a carrier of his intellectual attributes, which join in a womb with the female attributes to produce a fetus; an idea that echoes the Aristotelian concept of conception, whereby it is "for the male to have an idea, an artistic or artisanal conception, in the brain-uterus of the female" (Laqueur, *Making Sex*, 42). See also Idel, *Kabbalah and Eros*, 218 for examples of kabbalists associating intercourse with the Tree of Knowledge of good and evil (*'ets ha-da'at*).
24. On the zoharic sources of this juxtaposition, see Hellner-Eshed, *A River Flows from Eden*, 73. For examples of its use in Shneur Zalman's lore, see LT *Shelah* 47c; MAHZ 5562, i, 403; 5569, 180; 5572, 129.
25. Shneur Zalman uses the expression "fatigue such as a woman's" (*teshishut koah ki-nekevah*), which is derived from Rashi's commentary on Num. 11:15 and Deut. 5:25.
26. LT *Kedoshim* 29d.
27. On the doctrine of creation by means of divine speech in Hasidism, see Idel, "'Le-'olam ha-Shem,'" 219–86 and, in particular, 239–43, where he discusses Shneur Zalman. See also Foxbrunner, *Habad*, 104–5. The identification of the feminine aspect of the Godhead with the divine speech is a classical kabbalistic theme. See Scholem, *On the Mystical Shape*, 181–82
28. See, for example, Vital, *'Ets hayim*, Gate 34, chapter 2, 151; chapter 3, 156; Poppers, *Sefer ha-likutim*, Shir ha-shirim, par. 2, 336
29. LT *Kedoshim* 29d. Five is the numerical value of the letter *he*, which also stands for the "lower letter *he*," the final letter of the Tetragrammaton, identified with *Malkhut* and the divine speech.
30. See, for example, T2, 4:79b; TO 63c, 117d; LT *Emor* 38d, *Ba-midbar* 7c, *Hukat* 58d; *Seder tefilot* 236d. See Poppers, *Sefer ha-likutim*, Be-reshit,

par. 2, 15–16. This passage also correlated the five Judgments with the five "naked things" in a woman (bBerakhot 24a); see Ziii 142a.
31. See Biale, Eros and the Jews, 121–48, in particular, 141–45.
32. Seder tefilot 261c–264b. On the gender symbolism of the four species, see Wolfson, Language, Eros, Being, 151–52; Wolfson, Circle in the Square, 118–19.
33. Seder tefilot 134b.
34. Seder tefilot 115b, based on the zoharic saying that "Adam includes equally male and female" (Ziii, 145b). Shneur Zalman refers here to the numerical value of the name of Adam (45, related also to one of the divine names), and divides it into two strands: the Tetragrammaton (numerical value, 26) and Havah (19). See also, for example, LT Va-yikra 3d and Vital, 'Ets hayim, Gate 10, chapter 3, 140; Gate 38, chapter 2, 203.
35. See LT Shelah 41b; TO 44b. The world of the masculine corresponds to Binah in the sefirotic system, whereas the world of the feminine ('alma de-nukba) represents the sefirah of Malkhut. See Wolfson, "Min u-minut," 232; Wolfson, Circle in the Square, 89, 99–100; Scholem, "Le-heker kabalat r. Yitshak ben Ya'akov ha-Kohen," 40–41.
36. See TO 43d.
37. See LT Shelah 38b. Binah corresponds to thought, and Malkhut to speech and deeds. On the correlation between masculinity and spirit and femininity and materiality, see note 19, above.
38. One of the sayings that recurs in Shneur Zalman's writings is "There is no place void of him" (let atar panui mineh, in Tikune zohar, lvii, 91b), underscoring the divine omnipresence in the world. See, for example, T1, 21:26b, 40:54b, 51:71a; T2, 7:83b; T3, 5:95b; T4, 1:102a, 11:116b, 20:131b; TO53c. See Loewenthal, "Women and the Dialectic," which suggests that the mystical concept of Lower Unity, that is unity of God within the world, was used in twentieth-century Habad as a theoretical framework for opening up for women the possibility of fully participating in the Hasidic spiritual enterprise. See in particular 15*–19*.
39. Sefer yetsirah 1:7.
40. For the significance of this principle in Shneur Zalman's thought, see Foxbrunner, Habad, 74–77.
41. See, for example, Seder tefilot 46d: "It is also so according to the literal meaning [of the statement] that 'a woman is only for the sake of beauty' [bKetubot 59b]: since women are by way of the creation more beautiful than men in their nature, as is well known, this is a sign that the issue is to be understood in this way also on high. This is why they are more beautiful in their nature, because 'their end is fixed in their beginning' [Sefer yetsirah, 1:7] and they receive from the light of Keter." See also Idel, Kabbalah and Eros, 198, where he discusses a similar concept found in the teachings of the Maggid of Mezrich, and as transmitted by his student, Ze'ev Volf of Zhitomir, in Or ha-me'ir 10b, based on the same passage from bKetubot 59b: "All the worlds in general were created only in order that

the Holy One, blessed be he, will enjoy the lower degrees which are called Woman, which will receive an illumination from him, blessed be he."

42. For a discussion of this phenomenon in Habad, see Wolfson, *Open Secret*, 204–5. For references to kabbalistic sources, see Wolfson's *Language, Eros, Being*, 94–99; "Min u-minut," 231–62; Idel, *Kabbalah and Eros*, 82–83.

43. Following the *Zohar*, even *Malkhut*, the epitome of femininity in the *sefirotic* tree, goes by a masculine name "lad" (*na'ar*) until it receives the influx from the world of the masculine, when it takes the name of "maiden" (*na'arah*); see LT *Matot* 85c, *Tsav* 9d, based on Zii 38b. For an analogous example, where *Shekhinah* changes her name from *Tsedek* to *Tsedakah*, see MAHZ *Ketsarim*, 159.

44. See, for example, MAHZ *Parshiyot*, ii, 567; *Seder tefilot* 280d. In some relations, Israel can assume the masculine role, and God the feminine; see, for example, Dov Ber of Mezrich, *Magid devarav le-Ya'akov*, Or Torah 9a-b, par. 24, in which God and Israel are compared to father and a son, or master and a disciple. While imparting knowledge to a disciple is an active—and masculine—act, the fact that the father receives pleasure from the son's progress, shows his passive, feminine side. See also 83b, par. 287, in which God is described "as if a female [nekevah] for the righteous ones," on account of the delight caused by their deeds.

45. See, in particular, the contexts in which Shneur Zalman implements an alternative interpretation of the verse, "Moses charged us with the teaching [*torah*], as the heritage of the congregation of Jacob" (Deut. 33:4), which reads "betrothed" (*me'orasah*) instead of "heritage" (*morashah*), based on bBerakhot 57a and bPesahim. 49b. See, for example, TO 44d, 54d, 99c; LT *Shelah* 45b, 47c.

46. See, for example, TO 6d; LT *Be-shalah* 1a; *Seder tefilot* 132c, discussed in Magid, "The Ritual." See also Dov Ber of Mezrich, *Magid devarav le-Ya'akov*, Or Torah 71b, par. 235, which further complicated this division, explaining that before the Written Torah was given to Israel in ten (masculine) commandments (*diburim*), the Torah, according to which God had created the world, was feminine, as the world was created in ten (feminine) sayings (*amirot*).

47. MAHZ *Ketsarim*, 268–69.

48. See, for example, TO 63d–64a; MAHZ 5567, 40–42.

49. See MAHZ *Ketsarim*, 170–71.

50. See *Seder tefilot* 80d.

51. Mondshine, *Migdal 'oz*, 380–81, where this idea is set in the context of the polemics about Shneur Zalman's way of leadership as opposed to that of the Polish *tsadikim*. For a slightly different version of the discourse, see *Boneh Yerushalayim*, 60.

52. See mKidushin 1:1. The *tsadik*, however, can also be characterized in Hasidism as female from the vantage point of his relationship with God (see Idel, *Kabbalah and Eros*, 86–87, 97), a fact that further emphasizes the fluidity of genders in Hasidism.

53. A play on the double meaning of Hebrew root *kaf samekh pe* meaning both money or silver and yearning or love. For the overt use of this concept, see, for example, T1, 50:70b; LT *'Ekev* 16d.
54. Based on *Shulhan 'arukh*, Even ha-'ezer 27:9—a man can acquire a wife by way of the pleasure he derived from a monetary gift he received from her.
55. See LT *Be-shalah* 1c: "The Sages of blessed memory said: [mKidushin 1:1] 'A women is acquired by three means' [. . .] 'by document' [*bi-shetar*] refers to the letters constituting the Torah." See also MAHZ *Ketsarim*, 178–79: "[bKidushin 9a] He writes on paper or on a shard, [that is to say,] whether he studies kabbalah [and] *Zohar* or simple *Gemara*—she is sanctified unto him."
56. Mondshine, *Migdal 'oz*, 291–92. A similar concept of the relationship between the "male" *tsadik* and the "female" Hasid can be found in the writings of other Hasidic masters, including those who preceded Shneur Zalman. See Rapoport-Albert, *Women and the Heresy*, 273–74. In Hasidic literature the *tsadik* can be perceived as changing gender roles, being male as "donor" in relation to his followers but female as "recipient" when in relation to God, see Idel, *Kabbalah and Eros*, 97.
57. See LT *Ba-midbar* 7d, based on Vital, *Likute Torah*, Introduction to Ta'ame mitsvot, 34–35.
58. See *Bereshit rabah* 1:4: "[God's] thought of Israel preceded everything else."
59. *Seder tefilot* 109b.
60. TO 5a-b.
61. TO 5b. For more on the female as a factor determining the process of creation in Lurianic kabbalah, see Jacobson, "The Aspect of the 'Feminine.'" Other early Hasidic masters translate *ezer ke-negdo* explicitly as the matter that opposes and complements the form. See, for example, Ya'akov Yosef of Polnoye, *Tsofnat pa'neah*, Terumah 83a (359); Ya'akov Yosef of Polnoye, *Toledot Ya'akov Yosef*, ii, Matot, 1119; Menahem Nahum of Chernobyl, *Me'or 'enayim*, Likutim, 142b.
62. "If he is worthy, she will be a helper ['*ezer*]. If he is not worthy, she will be against him [*ke-negdo*]" (Rashi to Gen. 2:18. See also bYevamot 63a; *Bereshit rabah* 17:3, 11; *Pirke de-rabi Eli'ezer*, chapter 12, 11a). By contrast, Shneur Zalman states that even if Adam had not sinned at all, the helpmate would have remained in opposition to him, albeit in a *subtler* form. See TO 5b.
63. TO 5a.
64. TO 5a.
65. See Wolfson, *Open Secret*, 206–9; Polen, "Miriam's Dance," 6; Rapoport-Albert, "From Woman as Hasid," 433–35. In some of the discourses, Shneur Zalman talks about the equality of the male and the female rather than the supremacy of either at the time of redemption. See Wolfson, *Open Secret*, 206. For the list of relevant sources see Loewenthal, "Women and the Dialectic," *65n192.
66. LT *Shir ha-shirim*, 48b. See also TO 44d–45b and the more extensive version of this sermon in *Seder tefilot* 138b–39b, from a transcript

prepared by Shneur Zalman's son and successor, Dov Ber Shneuri. Dov Ber's competitor to the succession after Shneur Zalman's death, Aharon ha-Levi of Starosielce, also prepared a transcript of this sermon, which was later published in the collection of his teachings; see his *'Avodat ha-Levi*, iii, Likutim 86a-b.

67. LT *Shir ha-shirim*, 48b. For a discussion of this motif, see Levin, "Kol ha-kalah le-'atid," 365–68; Magid, "The Ritual," 206–11. The notion of the exile as the time when the congregation of Israel is speechless appears in Zi, 36a. See also Wiskind Elper, "Be-tselem Elohim," 21. See also Schwartzmann ("From Mystical Visions," 147–48), who argues against the interpretation of Shneur Zalman's words as an inclusive vision of women performing masculine rituals in the future.

68. For the voice as the drawing down and revelation of the divine influx, see, for example, LT *Shir ha-shirim* 15b, 48b; MAHZ 5566, ii, 677. It does not contradict Shneur Zalman's association of the female with articulated speech in other contexts (see note 29 of this chapter, above); in both these instances, the female is the receptive and limiting force of the infinite divine male influx. For the idea of silence as nullification, see, for example, TO 45c; LT *Tsav* 15c; MAHZ 5564, 238; *Seder tefilot*, 116a, 132c, 148c, 237d.

69. See MAHZ *Ketsarim* 69. See also Wolfson, *Open Secret*, 209, where he notes this transformation.

70. MAHZ *Hanahot ha-Rap*, 64–65.

71. See Foxbrunner, *Habad*, 65–66, and the sources enlisted there.

72. On various interpretations of the verse "Woman shall compass a man" in Jewish thought from ancient midrash to contemporary Israeli rabbis, see Schwartzmann, "From Mystical Visions," 149–56. See also a similar motif in Kalonimus Kalman Epstein's *Ma'or va-shemesh*, Be-shalah 13b–14a, based on the Lurianic notions of *'igulim ve-yosher* (circles and linearity) and the association with the ritual of *hakafot* (circle dances) on Simhat Torah, discussed and compared to Shneur Zalman in Polen, "Miriam's Dance."

73. On the custom of the wedding dance, see Friedhaber, "Dance with the Separating Kerchief," 65–69. For an overt use in Hasidic sources of the *mitsvah* dance as an allegory of the purifications of the holy sparks on the way to redemption, see *Keter shem tov*, par. 179, 23a, noted by Fishbane in "To Jump for Joy," 378n18.

74. See, for example, T1, 39:52b, 49:69a; TO 8d, 9a, 71c, 80c; LT *Va-yikra* 2d, *Naso* 28c, *Shelah* 47a, *Hukat* 48d, *Balak* 74c, *Tetse* 38b, *Rosh ha-shanah* 55b, *Shemini 'atseret* 90b.

75. See, for example, the commentary of David Kimhi (Radak) on Jer. 31:32: "'For the Lord has created something new on earth.' In the future a new thing will be created after you have sat for many years in the exile. What is the new thing? That the woman shall compass a man, for it is the custom of the world that the man woos [*mehazer*] and courts [*mesovev*] the woman, as the Sages said: 'The loser goes

in search [*mehazer*] of the lost article' [*b*Kidushin 2b]. But when the woman shall court her man, that is to say, when the children of Israel return to the Lord their God, he will redeem them, as is stated in the prophecy of Hosea [3:5]: 'Afterwards, the Israelites will turn back and will seek the Lord their God, and David their king—and they will thrill over the Lord and over his bounty in the days to come.'" On the exegetical difficulties posed by the ambiguity of the Hebrew word *tesovev*, see Schwartzmann, "From Mystical Visions," 149–50.

76. See also Elliot Wolfson's discussion of this motif in the context of kabbalistic readings of the Song of Songs, in his *Language, Eros, Being*, 367.
77. See Kallus, "The Theurgy of Prayer," 134–36.
78. See, for example, LT *Va-yikra* 3c-d. Shneur Zalman applies the distinction between these two names to his psychology (where 45 refers to the divine soul and 52 to the animal soul, for 52 equals *behemah*—animal; see, for example, T1, 46:66b; TO 18a, 47d, 76b; LT *Va-yikra* 3b-d, *Tsav* 8b, *Shemini 'atseret*, 19a, *Emor* 35d), as well as to divine service (where 45 represents Torah study and the ecstatic "great love" [*ahavah rabah*], whereas 52 stands for prayer and "worldly love" [*ahavat 'olam*], namely love of God that results from contemplation of the world. See TO 47d–48a. For a discussion of these two types of love, see T1, 43:62b and Foxbrunner, *Habad*, 178–85).
79. See TO 47d–48a.
80. On male and female waters see Scholem, *On the Mystical Shape*, 187–88; Wolfson, *Circle in the Square*, 110–15.
81. On different types of nullification in the Habad tradition, see Wolfson, *Open Secret*, 75–76.
82. LT *'Ekev* 15d.
83. LT *'Ekev* 15d. See *Tikune zohar*, Hakdamah, 3b.
84. See TO 99c–111b. The attribution of the lower nullification to Eliyahu in the same passage is based on the numerical value of his name (52), whereas Moses's relation to the upper annihilation is based on his question "And what are we?" (Exod. 16:7, 8), where the word *what* (*mah*) equals 45. The phrase is interpreted as an expression of his humility. Since Moses's words refer to both himself and Aaron, the latter, too, is comprised in the name of 45. However, Aaron is not on the same level as Moses, and therefore he is referred to as "52 of 45" and related to the purification of the lower worlds by *Malkhut*.
85. TO 111a.
86. Even though the name Elohim is often interpreted as meaning "nature" (both Elohim and *ha-teva'* equal 86), and therefore as related to the feminine *sefirah* of *Malkhut*, in the aforementioned *ma'amar*, Shneur Zalman casually interprets it as referring to the "essence of godliness" (*'atsmut elokut*), the aspect of the Godhead that is beyond its lower hypostasese.
87. See, for example, Vital, *'Ets hayim*, Gate 34, chapter 7, 165. See also Idel, "Higher than Time," 182–83.

88. TO 47d.
89. See T1, 41:58b; MAHZ 5567, 347.
90. Based on the zoharic saying that "in the night the gates of paradise are shut." Zi, 92a, 172a, 242b.
91. MAHZ 5566, i, 105–7. See also TO 12c. For another example of translating *teref* as 288+1 see TO 110. Elsewhere, Shneur Zalman explains that *teref* (pray) alludes to the power of Judgments by means of which *Malkhut* purifies the lower worlds "like a roaring lion ravening [the pray]" (Ezek. 22:25). See LT *Emor* 36b and MAHZ *Parshiyot*, ii, 678. He further compares this to sleeping: when a man is asleep, his emotional and intellectual faculties depart from him and are contracted into his heart. At the same time, his less vital faculties become active and he digests more intensively than while he is awake, digestion in turn functioning as a ubiquitous metaphor for purification in Shneur Zalman's lore. This is because digestion separates the life force from waste in food. See, for example, TO 47d; LT *Emor* 36a.
92. See MAHZ *Ketuvim*, ii, 239.
93. See also LT *Shir ha-Shirim* 9a, where Shneur Zalman explains the roles of the male and female in procreation: "As a matter of fact, the essence ['ikar] of the foetus comes from the seed of the woman, even though the woman is called the aspect of receiver, for she does not have the power to coagulate [her seed] and form a foetus of it. This can be done only by the seed of the man, which is like milk that coagulates when one adds rennet to it." Thus, the seed of a woman, of which the fetus is formed, is a passive matter shaped by the active power of the male seed. Consequently, pregnancy and birth are used as an allegory of exile and redemption, for they represent, on the one hand, the concealment and diminution of consciousness (*katnut de-mohin*), and on the other hand, the disclosure and augmentation of consciousness (*gadlut de-mohin*). See, for example, *Seder tefilot*, 295a-c. Similarly, birth pangs become the tribulations that would precede the coming of the Messiah, which arise from the purification and separation of the newborn (souls of Israel) from the impure female blood (husks). See MAHZ *Ketuvim*, i, 63–64; TO 106a-b, 55a-d.
94. As Shneur Zalman explains, Sabbath's feminine character is alluded to by the feminine personal pronoun *hi* (she) in the verse "For *she* [Sabbath] is holy for you" [*kodesh hi*; Exod. 31:14]; see MAHZ *Parshiyot*, ii, 671.
95. Maimonides, *Mishneh Torah*, Laws of Sabbath, 8:11–13, 21:17; *Shulkhan 'arukh Rabenu ha-Zaken*, Orah hayim, 319.
96. MAHZ *Parshiyot*, ii, 671. See also MAHZ 5568, 223–24; *Ethalekh*, 11; *Ketsarim*, 346–47.
97. See, for example, *Seder tefilot*, 188a. For a discussion of this issue, see Wolfson, *Luminal Darkness*, 146–47 and the literature listed there.
98. On the sexual connotations of the delight in Jewish mysticism, see Idel, "Ta'anug."

99. See, for example, LT *Ba-midbar* 16c. The relation between male and female on the regular days of the week also happens to be depicted in terms of marital union, but Shneur Zalman makes sure to stress the difference between these two types of union. Referring to the Lurianic work *Peri 'ets hayim*, he defines the union of male and female on weekdays as the union of "Jacob and Rachel," as opposed to the union of "Israel and Rachel" on the Sabbath. Through an invented etymology, he explains that the name of Jacob denotes the *sefirah Yesod* of the constellation of *Aba*, which descends to the lower world (*Ya'akov* consists of the letter *yud* denoting *Yesod*, and the word *'akev* [heel] denoting the lower worlds), and is linked to the provision of the divine vitality to the external forces. The name of Israel, conversely, denotes the constellation *Ze'ir anpin*, which ascends to receive the influx from the lights of *Aba*. Israel, who "has striven with God" (*sarita 'im Elohim*; Gen. 32:28) is beyond the name Elohim (nature) and therefore beyond the reach of the external forces. See LT *Balak* 72c. On both types of union in Lurianic kabbalah, see Fine, *Physician*, 199–200. See also MAHZ 5664, 184–85.
100. Ziii, 115b.
101. TO 100b. See also MAHZ 5564, 266, where the descent of *Malkhut* to the husk of *nogah* is interpreted as "the distancing of the impure blood," which echoes the medieval concept of the exile of the menstruant *Shekhinah*. See Koren, *Forsaken*, 75–97.
102. For the correspondence between the days of week and the attributes, see, for example, LT *Pekude* 5b; *Seder tefilot* 26d–27a.
103. See Wolfson, *Luminal Darkness*, 147 and the sources listed there. For the similar concept in the Gur Hasidism, arguably influenced by Shneur Zalman, see Jacobson, "Kedushat ha-hulin."
104. See, for example, TO 8c, 9b, 10a, 25c, 97c.
105. TO 10a.
106. See *Vayikra rabah* 27:10.
107. See, for example, *Seder tefilot* 141d.
108. LT *Tazri'a* 20d–21a. On the connection between circumcision and apophany, see Wolfson, *Circle in the Square*, 29–48.
109. See Wolfson, "Circumcision and the Divine Name," 87–90.
110. LT *Tazri'a* 21d. See also TO 13b, 31c.
111. See, for example, T2, 7:82a; TO 106a.
112. In LT *Tazri'a* 21d the eight days stands for the eight-string harp of the Messiah, made out of seven strings corresponding to the disclosure of light from seven "worldly days" (seven attributes from the World of Emanation corresponding to the seven days of the week), and from the radiance emanating from the "primordial days" (*yeme kedem*—namely *Adam kadmon* who precedes the division into attributes-days).
113. Gen. 36:31–39. On the relation of circumcision, Hadar, and the eight-string harp in later Habad, see Wolfson, *Open Secret*, 54–55. On the myth of the Edomite kings in the Lurianic kabbalah, see Wolfson,

"Min u-minut," 254n109, and the literature listed there, and Wolfson, *Language Eros Being*, 311.

114. See *Seder tefilot* 113c–14a.
115. *Seder tefilot* 114a.
116. See, for example, Wolfson, "Min u-minut," 232; Wolfson, *Circle in the Square*, 98–106.
117. See Wolfson, *Language, Eros, Being*, 142–89.
118. See LT *Hukat* 60c: "Woman is the aspect of 'Judgments,' the aspect of *Malkhut* whose [Prov. 5:5] 'feet go down to death' [. . .], the source and root of the grasp of the external forces." On the kabbalistic notion of the affinity between the *Shekhinah* and "the other side," see Tishby, *Wisdom of the Zohar*, i, 376–79 and ii, 469.
119. See LT *Hukat* 60c. For the source of the law, see Maimonides, *Mishneh Torah*, Laws of the Red Heifer, 10:6.
120. See, for example, LT *Emor* 32a, *Nitsavim* 52b.
121. This is because the eradication of the evil force does not diminish the divine pleroma. See, for example, MAHZ 5568, i, 194. Elsewhere, a similar function is ascribed to nails. See, for example, TO 7a-c, 12d, 26b, 63b; MAHZ *Ketsarim*, 69. For the use of the image of hair in Shneur Zalman's teachings on the contraction of the divine and its Maggidic sources, see Schwartz, *Mahashevet Habad*, 94n279. This view of hair and nails has a Lurianic source. On hair as the representation of Judgments (*Dinim*), see, for example, Vital, *Peri 'ets hayim*, Gate 2, chapter 6, 43. On nails, see, for example, Vital *'Ets hayim*, Gate 31, chapter 2, 112.
122. See, for example, *Seder tefilot*, 57a-b, where five colors of impure blood (see *m*Nidah 2:6) are depicted as "a level, which is entirely devoid of good." See also MAHZ 5564, 262; 5568, 194 and 199. TO 59d associates impure blood with strange thoughts.
123. TI, 14:20a. See also Rosman, "'Al nashim va-hasidut," 157n24.
124. *m*Kidushin 1:7; *b*Kidushin 29a, 34a; *y*Kidushin 1:7 (19a); *Sifre 'al sefer be-Midbar*, Shelah 115. On the rationale, provided by Jacob Anatoli in *Malmad ha-talmidim* and David b. Jehoshua Abudraham in *Sefer Abudraham*, see Fishman, "A Kabbalistic Perspective," 209.
125. MAHZ 5572, 136.
126. See, for example, TO 111b; *Seder tefilot* 75a; MAHZ 5567, 78; *Parshiyot*, i, 138 and 353; *Ketsarim*, 43. On the theosophic justification for the exemption in Lurianic kabbalah, see Vital, *Likute Torah*, Introduction to Ta'ame mitsvot, 34–35. For an earlier example of kabbalistic explanation for the exemption, found in a medieval Byzantine kabbalistic treatise *Sefer ha-Kanah*, see Fishman "A Kabbalistic Perspective."
127. See *Seder tefilot* 80d.
128. See Vital, *'Ets hayim*, Gate 50, chapter 4, 398.
129. See MAHZ 5572, 151; Wolfson, "Nequddat ha-Reshimu," 98–99n91.
130. See *m*Shabat 2:6; see also *Bereshit rabah* 17:8 and *Midrash Tanhuma*, Noah 1, where these three commandments are listed as having been given to

women in retribution for the sin of Eve. On the special role of a woman in respect of these commandments according to contemporary Habad, see Loewenthal, "'Daughter/Wife of Hasid,'" 24*–28*; Heilman and Friedman, *The Rebbe*, 176–80.

131. See *Shulhan 'arukh Rabenu ha-Zaken*, Orah hayim, 263:5, 173, based on yShabat 2:6 (20a); *Bereshit rabah* 17:8; *Midrash Tanhuma*, Noah 1, Metsora' 9; Zi 48b.
132. *Shulhan 'arukh Rabenu ha-Zaken*, Orah hayim, 263, Kuntres aharon 2, 177.
133. "Sihat motsa'e Shabat Kodesh Bereshit—li-neshe u-venot Yisra'el ti. [hyu] 5735" in Schneerson, *Sihot kodesh 5735*, i, 133. An abridged version of the talk was published in Shalom Dovber Levine, *Kuntres nerot Shabat Kodesh*, i, 5–12.
134. See TO 92d, where Shneur Zalman stresses that, contrary to popular opinion, sexual union is not repulsive; it is a "great thing," both in this world and in heaven. See also Loewenthal, "Women and the Dialectic," 19*n39.
135. TO 25b. On the concept of "great love" in Shneur Zalman's teachings, see Foxbrunner, *Habad*, 179–84. Ben Azzai was offered Rabbi Akivah's daughter as a wife. For Ben Azzai's conviction that the world should be preserved by others, see tYevamot 8:4; bYevamot 63b; *Bereshit rabah* 34:14.
136. See HTT 3:1, 841a and 3:2, 845b.
137. HTT, Kuntres aharon 3:1, 841a.
138. See bKetubot 62b and Ya'akov ben Asher, *Arba'ah turim*, Orah hayim, 240; Karo, *Shulhan 'arukh*, Orah hayim, 240:1; *Shulhan 'arukh Rabenu ha-Zaken*, Orah hayim, 280:1. In this passage, Shneur Zalman refers to the broader explication of the issue in paragraph 240 of his codex, which has not come down to us.
139. See Zi, 49b–50a; Zii, 89a-b; de Vidas, *Reshit hokhmah*, Gate of Holiness, chapter 16, 302–4. On this and other aspects of sexual union on the Sabbath in kabbalah, see Fine, *Physician*, 197, 414n32; Ginsburg, *Sabbath*, 134–35, 289–93; Tishby, *Wisdom*, 3:1357–58.
140. Since these are "the times of the lovers above" (Ezek. 16:8). This follows the idea that the 'Amidah prayer is an aspect of the Sabbath. See, for example, TO 9b; LT *Be-har* 44a, *Yom ha-kipurim* 68b, *Shir ha-shirim* 19a; *Seder tefilot* 213a. Shneur Zalman adds that "during the daily 'Amidah of the morning service 'something of this nature' occurs" (*Seder tefilot* 54d).
141. *Seder tefilot*, 54d.
142. For the discussion of this idea in the teachings of Menahem Mendel Schneerson, see Wolfson, *Open Secret*, 220–23.
143. See Rapoport-Albert, *Women and the Messianic Heresy*, 121–23; Rapoport-Albert, "From Woman as Hasid," 434–35. See also Magid, "The Ritual," which presents Shneur Zalman's image of the future reversal of the gender hierarchy in wedding blessings as a consciously constructed infeasible fantasy.
144. T4, 26:143a-b.
145. Based on bShabat 30b, where Rabbi Gamliel interprets the verse in Jer. 31:8 (*harah ve-yoledet yahdav*) as meaning "she, who conceives and gives birth concurrently."

146. Since a woman is considered ritually impure during twelve days following childbirth. An alternative interpretation given by Menahem Mendel Schneerson reads *mi-bi'ah ahat* as *mevi'ah ahat*, "she shall bring one [offering]." See *Igerot kodesh*, xxiii, 296–97; *Likute sihot*, xii, 178, and Wineberg, *Lessons in Tanya*, v, 130–31.
147. An idea based on the word play *nidah—nad heh*: the letter *he* representing the *Shekhinah*, which has wandered. See Schneersohn (*Tsemah Tsedek*), *Or ha-Torah*, Be-reshit, i, 51a; Schneersohn, *Be'ure ha-Zohar*, ii, 945.
148. See, for example, *Seder tefilot* 57a-b.
149. MAHZ *Ketsarim*, 534.
150. Wolfson, *Open Secret*, 220.

BIBLIOGRAPHY

Primary Literature

Shneur Zalman of Liady. *Boneh Yerushalayim*. Jerusalem, Israel: Y. Verker, 1926.
———. *Likute amarim: Tanya*. London, UK: Soncino, 1973.
———. *Likute amarim: mahadura kama*. Brooklyn, NY: Kehot, 1981.
———. *Likute Torah*. Brooklyn, NY: Kehot, 2002.
———. *Ma'amre Admor ha-Zaken*. Brooklyn, NY: Kehot, 1976–2008.
———. *Seder tefilot mi-kol ha-shanah*. Brooklyn, NY: Kehot, 1986.
———. *Shulhan 'arukh Rabenu ha-Zaken*, vols. i-iv. Brooklyn, NY: Kehot, 1987.
———. *Torah or*. Brooklyn, NY: Kehot, 1991.

Other Sources

Alshekh, Moshe. *Torat Moshe*. Warsaw, Poland: Lebensohn, Gershon & Pesah, 1861.
Arama, Yitshak. *'Akedat Yitshak*. Lviv, Ukraine: A. Y. Madpis, 1868.
Aristotle. *Physics*. Oxford, UK: Oxford University Press, 1996.
Avot de-rabi Natan. Jerusalem, Israel: Sefarim toraniyim, 1986.
Avraham of Tulczyn. *Avaneha barzel: sihot ve-sipurim mi-Nahman mi-Bratslav*. Bnei Brak, Israel: Agudat haside Bratslav be-Yisra'el, 1961.
Bahya bar Asher. *Midrash Rabenu Bahya 'al Hamishah Humshe Torah*. Nagyvarad (Oradea), Romania: Rubinstein, 1942.
Buber, Salomon, ed. *Pesikta de-Rav Kahana*. Lyck (Ełk), Poland: Mekize Nirdamim, 1868.
Cordovero, Moshe. *Pardes rimonim*. Jerusalem, Israel: Yerid ha-sefarim, 2000.
———. *Tefilah le-Moshe*. In *Sidur tefilah ke-minhag Sefarad: helek rishon 'im perush Tefilah le-Moshe*. Przemyśl, Poland: Zupnik, Knoller, Hamershmit, 1892.

Dov Ber of Mezrich. *Magid devarav le-Ya'akov ve-hu Likute amarim: Or Torah.* Brooklyn, NY: Kehot, 1972.

———. *Or ha-emet.* Bnei Brak, Israel: Yahadut, 1966.

Eidels, Shmuel (Maharsha). *Hidushe agadot.* Frankfurt, Germany: Literis Blasii Ilsneri, 1682.

Epstein, Kalonimus Kalman. *Ma'or va-shemesh.* Warsaw, Poland: Fayvel Munk, 1877.

Friedmann, Meir, ed. *Pesikta rabati.* Vienna, Austria: Y. Kaizer, 1880.

Gersonides (Levi ben Gershon). *Milhamot ha-Shem.* Riva, Italy: Y. Marcaria, 1560.

Green, Arthur, Ebn Leader, Ariel Evan Mayse, and Or N. Rose. *Speaking Torah: Spiritual Teachings from around the Maggid's Table.* Woodstock, VT: Jewish Lights, 2013.

Grossfeld, Bernard, ed. *Two Targums of Esther. The Aramaic Bible,* xviii. Collegeville, MN: Liturgical Press, 1991.

Heller, Meshulam Fayvush. *Derekh emet: Yosher divre emet.* Monsey, NY: Va'ad le-hafatsat sifre Ba'al Shem Tov ha-kadosh ve-talmidav, 1993.

Hillman, David Zvi, ed. *Igerot Ba'al ha-Tanya u-vene doro.* Jerusalem, Israel, 1953.

Horovits, Aharon ha-Levi of Starosielce. *Sha'are ha-yihud veha-emunah.* Shklov, Belarus: A. Zelig, 1820.

———. *'Avodat ha-Levi.* Lviv: Hayim Refa'el; Warsaw, Poland: Bumritter and Rothblat, 1842–66.

Horovits, Yesha'yahu. *Shene luhot ha-berit,* Amsterdam, The Netherlands: 'Imanuel ben Yosef 'Atias, 1698.

Karo, Yosef. *Shulhan 'arukh.* Vilnius, Lithuania: Romm, 1895–96.

———. *Keter shem tov.* Brooklyn, NY: Kehot, 2004.

Kimhi, David. *Perush ha-Radak 'al Yirmiyahu.* In *Mikra'ot gedolot 'Ha-keter,'* edited by M. Cohen. Ramat Gan, Israel: Bar-Ilan University Press, 2012.

Levi Yitshak of Berdichev. *Kedushat Levi.* Warsaw, Poland: Yisra'el Rozumovski, 1902.

Levine, Shalom Dovber. *Igerot kodesh me-et k.k. Admor ha-Zaken, k.k. Admor ha-Emtsa'i, k.k. Admor ha-"Tsemah Tsedek."* Brooklyn, NY: Kehot, 1987–93.

Luzzatto, Moshe Hayim. *Sefer adir ba-marom ha-shalem.* Jerusalem, Israel: [Yosef Spiner], 1995.

Mekhilta de-Rabi Yishma'el. Jerusalem, Israel: [Ha-mesorah], 1954.

Menahem Mendel of Vitebsk. *Peri ha-'ets.* Krakow, Poland: Aharon Tsevi Lipshits, 1937.

Menahem Nahum of Chernobyl. *Me'or 'enayim.* Slavuta, Ukraine: Eliyahu Kats, 1798.

———. *Midrash rabah.* Vilnius, Lithuania: Romm, 1878.

———. *Midrash Tanhuma 'al Hamishah Humshe Torah.* Jerusalem, Israel: Ha-ahim Levin-Epshtein, 1973.

Maimonides, Moses. *Mishneh Torah.* Jerusalem, Israel: Mossad Harav Kook, 1985.

———. *Moreh nevukhim.* Jerusalem, Israel: Mossad Harav Kook, 2000.

Moshe ben Nachman, *Perush ha-Ramban 'al ha-Torah*. In *Mikra'ot gedolot 'Ha-keter,'* edited by M. Cohen. Ramat Gan, Israel: Bar-Ilan University Press, 2012.
Odeberg, Hugo, ed. *3 Enoch or the Hebrew Book of Enoch*. Cambridge, UK: Cambridge University Press, 1928.
———. *Pirke de-Rabi Eli'ezer*. Warsaw, Poland: Zisberg, 1874.
Poppers, Meir. *Sefer ha-likutim 'al Torah Nevi'im Ketuvim leha-tana ha-eloki rabenu ha-kadosh mo.ha-r. Yitshak Luria Ashkenazi*. Jerusalem, Israel,1988.
Ragoler, Avraham. *Ma'alot ha-Torah*. Pressburg (Bratislava), Slovakia: Kottritsch & Zimmerman, 1875.
Sa'adyah Ga'on. *Sefer emunot ve-de'ot*. Istanbul, Turkey: Shlomo Ya'abets, 1562.
Schneersohn, Menahem Mendel (the Tsemah Tsedek). *Be'ure ha-Zohar*. Brooklyn, NY: Kehot, 1978.
———. *Derekh mitsvotekha hu Sefer ta'ame ha-mitsvot*, Brooklyn, NY: Kehot, 2006.
———. *Or ha-Torah*. Brooklyn, NY: Kehot, 1960–71.
———. *Sefer ha-hakirah*. Brooklyn, NY: Kehot, 2003.
Schneersohn, Shalom Dovber. *Be-sha'ah she-hikdimu*. Brooklyn, NY: Kehot, 1992.
———. *Kuntres 'ets ha-hayim*. Brooklyn, NY: Kehot, 2000.
Schneersohn, Yosef Yitshak. *Igerot kodesh*. Brooklyn, NY: Kehot, 1982–2011.
———. *Likute diburim*. Brooklyn, NY: Kehot, 2009.
———. *Lyubavitcher Rebens zikhroynes*. Brooklyn, NY: Kehot, 1947.
Schneerson, Menahem Mendel, ed. *Ha-yom yom*, Brooklyn, NY: Kehot, 1957.
———. *Igerot kodesh*. Brooklyn, NY: Kehot, 1988–2006.
———. *Likute sihot*. Brooklyn, NY: Kehot, 1968–2006.
———. *Sihot kodesh mi-k.k. Admor shlita mi-Lyubavitsh*. Brooklyn, NY, 1985-.
———. *Sefer ha-hinukh*. Jerusalem, Israel: Eshkol, 1958.
———. *Sefer ha-Zohar 'al Hamishah Humshe Torah meha-tana ha-eloki Rabi Shimon Ben Yohai z.l*. Vilnius, Lithuania: Romm, 1882.
———. *Sefer yetsirah . . . im 4 be'urim . . . perush Ra'avad*. Jerusalem, Israel: Levin-Epshtein, 1965.
Shneuri, Dov Ber. *Imre binah*. Kopys, Belarus: Yisra'el Yafeh, 1821.
———. *Ma'amre Admor ha-Emtsa'i*, Brooklyn, NY: Kehot, 1989–1994.
———. *Perush ha-milot*, Warsaw, Poland: Natan Shriftgisser, 1887.
———. *Pokeah 'ivrim*, Brooklyn, NY: Kehot, 2003.
———. *Sifra de-ve Rav hu sefer Torat kohanim*. Jerusalem, Israel: Sifra, 1959.
———. *Sifre 'al sefer be-Midbar*. Jerusalem, Israel: Mif'al Torat hakhme Lita, 1993.
Singer, Simeon, ed. *The Authorised Daily Prayer Book of the Hebrew Congregations of the Commonwealth. With New Translation and Commentary by Chief Rabbi Sir Jonathan Sacks*. London, UK: Collins, 2007.
Sternharts, Natan. *Haye Moharan . . . hugah be-hagahah meduyeket, ve-hukhnesu bo kamah hashmatot she-nishmetu mi-defus rishon. . . .* Jerusalem, Israel: Keren hadpasah de-haside Breslav, 1976.

———. *Ha-tamim*. Kfar Chabad, Israel: Kehot, 1984.
———. *Tanakh: The Holy Scriptures. The New JPS Translation According to the Traditional Hebrew Text*. Philadelphia, PA: Jewish Publication Society of America, 1985.
———. *Tana de-ve Eliyahu*. Warsaw, Poland: Shmuel Shmelke Pilitser, 1912.
———. *Tikune Zohar meha-tana ha-eloki Rabi Shimon ben Yohai*. Jerusalem, Israel: Mekhon Da'at Yosef, 2005.
Tobiah ben Eliezer. *Pesikta zutarta*. Venice, Italy: Daniel Bomberg, 1546.
Vidas, Eliyahu de. *Reshit hokhmah*. Warsaw, Poland: Shne'ur, 1937.
Vital, Hayim. *'Ets hayim*. Jerusalem, Israel, 1988.
———. *Likute Torah: Torah Nevi'im u-Khetuvim ve-nilvah elav Sefer Ta'ame ha-mitsvot*. Jerusalem, Israel: n.p., 1988.
———. *Peri 'ets hayim*, Jerusalem, Israel, 1988
Ya'akov Ben Asher. *Arba'ah turim*. Jerusalem, Israel: Kiryah ne'emanah, 1961–64.
Ya'akov Yosef of Polnoye. *Tsofnat pa'neah*, edited by G. Nigal. Jerusalem, Israel: ha-Makhon le-heker ha-sifrut ha-hasidit, 1989.
———. *Toledot Ya'akov Yosef*. Jerusalem, Israel: Mishpahat Aikhen, 2010.
Ze'ev Volf of Zhitomir. *Or ha-me'ir*. Warsaw, Poland: Meir Yehi'el Halter, 1883.

Secondary Literature

Afterman, Adam. "Time, Eternity and Mystical Experience in Kabbalah." In *Time and Eternity in Jewish Mysticism*, edited by B. Ogren, 162–78. Leiden, The Netherlands: Brill, 2015.
Ashkenazi, Mordekhai Shmuel. *Hilkhot talmud Torah mi-Shulhan 'arukh Admor ha-Zaken 'im hosafot 'im he'arot ve-tsiyunim*. Brooklyn, NY: Kehot, 2000.
Balakirsky Katz, Maya. "An Occupational Neurosis: A Psychoanalytic Case History of a Rabbi." *AJS Review* 34, no. 1 (2010): 1–31.
———. "A Rabbi, a Priest, and a Psychoanalyst: Religion in the Early Psychoanalytic Case History." *Contemporary Jewry* 31, no. 1 (2011): 3–24.
———. *The Visual Culture of Chabad*. Cambridge, UK: Cambridge University Press, 2010.
Barr, James. *Comparative Philology and the Text of the Old Testament*. Oxford, UK: Clarendon, 1968.
Biale, David. *Eros and the Jews: from Biblical Israel to Contemporary America*. Berkeley, CA: University of California Press, 1997.
Biale, David, David Assaf, Benjamin Brown, Uriel Gellman, Samuel Heilman, Moshe Rosman, Gadi Sagiv, Marcin Wodziński, and Arthur Green. *Hasidism: A New History*. Princeton, NJ: Princeton University Press, 2018.
Bilu, Yoram. *Itanu yoter mi-tamid: hankahat ha-Rabi be-Habad ha-meshihit*. Ra'anana, Israel: ha-Universitah ha-petuhah, 2016.
Brawer, Naftali. *Resistance and Response to Change: The Leadership of Rabbi Shalom DovBer Schneersohn (1860–1920)*. PhD diss., University College London, 2004.

---. "Yisudah shel yeshivat 'Tomkhe Temimim' ve-hashpa'atah 'al tenu'at Habad." In *Yeshivot u-vate midrashot*, edited by I. Etkes, 357–68. Jerusalem, Israel: Zalman Shazar Center, 2006.
Breslauer, S. Daniel. "Zebulun and Issachar as an Ethical Paradigm." *Hebrew Annual Review* 8 (1985): 13–23.
Brown, Benjamin. "Substitutes for Mysticism: A General Model for the Theological Development of Hasidism in the Nineteenth Century." *History of Religions* 56, no. 3 (2017): 247–88.
Bunin, Hayim Yitshak. *Mishneh Habad*. Warsaw, Poland: Ha-va'ad le-hotsa'at Mishneh Habad, 1936.
Cooper, Levi. "Towards a Judicial Biography of Rabbi Shneur Zalman of Liady." *Journal of Law and Religion* 30, no. 1 (2015): 107–35.
---. "Mysteries of the Paratext: Why Did Rabbi Shneur Zalman of Liady Never Publish His Code of Law?" *Dine Israel* 31 (2017): 43*–84*.
Dahan, Alon. 'Dirah ba-tahtonim': mishnato ha-meshihit shel R. Menahem Mendel Schneerson (ha-Rabi mi-Lyubavitsh). PhD diss., Hebrew University of Jerusalem, 2006.
---. "Yahaso shel R. Menahem Mendel Schneerson le-tsiyonut, le-Erets Yisra'el uli-medinat Yisra'el." In *Habad: historyah, hagut ve-dimui*, edited by J. Meir and G. Sagiv, 301–22. Jerusalem, Israel: Zalman Shazar Center, 2016.
Dan, Joseph. "Kefel ha-panim shel ha-meshihiyut ba-hasidut." In *Be-ma'gele Hasidim: kovets mehkarim le-zikhro shel Profesor Mordecai Wilensky*, edited by I. Etkes, I. Bartal, D. Assaf, E. Reiner, and M. Wilensky, 299–315. Jerusalem, Israel: Bialik Institute, 1999.
Dan, Joseph, and Isaiah Tishby. "Torat ha-hasidut." In *Ha-Entsiklopedyah ha-'Ivrit*, edited by Y. Leibowitz, 769–821. Jerusalem, Israel: Encyclopaedia Publishing, 1965.
Dauber, Jonathan. *Knowledge of God and the Development of Early Kabbalah*. Leiden, The Netherlands: Brill, 2012.
Davidson, Herbert A. *Moses Maimonides: The Man and His Works*. Oxford, UK: Oxford University Press, 2005.
Dein, Simon. *Lubavitcher Messianism: What Really Happens When Prophecy Fails?* London, UK: Continuum, 2011.
Dvir-Goldberg, Rivka. "Ha-Besht u-'mahbarto ha-tehorah.' Ha-yahas le-nashim ba-siporet ha-hasidit." *Massekhet* 3 (2005): 45–62.
---. "Kolo shel ma'ayan tat-karka'i: demutah shel ishah mi-ba'ad la-sipur ha-hasidi." *Mehkere Yerushalayim be-folklor Yehudi* 21 (2001): 27–44.
Dynner, Glenn. *Men of Silk: The Hasidic Conquest of Polish Jewish Society*. Oxford, UK: Oxford University Press, 2009.
Ehrlich, M. Avrum. *The Messiah of Brooklyn: Understanding Lubavitch Hasidism Past and Present*. Jersey City, NJ: KTAV Publishing House, 2004.
Elior, Rachel. "HaBaD: The Contemplative Ascent to God." In *Jewish Spirituality from the Sixteen-Century Revival to the Present*, edited by A. Green, 157–205. New York: Crossroad, 1987.

———. "Mekomo shel ha-adam be-'avodat ha-Shem ha-Habadit." *Daat* 12 (1988): 493–506.

———. "The Lubavitch Messianic Resurgence: The Historical and Mystical Background 1939–1996." In *Toward the Millennium: Messianic Expectations from the Bible to Waco*, edited by P. Schaefer and M. Cohen, 383–408. Leiden, The Netherlands: Brill, 1998.

———. *The Paradoxical Ascent to God*. Albany, NY: State University of New York Press, 1993.

———. "Vikuah Minsk." *Mehkere Yerushalayim be-mahashevet Yisra'el* 1 (1981): 179–207.

Torat ha-Elohut ba-dor ha-sheni shel hasidut Habad. Jerusalem, Israel: Magnes, 1982.

Etkes, Immanuel. *Rabbi Shneur Zalman of Liady: The Origins of Chabad Hasidism*. Waltham, MA: Brandeis University Press, 2015.

———. "Darko shel R. Shneur Zalman mi-Liadi ke-manhig shel Hasidim." *Zion* 50 (1985): 321–54.

———. *Rabbi Shneur Zalman of Liady: The Origins of Chabad Hasidism*. Waltham, MA: Brandeis University Press, 2015.

———. "The War of Lyady Succession: R. Aaron Halevi versus R. Dov Baer." *Polin* 25 (2013): 93–133.

Faierstein, Morris. "Personal Redemption in Hasidism." In *Hasidism Reappraised*, edited by A. Rapoport-Albert, 214–24. London, UK: Littman, 1997.

Ferziger, Adam S. *Beyond Sectarianism: The Realignment of American Orthodox Judaism*. Detroit, MI: Wayne State University Press, 2015.

Fine, Lawrence. *Physician of the Soul, Healer of the Cosmos: Isaac Luria and His Kabbalistic Fellowship*. Stanford, CA: Stanford University Press, 2003.

Fishbane, Michael. "To Jump for Joy: The Rites of Dance According to R. Nahman of Bratzlav." *Journal of Jewish Thought and Philosophy* 6, no. 2 (1997): 371–87.

Fishkoff, Sue. *The Rebbe's Army: Inside the World of Chabad-Lubavitch*. New York: Schocken Books, 2003.

Fishman, David E. "Preserving Tradition in the Land of Revolution: The Religious Leadership of Soviet Jewry, 1917–1930." In *The Uses of Tradition: Jewish Continuity in the Modern Era*, edited by J. Wertheimer, 85–118. New York: Jewish Theological Seminary of America, 1992.

———. *Russia's First Modern Jews*. New York: New York University Press, 1995.

Fishman, Talya. "A Kabbalistic Perspective on Gender-Specific Commandments: On the Interplay of Symbols and Society." *AJS Review* 17, no. 2 (1992): 199–245.

Foxbrunner, Roman A. *Habad. The Hasidism of R. Shneur Zalman of Lyady*. Tuscaloosa, AL: University of Alabama Press, 1992.

Friedhaber, Zvi. "Dance with the Separating Kerchief." *Dance Research Journal* 17/18, no. 1-1 (1985–86): 65–69.

Garb, Jonathan. *Yearnings of the Soul: Psychological Thought in Modern Kabbalah*. Chicago, IL: Chicago University Press, 2015.

———. "Rabbi Kook and His Sources: from Kabbalistic Historiosophy to National Mysticism." In *Studies in Modern Religions, Religious Movements and the Babi-Bahai Faiths*, edited by M. Sharon, 77–96. Leiden, The Netherlands: Brill, 2004.

———. *Shamanic Trance in Modern Kabbalah*. Chicago, IL: Chicago University Press, 2011.

Giller, Pinchas. *Reading the Zohar: The Sacred Text of the Kabbalah*. New York: Oxford University Press, 2000.

Ginsburg, Elliot K. *Sabbath in the Classical Kabbalah*. Oxford, UK: Littman, 2008.

Glitzenstein, Avraham Hanokh. *Sefer ha-toldot: Rabi Shneur Zalman mi-Liadi*. Brooklyn, NY: Kehot, 1967.

Gotlieb, Ya'akov. *Sekhaltanut bi-levush hasidi: demuto shel ha-Rambam be-hasidut Habad*. Ramat Gan, Israel: Bar-Ilan University Press, 2009.

Green, Arthur. "Around the Maggid's Table: *Tsaddik*, Leadership, and Popularization in the Circle of Dov Baer of Miedzyrzecz." In Arthur Green, *The Heart of the Matter: Studies in Jewish Mysticism and Theology*, 119–66. Philadelphia, PA: Jewish Publication Society of America, 2015.

———. *Tormented Master: A Life of Rabbi Nahman of Bratslav*. Tuscaloosa, AL: University of Alabama Press, 1978.

Greenberg, Gershon. "Menahem Mendel Schneerson's Response to the Holocaust." *Modern Judaism* 34, no. 1 (2014): 86–122.

Greenstein, Edward, L. "Wordplay, Hebrew." In *The Anchor Bible Dictionary*, edited by D. N. Freedman, vi, 968–71. New York: Doubleday, 1992.

Gries, Zeev. "The Hasidic Managing Editor." In *Hasidism Reappraised*, edited by A. Rapoport-Albert, 141–55. London, UK: Littman, 1997.

Halbertal, Moshe. *Maimonides: Life and Thought*. Princeton, NJ: Princeton University Press, 2014.

Hallamish, Moshe. "'Al ha-shetikah ba-kabalah uva-hasidut." In *Dat ve-safah: ma'amarim be-filosofyah kelalit ve-Yehudit*, edited by M. Hallamish and Asa Kasher, 79–89. Tel Aviv, Israel: Mif'alim universita'im le-hotsa'ah la-or, 1981.

———. *An Introduction to the Kabbalah*. Albany, NY: State University of New York Press, 1999.

———. "Ha-hasidut ve-Erets Yisra'el: tefisat 'olam be-mivhan ha-metsi'ut—shene degamim." In *Erets Yisra'el ba-hagut ha-Yehudit ba-'et ha-hadashah*, edited by A. Ravitsky, 225–55. Jerusalem, Israel: Yad Izhak Ben-Zvi, 1998.

———. Mishnato ha-'iyunit shel r. Shneur Zalman mi-Ladi (ve-yahasah le-torat ha-kabalah ule-reshit ha-hasidut). PhD diss., Hebrew University of Jerusalem, 1976.

———. "Shulhan 'arukh ha-rav—ben kabalah le-halakhah." In *Habad: historyah, hagut ve-dimui*, edited by J. Meir and G. Sagiv, 75–96. Jerusalem, Israel: Zalman Shazar Center, 2016.

———. "The Teachings of R. Menahem Mendel of Vitebsk." In *Hasidism Reappraised*, edited by A. Rapoport-Albert, 268–87. London, UK: Littman, 1997.
———. "Torat ha-tsedakah be-mishnat rabi Shneur Zalman mi-Lyadi." *Daat* 1 (1977): 121–93.
———. "Yahase tsadik ve-'edah be-mishnat R. Shneur Zalman mi-Ladi." In *Hevrah ve-historyah*, edited by Y. Cohen, 79–92. Jerusalem, Israel: Misrad ha-hinukh, 1980.
Haran, Raya. "Mishnato shel R. Avraham mi-Kalisk: ha-derekh li-devekut he-nahalatam shel bene ha-'aliyah." *Tarbiz* 66, no. 4 (1997): 517–41.
Harvey, Warren Zev. *Physics and Metaphysics in Hasdai Crescas*. Amsterdam, The Netherlands: J. C. Gieben, 1998.
Heilman, Hayim Meir. *Bet rabi*. Berdichev, Ukraine: H. Y. Sheftel, 1902.
Heilman, Samuel, and Menachem Friedman. *The Rebbe: The Life and Afterlife of Menachem Mendel Schneerson*. Princeton, NJ: Princeton University Press, 2010.
Heinemann, Yitshak. *Darkhe ha-agadah*. Jerusalem, Israel: Magnes, 1949.
Hellner-Eshed, Melila. *A River Flows from Eden: The Language of Mystical Experience in the Zohar*. Stanford, CA: Stanford University Press, 2009.
Horodecky, Shmuel Abba. *Ha-hasidut veha-hasidim*. Jerusalem, Israel: Dvir, 1923.
Huss, Boaz. "Mysticism versus Philosophy in Kabbalistic Literature." *Micrologus* 9 (2001): 125–35.
Idel, Moshe. "'*Adonai Sefatai Tiftah*.' Models of Understanding Prayer in Early Hasidism." *Kabbalah* 18 (2008): 7–111.
———. *Enchanted Chains: Techniques and Rituals in Jewish Mysticism*. Los Angeles, CA: Cherub, 2005.
———. "Female Beauty: A Chapter in the History of Jewish Mysticism." In *Be-ma'gele Hasidim. Kovets mehkarim le-zikhro shel Profesor Mordekhai Vilenski*, edited by I. Etkes, I. Bartal, D. Assaf, E. Reiner, and M. Wilensky, 317–34. Jerusalem, Israel: Bialik Institute, 1999.
———. *Hasidism: Between Ecstasy and Magic*. Albany, NY: State University of New York Press, 1995.
———. "'Higher than Time': Observation on Some Concepts of Time in Kabbalah and Hasidism." In *Time and Eternity in Jewish Mysticism*, edited by B. Ogren, 179–210. Leiden, The Netherlands: Brill, 2015.
———. *Kabbalah and Eros*. New Haven, CT: Yale University Press, 2005.
———. *Kabbalah: New Perspectives*. New Haven, CT: Yale University Press, 1990.
———. "'Le-'olam ha-Shem devarekha nitsav ba-shamayim.' 'Iyunim be-torah mukdemet shel ha-Besht ve-gilguleha ba-hasidut." *Kabbalah* 20 (2009): 219–286.
———. *Messianic Mystics*. New Haven, CT: Yale University Press, 1998.
———. "Multiple Forms of Redemption in Kabbalah and Hasidism." *Jewish Quarterly Review* 101, no. 1 (2011): 27–70.
———. "Mystical Redemption and Messianism in R. Israel Ba'al Shem Tov's Teachings." *Kabbalah* 24 (2011): 7–122.

———. "On Paradise in Jewish Mysticism." *Journal for the Study of Religions and Ideologies* 10, no. 30 (2011): 3–38.

———. "Sabbath: on Concepts of Time in Jewish Mysticism." In *Sabbath: Idea, History, Reality*, edited by G. J. Blidstein, 57–93. Beer Sheva, Israel: Ben Gurion University Press, 2004.

———. "Some Concepts of Time and History in Kabbalah." In *Jewish History and Jewish Memory: Essays in Honour of Yoseph Haim Yerushalmi*, edited by E. Carlebach, J. M. Ephron, and D. N., Myers, 153–88. Hanover, NH: Brandeis University Press, 1998.

———. "Ta'anug: Erotic Delights from Kabbalah to Hasidism." In *Hidden Intercourse: Eros and Sexuality in the History of Western Esotericism*, edited by W. J. Hanegraaff and J. J. Kripal, 111–51. Leiden, The Netherlands: Brill, 2008.

Jacobs, Louis. "Divine Foreknowledge and Human Free Will." *Conservative Judaism* 34, no. 1 (1980): 4–16.

———. "Eating as an Act of Worship in Hasidic Thought." In *Studies in Jewish Religious and Intellectual History*, edited by S. Stein and R. Loewe, 157–66. Tuscaloosa, AL: University of Alabama Press, 1979.

———. *Hasidic Prayer*. London, UK: Routledge, 1972.

———. "Hasidism and the Dogma of the Decline of the Generations." In *Hasidism Reappraised*, edited by A. Rapoport-Albert, 208–13. London, UK: Littman, 1997.

———. "The Uplifting of Sparks in Later Jewish Mysticism." In *Jewish Spirituality from the Sixteenth-Century Revival to the Present*, edited by A. Green, 99–126. New York: Crossroad, 1987.

Jacobson, Yoram. "Bi-mevokhe ha-'ain' uvi-mevokhe ha-'yesh': 'iyun be-sifrah shel Rachel Elior: 'Torat ahdut ha-hafakhim,' Yerushalaim 5753." In *Asufat kiryat sefer: mehkarim be-mada'e ha-Yahadut u-vikorot sefarim*, edited by Y. Rozenberg, 229–45. Jerusalem, Israel: Beit ha-sefarim ha-leumi ve-ha-universita'i, 1998.

———. "Galut u-ge'ulah be-hasidut Gur." *Daat* 2/3 (1977–79): 175–215.

———. "Kedushat ha-hulin be-hasidut Gur: 'iyunim bi-tefisat ha-shabat bi-derushe 'Sefat Emet." In *Tsadikim ve-anshe ma'aseh: mehkarim be-hasidut Polin*, edited by R. Elior, I. Bartal, Ch. Shmeruk, 241–77. Jerusalem, Israel: Bialik Institute, 1994.

———. "Mi-ne'urim le-hanhagah umi-kabalah le-hasidut: shelavim be-hitpathuto shel ba'al 'Sefat Emet'." *Jerusalem Studies in Jewish Thought* 13 (1996): 429–46.

———. "The Aspect of the 'Feminine' in the Lurianic Kabbalah." In *Gershom Scholem's Major Trends in Jewish Mysticism 50 Years After: Proceedings of the Sixth International Conference on the History of Jewish Mysticism*, edited by P. Schäfer and J. Dan, 229–45. Tübingen, Germany: Mohr Siebeck, 1993.

Kahana, Maoz, and Ariel Evan Mayse. "Hasidic Halakhah: Reappraising the Interface of Spirit and Law." *AJS Review* 41, no. 2 (2017): 375–408.

Kallus, Menahem. *The Theurgy of Prayer in the Lurianic Kabbalah*. PhD diss., Hebrew University of Jerusalem, 2002.

Kauffman, Tsippi. *Be-khol derakheha da'ehu: tefisat ha-Elohut veha-'avodah be-gashmiyut be-reshit ha-hasidut*. Ramat Gan, Israel: Bar-Ilan University Press, 2009.

Klausner, Joseph. *The Messianic Idea in Israel: From Its Beginning to the Completion of the Mishnah*. London, UK: Allen & Unwin, 1956.

Koren, Sharon Faye. *Forsaken: The Menstruant in Medieval Jewish Mysticism*. Waltham, MA: Brandeis University Press, 2011.

Kravel-Tovi, Michal and Yoram Bilu. "The Work of the Present: Constructing Messianic Temporality in the Wake of a Failed Prophecy in Chabad." *Religion* 39, no. 3 (2009): 248–69.

Korf, Yehoshua Gedalyah. *Likute be'urim be-Sefer ha-Tanya*, helek i. Brooklyn, NY: Kehot, 1984.

Kraus, Yitshak. *Ha-shevi'i: meshihiyut ba-dor ha-shevi'i shel Habad*. Tel-Aviv, Israel: Yedi'ot aharonot, 2007.

Lamm, Norman. *Torah Lishmah: Torah for Torah's Sake in the Works of Rabbi Hayyim of Volozhin and His Contemporaries*. Hoboken, NJ: Ktav, 1989.

Laquer, Thomas. *Making Sex: Body and Gender from the Greeks to Freud*. Cambridge, MA: Harvard University Press, 2003.

Levin, Yael. "Kol ha-kalah le-'atid." *Kovets ha-Tsiyonut ha-datit* 4 (2001): 365–68.

Levine, Shalom Dovber. *Kuntres nerot Shabat Kodesh*. Brooklyn, NY, 1975.

———. *Toledot Habad*. Brooklyn, NY: Kehot, 1988–2011.

Lewis, Justin Jaron. *Imagining Holiness: Classic Hasidic Tales in Modern Times*. Montreal, QC: McGill-Queen's University Press, 2009.

———. *Likute hagahot le-Sefer ha-Tanya*. Brooklyn, NY: Kehot, 1974.

Liwer, Amira. *Torah shebe-'al peh be-khitve R. Tsadok ha-Kohen mi-Lublin*. PhD diss., Hebrew University of Jerusalem, 2006.

Loewenthal, Naftali. "Communicating Jewish Spirituality to Women and Girls in Riga, 1937–1941: A Model for Today?" In *Jews in a Changing World: Materials of the First International Conference, Riga, August 28–29, 1995*, edited by H. Branover and R. Ferber, 188–96. Riga, Latvia: M. Dubin Foundation "Shamir," 1997.

———. *Communicating the Infinite: The Emergence of the Habad School*. Chicago, IL: University of Chicago Press, 1990.

———. "Contemporary Habad and the Paradox of Redemption." In *Perspectives on Jewish Thought and Mysticism*, edited by A. L. Ivry, E.R. Wolfson, and A. Arkush, 381–402. Amsterdam, The Netherlands: Harwood, 1998.

———. "'Daughter/Wife of Hasid' or 'Hasidic Woman'?" *Jewish Studies* 40 (2000): 21*–28*.

———. "Finding the Radiance in the Text: A Habad Hasidic Interpretation of the Exodus." In *Scriptural Exegesis: The Shapes of Culture and the Religious Imagination. Essays in Honour of Michael Fishbane*, edited by D. A. Green and L. S. Lieber, 299–309. New York: Oxford University Press, 2009.

———. "Habad Messianism: A Combination of Opposites." In *Jewish Studies in a New Europe*, edited by U. Haxen, H. Trautner-Kromann, and K. L. Goldschmidt Salamon, 498–511. Copenhagen, Denmark: C. A. Reitzel, 1998.

———. "'Reason' and 'Beyond Reason' in Habad Hasidism." In *'Ale shefer: mehkarim be-sifrut he-hagut ha-Yehudit mugashim li-khevod ha-rav Dr. Alexander Safran*, edited by M. Hallamish, 109–126. Jerusalem, Israel: Bar-Ilan University Press, 1990.

———. "Self-sacrifice of the Zaddik in the Teaching of R. Dov Ber, the Mitteler Rebbe." In *Jewish History: Essays in Honour of Chimen Abramsky*, edited by A. Rapoport-Albert and S. J. Zipperstein, 457–94. London, UK: Halban, 1988.

———. "The Ba'al Shem Tov's 'Iggeret ha-kodesh' and contemporary Habad 'outreach.'" In *Yashan mi-pene hadash: mehkarim be-toldot Yehude mizrah Eropah uve-tarbutam. Shai le-Immanuel Etkes*, edited by David Assaf and Ada Rapoport-Albert, i, 69–101. Jerusalem, Israel: Zalman Shazar Center, 2009.

———. "The Image of Maimonides in Habad Hasidism." In *Traditions of Maimonideanism*, edited by C. Fraenkel, 277–312. Leiden, The Netherlands: Brill, 2009.

———. "'The Thickening of the Light': The Kabbalistic-Hasidic Teachings of Rabbi Shalom Dovber Schneersohn in Their Social Context." In *Habad: historyah, hagut ve-dimui*, edited by J. Meir and G. Sagiv, 7–43. Jerusalem, Israel: Zalman Shazar Center, 2016.

———. "Women and the Dialectic of Spirituality in Hasidism." In *Be-ma'gele Hasidim: kovets mehkarim le-zikhro shel Profesor Mordekhai Vilenski*, edited by I. Etkes, I. Bartal, D. Assaf, E. Reiner, M. Wilensky, 7*–65*. Jerusalem, Israel: Bialik Institute, 1999.

Lurie, Ilia. "Ben dat le-politikah: R. Shalom Dovber Shneersohn ke-manhig ortodoksi." In *Habad: historyah, hagut ve-dimui*, edited by J. Meir and G. Sagiv, 201–21. Jerusalem, Israel: Zalman Shazar Center, 2016.

———. *'Edah u-medinah: hasidut Habad ba-Imperyah ha-Rusit 5580–5643*. Jerusalem, Israel: Magnes, 2006.

———. "Hinukh ve-ide'ologyah: reshit darkah shel ha-yeshivah ha-habadit." In *Yashan mi-pene hadash: mehkarim be-toldot Yehude mizrah Eropah uve-tarbutam. Shai le-Immanuel Etkes*, edited by David Assaf and Ada Rapoport-Albert, i, 185–221. Jerusalem, Israel: Zalman Shazar Center, 2009.

———. *Milhamot Lyubavich: hasidut Habad be-Rusyah ha-Tsarit*. Jerusalem, Israel: Zalman Shazar Center, 2018.

Magid, Shaul. "The Ritual Is Not the Hunt: The Seven Wedding Blessings, Redemption, and Jewish Ritual as Fantasy." In *Liturgy, Time, and the Politics of Redemption*, edited by R. Rashkover and C. C. Pecknold, 188–211. Grand Rapids, MI: Eerdmans, 2006.

Margolin, Ron. *Mikdash adam: ha-hafnamah ha-datit ve-'itsuv haye ha-dat ha-penimiyim be-reshit ha-hasidut*. Jerusalem, Israel: Magnes, 2005.

Mark, Zvi. *Megilat setarim: ha-hazon na-meshihi ha-sodi shel R. Nahman bi-Breslav*. Ramat-Gan, Israel: Bar-Ilan University Press, 2006.

———. *Mysticism and Madness: The Religious Thought of Rabbi Nachman of Bratslav*. London, UK: Continuum, 2009.

———. *The Scroll of Secrets: The Hidden Messianic Vision of R. Nachman of Breslav*. Boston, MA: Academic Studies Press, 2010.

Mayse, Ariel Evan. Beyond the Letters: The Question of Language in the Teachings of Rabbi Dov Baer of Mezritch. PhD diss., Harvard University, 2015.

———. "Eternity in Hasidism: Time and Presence." In *Eternity: A History*, edited by Y. Melamed, 231–38. Oxford, UK: Oxford University Press, 2016.

Mayse, Ariel Evan, and Daniel Reiser. "Derashato ha-aharonah shel ha-rabi mi-Gur 'Ba'al ha-Sefat Emet'—u-mashma'ut sefat ha-Yidish le-heker ha-derashah ha-hasidit." *Kabbalah* 30 (2013): 127–60.

———. "Sefer Sefat Emet, Yiddish Manuscripts and the Oral Homilies of R. Yehudah Aryeh Leib of Ger." *Kabbalah* 33 (2015): 9–44.

———. "Territories and Textures: The Hasidic Sermons as the Crossroad of Language and Culture," *Jewish Social Studies* 24, no.1 (2018): 127–60.

Meir, Jonatan. "Reformed Hasidism: The Image of Habad in Haskalah Literature." *Modern Judaism* 37, no. 3 (2017): 297–315.

Miller, Chaim. *Turning Judaism Outward: A Biography of Rabbi Menachem Mendel Schneerson, the Seventh Lubavitcher Rebbe*. Brooklyn, NY: Kol Menachem, 2014.

Mindel, Nissan. *Rabbi Schneur Zalman of Liadi*. Brooklyn, NY: Kehot, 1969–1973.

Mondshine, Yehoshua. "Ha-ma'asar ha-rishon." *Kerem Habad* 4, no. 1 (1992): 27–76.

———. *Ha-masa' ha-aharon: matayim shanah le-masa'o shel ha-Admor Rabi Shneur Zalman Ba'al ha-Tanya be-ṣitsumah shel milhemet Napoleon 572–772*. Jerusalem, Israel: Knizhniki, 2012.

———. *Ha-ma'asar ha-rishon: ma'asaro ha-rishon shel Admor Rabi Shneur Zalman Ba'al ha-Tanya*. Jerusalem, Israel: Knizhniki, 2012.

———. "Ha-ma'asar ha-sheni." *Kerem Habad* 4, no. 1 (1992): 77–110.

———. "Ha-shavu'on la-yeladim 'ha-Ah,'" *Kerem Habad* 1 (1986), 118–20.

———. "Igeret mi-bat Rabenu marat Freyda(?) le-ahiha mo.ha-r.d." *Kerem Habad* 1 (1986): 101.

———. *Masa' Berditshov: matayim shanah le-masa'o shel Admor ha-Zaken le-Berditshov, Breslav u-Mezhbuzh 570–770*. Kiryat Malakhi, Israel: Hazak, 2010.

———. *Migdal 'oz*. Kfar Chabad, Israel: Makhon Lubavitch, 1990.

———. *Likute amarim hu Sefer ha-Tanya: mahadurotav, tirgumav u-ve'urav*. Brooklyn, NY: Kehot, 1981.

———. *Sifre ha-halakhah shel Admor ha-Zaken (Ba'al ha-Tanya veha-Sh.'a.) Biblyografyah*. Brooklyn, NY: Kehot, 1984.

Morris, Bonnie J. *Lubavitcher Women in America: Identity and Activism in the Postwar Era*. Albany, NY: State University of New York Press, 1998.

Niger, Shmuel, and Yankev Shatzky. *Leksikon fun der nayer Yidisher literatur*. New York: Alveltlekher Yidisher Kultur-Kongres, 1956–81.

Nigal, Gedalyah. *Ledat ha-Hasidut*. Jerusalem, Israel: Ha-makhon le-heker ha-sifrut ha-hasidit, 2004.

Novak, David. *The Image of the Non-Jew in Judaism: The Idea of Noahide Law*. Oxford, UK: Littman, 2011.

Ornet, Leah. *Ratso va-shov: yesodot etiyim u-mistiyim be-torato shel R. Shneur Zalman mi-Ladi. 'Iyun hashva'ati.* Tel-Aviv, Israel: Hakibuts ha-me'uhad, 2007.
Perl, Joseph. *Uiber das Wesen der Sekte Chassidim.* Jerusalem, Israel: Israel Academy of Sciences and Humanities, 1977.
Polen, Nechemia. "Charismatic Leader, Charismatic Book: Rabbi Shneur Zalman's *Tanya* and His Leadership." In *Rabbinic and Lay Communal Authority*, edited by S. Last Stone, 53–64. New York: Yeshiva University Press, 2006.
———. "Miriam's Dance: Radical Egalitarianism in Hasidic Thought." *Modern Judaism* 12 (1992): 1–21.
Rapoport-Albert, Ada. "From Woman as Hasid to Woman as 'Tsadik' in the Teachings of the Last Two Lubavitcher Rebbes." In A. Rapoport-Albert, *Hasidic Studies: Essays in History and* Gender, 427–70. Liverpool, UK: Littman, 2018.
———. "Hagiography with Footnotes: Edifying Tales and the Writing of History in Hasidism." In A. Rapoport-Albert, *Hasidic Studies: Essays in History and* Gender, 199–268. Liverpool, UK: Littman, 2018.
———. "Hasidism after 1772: Structural Continuity and Change." In A. Rapoport-Albert, *Hasidic Studies: Essays in History and* Gender, 23–123. Liverpool, UK: Littman, 2018.
———. "On Women in Hasidism: S. A. Horodecky and The Maid of Ludmir Tradition." In A. Rapoport-Albert, *Hasidic Studies: Essays in History and Gender*, 318–67. Liverpool, UK: Littman, 2018.
———. "The Emergence of a Female Constituency in Twentieth-Century HaBaD." In A. Rapoport-Albert, *Hasidic Studies: Essays in History and Gender*, 368–426. Liverpool, UK: Littman, 2018.
———. *Women and the Messianic Heresy of Sabbatai Zevi.* Oxford, UK: Littman, 2011.
Rapoport-Albert, Ada, and Gadi Sagiv. "Habad ke-neged hasidut 'Polin': le-toldotav shel dimui." In *Habad: historyah, hagut ve-dimui*, edited by J. Meir and G. Sagiv, 223–66. Jerusalem, Israel: Zalman Shazar Center, 2016.
Ravitzky, Aviezer. "'To the Utmost Human Capacity': Maimonides on the Days of the Messiah." In *Perspectives on Maimonides*, edited by J. Kraemer, 221–56. Oxford, UK: Oxford University Press, 1990.
Reiser, Daniel. "Ha-derashah ha-hasidit—ben Yidish le-'Ivrit." *Judaica Petropolitana* 6 (2016): 3–23.
———. *Ha-Mar'eh ka-mar'ah: tekhnikat ha-dimyon ba-mistikah ha-Yehudit ba-me'ah ha-'esrim.* Los Angeles, CA: Cherub, 2014.
———. "The Encounter in Vienna: Modern Psychotherapy, Guided Imagery, and Hasidism Post-World War I." *Modern Judaism* 36, no. 3 (2016): 277–302.
Reisen, Zalman. *Leksikon fun der Yidisher literature, prese un filologye.* Vilnius, Lithuania: B. Kletskin, 1926–29.
Rodkinson, Michael Levi. *Toledot 'amude Habad.* Koenigsberg (Kaliningrad), Russia: Hirsh Fettsoll, 1876.

Rosman, Moshe. "'Al nashim va-hasidut: he'arot le-diyun." In *Yashan mi-pene hadash: mehkarim be-toldot Yehude mizrah Eropah uve-tarbutam. Shay le-Immanuel Etkes*, edited by D. Assaf, and A. Rapoport-Albert, i, 151–64. Jerusalem, Israel: Zalman Shazar Center, 2009.

———. *Founder of Hasidism. A Quest for the Historical Ba'al Shem Tov*. Berkeley, CA: University of California Press, 1996.

Roth, Ariel. *Ketsad li-kero et safrut Habad*. Ramat Gan, Israel: Bar-Ilan University Press, 2017.

Rubenstein, Jeffrey. "Mythic Time and the Festival Cycle." *Journal of Jewish Thought and Philosophy* 6, no. 1 (1997): 157–83.

Rudavsky, Tamar M. *Time Matters: Time, Creation and Cosmology in Medieval Jewish Philosophy*. Albany, NY: State University of New York Press, 2000.

Sagiv, Gadi. *Ha-shoshelet: bet Chernobil u-mekomo be-toledot ha-hasidut*. Jerusalem, Israel: Zalman Shazar Center, 2014.

Saperstein, Marc. *Jewish Preaching 1200–1800: An Anthology*. New Haven, CT: Yale University Press, 1989.

———. "The Sermon as Oral Performance." In *Transmitting Jewish Traditions: Orality, Textuality, and Cultural Diffusion*, edited by Y. Elman and I. Gershoni, 248–77. New Haven, CT: Yale University Press, 2000.

Schatz Uffenheimer, Rivka. *Hasidism as Mysticism*. Princeton, NJ: Princeton University Press, 1993.

Scholem, Gershom. *Ha-shalav ha-aharon: mehkere ha-hasidut shel Gershom Scholem*. Tel Aviv, Israel: 'Am 'oved; Jerusalem: Magnes, 2008.

———. *Kabbalah*. Jerusalem, Israel: Keter, 1974.

———. "Le-heker kabalat r. Yitshak ben Ya'akov ha-Kohen. 2. Hitpathut torat ha-'olamot be-kabalat ha-rishonim (Sof)." *Tarbiz* 3 (1931): 33–66.

———. *Major Trends of Jewish Mysticism*. New York: Schocken Books, 1941.

———. *On the Mystical Shape of the Godhead: Basic Concepts in Kabbalah*. New York: Schocken Books, 1976.

———. *The Messianic Idea in Judaism and Other Essays on Jewish Spirituality*. New York: Schocken Books, 1995.

Schwartz, Dov. *Dilug el ha-or: musage yesod be-hagut Habad*. Alon Shvut, West Bank: hotsa'at *Mikhlelet Herzog—Tevunot*, 2017.

———. *Mahashevet Habad me-reshit ve-'ad aharit*. Ramat Gan, Israel: Bar-Ilan University Press, 2010.

Schwartzmann, Julia. "From Mystical Visions to Gender Equality Aspirations: A Hermeneutical Journey of Two Biblical Verses." *Journal of Jewish Studies* 66, no. 1 (2015): 138–56.

———. "Rabbi Yitzchak Ginsburgh and his Feminine Vision of the Messianic Age." *Journal of Modern Jewish Studies* 12, no. 1 (2013): 52–70.

Seidman, Naomi. *Sarah Schenirer and the Bais Yaakov Movement*. Liverpool, UK: Littman, 2019.

Shandler, Jeffrey. *Jews, God and Videotape: Religion and Media in America*. New York: New York University Press, 2009.

Shuchat, Raphael B. *'Olam nistar bi-memade ha-zeman: torat ha-ge'ulah shel*

ha-Gra mi-Vilnah mekoroteha ve-hashpa'atah le-dorot. Ramat Gan, Israel: Bar-Ilan University Press, 2008.
Shapiro, Marc B. *The Limits of Orthodox Theology: Maimonides' Thirteen Principles Reappraised*. Oxford, UK: Littman, 2004.
Stamler, Yossef. Sekhel, filosofyah ve-emunah be-haguto shel Rabi Shneur Zalman mi-Ladi. PhD diss., Haifa University, 2012.
Stern, Sacha. "The Rabbinic Concept of Time from Late Antiquity to the Middle Ages." In *Time and Eternity: The Medieval Discourse*, edited by G. Jaritz and G. Moreno-Riaño, 129–45. Turnhout, Belgium: Brepols, 2003.
———. *Time and Process in Ancient Judaism*. Oxford, UK: Littman, 2003.
Teitelbaum, Mordekhai. *Ha-rav mi-Ladi u-mifleget Habad*. Warsaw, Poland: Tuschijah, 1910–13.
Tirosh-Samuelson, Hava. "Gender in Jewish Mysticism." In *Jewish Mysticism and Kabbalah; New Insights and Scholarship*, edited by F. E. Greenspahn, 191–230. New York: New York University Press, 2011.
Tishby, Isaiah. "Ha-ra'ayon ha-meshihi veha-megemot ha-meshihiyot bi-tsemihut ha-hasidut." *Zion* 32 (1967): 1–45.
———. *Hikre kabalah u-sheluhoteha*. Jerusalem, Israel: Magnes, 1982–93.
———. *The Wisdom of the Zohar*. Oxford, UK: Oxford University Press for the Littman Library, 1989.
Turov, Igor. *Rannyi khasidizm: istoriya, veroucheniye, kontakty so slavyanskim okruzheniyem*. Kiev, Ukraine: Dukh i litera, 2003.
Tworek, Wojciech. "Between Hagiography and Historiography: Chabad, Scholars of Hasidism, and the Case of the Portrait of Rabbi Shneur Zalman of Liady." *East European Jewish Affairs* 47, no. 1 (2017): 3–27.
———. "Beyond Hagiography with Footnotes: Writing Biographies of the Habad Rebbe in the Post-Schneerson Era." *AJS Review* 43, no. 2 (forthcoming).
———. "*The Scroll of 19 Kislev* and the Construction of an Imagined Chabad-Lubavitch Community in Interwar Poland." *Polin* 33 (forthcoming).
Urbach, Efraim. *The Sages, Their Concepts and Beliefs*. Jerusalem, Israel: Magnes, 1979.
Weiss, Joseph. *Studies in East European Jewish Mysticism & Hasidism*. London, UK: Littman, 1997.
Wertheim, Aaron. *Law and Custom in Hasidism*. Hoboken, NJ: Ktav, 1988.
Wilensky, Mordecai L. "Hasidic-Mitnaggedic Polemics in the Jewish Communities of Eastern Europe: The Hostile Phase." In *Essential Papers on Hasidism: Origins to Present*, edited by G. D. Hundert, 244–71. New York: New York University Press, 1991.
Wineberg, Yosef. *Lessons in Tanya*. Brooklyn, NY: Kehot, 1987–93.
Wiskind Elper, Ora. "Be-tselem Elohim bara otah: motivim shel nashiyut bi-yetsirat R. Nahman mi-Breslav." *Massekhet* 5 (2006): 11–26.
Wodziński, Marcin. *Hasidism: Key Questions*. Oxford, UK: Oxford University Press, 2018.
Historical Atlas of Hasidism. Princeton, NJ: Princeton University Press, 2018.
———. "Women and Hasidism: A "Non-Sectarian" Perspective." *Jewish History* 27, no. 2–4 (2013): 399–434.

Wodziński, Marcin, and Wojciech Tworek, "Hasidic Attitudes to the Non-Jewish World." *Jewish Social Studies* (forthcoming).
Wolfson, Elliot R. *A Dream Interpreted within a Dream: Oneiropoiesis and the Prism of Imagination*. New York: Zone Books, 2011.
———. "Achronic Time, Messianic Expectation, and the Secret of the Leap in Habad." In *Habad: historyah, hagut ve-dimui*, edited by J. Meir and G. Sagiv, 45–86. Jerusalem, Israel: Zalman Shazar Center, 2016.
———. *Alef, Mem, Tau: Kabbalistic Musings on Time, Truth and Death*. Los Angeles, CA: University of California Press, 2006.
———. *Circle in the Square: Studies in the Use of Gender in Kabbalistic Symbolism*. Albany, NY: State University of New York Press, 1995.
———. "Circumcision and the Divine Name. A Study in the Transmission of Esoteric Doctrine." *Jewish Quarterly Review* 78 (1987): 77–112.
———. "Eternal Duration and Temporal Discourse: The Influence of Habad on Joseph B. Soloveitchik." In *The Value of the Particular: Lessons from Judaism and the Modern Jewish Experience. Festschrift for Steven T. Katz on the Occasion of His Seventieth Birthday*, edited by M. Zank and I. Anderson, 195–238. Leiden, The Netherlands: Brill, 2015.
———. *Language, Eros, Being: Kabbalistic Hermeneutics and Poetic Imagination*. New York: Fordham University Press, 2005.
———. *Luminal Darkness: Imaginal Gleanings from Zoharic Literature*. Oxford, UK: Oneworld, 2007.
———. "Min u-minut be-heker ha-kabalah." *Kabbalah* 6 (2002): 231–62.
———. "'Neqqudat ha-Reshimu'—The Trace of Transcendence and the Transcendence of the Trace, the Paradox of 'Simsum' in the RaShaB's 'Hemshekh Ayin Beit.'" *Kabbalah* 30 (2013): 75–120.
———. "Oneiric Imagination and Mystical Annihilation in Habad Hasidism." *ARC: Journal of the Faculty of Religious Studies* 35 (2007): 131–57.
———. *Open Secret: Postmessianic Messianism and the Mystical Revision of Menahem Mendel Schneerson*. New York: Columbia University Press, 2009.
———. "Revealing and Re/veiling: Menahem Mendel Schneerson's Messianic Secret." *Kabbalah* 26 (2012): 25–96.
———. "Walking as a Secret Duty: Theological Transformation of Social Reality in Early Hasidism." In *Hasidism Reappraised*, edited by A. Rapoport-Albert, 180–207. London, UK: Littman, 1997.
Wolfson, Harry Austryn. *Crescas' Critique of Aristotle: Problems of Aristotle's Physics in Jewish and Arabic Philosophy*. Cambridge, MA: Harvard University Press, 1929.
———. *The Philosophy of Spinoza: Unfolding the Latent Processes of His Reasoning*. Cambridge, MA: Harvard University Press, 1934.
Yerushalmi, Yosef Chaim. *Zakhor: Jewish History and Jewish Memory*. Seattle, WA: University of Washington Press, 1982.

INDEX

Aaron, 138
Abbahu, Rabbi, 17
Abraham (the Patriarch), 48, 96–97, 198n158
Abulafia, Abraham, xxiii
Afterman, Adam, xxiii
Aharon ha-Levi of Starosielce, 172n12, 192n67, 218n66
Aharon of Karlin, xv
Alter, Yehudah Aryeh Leib (the Sefat Emet), 66–67, 185n190
Amalek, 172n8, 191n60; and annihilation of, 73, 78, 148; and the counterpart of the *sefirot*, 38, 40–42, 175n33
Arama, Yitshak, 19–20
Aristotle, xxii, 3, 15, 19, 28, 115, 214n23
Avraham "the Angel," xv
Avraham of Kalisk: his conflict with the Maggid, xv; emigration to Palestine, xvi; his conflict with Shneur Zalman, xvii–xviii, xxiv–xxv
Azriel of Gerona, xxiii

Ba'al Shem Tov, Israel, xiv, xxv, 66, 80, 157n26, 189n38, 193n83, 196n118

Beinoni: difference from the *tsadik*, 65, 108–9, 114, 202n14; elevation of strange thoughts by, 213n13; and repentance, 206n49; their worship, 55, 57, 89, 114
Biale, David, 129
Bitul (nullification): of gentile nations, 191n60; of physical reality, 7, 111–12, 149, 182n166; of the self, 74, 77, 106, 114–16, 119, 189n35, 189n42, 203n18; types of, 138, 220n84
Body: as a barrier separating from God, 115–16, 118; divestment from corporeality, xxv; divine, 86, 127–28, 145; exile of the divinity in, 36–37; female, 125–27, 135–36; male, 145; performing commandments through, xxv, 56–57, 60–62; prison of the soul, 45, 52, 82–83, 85; and the realm of husks, 36, 143, 174n23, 183n168; as a redemptive tool, xxiv, xxv, 53–55, 62, 64; sublime, 72–73, 77; 86; 187n31, 188n32
Breaking of the vessels (*shevirat ha-kelim*), 33–34, 36, 47, 51, 53, 56, 62, 90, 110, 138, 142–43, 175n50, 191n60

Charity, 57, 59–62, 64, 81, 83, 131, 182n163, 204n28, 207n80
Circumcision: and the female, 142–43, 149; of hearts, 86; and redemption, 96–97, 141–43, 149, 200n182; transcending time, 98, 141
Commandments: in the "footsteps of the Messiah," 81; blessings before, 180n133, 187n24; corporeal, xxv; build the sanctuary to, 110–11; embodiment of divinity, as 8–9, 40, 56, 60, 95, 115, 165n41; Noahide, 99–100; observance by gentiles, 75–76; observance by women, 76, 144–48, 150; observance in the Messianic days, 69–71, 75–76, 97, 197n135; performance in spirituality, 48, 130, 178n90; pertinent to sexuality, 125, 140, 146–47; practical observance of, 48–49, 60–61, 65, 113, 131, 178n90, 187n24; their rationales, 51, 59, 76, 103, 182n163; redemptive value of, xx, xxiv, 54–57, 62, 64, 65, 82–83, 90, 110, 173n15; to remember Exodus, 42–43, 106, 186n9; reward for, 54–55, 72–73, 92, 187n24; time-bound, xiii, xxix, 83, 144–48
Contraction. See *tsimtsum*
Cordovero, Moshe, xxiii, 25, 109
Creation: as concealment, 84–85; continuous, 20–24, 25, 27, 29, 31, 98, 152, 171n138; days of creation, xxiii; and the divine names, 10–11, 13, 66; through the divine speech, 26, 43–44, 129; as exile, 35–37, 43–45, 49, 52, 63; 66 94, 176n59; *ex-nihilo*, 5, 35–36, 166n49; female, and 132; of the four kabbalistic worlds, 15, 16, 25, 43; and God's infinity, 3–4, 5; its purpose, 32, 34–35, 63, 66, 69, 71, 82, 132–34; 174n20; Lurianic model of, 33–34; and *Malkhut*, 12, 32, 43; ritualistic re-enactment; xxi; 60; time, of 4–5, 13, 18–19, 164n25; timing of creation, 4–5, 17–20, 164n26; and the Torah, 8–9
Crescas, Hasdai, xxii, 18–20

Dan, Joseph, xxvii, 159n39, 196n116
Dauber, Jonathan, xxii
Derbaremdiker, Eliezer, xv
Devekut: to God, xiv, xvi, 58, 60, 116, 125–26; to *halakhah*, 107; to the *tsadik*, 88, 196n116, 196n125
Devorah (Shneur Zalman's granddaughter), xv
Dov Ber of Mezrich (the Maggid): and engagement in physical world, 118–19; and gazing at women, 126; his circle, xiv–xvi, xviii, xxv, 34, 54, 157n26, 206n52; and redemption, 34, 54, 80; and time, xxiv, 4–7, 8, 22–23, 80, 163n24, 166n33, 169n112; relationship with Shneur Zalman, xiv–xv, 34, 115, 118, 155n9, 157n26, 196n121; and Torah study, 207n82
Dvir-Goldberg, Rivka, 124

Ecstasy (*hitpa'alut*), 86, 106–8, 115, 118, 121
Eden, Garden of: biblical, 34–35, 179n97; Lower and Upper, 72, 74, 92–94, 98, 186n19, 199n167, 211n122
Eleazar ben Durdaya, 82, 197n141, 206n49
Eliade, Mircea, xxi–xxii
Eliezer, Rabbi, 4, 26
Elijah, the prophet, 82
Elimelekh of Lizhensk, xv; xvi, xxiv, 206n52
Elisha ben Avuya, 93
Eliyahu ben Shlomo Zalman. *See* Vilna Gaon
Epstein, Kalonimus Kalman, 199n172

Etkes, Immanuel, xvi
Exile: and the divine names, 176n71; and gender, 135–36, 140–41, 148; cognition during, 85, 86; as creation, 36, 66, 94, 190n53; current exile, 6, 50–51, 62–63, 181n141; of the Divine, 35–38, 40–48, 111, 148, 174n24, 178n97; Egyptian, xxviii, 38, 42–48, 50–51, 58–59, 63–64, 83–84, 106, 176n59; embodiment of, 36, 38, 84; historical exiles, 32, 35, 38–42; state of confusion, 81, 86, 181n141, 198n141; subjugation to gentile nations, as 37–38, 71, 74, 78–79; worship in, 54, 56, 58–59, 62, 71, 76, 95, 173n18

Exodus: as the prefiguration of the redemption, 38; 42–51, 58–59, 76; 177n71, 186n15; personal, 82–84, 106

Faith: during exile, 86; in God's unity, 1, 83–84, 162n5; and intellectualism, 1, 194n93; Jewish vs. gentile, 21; simple faith, xviii, xxv, 55
Foxbrunner, Roman A., xxvii

Garb, Jonathan, 57
Gehinom, 92–93, 98, 198n158
Gender: association with the divine speech, 129, 135; female as the constricting factor, 129, 132; female aspect of the divine body, 127–28; female impurity, 143, 147–48; femininity as receptiveness, 129–31, 135, 142, 149; fluidity of gender categories, 130–31, 142; genders in the future-to-come, 134–36, 141–45; interdependence of femininity and masculinity, 129–30, 133–37; in kabbalistic imagery, 126–29; masculine and feminine worship; 131; and time, 130–50, 152

Gentiles: biblical gentile nations, 41–42; 49; conversion to Judaism, 76–77, 190n53; and eschatology, 39, 49, 74–79, 87, 88, 99–100; faith of, 21–22; gentile/Jewish difference, 22, 74–75, 88; lands of, 100, 188n38; Noahide commandments, 99–100; relations with Jews, 38, 67, 71, 74, 78; Torah study by, 75–77, 78, 87; wisdom of, 1–2, 5, 40, 48, 174n33

Gershon of Kuty, 66

Habad: inclusivism, xvii, 119–20; origins, xiv–xviii; rank-and-files, xvi–xvii, xxix, 101–14, 121–22, 131, 152, 182n163, 202n13, 202n14, 207n80, 210n122; scholarly class, 103, 107, 108–13, 119–22, 131, 182n163, 183n168, 207n80; structure, xvii, 156n22, 192n67; in twentieth century, xiv, xix–xx, 64–66, 97, 159n39

Hadiach, xviii
Hagiography, xxix, 124–25, 156n10, 157n26

Halakhah: and gender, 143–48; God's revelation in, 62, 111; Messianic, 69–70; 185n4; Shneur Zalman's, xx, 101–8, 110, 112; study by gentiles, 76, 190n53; study of, 58–59, 69–70, 76, 118, 203n22. *See also* Commandments, Torah; Torah study

Hasidism: beginnings of, xiv–xv; conflict with *mitnagedim*, xiii, xv, xviii; xxvi, 119; in the Land of Israel, xvi, xvii, xxvi, 60–61, 63, 89, 120; neutralization of Messianism in, xiii–xiv; women in, 123–24. *See also* Habad, Tsadik

Heilman, Hayim Meir, 125

Hillel, rabbi, 42
Husks: and charity, 60; and corporeality, 37, 53, 56, 62, 74, 220n93; and gentile nations, 49, 74, 76; and God's silence, 177n90; and impure husks, 56, 74, 174n23; *Nogah*, 53–54, 74, 76, 109, 140, 174n23; and nondivine beings, 36, 47, 49, 52; subjugation of, 57, 62, 73, 83. See also Sparks, purification of

Idel, Moshe, xiv, xxi, xxii–xxiv, 31
Idolatry, 37, 41–42, 76–77, 190n55
Jacob (the Patriarch), 44, 78
Jacobson, Yoram, 66
Jewish law. See Halakhah

Kabbalah: evil in, 36; genders in, 130; Lurianic messianism xiv, 79, 173n20; Lurianic myth of creation, 10, 16, 33, 36, 51; and philosophy, 2, 33–34, 162n1, 163n19; Safedian kabbalists on God's immanence, 110–11; time in, xxiii–xxiv; 16–17, 25, 27, 31, 138–39; and time, 3, 144, 163n16; worlds in, 2, 14–15, 16, 18–20, 43, 47, 80, 82, 111, 130, 132, 138, 176n59. See also Breaking of the vessels, *Sefirot*; Sparks, purification of; *Partsufim*; Radiance
Keter, 8–9, 15, 53, 60, 72, 82, 95–96, 167n73, 174n33, 193n75

Lamm, Norman, 110
Levi Yitshak of Berdichev, xv, xvi, xxiv, 21, 206n52
Liady: xviii
Light, divine: and circumcision, 141; contraction of, 10–11, 14, 44, 63, 133–34; direct light and refracted light (*or yashar* and *or hozer*), 109–10, 133; of the divine Wisdom, 38; drawn down in Torah study, 109–10, 112–13, 121–22; of *Ein Sof*, 3, 5, 7, 36, 47, 54–55, 60, 62, 72, 74, 82–83, 86, 88, 98, 112–13, 117, 167n77, 210n120; in the end of days, 77–79, 85, 97–98, 221n112; external and internal lights (*orot makifim and penimiyim*), 40; in Gan Eden, 74, 98, 186n19; Memale *kol 'almin* and Sovev *kol 'almin* (filling light and surrounding light): 11–12, 14, 46, 49, 57–58, 73, 90–91, 95, 117–18, 136, 183n171; and the Sabbath candles, 65, 146; and time, 27–29; and the vessels (*kelim*), 33–34
Liozna (Łoźna): Shneur Zalman's seat, xiv, xvi; Liozna Ordinances, xvi, 119–20, 161n77
Loewenthal, Naftali, xvi, xxi
Luzzatto, Moshe Hayim, 172n10, 200n185, 208n94
Lyubavichi, xviii.

Maggid, the. See Dov Ber of Mezrich
Maimonides, Moses, xiii, xxii, 2, 6, 70, 75, 100, 102, 169n103, 170n114, 189n50
Malkhut, 8, 12–16, 19–20, 25–29, 32, 37, 43, 45–51, 76, 111, 117–18, 125, 128–30, 132–36, 138–44, 149, 152–53; 167n77, 172n130, 173n18, 177n73, 177n90; 203n18, 205n42
Mark, Zvi, 55
Mayse, Ariel Evan, 118
Meir, Rabbi, 93, 190n53
Menahem Mendel of Vitebsk: and creation, 21; and worship, xxv, 52; emigration to Palestine, xvi, 120; as a Hasidic leader, xvi, 32
Menahem Nahum of Chernobyl: in the Maggid's circle, xv, xxiv, 54
Messiah: advent of, xiii, xx, xxv,

50–63, 69, 80, 99; birth pangs of, 220n93; collective, 54–55; "footsteps of," 61, 79–82, 97–99, 130; messianic days, 35, 52, 54–56, 69–72, 75–78, 79–97, 98–99, 145, 147–49, 152–53; personal, xxv, xxviii, 39, 52, 54–55, 75, 78, 86–87; See also Messianism; Redemption; Resurrection

Messianism: harmonistic, xxv, 89; heretical messianism; xiv; 159n39; in Maimonides, 70; messianic calculations, 79; messianic effort, 50, 54–55, 82, 152; and Nahman of Bratslav, xxv, 88–89; neutralization of, xiii–xiv; and Shneur Zalman, xxv, 88–89, 97; in twentieth-century Habad, xiv, xx, 64–66, 97,. See also Messianism; Redemption; Resurrection; Repentance.

Mezhbizh (Międzybórz), xiv

Miracles: God's 177n71; of Purim, 84, 194n90; Shneur Zalman's reluctance, xvi, xvii

Mitnagedim: conflict with Hasidim, xiii, xv; xviii, xxvi, 32; elitism, 210n122; messianism, 200n185; and Torah study, 119, 182n163

Mitsvah tants, 136–37

Mordekhai of Chernobyl, his ties with Shneur Zalman, xv

Moses, 48, 65, 106, 114, 116, 138

Nahman of Bratslav: xvii; and messianism, xxv, 54–55, 88–89

Napoleon, xviii, 32, 171n4

Nothingness, 36, 117, 119, 203n18; creation *ex-nihilo*, 5, 21, 35–36, 166n49, 182n66, 191n60

Partsufim, 126, 138, 167n73, 204n35, 220n93; Nukba, xxix, 76, 117, 132, 142, 144, 149, 215n35; *Ze'ir Anpin*, 14, 25, 27, 49, 51, 117–18, 125, 129,

132–33, 135, 138, 140–42, 144, 145, 170n113, 220n93, 221n99. See also *Sefirot*

Passover, 43, 50, 187n13

Perl, Yosef, xvii

Person, Avraham Abba, 213n11

Philosophy: in Habad, xix, 17, 18; medieval, xix, xxii, 1–3, 28; non-Jewish, 1–2, 5, 40, 48; relation to kabbalah, 2, 7, 25, 33–34, 104, 114, 162n1, 163n19

Pinhas of Korets, 157n26

Plato, 88

Prayer: *'Amidah*, 115, 135, 180n132, 181n133; delaying of, xiii, 209n120; as part of the worship routine, xxix, 61, 111, 112, 116–19, 122; as personal redemption, 46, 56–58, 64, 82–83; as preparation for study, 102, 105, 114–19; re-enactment of the Exodus in, 50; and *sefirot*, 175n39; *Shema'*, 8, 12, 23, 57, 82–84, 104, 114–15, 116; time-bound, 116–18; transformation of evil into good in, 62

Providence, 21–22, 89

Ragoler, Avraham, 210n122

Rapoport-Albert, Ada, 147

Rashi, 33, 61, 76, 102

Ratso va-shov, 21, 23–25, 28, 29, 31, 47, 55–56, 95, 114–15, 117, 121–22; 146, 151, 170n114

Rava, 101

Red heifer, 55–56, 88, 143

Redemption: collective, 42, 54, 57, 64–65, 81–83; 99, 153, 198n153; *dirah ba-tahtonim*, 34–35, 46, 54, 58, 60–65, 94, 111–12, 118, 132, 172n15, 183n168, 187n28, 188n38; as the eight day, 96–98, 141–42, 221n112; future-to-come; xxx, 59, 70, 77, 86–87, 95–96, 123, 126, 132, 132–137, 141, 144, 147–49, 153; of the gentiles, 74–79, 87;

Redemption (continued): as a journey, 49–50; personal, 46, 56–58, 64, 82–84, 98–99,106, 153; Sabbath, xxix, 95–97, 98, 137, 140–41; transformation of cognition, 5–6, 84–85, 186n16; transparency of language in, 85–86; world-to-come; 2, 70–71; 74–79, 82, 89–94, 134, 145, 148. See also Exodus; Messiah; Messianism; Repentance; Resurrection.

Repentance (*teshuvah*): penitents (*ba'ale teshuvah*), 86, 108, 202n14; redemptive significance of, 82, 86–87, 193n80, 195n104; return to God, 105–6; theurgical, 107–8, 121; transcending time, 82, 98, 197n141

Resurrection, 35, 54, 69, 71–74, 77–78, 85, 95, 97–99, 152, 186n15; exclusion from; 78–79, 188n35, 191n60; at Mt. Sinai, 77, 187n20

Revelation: and circumcision, 86; in creation, 16, 32, 36, 44; in the future, 35, 53–55, 58–59, 60, 73–74, 77, 86, 96, 97, 152, 187n20; of *da'at* (knowledge), 84; the female's role in, 133, 135; Sinaitic, 6–7, 9, 35, 43, 47–48, 50–51, 58–59, 81, 85–86, 106, 111, 117, 187n20, 178n93

Riga, 119

Ritual objects, xx, 8–9, 23, 48, 56–57, 61–62, 65, 95, 182n166

Rubenstein, Jeffrey L., xxi–xxii

Sabbateanism, xiv
Sanctuary (*mishkan*), 110–12, 121
Sarah (Shneur Zalman's granddaughter), xv
Schneersohn, Menahem Mendel (Tsemah Tsedek), xviii–xix, xxvi, 4, 17–20, 100, 148, 161n77–78, 210n122

Schneersohn, Shalom Dovber, xix
Schneersohn, Yosef Yitshak: emigration from USSR, xix; hagiography, 126, 157n26, 213n16; leadership, 202n15; messianism xx; outreach, 184n176; Torah study at set times, 119; women in the teachings of, 124

Schneerson, Menahem Mendel: leadership, xix–xx, 184n176; messianism, xx, 64–66, 99–100, 159n39, 184n180, 193n80, 194n95, 195n115; women in the teachings of, 124–25, 146, 149; writings of, 124

Scholem, Gershon: neutralization of messianism, xiii–xiv, 98

Schwartz, Dov, 64

Sefat Emet: See Alter, Yehudah Aryeh Leib

Sefirot: and exile, 38, 41–42; and gender, xxix; and the days of creation, xxiii–xxiv, 25, 27, 141; impure *sefirot*: 38, 174n28, 175n33, 176n44, 176n50; intellectual, 1, 8–9, 27, 39, 44, 53, 80, 84, 109, 113, 131–32, 139–41, 144–45, 162n2, 175n50, 183n168, 195n100; the order of, 2, 5, 9, 18–19, 20, 23–25, 28, 29, 39, 44, 72, 80–81, 117, 174n33, 191n66; and prayer, 39, 175n39; and *ratso va*-shov, 23–24; and time, xxiv; 24–25, 27, 29, 51. See also *Malkhut*; *Keter*; *Partsufim*

Sermons: xvi, xviii, xxv, xxvii, 66, 75, 87, 94, 101, 105, 119, 121, 124, 135, 144, 161n69–71

Shekhinah: bestowment of *Sh.* on Israel, 47; divine speech, 114–15; exile of, 36–37, 40, 43, 53, 111, 148, 178n97; and the female, 133, 138, 140, 147, 148; and time, 26; radiance of, 74, 98, 186n19; receptivity of, 60

Shevirat ha–kelim. See Breaking of the vessels

Shimon bar Yohai, Rabbi, 87, 173n19
Shimon ben Azzai, 146
Shimon ha-Tsadik, 57
Shlomo Efraim (Nahman of Bratslav's son), 54
Shneuri, Dov Ber, xxvi, xxvii; 118, 161n71–72, 164n25, 168n77
Shterna, rabbanit (Shneur Zalman's wife), 125
Solomon, the king, 75
Soul: after death, 72–74, 92–94, 98; and angels, 90; animal and divine souls, xxv, 22, 1, 22, 36–37, 45, 52–53, 57, 62, 74, 116, 174n23, 219n78; collective, 61–62, 183n169; its "garments," 37, 40, 57, 85, 92, 113; gentile vs. Jewish, 22, 67, 74, 78, 191n53; God's sanctuary, 111; hierarchy of, 78, 80–81, 108, 191n66, 192n67, 204n28, 210n120; incarnated, 45, 52–53, 55, 62, 82–83, 183n168; pre-incarnated, 53; sacrifice of in prayer, 118; and the *sefirotic* structure, 80; and temporality, xxiii–xxiv; *tsadik*'s, 87–88, 94; and *tsimtsum*, 172n10; union with God, 60, 108, 114–15, 131, 146; as a universal category, 6–7, 14, 28–29, 41, 66–67; in the world-to-come, 74, 78; of the wicked, 92–94
Space: as created entity, 13; as included in divinity, 11–12; in the future-to-come, 79; purification of, 60, 62; its source in *Malkhut*, 28–29; spatio-temporal realm, 6–14, 43–45, 67, 83–84, 94–95; transcending in ritual, 83; as a universal category, 6–8, 14, 27–28, 29, 66–67
Sparks, purification of: 51–53, 57, 59, 62–63, 76, 79, 81, 90, 95, 110, 136, 137–40, 178n91, 181n141, 183n168, 186n13, 188n39

Speech: and circumcision, 86, 96–97; divine, 26–27, 45, 49, 86, 115, 129, 171n130, 203n18, 205n42; female voice, 129, 135, 218n68; as human faculty, 115; idle speech, 178n91; inarticulate, 84, 194n90; recitation of Torah and prayer, 46, 57, 84, 107, 112–13; silence, 177n90; soul's garment, 37, 57, 88, 112–13, 130
Stamler, Yosef, 2
Stern, Sacha, xxi–xxii, 17

Tanhuma, Rabbi, 4
Time: Aristotelian definition of, xxii, 3, 151; as a created entity, 3–5, 11, 13, 18–19; control over, 23, 153; cyclical, xxi–xxiii, 21, 23, 31; eternity, xxiii, 5, 13, 15, 95, 117–18, 132, 145, 167n77; in Hasidism, xxiv–xxv; history, xxviii; in kabbalah, xxiii–xxiv; in kabbalah research, xxi; its source, 7, 12–16, 20, 27–29, 117–18, 144, 152–53, 167n77, 180n133; linear, xxi–xiii, 31–32; and multiplicity, 2–3, 5, 15, 17, 23, 117; order of time, xxiv, 15, 16–19, 20, 23–24, 28–29; as *ratso va-shov*, 23–25, 28, 29, 31, 95, 171n114; and ritual calendar, xxi, 4; and sanctification of, 62; supratemporal reality, xxi, xxiii–xxiv, 3–6, 9, 12, 15, 23, 28–29, 45, 51, 82, 141, 151–52, 167n77; Tetragrammaton, 6–7, 10–13; as a universal category, 6–7, 14, 27–28, 29, 66–67. *See also* Space
Tishby, Isaiah: xxvii, 79, 192n67
Torah study: and *bitul* (self-nullification), 116; as God's revelation, 9, 46, 77, 95, 111, 114, 117; for its own sake (*li–shmah*), 113, 114, 181n141, 182n163, 207n80, 207n82; by gentiles, 75–77, 78, 87, 190n53

Torah study *(continued)*: laws concerning, xxvi, 2, 101–107, 124; in *mitnagedic* Judaism, 182n163, 210n122; in the Messianic days, 75–76, 78, 87, 100, 111; as recitation, 46, 56–57, 109, 111, 112–13, 115, 203n18, 203n18; redemptive value of, 35, 56–59, 61–62, 64, 83, 88, 152–53; at set times: xxix, 23, 101–22, 152–53, 204n28, 207n80, 211n123; and sexual purity, 146–47; study of halakhah, 58–59, 76, 118; transcending time, 117–18; by women, 124. *See also* Torah; Commandments

Torah: blueprint for creation, xxii, 8; eternal, 8–9, 117–18, 122; gender of, 130–31, 142; Giving of, 35, 43, 47–48, 50, 51, 58–59, 77, 81, 85, 86, 106; as God's wisdom, 8–9, 40; innermost aspect of, 51 87, 97; a link between transcendence and immanence, 8–9, 13, 40, 115, 116, 165n41; scroll of, 48, 62; supra-temporal, 116–17; as united with God, 116; 175n44. *See also* Torah study.

Tsadik: his death, 88; elevation of strange thoughts by, 213n13; his functions, xvi–xviii, xxiv–xxv, xxvii, 88–89, 112, 131; meeting with, xxvii, 131; and messianism, xxv, 54–55, 65, 87–89, 184n180, 196n116; Shneur Zalman as a *tsadik*, xvi, 120; types of, 87–88; 196n121, 197n141; vs. *beinoni*, 65, 108, 202n14, 206n52. *See also* Beinoni

Tsemah Tsedek. *See* Schneersohn, Menahem Mendel

Tsimtsum (contraction), 10–11, 12–13, 29, 33, 35–36, 44, 132, 172n10, 172n15

Vidas, Eliyahu de, 147
Vital, Hayim, 4, 18, 163n25

Will, free, *See Yedi'ah u-vehirah*
Wolfson, Elliot R., 13, 26, 27, 64, 149
Women, xxix–xxx, 123–50; faith in God, 1; gazing at, 125–26; in Hasidic community, 123–25; laws and customs pertaining to, 143, 147–48; in Messianic days, 70; women's commandments, 76, 144–48
Worship through corporeality (*'avodah be-gashmiyut*), 54, 60, 130

Ya'akov Yisra'el of Cherkasy, xv
Yedi'ah u-vehirah, 91
Yehoshua, Rabbi, 4, 82
Yehuda Leib of Yanovitch, 161n70–71
Yehudah bar Simon, Rabbi, 17
Yiddish: xxv, xxvii, 124

Ze'ev Volf of Zhitomir, xxiv
Zionism, 67, 100

www.ingramcontent.com/pod-product-compliance
Lightning Source LLC
Chambersburg PA
CBHW030531230426
43665CB00010B/849